THE PSEUDEPIGRAPHA
AND
MODERN RESEARCH
WITH A SUPPLEMENT

SOCIETY OF BIBLICAL LITERATURE
SEPTUAGINT AND COGNATE STUDIES SERIES
George W. E. Nickelsburg
and
Harry M. Orlinsky, Editors

Number 7S
THE PSEUDEPIGRAPHA AND MODERN RESEARCH
NEW EDITION WITH A SUPPLEMENT
by
James H. Charlesworth

THE PSEUDEPIGRAPHA AND MODERN RESEARCH WITH A SUPPLEMENT

by

James H. Charlesworth

assisted by

P. Dykers and M.J.H. Charlesworth

Published by
SCHOLARS PRESS
for
The Society of Biblical Literature

THE PSEUDEPIGRAPHA AND MODERN RESEARCH
WITH A SUPPLEMENT
by
James H. Charlesworth

A reprint with supplement of the 1976 edition

Copyright ©1981
James H. Charlesworth

Library of Congress Cataloging in Publication Data

Charlesworth, James H.
  The pseudepigrapha and modern research with a
supplement.

  (Septuagint and cognate studies ; no. 060407S)
  Bibliography: p.
  Includes index.
  1. Apocryphal books (Old Testament) —Criticism,
interpretation, etc. I. Dykers, P. II. Charlesworth,
M.J.H. III. Title. IV. Series.
BS1700.C45   1981   229'.06   81-5695
ISBN 0-89130-440-1   AACR2

Printed in the United States of America
          1   2   3   4   5
        Edwards Brothers Inc.
     Ann Arbor, Michigan 48106

In Memory of

Dwight L. Phillips,

a philanthropist who succeeded in realizing dreams;

and

in recognition of

my colleagues in the SBL Pseudepigrapha Group

and

my graduate students at Duke,

from whom I continue to learn.

PREFACE

The documents discussed herein are called collectively the Pseudepigrapha; but this designation is unsatisfactory to many interested readers. To some specialists it is so regarded because some of these documents are not attributed pseudonymously to an Old Testament figure, while several books in the Old Testament and Apocrypha are pseudepigraphical; likewise, others received pseudepigraphical attribution from late editors. It is unjust, furthermore, to perpetuate a title that tends to intimate something is false about these documents. To non-specialists the term frequently is both hard to pronounce and confusing.

Attempts to propose other names have met with even less success. "The Lost Books of the Bible" and "The Books Jesus Read" are inaccurate and journalistic. "The Intertestamental Books," which is acceptable to some scholars, can be misleading since some documents are contemporaneous with the most recent books in the Old and others postdate the latest books in the New Testament. "Intertestamental," moreover, would have been meaningless and anachronistic to the authors themselves and can be offensive from the Jewish perspective. For some time I followed Torrey's lead and referred to the compositions discussed herein as "apocryphal literature." It became evident, however, that more than one person misunderstood this designation.

To many persons the least unsatisfactory titles have proved to be "The Extra-Biblical Books" and "The Writings Contemporaneous with Jesus." The title "Pseudepigrapha," nevertheless, is used for the present collection because it is the one we have inherited (at least for the thirteen books common to the editions by Kautzsch and Charles), because almost all of the compositions that are considered below are pseudonymously attributed to an Old Testament figure, and because most of the recent series, projects, and publications in this area have retained the name.

The quantity of recent publications listed below--1618 entries--is indicative of an international re-appreciation for these writings. The impression received from these publications is occasionally one of cooperation and advancement, but also, unfortunately, of yoked horses pulling in contrary ways. Regretfully the Pseudepigrapha is frequently treated cavalierly by New Testament and rabbinic scholars. All too frequently exciting titles promise more than they deliver: C. Mesters' *Eden: Golden Age or Goad to Action?* (trans. P'.J. Leonard. Maryknoll, N.Y.: Orbis, 1974) is limited to the Old Testament, ignoring completely the rich development of symbolism in the Pseudepigrapha; and M.D. Conway's *Solomon and Solomonic Literature* (New York: Haskell House, 1973) makes no mention of the Odes of Solomon, the Psalms of Solomon, the Testament of Solomon, or other works in the Solomonic cycle.

The present work is not meant only for specialists, but hopefully also for the growing, albeit select, group of scholars and laymen interested in the Pseudepigrapha.

Let me conclude by requesting assistance in keeping the report updated. Please send additions, corrections, and news of forthcoming publications to

J. H. Charlesworth
Box 4735
Duke University
Durham, N.C. 27706

May, 1976

ACKNOWLEDGMENTS

I wish to express my appreciation for the cooperation received during the preparation of this report. Requests for information were almost always answered promptly, fully, and courteously. Certainly such cooperation from scholars in every country in which research in this field is progressing is ample evidence that the subject matter is extremely important and, as my colleague Roland Murphy has written recently, that an individual working alone can no longer convincingly reconstruct this period in history (*CBQ* 36 [1974] 407-09).

It is impossible to mention every scholar who has supplied information incorporated herein--the sources for some facts can no longer be recalled from memory. My special debt and appreciations for advice, assistance, and encouragement are expressed to the following colleagues: F. Andersen, J. Collins, W.D. Davies, G. Delling, A.-M. Denis, D.J. Harrington, M. de Jonge, R.A. Kraft, W.G. Kümmel, M. McNamara, G.W. MacRae, B.M. Metzger, R.E. Murphy, M. Philonenko, J.A. Sanders, D.M. Smith, Jr., H.F.D. Sparks, M.E. Stone, J. Strugnell, and O. Wintermute.

I am grateful to the SBL authorities for accepting this work for publication. Marie Smith has been my faithful and excellent secretary. Louise G. Upchurch, who assisted me during the initial phases of this work, and Patricia Dykers, who helped me until its completion, were invaluable and indefatigable assistants. Without them this demanding task would have remained unfinished. The staffs of Duke's Perkins Library, Interlibrary Loan Office, and Divinity School Library have faithfully rendered significant assistance. The Phillips family of Charlotte, N.C., and the Duke Research Council have graciously supported this research.

TABLE OF CONTENTS

ABBREVIATIONS

1. *Periodicals, Series, Encyclopedias, and Societies*

AAR	American Academy of Religion
AcOr	*Acta orientalia*
AGAJU	Arbeiten zur Geschichte des antiken (späteren) Judentums und des Urchristentums
ALBO	Analecta lovaniensia biblica et orientalia
ALGHJ	Arbeiten zur Literatur und Geschichte des hellenistischen Judentums
ALUOS	*Annual of the Leeds University Oriental Society*
AnBib	Analecta biblica
ANF	Roberts, A. and J. Donaldson, eds. *The Ante-Nicene Fathers: Translations of the Writings of the Fathers Down to A.D. 325.* 10 vols. Edinburgh: Clark, 1868-1872; rev. and repr. Grand Rapids, Mich.: Eerdmans, 1950-1952.
ASOR	American Schools of Oriental Research
ASTI	*Annual of the Swedish Theological Institute*
ATANT	Abhandlungen zur Theologie des Alten und Neuen Testaments
ATR	*Anglican Theological Review*
AusBR	*Australian Biblical Review*
BA	*The Biblical Archaeologist*
BASOR	*Bulletin of the American Schools of Oriental Research*
BDT	Harrison, E.F., *et al.*, eds. *Baker's Dictionary of Theology.* Grand Rapids, Mich.: Baker, 1960.
BEvT	Beiträge zur evangelischen Theologie
BHH	Reicke, B. and L. Rost, eds. *Biblisch-historisches Handwörterbuch.* 3 vols. Göttingen: Vandenhoeck & Ruprecht, 1962-1966.
Bib	*Biblica*
BibSt	Biblische Studien
BIFAO	*Bulletin de l'institut français d'archéologie orientale*
BiKi	*Bibel und Kirche*
BIOSCS	*Bulletin of the International Organization for Septuagint and Cognate Studies*

BJRL, BJRULM	*Bulletin of the John Rylands Library, Bulletin of the John Rylands University Library of Manchester*
B-L^2	Haag, H., ed. *Bibel-Lexikon*, 2d. ed. Zurich: Benziger, 1968.
BLE	*Bulletin de littérature ecclésiastique*
BO	*Bibliotheca orientalis*
BR	*Biblical Research*
BSOAS	*Bulletin of the School of Oriental and African Studies*
BZ	*Biblische Zeitschrift*
BZAW	Beihefte zur Zeitschrift für die alttestamentliche Wissenschaft
BZNW	Beihefte zur Zeitschrift für die neutestamentliche Wissenschaft und die Kunde der älteren Kirche
CB	*Cultura bíblica*
CBQ	*Catholic Biblical Quarterly*
CETEDOC	Centre de traitement électronique des documents
CSCO	Corpus scriptorum christianorum orientalium
CTM	*Concordia Theological Monthly*
DB	Vigouroux, F., ed. *Dictionnaire de la Bible*. 5 vols. Paris: Letouzey et Ané, 1895-1912.
DBSup	Pirot, L., *et al.*, eds. *Dictionnaire de la Bible, Suppléments*. Paris: Letouzey et Ané, 1928-.
DJD	*Discoveries in the Judaean Desert*
DTT	*Dansk teologisk Tidsskrift*
EBib	Etudes bibliques
EJ	*Eranos-Jahrbuch*
Enciclopedia de la Biblia	Gutiérrez-Larraya, J.A., ed. *Enciclopedia de la Biblia*. 6 vols. Barcelona: Garriga, 1963.
Encyclopedia of Christianity	Palmer, E.H., *et al.*, eds. *The Encyclopedia of Christianity*. Wilmington, Del.: National Foundation for Christian Education, 1964-.
EncyJud	Roth, C., *et al.*, eds. *Encyclopedia Judaica*. 16 vols. New York: Macmillan, 1971-1972.
ETL	*Ephemerides theologicae lovanienses*
EvT	*Evangelische Theologie*
FBBS	Facet Books, Biblical Series
FRLANT	Forschungen zur Religion und Literatur des Alten und Neuen Testaments

GamPseud	Hammershaimb, E., *et al.*, eds. *De Gammeltestamentlige Pseudepigrapher: I Oversaettelse med Inledning og Noter*. Copenhagen: Gads, 1953-.
GCS	Die griechischen christlichen Schriftsteller der ersten drei Jahrhunderte
GDBL	Nielsen, E. and B. Noack, eds. *Gads Danske Bibel Leksikon*. 2 vols. Copenhagen: Gads, 1965-1966.
GNT	Grundrisse zum Neuen Testament
Hastings	Hastings, J., ed. *Dictionary of the Bible*, rev. ed. by F.C. Grant and H.H. Rowley. New York: Scribner, 1963.
HAW	Handbuch der Altertumswissenschaft
HeyJ	*Heythrop Journal*
HNT	Handbuch zum Neuen Testament
HTKNT	Herders theologischer Kommentar zum Neuen Testament
HTR	*Harvard Theological Review*
HTS	Harvard Theological Studies
HUCA	*Hebrew Union College Annual*
IB	Buttrick, G.A., *et al.*, eds. *The Interpreter's Bible*. 12 vols. New York: Abingdon, 1952-1957.
IDB	Buttrick, G.A., *et al.*, eds. *The Interpreter's Dictionary of the Bible*. 4 vols. New York: Abingdon, 1962.
IEJ	*Israel Exploration Journal*
Int	*Interpretation*
IOCB	Laymon, C.M., ed. *The Interpreter's One-Volume Commentary on the Bible*. New York: Abingdon, 1971.
ITQ	*Irish Theological Quarterly*
JA	*Journal asiatique*
JAAR	*Journal of the American Academy of Religion*
JAC	*Jahrbuch für Antike und Christentum*
JAL	Jewish Apocryphal Literature
JAOS	*Journal of the American Oriental Society*
JBC	Brown, R.E., J.A. Fitzmyer, and R.E. Murphy, eds. *The Jerome Biblical Commentary*. Englewood Cliffs, N.J.: Prentice-Hall, 1968.
JBL	*Journal of Biblical Literature*
JBLMS	Journal of Biblical Literature Monograph Series
JJS	*Journal of Jewish Studies*

JNES	*Journal of Near Eastern Studies*
JQR	*Jewish Quarterly Review*
JRAS	*Journal of the Royal Asiatic Society*
JSHRZ	Kümmel, W.G., *et al.*, eds. *Jüdische Schriften aus hellenistisch-römischer Zeit*. Gütersloh: Mohn, 1973-.
JSJ	*Journal for the Study of Judaism*
JSS	*Journal of Semitic Studies*
JThC	*Journal for Theology and the Church*
JTS	*Journal of Theological Studies*
Kommentar	Strack, H.L. and P. Billerbeck. *Kommentar zum Neuen Testament aus Talmud und Midrasch*. 5 vols. Munich: Beck, 1922-1956.
KS	*Kirjath Sepher*
LCL	Loeb Classical Library
LD	Lectio divina
LTK^2	Buchberger, M., J. Höfer, and K. Rahner, eds. *Lexikon für Theologie und Kirche*, 2d. ed. 11 vols. Freiburg: Herder, 1957-1967.
LUOS MS	Leeds University Oriental Society Monograph Series
McCQ	*McCormick Quarterly*
NCCHS	Fuller, R.C., *et al.*, eds. *A New Catholic Commentary on Holy Scripture*. London: Nelson, 1969.
NCE	McDonald, W.J., *et al.*, eds. *New Catholic Encyclopedia*. 15 vols. New York: McGraw-Hill, 1967-.
NEB	New English Bible
NovT	*Novum Testamentum*
NovTSup	Novum Testamentum, Supplements
NTS	*New Testament Studies*
NTTS	New Testament Tools and Studies
Or	*Orientalia*
OrSyr	*L'orient syrien*
OTS	Oudtestamentische Studiën
Pauly-Wissowa n.B.	Wissowa, G., *et al.*, eds. *Paulys Real-Encyclopädie der classischen Altertumswissenschaft*, neue Bearbeitung. Stuttgart [or Munich]: Metzler [or Druckenmüller], 1893-1972.
PCB	Peake, A.S., M. Black, and H.H. Rowley, eds. *Peake's Commentary on the Bible*. London, New York: T. Nelson, 1962.
PEQ	*Palestine Exploration Quarterly*

PETSE	Papers of the Estonian Theological Society in Exile
Peshiṭta	*The Old Testament in Syriac According to the Peshiṭta Version.* Leiden: Brill, 1966-.
PG	Patrologia graeca, ed. J. Migne.
PIOL	Publications de l'institut orientaliste de Louvain
PVTG	Pseudepigrapha Veteris Testamenti Graece
RAC	Klauser, T., *et al.*, eds. *Reallexikon für Antike und Christentum: Sachwörterbuch zur Auseinandersetzung des Christentums mit der antiken Welt.* Stuttgart: Hiersemann, 1950-.
RB	*Revue biblique*
RBen	*Revue bénédictine*
RechBib	Recherches bibliques
REJ	*Revue des études juives*
RESl	*Revue des études slaves*
RevExp	*Review and Expositor*
RevistB	*Revista bíblica*
RevSem	*Revue sémitique*
*RGG*³	Galling, K., *et al.*, eds. *Die Religion in Geschichte und Gegenwart*, 3rd. ed. 6 vols. plus index. Tübingen: Mohr, 1957-1965.
RHPR	*Revue d'histoire et de philosophie religieuses*
RHR	*Revue de l'histoire des religions*
RivB	*Rivista biblica*
RQ	*Revue de Qumran*
RSR	*Recherches de science religieuse*
RSV	Revised Standard Version
RTP	*Revue de théologie et de philosophie*
Sacramentum Mundi	Rahner, K., *et al.*, eds. *Sacramentum Mundi: An Encyclopedia of Theology.* 6 vols. New York: Herder, 1968-1970.
SBFLA	*Studii biblici franciscani liber annuus*
SBLDS	Society of Biblical Literature Dissertation Series
SBLMS	Society of Biblical Literature Monograph Series
SBS	Stuttgarter Bibelstudien
SBT	Studies in Biblical Theology
SC	Sources chrétiennes
ScEs	*Science et esprit*
SEA	*Svensk exegetisk Årsbok*

6

Sem	*Semitica*
SJT	*Scottish Journal of Theology*
SNTS MS	Studiorum Novi Testamenti Societas Monograph Series
SPB	Studia postbiblica
StANT	Studien zum Alten und Neuen Testament
Sup *Numen*	Supplements to *Numen*
SVTP	Studia in Veteris Testamenti Pseudepigrapha
T&S	Texts and Studies
T&T	Texts and Translations
TBT	*The Bible Today*
TED	Translations of Early Documents
ThĒE	Martinos, A., ed. *Thrēskeutikē kai Ēthikē Enkuklopaideia.* 12 vols. Athens, 1962-1968.
ThRu	*Theologische Rundschau*
TLZ	*Theologische Literaturzeitung*
TQ	*Theologische Quartalschrift*
TU	Texte und Untersuchungen
TZ	*Theologische Zeitschrift*
USQR	*Union Seminary Quarterly Review*
VC	*Vigiliae christianae*
VT	*Vetus Testamentum*
WUNT	Wissenschaftliche Untersuchungen zum Neuen Testament
WZHalle	*Wissenschaftliche Zeitschrift der Martin-Luther-Universität, Halle-Wittenberg. Gesellschafts- und Sprachwissenschaftliche Reihe*
WZJena	*Wissenschaftliche Zeitschrift der Friedrich-Schiller-Universität, Jena. Gesellschafts- und Sprachwissenschaftliche Reihe*
WZKM	*Wiener Zeitschrift für die Kunde des Morgenlandes*
ZAW	*Zeitschrift für die alttestamentliche Wissenschaft*
ZDMG	*Zeitschrift der deutschen morgenländischen Gesellschaft*
ZKG	*Zeitschrift für Kirchengeschichte*
ZNW	*Zeitschrift für die neutestamentliche Wissenschaft und die Kunde der älteren Kirche*
ZPEB	Tenney, M.C., ed. *The Zondervan Pictorial Encyclopedia of the Bible.* 5 vols. Grand Rapids, Mich.: Zondervan, 1975.
ZRGG	*Zeitschrift für Religions- und Geistesgeschichte*

ZTK	*Zeitschrift für Theologie und Kirche*

2. Books

Agrapha	Resch, A., ed. *Agrapha: Aussercanonische Schriftfragmente* (TU 30.3-4) Leipzig: Hinrichs, 1906; repr. Darmstadt: Wissenschaftliche Buchgesellschaft, 1967.
APAT	Kautzsch, E., ed. *Die Apokryphen und Pseudepigraphen des Alten Testaments.* 2 vols. Tübingen: Mohr, 1900.
Apoc. Lit.	Torrey, C.C. *The Apocryphal Literature: A Brief Introduction.* New Haven, Conn.: Yale University, 1945; repr. Hamden, Conn.: Archon, 1963.
Apocrifi del NT	Erbetta, M. *Gli Apocrifi del Nuovo Testamento.* 3 vols. [?] Turin: Marietti, 1966 [vol. 2], 1969 [vol. 3].
APOT	Charles, R.H., ed. *The Apocrypha and Pseudepigrapha of the Old Testament in English.* 2 vols. Oxford: Clarendon, 1913; repr. 1963 etc.
Biblia Sacra	Weber, R., *et al. Biblia Sacra: Iuxta Vulgatam Versionem.* 2 vols. Stuttgart: Württembergische Bibelanstalt, 1969.
Clarendon edition	An expanded version of *APOT* 2 which is being published by Clarendon Press under the editorship of H.F.D. Sparks.
Crucible	Toynbee, A., ed. *The Crucible of Christianity: Judaism, Hellenism and the Historical Background to the Christian Faith.* New York: World, 1969.
Dogmengeschichte[4.]	Harnack, A. *Lehrbuch der Dogmengeschichte,* 4th ed. 3 vols. Tübingen: Mohr, 1909-1910.
Doubleday edition	A full collection of the Pseudepigrapha in English translations which is being published by Doubleday & Company, Inc., under the editorship of J. H. Charlesworth.
Exégèse biblique et judaïsme	Ménard, J.-E., ed. *Exégèse biblique et judaïsme.* Strasbourg: Faculté de théologie catholique, 1973.
Falasha Anthology	Leslau, W. *Falasha Anthology* (Yale Judaica Series 6) New Haven: Yale University, 1951; repr. New York: Schocken, 1969.
Geschichte [Baumstark]	Baumstark, A. *Geschichte der syrischen Literatur mit Ausschluss der christlich-palästinensischen Texte.* Bonn: A. Marcus und E. Weber, 1922.

8

Geschichte [Graf]   Graf, G. "Apokryphen und Pseudepigraphen," *Geschichte der christlichen
arabischen Literatur* (Studi e Testi
118) Vatican: Biblioteca Apostolica
Vaticana, 1944. Vol. 1, pp. 196-297.

GLAJJ   Stern, M., ed. *Greek and Latin Authors
on Jews and Judaism*. Vol. 1: *From Her-
odotus to Plutarch*. Jerusalem: Israel
Academy of Sciences and Humanities,
1974.

Goodenough Festschrift Neusner, J., ed. *Religions in Antiquity:
Essays in Memory of Erwin Ramsdell
Goodenough* (Sup *Numen* 14) Leiden:
Brill, 1968.

Gottesvolk   Janssen, E. *Das Gottesvolk und seine
Geschichte: Geschichtsbild und Selbst-
verständnis im palästinensischen
Schrifttum von Jesus Sirach bis Jehuda
ha-Nasi*. Neukirchen-Vluyn: Neukirchener, 1971.

Gunkel Festschrift   Schmidt, H., ed. *Eucharistērion: Studien
zur Religion des Alten und Neuen Testa-
ments*. H. Gunkel Festschrift. Part 2:
*Zur Religion und Literatur des Neuen
Testaments*. Göttingen: Vandenhoeck &
Ruprecht, 1923.

History [Pfeiffer]   Pfeiffer, R.H. *History of New Testament
Times with an Introduction to the
Apocrypha*. New York: Harper and Row,
1949.

History [Schürer]   Schürer, E. *A History of the Jewish
People in the Time of Jesus Christ*,
trans. J. MacPherson. 5 vols. plus index. Edinburgh: T. & T. Clark, 1897-1898.

History...The Time of Hausrath, A. *A History of New Testament
the Apostles*   Times: The Time of the Apostles*.
4 vols., trans. L. Huxley. London:
Williams and Norgate, 1895.

HSW   Hennecke, E., W. Schneemelcher, and R.
McL. Wilson, eds. *New Testament Apoc-
rypha*. 2 vols. London: Lutterworth,
1963-1965.

Intr. to the Apoc.   Metzger, B.M. *An Introduction to the
Apocrypha*. New York: OUP, 1957.

Introduction   Denis, A.-M. *Introduction aux pseudépigraphes grecs d'Ancien Testament* (SVTP
1) Leiden: Brill, 1970.

Jewish Symbols   Goodenough, E.R. *Jewish Symbols in the
Greco-Roman Period*. 12 vols. New York:
Random House, 1953-1968.

Judaic Tradition   Glatzer, N.N. *The Judaic Tradition:
Texts Edited and Introduced*. Boston:
Beacon, 1969.

Kuhn Festschrift   Jeremias, G., H.-W. Kuhn, and H. Stege-
mann, eds. *Tradition und Glaube: Das
frühe Christentum in seiner Umwelt.
Festgabe für Karl Georg Kuhn zum 65.
Geburtstag.* Göttingen: Vandenhoeck &
Ruprecht, 1971.

LAOT   James, M.R. *The Lost Apocrypha of the
Old Testament* (TED) London: S.P.C.K.,
1920.

Legends   Ginzberg, L. *The Legends of the Jews.*
7 vols., trans. H. Szold. Philadelphia:
Jewish Publication Society of America,
1909-1938; repr. 1937-1966.

Literatur und Religion Maier, J. and J. Schreiner, eds. *Litera-
des Frühjudentums*   *tur und Religion des Frühjudentums.*
Gütersloh: Mohn, 1973.

M. Smith Festschrift   Neusner, J., ed. *Christianity, Judaism
and Other Greco-Roman Cults: Studies
for Morton Smith at Sixty.* 4 parts
(Studies in Judaism in Late Antiquity
12) Leiden: Brill, 1975.

Missionsliteratur   Dalbert, P. *Die Theologie der hellenistisch-jüdischen Missionsliteratur
unter Ausschluss von Philo und Josephus.* Hamburg-Volksdorf: Herbert
Reich-Evangelischer Verlag, 1954.

Les origines   Roncaglia, M. *Histoire de l'église copte.*
Vol. 1: *Les origines du christianisme
en Egypte.* Lebanon: Dar Al-Kalima,
1966.

Pseud I   Fritz, K. von, ed. *Pseudepigrapha I:
Pseudopythagorica, Lettres de Platon,
Littérature pseudépigraphe juive*
(Entretiens sur l'antiquité classique
18) Geneva: Fondation Hardt, 1972.

Pseudépigraphes   Philonenko, M., *et al. Pseudépigraphes
de l'Ancien Testament et manuscrits
de la Mer Morte* (Cahiers de la RHPR
41) Paris: Presses universitaires de
France, 1967.

SBL 1971 Seminar   *The Society of Biblical Literature One
Papers*   *Hundred Seventh Annual Meeting Seminar
Papers--28-31 October 1971, Regency
Hyatt House--Atlanta, Ga.* 2 vols.
[Missoula, Mont.]: SBL, 1971.

SBL 1972 Seminar   McGaughy, L.C., ed. *The Society of Bib-
Papers*   *lical Literature One Hundred Eighth
Annual Meeting Book of Seminar Papers:
Friday-Tuesday, 1-5 September 1972,
Century Plaza Hotel--Los Angeles, Ca.*
2 vols. [Missoula, Mont.]: SBL, 1972.

SBL 1974 Seminar Papers	MacRae, G., ed. *Society of Biblical Literature 1974 Seminar Papers: One Hundred Tenth Annual Meeting, 24-27 October 1974, Washington Hilton, Washington, D.C.* 2 vols. Cambridge, Mass.: SBL, 1974.
SCS 2	Kraft, R.A., ed. *1972 Proceedings: International Organization for Septuagint and Cognate Studies and the Society of Biblical Literature Pseudepigrapha Seminar* (Septuagint and Cognate Studies 2) [Missoula, Mont.]: SBL, 1972. [A new expanded edition of the material on Abraham is in preparation.]
SCS 4	Nickelsburg, G.W.E. Jr., ed. *Studies on the Testament of Moses: Seminar Papers* (Septuagint and Cognate Studies 4) Cambridge, Mass.: SBL, 1973.
SCS 5	Nickelsburg, G.W.E. Jr., ed. *Studies on the Testament of Joseph* (Septuagint and Cognate Studies 5) Missoula, Mont.: Scholars Press, 1975.
Septuaginta	Rahlfs, A., ed. *Septuaginta: Id est Vetus Testamentum graece iuxta LXX interpretes.* 2 vols. Stuttgart: Württembergische Bibelanstalt, 1935; repr. 1965.
Studien	Eltester, W., ed. *Studien zu den Testamenten der zwölf Patriarchen* (BZNW 36) Berlin: Töpelmann, 1969).
Studies on T12P	Jonge, M. de. *Studies on the Testaments of the Twelve Patriarchs: Text and Interpretation* (SVTP 3) Leiden: Brill, 1975.
UWOT	Issaverdens, J. *The Uncanonical Writings of the Old Testament.* Venice: Armenian Monastery of St. Lazarus, 1901; repr. 1907.
VTSup 22	Boer, P.A.H. de, ed. *Congress Volume: Uppsala 1971* (Supplements to Vetus Testamentum 22) Leiden: Brill, 1972.
Widengren Festschrift	Bergman, J., *et al.*, eds. *Ex Orbe Religionum: Studia Geo Widengren.* 2 vols. (Studies in the History of Religions 21, 22) Leiden: Brill, 1972.

3. Bible and Apocrypha

Gen	Eccl (Qoh)	Tob	Gal
Ex	Song	Jdt	Eph
Lev	Isa	AddEsth	Phil
Num	Jer	WisSol	Col
Deut	Lam	Sir	1Thes
Josh	Ezek	1Bar	2Thes
Judg	Dan	LetJer	1Tim
Ruth	Hos	PrAzar	2Tim
1Sam	Joel	Sus	Tit
2Sam	Amos	Bel	Phlm
1Kgs	Obad	1Mac	Heb
2Kgs	Jonah	2Mac	Jas
1Chr	Micah	Mt	1Pet
2Chr	Nah	Mk	2Pet
Ezra	Hab	Lk	1Jn
Neh	Zeph	Jn	2Jn
Esth	Hag	Acts	3Jn
Job	Zech	Rom	Jude
Ps(s)	Mal	1Cor	Rev
Prov	2Ezra	2Cor	

4. Dead Sea Scrolls

All abbreviations are according to J. A. Fitzmyer, S.J., *The Dead Sea Scrolls: Major Publications and Tools for Study* ([Sources for Biblical Study 8] Missoula, Mont.: SBL and Scholars Press, 1975).

5. Pseudepigrapha

ApAb	Apocalypse of Abraham
TAb	Testament of Abraham
ApAdam	Apocalypse of Adam
TAdam	Testament of Adam
LAE	Life of Adam and Eve
Ah	Ahiqar
AnonSam	An Anonymous Samaritan Text
LetAris	Letter of Aristeas
ArisEx	Aristeas the Exegete
Aristob	Aristobulus
Art	Artapanus
2Bar	2 (Syriac) Baruch
3Bar	3 (Greek) Baruch
4Bar	4 Baruch
CavTr	Cave of Treasures
ClMal	Cleodemus Malchus
Dem	Demetrius

ElMod	Eldad and Modad
ApEl	Apocalypse of Elijah
1En	1 (Ethiopic) Enoch
2En	2 (Slavonic) Enoch
3En	3 (Hebrew) Enoch
Eup	Eupolemus
Ps-Eup	Pseudo-Eupolemus
ApocEzek	Apocryphon of Ezekiel
ApEzek	Apocalypse of Ezekiel
EzekTrag	Ezekiel the Tragedian
4Ezra	4 Ezra
GkApEzra	Greek Apocalypse of Ezra
QuesEzra	Questions of Ezra
RevEzra	Revelation of Ezra
VisEzra	Vision of Ezra
HecAb	Hecataeus of Abdera
Ps-Hec	Pseudo-Hecataeus
THez	Testament of Hezekiah
FrgsHistWrks	Fragments of Historical Works
TIsaac	Testament of Isaac
AscenIs	Ascension of Isaiah
MartIs	Martyrdom of Isaiah
VisIs	Vision of Isaiah
LadJac	Ladder of Jacob
TJac	Testament of Jacob
JanJam	Jannes and Jambres
TJob	Testament of Job
JosAsen	Joseph and Asenath
PrJos	Prayer of Joseph
TJos	Testament of Joseph
Jub	Jubilees
LAB	*Liber Antiquitatum Biblicarum*
LosTr	The Lost Tribes
3Mac	3 Maccabees
4Mac	4 Maccabees
5Mac	5 Maccabees
PrMan	Prayer of Manasses
Ps-Men	Pseudo-Menander
ApMos	Apocalypse of Moses

AsMos	Assumption of Moses
PrMos	Prayer of Moses
TMos	Testament of Moses
BkNoah	Book of Noah
Ps-Orph	Pseudo-Orpheus
PJ	*Paraleipomena Jeremiou*
PhEPoet	Philo the Epic Poet
Ps-Philo	Pseudo-Philo
Ps-Phoc	Pseudo-Phocylides
FrgsPoetWrks	Fragments of Poetical Works
LivPro	Lives of the Prophets
ApSedr	Apocalypse of Sedrach
TrShem	Treatise of Shem
SibOr	Sibylline Oracles
OdesSol	Odes of Solomon
PssSol	Psalms of Solomon
TSol	Testament of Solomon
5ApocSyrPss	Five Apocryphal Syriac Psalms
Thal	Thallus
Theod	Theodotus
T12P	Testaments of the Twelve Patriarchs
TReu	Testament of Reuben
TSim	Testament of Simeon
TLevi	Testament of Levi
TJud	Testament of Judah
TIss	Testament of Issachar
TZeb	Testament of Zebulun
TDan	Testament of Dan
TNaph	Testament of Naphtali
TGad	Testament of Gad
TAsh	Testament of Asher
TJos	Testament of Joseph
TBenj	Testament of Benjamin
ApZeph	Apocalypse of Zephaniah
ApZos	Apocalypse of Zosimus

6. Patristics, Rabbinics, and Josephus
[selected]

Clement of Alexandria	Protr.	Protrepticus
	Quis dives salv.	Quis dives salvetur
	Strom.	Stromata
Epiphanius	Haer.	Contra Haereses (Panarion)
Eusebius	H.E.	Historia ecclesiastica
	Pr.ev.	Praeparatio evangelica
Josephus	Contr. Ap.	Contra Apionem
	Ant.	Antiquitates
Origen	Philoc.	Philocalia
Pseudo-Justin	de Mon.	De monarchia
Rabbinics	Lev. R.	Leviticus Rabba
	Sanh.	Sanhedrin
Shepherd of Hermas	Vis.	Visions
Theophilus of Antioch	Ad Autol.	Ad Autolycum

INTRODUCTION

The year 1970 could be considered the beginning of a new era of research upon the Pseudepigrapha. While 1969 was the year for the publication of G. Delling's important *Bibliographie zur jüdisch-hellenistischen und intertestamentarischen Literatur*, 1970 was the year for the appearance of A.-M. Denis' *Introduction aux pseudépigraphes grecs d'Ancien Testament*, his *Concordance de l'Apocalypse grecque de Baruch*, the completion of L. Rost's *Einleitung*, fascicle one of Pseudepigrapha Veteris Testamenti Graece,[1] volume one of *Journal for the Study of Judaism in the Persian, Hellenistic and Roman Period*, and the first section of papers on the Pseudepigrapha at the annual meeting of the AAR and SBL. Projects and publications have multiplied so that it is apposite to attempt a report of contemporary research on the Pseudepigrapha.

Focus of This Report

A bibliographic report, if it is to serve a specific function, must be focused. An explanation of the guidelines for this process facilitates the use of the report.

Since Delling's *Bibliographie* attempts to include publications up to 1965, the enclosed data represent publications from 1960 to 1975, almost always excluding items from 1960 to 1965 that are listed by Delling.

Some volumes are excluded because their primary concern is not with the Pseudepigrapha, because the information provided is characteristically marginal, or because a multi-volumed work is only partly completed. Hence, for example, not included are the *Theologisches Wörterbuch zum Neuen Testament* edited by G.

---

[1]The series had begun in 1967 with the publication of PVTG 2. In 1970, however, were published M. de Jonge's *Testamenta XII Patriarcharum*[2] (PVTG 1), and M. Black's *Apocalypsis Henochi Graece* with A.-M. Denis' *Fragmenta pseudepigraphorum quae supersunt graeca* (PVTG 3).

Kittel and G. Friedrich (10 vols., 1933-1975; ET by G. W.
Bromiley, 1964-1974), the second edition of *The Oxford Diction-
ary of the Christian Church* edited by F. L. Cross and E. A.
Livingstone, and *Enciclopedia delle Religioni*, edited by M.
Gozzini and others.

Reprints of earlier publications are not usually cited unless accompanied by recent additions, or unless they are reproductions of important or virtually inaccessible text editions,
such as those by Tischendorf, concordances, like that by Wahl,
or premier collections, like those by Charles and Riessler.
Books in foreign languages that predate 1960 are excluded, of
course, but an English translation published since then is
reported.

Only publications, or portions of them, that deal directly
with or are essential to research upon the Pseudepigrapha are
included. Works on books included in our definition of Pseudepigrapha but sometimes included also with the Apocrypha do not
receive a list of all publications since there are good reference and bibliographical aids for the Apocrypha and the Septuagint (e.g., see S.P. Brock, C.T. Fritsch, and S. Jellicoe,
A Classified Bibliography of the Septuagint [ALGHJ 6] Leiden:
Brill, 1973). The Psalms of Solomon, although included by A.
Rahlfs in the *Septuaginta*, belongs only in the Pseudepigrapha,
and is not treated as the documents just mentioned.

The Dead Sea Scrolls are not cited, except for the editions of and studies upon the fragments of the pseudepigrapha[2]
found in the Qumran caves. These entries are listed under the
appropriate pseudepigraphon (1 Enoch, Jubilees, 5 Apocryphal
Syriac Psalms, or Testaments of the Twelve Patriarchs), and
under the heading "The Pseudepigrapha and the Dead Sea Scrolls."

Works that belong to the New Testament Apocrypha are
excluded. Hence, the now lost Apocalypse of Zechariah[3] is not

---

[2]This term is capitalized only when it refers to the collection of writings. The Pseudepigrapha was, of course, not
found at Qumran, but fragments of early versions or prototypes
of some pseudepigrapha have been discovered there.

[3]Mentioned in the List of Sixty Books between ApZeph and
GkApEzra, and noted in Pseudo-Athanasius and Nicephorus as a

included, since it refers neither to the prophet nor to the
unknown "Zechariah the son of Barachiah" who was murdered
"between the sanctuary and the altar" (Mt 23:35), but to the
father of John the Baptist.

Publications dealing with subjects germane to the Pseudepigrapha, such as Apocalypticism and Gnosticism, are included
only if they significantly discuss one or more of the documents
in the Pseudepigrapha. Hence, articles on apocalyptic as the
mother of Christian theology, like those by E. Käsemann and R.
Bultmann, are not included.

These decisions evolved out of a prior definition of
Pseudepigrapha. It is to this concept that our attention has
been moving.

A Definition of Pseudepigrapha

To compile a bibliographic report on the Pseudepigrapha
does not demand a fully refined definition of this category,
but it implies a coherent and workable one.[4] In attempting to
define Pseudepigrapha as a category, we are primarily concerned
with content--what to include or exclude--but this decision, of
course, presupposes a scholarly judgment upon the characteristics of a pseudepigraphon. Fortunately our task is assisted by
previous decisions on content and characteristics. Exclusive
definitions of content were offered by the first modern editors
of this literature. E. Kautzsch[5] included only thirteen

---

pseudepigraphon on Zechariah, the father of John, the Apocalypse
of Zechariah may have been quoted by Origen in more than one
place. The work is mentioned neither in the volumes of *ANF*
(not even in vol. 8, which contains the "Apocrypha of the New
Testament," nor in the "Added Volume," which contains several
apocalypses), nor in M.R. James' *The Apocryphal New Testament*
(Oxford: Clarendon, 1924), nor in HSW. See the discussions and
bibliographical information in M.R. James' *LAOT*, pp. 74-77; in
M. Erbetta's *Apocrifi del NT*, vol. 3, p. 445; and in A.-M.
Denis' *Introduction*, pp. xiiif., 293, 312.

[4]For a discussion of some problems inherent in defining
the Pseudepigrapha see my "The Renaissance of Pseudepigrapha
Studies: The SBL Pseudepigrapha Project," *JSJ* 2 (1971) 107-14,
esp. pp. 113f.

[5]*Die Apokryphen und Pseudepigraphen des Alten Testaments.*
2 vols. Tübingen: Mohr, 1900.

documents, while R. H. Charles[6] selected seventeen. Their re-
ductional definition of Pseudepigrapha was as follows:

Kautzsch	Charles
Der Aristeasbrief	Letter of Aristeas
Das Buch der Jubiläen	Jubilees
Das Martyrium Jesajae	Martyrdom of Isaiah
Die Psalmen Salomos	Psalms of Solomon
Das sogen. vierte Buch der Makkabäer	4 Maccabees
Die Sibyllinen	Sibylline Oracles
Das Buch Henoch	1 Enoch
Die Himmelfahrt Moses	Assumption of Moses
Das 4. Buch Esra	4 Ezra
Die syrische Baruchapokalypse	2 (Syriac) Baruch
Die griechische Baruchapokalypse	3 (Greek) Baruch
Die Testamente der 12 Patriarchen	Testaments of XII Patriarchs
Das Leben Adams und Evas	Books of Adam and Eve
	2 Enoch
	Ahiqar
	A Zadokite Work
	Pirkē Aboth

The chart reveals the four additional books chosen by Charles;
before discussing these, however, it is best to note the thirteen books common to each. Few would question that these thirteen books all belong in the Pseudepigrapha, although some
would wish to place 4 Ezra in the Apocrypha. It would be misleading, however, to call them the core of this category since
no specialist today would reduce the Pseudepigrapha to thirteen
books. The question concerns those that should be added. My[7]

---

[6]*The Apocrypha and Pseudepigrapha of the Old Testament.*
2 vols. Oxford: Clarendon, 1913; repr. 1963 etc.

[7]I must confess uneasiness in being forced to state what
should be placed in the Pseudepigrapha and venture to do so
only because of insistence and encouragement from my colleagues.
Perhaps the best way to obtain a clear understanding among international scholars over what is meant by "Pseudepigrapha" is
for one person to suggest a workable model with the expectation
that following discussions will mold and polish it. The task
is frustrated because the core of the Pseudepigrapha contains
heterogeneous documents, and because unlike working with the
Old and New Testaments the mandate is not to describe what is

attempt to answer this question, like all others, depends upon many historical and theological conclusions that cannot be conveniently articulated in the brief space allowed here.

Compiling a list of books that should be in the Pseudepigrapha is facilitated by other categories of biblical and quasi-biblical works. Councils, which merely formalized in a canon the writings claimed authoritative by religious communities, have bequeathed us a definitive "Old Testament" and "New Testament."[8] The Greek "Old Testament" contains some documents not found in the Hebrew; although these are called the Apocrypha their number varies among manuscripts. An exclusive definition of Apocrypha, I believe, must be maintained in order to be consistent with the burgeoning consensus that today we need an inclusive definition of Pseudepigrapha. This decision also clarifies the confusing discrepancies among the collections of "Apocrypha."[9] Thus, only the extra writings in almost all Septuagint manuscripts, and not those in the Vulgate, should be in the Apocrypha, which should not contain the Psalms of Solomon, the Prayer of Manasses, 4 Ezra, 3 Maccabees, 4 Maccabees, and Psalm 151. Our definition of the Apocrypha,[10] therefore, agrees with that of R.H. Pfeiffer,[11] except that he includes

---

already collected but to select according to representative criteria what should be included.

[8]We must bar for the present the intriguing historical, theological, and existential concerns of canonical criticism. See the publications listed below under 5ApocSyrPss, especially the publications by J.A. Sanders, and his *Torah and Canon* (Philadelphia: Fortress, 1972).

[9]While the RSV and NEB Apocrypha are similar, the Jerusalem Bible excludes 4 Ezra (= 2 Esdras) and PrMan, and the Dartmouth Bible reduces the list to nine, omitting 4Ezra, PrMan, AddEsth, 1Bar, LetJer, and PrAzar (with the Song of the Three Young Men).

[10]The Apocrypha hence includes the following thirteen documents: 2 Ezra (= 1 Esdras), Tobit, Judith, Additions to Esther, Wisdom of Solomon, Sirach, 1 Baruch, Letter of Jeremiah, the Prayer of Azariah with the Song of the Three Young Men, Susanna, Bel and the Dragon, 1 Maccabees, and 2 Maccabees.

[11]This definition is found in his *History of New Testament Times with an Introduction to the Apocrypha* (New York: Harper, 1949) but not in his "The Literature and Religion of the Apocrypha" (*IB* 1 [1952] 391-419), which also includes 4Ezra.

the Prayer of Manasses, and with the Roman Catholic *La Bible de Jérusalem* (*The Jerusalem Bible*), except that it excludes 2 Ezra (= 1 Esdras). The Pseudepigrapha, therefore, should contain the following documents that are sometimes placed in the Apocrypha: Psalms of Solomon; 4 Ezra (= 4,5,6); 4, and 3 Maccabees; the Prayer of Manasses; and Psalm 151. Thus, added to the thirteen documents common to Kautzsch and Charles, which include the first three in this list, are three more documents bringing the total to sixteen.

Problematic for a collection of Jewish apocryphal works are the publications *en bloc* of works grouped together primarily because they were discovered supposedly in the same geographical area; this is especially true of the Dead Sea Scrolls and the Nag Hammadi Codices. The latter group contains a text, the Apocalypse of Adam, that should be placed within the Pseudepigrapha. Five reasons why such a document should be included are given below; essentially the Apocalypse of Adam is included not primarily because it is attributed to an Old Testament figure, but because it apparently emanates from a milieu appreciably different from that of the other Coptic Codices; that is, it may derive ultimately from a very early Syrian-Palestinian baptist sect.

Nothing found solely among the Dead Sea Scrolls should be added for the present to the Pseudepigrapha, although discussions in the future must take seriously the inclusion of such apocryphal, non-sectarian texts as the Genesis Apocryphon (1QapGen, 6QapGen ar), the Sayings of Moses (1QDM), the Book of Mysteries (1QMyst), an apparent apocryphon of Moses (2QapMos), a supposed apocryphon of David (2QapDavid), a prophetic apocryphon (2QapProph, cf. 6QapProph), the Description of the New Jerusalem (2QJN ar, 5QJN ar, 11QJN ar), a Hymn of Praise (3QHymn), many ill-defined texts and fragments from Cave 3, the Copper Scroll (3QTreasure), an apocryphon of Malachi (5QapMal), a Samuel-Kings Apocryphon (6QapSam/Kgs), the Allegory of the Vine (6QAllegory), an apocalyptic text (6QApoc ar), the Prayer of Nabonidus (4QPrNab, 4QPsDan ar), the Vision of ʿAmram (4Q ʿAmram, 4QTQahat), the Psalms of Joshua (4QPssJosh), the Melchizedek Scroll (11QMelch), and the recently recovered Temple Scroll. Not all of these, of course, are equal

candidates, and no writing which is peculiar to the Qumran
Essenes should be included.

Seventeen documents are hereby considered to belong to the
Pseudepigrapha. How many others should also be considered from
the remaining list? As can be seen by reading the discussions
of cycles below, the documents remaining to be considered total
over one hundred. It is inaccurate to limit the Pseudepigrapha
to a mere seventeen documents since there are others that pos-
sess features similar to those already included. The criteria
which I have used to recognize among the remaining group documents that probably should be considered within the Pseudepigrapha are the following: First, the work must be at least partially, and preferably totally, Jewish or Jewish-Christian.
Second, it should date from the period 200 B.C. to A.D. 200.
Third, it should claim to be inspired. Fourth, it should be
related in form or content to the Old Testament. Fifth, it
ideally is attributed to an Old Testament figure,[12] who often
claims to be the speaker or author. It is important to note
that the documents collected according to these criteria are
predominantly apocalyptic, or related to this genre, and some
are expansions of Old Testament narratives.

Applying these five criteria helps distinguish between
those writings which should be included in the Pseudepigrapha,
those which probably should be included, and those which might
be included. The latter group consists of works that are
really beyond the chronological limits, or are included because
of the default of other categories. The following chart clarifies these three groups (for an explanation of the abbreviations see ABBREVIATIONS).

---

[12]Sometimes the author intended his composition to be
pseudepigraphical, as in the WisSol; but at others he may not
have, and we must be cautious, allowing for the possibility
that pseudepigraphical attribution emanates from a later time,
as may be the case with the so-called OdesSol. M. Smith correctly warns against confusing the claim to antiquity with a
claim of authorship, and argues that pseudepigraphy does not
necessarily depend on the concept of intellectual property.
See his recent "Pseudepigraphy in the Israelite Literary Tradition," *Pseud* I, pp. 189-215; also see p. 310.

Primary

ApAb	2En	4Mac
TAb	4 (=4,5,6) Ezra	PrMan
ApAdam	AscenIs (MartIs,	AsMos (=TMos; frgs.)
LAE (ApMos)	THez, VisIs)	LivPro
LetAris	JanJam (frgs.)	TrShem
2Bar	TJob	SibOr
3Bar	JosAsen	OdesSol
4Bar	PrJos (frgs.)	PssSol
ApEl	Jub	5ApocSyrPss
1En	3Mac	T12P

Secondary

TAdam	VisEzra	Ps-Philo
AnonSam (frgs.)	TIsaac	Ps-Phoc (frgs.)
ElMod (not extant)	LadJac (frgs.)	ApSedr
ApocEzek (frgs.)	TJac	ApZeph
GkApEzra	LosTr (not extant)	ApZos
RevEzra	5Mac	

Tertiary

Ah	QuesEzra	FrgsHistWrks
3En	TSol	FrgsPoetWrks

It would be presumptuous for one individual to suggest that his
own list could be anything more than a prolegomenon toward a
definition of the contents of the Pseudepigrapha. The list,
however, should illumine the basis from which the report has
evolved.

It is obvious that only two of the four books which
Charles added to Kautzsch's list have been included, namely
2 Enoch and Ahiqar. A. Weiser[13] and O. Eissfeldt[14] accepted
only the former into their lists; L. Rost[15] accepted it along

---

[13]*Einleitung in das Alte Testament*, 6th ed. Göttingen:
Vandenhoeck & Ruprecht, 1966.

[14]*The Old Testament: An Introduction*, trans. P. R. Ackroyd.
New York: Harper and Row, 1965.

[15]*Einleitung in die alttestamentlichen Apokryphen und
Pseudepigraphen einschliesslich der grossen Qumran-Handschriften*. Heidelberg: Quelle & Meyer, 1971.

with 3 Maccabees. C.C. Torrey,[16] however, rejected 2 Enoch,
the Letter of Aristeas, and 3 Baruch from his list of "apocryphal literature"; but he added 3 Maccabees, the Lives of the
Prophets, and the Testament of Job. S. Zeitlin[17] accepted into
"Jewish Apocryphal Literature" 2 Enoch, along with 3 Maccabees,
the Lives of the Prophets, the Testament of Job, Pseudo-Philo,
and portions of some of the Fragments of Historical and Poetical Works. R.H. Pfeiffer[18] included 2 Enoch, along with 3
Maccabees, the Testament of Job, the Lives of the Prophets,
Paraleipomena Jeremiou, and Cantica (Odes); but he dropped
4 Ezra from the thirteen works found in both Kautzsch and
Charles.

The precursor of the inclusive definition of Pseudepigrapha was P. Riessler, who compiled an impressive collection of
Altjüdisches Schrifttum ausserhalb der Bibel. Six documents
in his list, however, should not be added to the Pseudepigrapha. The Eighteen Benedictions, the Scroll for Fasting, and
Pirkē Aboth belong within and are today customarily assigned to
the corpus of rabbinic literature. The Zadokite Work belongs
to the Dead Sea Scroll Literature, since it received at least
its final form at Qumran, and since it contains many of the
peculiar features of Qumran theology. The Fragment of Diphilus
of Sinope and the Letters of Heraclitus are not Jewish (see
no. 86 below).

It is unfortunate that there is such confusion in nomen-
clature. For example, 4 Ezra is referred to as 2 Esdras,
2 Ezra, 4 Esdras, Apocalypse of Ezra, and Apocalypse of Sheal-
tiel. Calling it 4 Ezra allows for the accepted custom of referring to the prefixed and suffixed chapters respectively as

---

[16]*The Apocryphal Literature*. New Haven, Conn.: Yale University, 1945; repr. Hamden, Conn.: Archon, 1963.

[17]"Jewish Apocryphal Literature," *JQR* n.s. 40 (1950)
88-115; repr. *Studies in the Early History of Judaism*. New
York: KTAV, 1974. Vol. 2, pp. 223-50.

[18]"The Literature and Religion of the Pseudepigrapha,"
IB 1 (1952) 421-36.

5 and 6 Ezra; and distinguishes it from the later Apocalypse
of Ezra, which is extant in Greek.

The arrangement of these books raises numerous problems.
Their organization according to provenance, as in the publications by J.B. Frey,[19] R.H. Pfeiffer,[20] and L. Rost,[21] is problematic because the geographical origin of a composition is
usually the most difficult issue to resolve.[22] It is occasionally possible, for example, to make an intelligent guess that
the original language is probably Hebrew or Greek, but this
conclusion does not therefore indicate a Palestinian or diasporic provenance. Not only was Palestine deeply hellenized,[23]
at least in scattered sections, but the diaspora itself contained islands of Jews loyal to Torah and traditions.[24] An
arrangement according to genre, as attempted by S. Zeitlin[25]

---

[19]"Apocryphes de l'Ancien Testament," *DBSup* 1, cols. 354-
460.

[20]*IB* 1 (1952) 421-36.

[21]See note 15 above.

[22]"Let me begin by confessing uneasiness about the common
distinction between Palestinian and diasporic pseudepigrapha"
(M. Smith, *Pseud* I, p. 191).

[23]Approximately thirty years ago W.D. Davies succeeded in
demonstrating that there is "no justification for making too
rigid a separation between the Judaism of the Diaspora and that
of Palestine..." Hellenistic Greek influences penetrated deep
into Palestine, "there was a Graeco-Jewish 'atmosphere' even at
[the protected, mountainous, and isolated] Jerusalem..." (*Paul
and Rabbinic Judaism.* London: S.P.C.K., 1948; repr. in 1967 by
Harper and Row of New York with an important new introduction,
"Paul and Judaism Since Schweitzer"; quotation is from p. 8).
Thanks to Davies' publications and those of others, especially
M. Smith, S. Lieberman, and E.R. Goodenough, the hellenization
of "Palestinian" Judaism is now acknowledged. For the most re-
cent demonstration of this fact see M. Hengel's *Judaism and
Hellenism: Studies in their Encounter in Palestine During the
Early Hellenistic Period* (2 vols., trans. J. Bowden. London:
SCM; Philadelphia: Fortress, 1974).

[24]V. Tcherikover amasses impressive data to demonstrate
that while there were no Hellenistic Jewish ghettos, the diaspora Jews organized in culturally separate miniature kingdoms;
cf. *Hellenistic Civilization and the Jews*, trans. S. Applebaum.
New York: 1970; see esp. pp. 296-377.

[25]See note 17 above.

and advocated in private correspondence with M.E. Stone and R. A. Kraft, has proved an effective pedagogical tool[26] and is the proper approach for the future. For the present I have listed the books alphabetically according to pseudonyms or first key words.

In summary, the definition of Pseudepigrapha presently defended is in contrast to that found in *Webster's Third New International Dictionary* (1961), which describes the category as consisting of "spurious works purporting to emanate from biblical characters." Rather than being spurious the documents considered as belonging to the Pseudepigrapha are works written in honor of and inspired by Old Testament heroes. It is anachronistic and misrepresentative to suggest that there is anything innately fraudulent about the Pseudepigrapha.

The Importance of the Pseudepigrapha

The Pseudepigrapha is important to the Humanist, Jew, and Christian. All three find these documents valuable because of their importance in the history of ideas since they advance significantly man's understanding of sin and the origin of evil, man's awareness of God's grandeur with the exaltation of Him progressively to more distant heavens, and man's belief in a resurrection with the subsequent speculation upon the place and qualities of paradise. The often bizarre, usually rich apocalyptic traditions upon which the Pseudepigrapha almost has a monopoly were determinative for the thoughts of Dante, Bunyan, and Milton.

The Jew is attracted to the Pseudepigrapha for at least four reasons. The documents contained therein represent an important, but neglected, chapter in the history of Jewish ideas, and perception of these ideas and images is a prerequisite for the comprehension of later movements such as medieval mysticism. They mirror, it is now acknowledged, a central and major aspect of pre-rabbinic Judaism. They contain significant

---

[26]My students have found helpful the following arrangement: Wisdom (Ah, 3Mac, 4Mac, etc.), Edifying Expansion of Hebrew Scriptures (LetAris, Jub, BkNoah, MartIs, etc.), Testaments (T12P, TJob, TAb, etc.), Apocalyptic Proper (1En, 2En, 4Ezra, ApAb, 2Bar, AsMos, etc.), Prayers and Psalms (PrMan, PssSol, OdesSol, 5ApocSyrPss, PrJos, etc.), and *Alia* (PhEPoet, Theod, EzekTrag, etc.).

early reflections upon and expansions of the Hebrew scriptures. They clarify that by the first century mutually exclusive definitions of Judaism had evolved, signifying that Judaism is more than a philosophy or a core of beliefs.

The Christian also is excited about these writings because of four main reasons. Some antedate the latest book in the Old and others postdate the last book in the New, hence the Pseudepigrapha is a spectrum of compositions that cumulatively bridge the chasm of over two hundred years that separates the two sacred testaments. They come from Jesus' time, providing an invaluable link with his milieu. This feature is highly significant since there is growing awareness that the proper approach to the historical Jesus is via documents and traditions contemporaneous with him. Some New Testament authors, especially John, Paul, Jude, and the author of Revelation, and many early Fathers, notably Origen, Clement of Alexandria, Eusebius, and Ephrem Syrus, considered some pseudepigrapha canonical or authoritative. Many pseudepigrapha contain long Christian passages, often revealing a precious glimpse of Christianity that is contemporaneous with the New Testament authors, and others are more 'Christian' and less 'Jewish' than readily admitted, since it is frequently impossible to distinguish between Jewish and Christian compositions written around the first century A.D.

Contemporary Text and Translation Projects

Worthy of special note are the projects underway for the publication of the Pseudepigrapha. From Denmark come the fascicles of *De Gammeltestamentlige Pseudepigrafer*, edited by E. Hammershaimb and others, which began in 1953 and appear approximately every other year. In Ireland M. McNamara has drawn attention to Irish texts of the pseudepigrapha in Latin and Irish; the latter may contain the "richest crop" of these documents in any vernacular language.[27] These documents are important since, *inter alia*, they intermittently reveal relationships with the East, especially the Syrian Chruch.[28] In order

---

[27] It is surprising and interesting to observe that an eighth-century Irish work, the *Liber de numeris*, considered as canonical 1,2,3 and 4 Mac.

[28] McNamara points to the Theodorean Psalm headings in

to facilitate a systematic study of the Pseudepigrapha in Ireland he has published *The Apocrypha in the Irish Church* (Dublin: Dublin Institute for Advanced Studies, 1975), which is a
catalogue of the documents preserved in Ireland with notes regarding extant manuscripts and published research.   In England
H.F.D. Sparks has organized a team of specialists who have
nearly finished for the Clarendon Press a revision of the books
published in R.H. Charles' *Pseudepigrapha* and of other compositions that should have been included therein.

In France M. Philonenko has inaugurated a new series entitled "Textes et études pour servir à l'histoire du judaïsme
intertestamentaire."[29]   In Germany W.G. Kümmel is chairman of a
committee that is publishing new introductions to and translations of most of the works contained in Kautzsch and Riessler.
Publication by Mohn is in fascicles under the title *Jüdische
Schriften aus hellenistisch-römischer Zeit (JSHRZ)*.   In Greece
S. Agourides has begun a series of publications on the Pseudepigrapha, consisting of an introduction and text, which is
addressed to the theological student and interested public.[30]

In Holland and Belgium there are two new series edited by
A.-M. Denis and M. de Jonge, Pseudepigrapha Veteris Testamenti
Graece and Studia in Veteris Testamenti Pseudepigrapha; a ser-
ies containing some Syriac apocryphal works published by the

Latin manuscripts copied and preserved in Ireland and shows
that Theodore of Mopsuestia's work on the Psalms influenced
profoundly Irish exegesis at least as early as the seventh century when the Theodorean commentary on the Psalms was unknown
elsewhere in the West (cf. his *Psalter Text and Psalter Study
in the Early Irish Church (A.D. 600-1200)* [Proceedings of the
Royal Irish Academy 73.C,7] Dublin: Royal Irish Academy, 1973).

[29]*La Bible Apocryphe*, ed. J. Bonsirven ([Textes pour l'histoire sacrée] Paris: Cerf-Fayard, 1953), was republished in
1975 with a prefixed "Avertissement" and bibliographical notes
up to 1973.

[30]See Agourides' edition of T12P (Athens: Theologikēs
Scholēs, 1973 [in Greek]).   After the present work was completed Agourides graciously thought to send me his *The Apocrypha of the Old Testament*, vol. 1 (Athens, 1973 [in Greek;
critical introductions and translations of the following documents are included: Jub, T12P, 1En, LetAris. The publication
is scholarly, informed, and beautifully printed.]).

Peshiṭta Institute in Leiden, which is directed by P.A.H. de Boer; and computer-produced concordances of Latin and Greek pseudepigrapha by the Centre de traitement électronique des documents (CETEDOC) in Louvain, which is directed by P. Tombeur. In Israel M.E. Stone has established a new series, Apocrypha Veteris Testamenti in Lingua Armeniaca Conservata. In Czechoslovakia translations of some of the Pseudepigrapha are being considered by the New Czechoslovakian Bible Translation Team, headed by J. Mánek. In Japan a new edition of the Apocrypha and Pseudepigrapha in Japanese will begin appearing, according to T. Muraoka.

In the United States there are five projects involving translations. B.M. Metzger is chairing the committee that is preparing a revised translation of the Apocrypha for the RSV. The series entitled "Jewish Apocryphal Literature," centered at Dropsie University with S. Zeitlin as Editor-in-Chief, continues as a significant vehicle for producing convenient text editions, translations, introductions, and commentaries on the apocryphal books. The series *Hermeneia* will contain translations and commentaries on a few pseudepigrapha. Analogous to their edition of the Jerusalem Bible, Doubleday & Co., Inc., is publishing a new translation of the Pseudepigrapha, with introductions directed to the average intelligent reader. The work is centered at Duke University under my editorship and with an advisory board consisting of W.D. Davies, R.E. Murphy, B.M. Metzger, R.E. Brown, and W. Harrelson. Under the guidance of the SBL Pseudepigrapha Group Steering Committee[31] and specifically under the editorship of R.A. Kraft, the SBL Texts and Translations, Pseudepigrapha Series, has begun publishing inexpensive, working editions of some of the Pseudepigrapha.

The *Interpreter's Dictionary of the Bible, Supplementary Volume*, will contain numerous contributions on or related to the Pseudepigrapha. Noteworthy are the following: "Apocalypse of Adam" by G.W. MacRae, "Apocalypse" and "Apocalypticism" by P. Hanson, "Jewish Messiah" by E. Rivkin, "Messianic Banquet" by J. Priest, "Odes of Solomon" by J.H. Charlesworth,

---

[31]The SBL Pseudepigrapha Group is discussed in publications numbered 16 and 17; also see nos. 14, 15, 18, 19.

"Pseudepigrapha" and "Testaments of the Twelve Patriarchs" by
M.E. Stone.

In conclusion, the following list juxtaposes the documents
that are included in the collections to be published by Clarendon, Doubleday, and Mohn (asterisks denote that the pseudepigraphon is not included).

Pseudepi- grapha	Clarendon	Doubleday	Mohn
ApAb	A.Pennington	R.Rubinkiewicz	L.Müller and O.Betz
TAb	N.Turner	E.P.Sanders	E.Janssen
ApAdam	*	G.W.MacRae	*
LAE(ApMos)	W.Whittaker	M.D.Johnson	*
Ah	*	J.M.Lindenberger	*
AnonSam	*	(uncertain)	*
LetAris	*	R.J.H.Shutt	N.Meisner
2Bar	L.H.Brockington	A.F.J.Klijn	A.F.J.Klijn
3Bar	R.Thanhill	H.E.Gaylord	Hage
4Bar	A.W.Argyle	A.-E.Purintun	B.Schaller
ApEl	*	O.Wintermute	W.Schrage
1En	M.A.Knibb	E.Isaac	Rau
2En	A.Pennington	F.Andersen	F.v.Lilienfeld
3En	*	P.Alexander	*
ApEzek	*	(uncertain)	Eckart
4Ezra(4,5,6)	*	B.M.Metzger	Schreiner(4) H.Stegemann(5&6)
GkApEzra	R.J.H.Shutt	M.E.Stone	U.Müller
QuesEzra	*	M.E.Stone	*
VisEzra	R.J.H.Shutt	(uncertain)	*
FrgsHistWrks	*	B.Z.Wacholder	N.Walter
TIsaac	K.H.Kuhn	W.F.Stinespring	W.Müller
AscenIs	J.M.T.Barton	M.A.Knibb	E.Hammershaimb (MartIs only)
LadJac	A.Pennington	R.Rubinkiewicz	*
TJac	K.H.Kuhn	W.F.Stinespring	*
JanJam	*	(uncertain)	*
TJob	R.Thanhill	R.Spittler	B.Schaller
JosAsen	D.Cook	C.Burchard	C.Burchard
PrJos	*	J.Z.Smith	*
Jub	C.Rabin	O.Wintermute	[K.]Berger

3Mac	*	H.Anderson	K.Müller
4Mac	*	H.Anderson	Wickert
PrMan	*	J.H.Charlesworth	E.Osswald
AsMos	J.P.M.Sweet	J.Priest	E.Brandenburger
Ps-Philo	*	D.J.Harrington	C.Dietzfelbinger
Ps-Phoc	*	P.W.van der Horst	N.Walter
FrgsPoetWrks	*	(uncertain)	N.Walter
LivPro	*	D.R.A.Hare	Elze
ApSedr	R.J.H.Shutt	S.Agourides	*
TrShem	*	J.H.Charlesworth	*
SibOr	*	J.Collins	Schwark
OdesSol	J.A.Emerton	J.H.Charlesworth	*
PssSol	S.P.Brock	R.B.Wright	S.Holm-Nielsen
TSol	M.Whittaker	(uncertain)	*
5ApocSyrPss	*	J.H.Charlesworth and J.A.Sanders	A.S.van der Woude
Tl2P	M.de Jonge	H.C.Kee	J.Becker
ApZeph	*	O.Wintermute	Altendorf
ApZos	*	J.H.Charlesworth	*

The Purpose and Limits of the Introductions

Each entry begins with an introduction which is directed
primarily to the beginning English-speaking student. Only the
most important extant versions are noted with references to
their best edition, and English translations are selected and
listed according to the version that has served as the base.
Where appropriate and possible a brief discussion is centered
upon the probable date, provenance, and original language of
the document. Scholarly discussions prior to 1960 are cited
only when demanded by their intrinsic importance or by the
paucity of recent comments; publications since 1960, if not
included in Delling's *Bibliographie*, are cited by their entry
number. Sometimes it is wise, because of the nature of the
work, to note its possible relationships to the Dead Sea
Scrolls and a judgment regarding its inclusion within the
Pseudepigrapha. A brief summary of the contents of the document concludes the introduction.[32]

---

[32]After this monograph was nearly finished I decided that
it would be wise to include a discussion of the cycles represented by some documents. In a second edition the number and
extent of these discussions should be expanded.

Efficient Use of the Bibliographical Report

A few words about the format of the following report and some advice about its use are appropriate. The title of a pseudepigraphon is followed by a brief introduction, a note on known work in progress, cross references by number to publications listed elsewhere, and the pertinent bibliographical data for publications that appeared from 1960 to 1975 (inclusive only of 1975 contributions available).[33] The report attempts to list all publications of fragments of the pseudepigrapha found among the Dead Sea Scrolls, and to note all appropriate entries in E.R. Goodenough's *Jewish Symbols in the Greco-Roman Period* (12 vols. New York: Random House, 1953-1968), since Delling lists only the early volumes and only under "Die Religion in der Kunst." Even though some antedate 1960 all volumes of the third edition of *Religion in Geschichte und Gegenwart* and the second edition of *Lexikon für Theologie und Kirche* are included. Only when necessary are foreign words transliterated or translated.

For further information regarding history, the relation between the Pseudepigrapha and the Dead Sea Scrolls, and related special themes--such as theology, dualism, messianism, resurrection, eschatology, and sin--see the bibliographies on the Dead Sea Scrolls published by C. Burchard, J.A. Fitzmyer, S.J., A.M. Habermann, B. Jongeling, W.S. LaSor, and M. Yizhar.[34] Also to be consulted with profit are the bibliographical reports published in *Elenchus Bibliographicus*, *Internationale Zeitschriftenschau für Bibelwissenschaft und Grenzgebiete*, *Journal for the Study of Judaism*, *Revue de Qumran*, and *Recherches de science religieuse*. For additional guidance on publications on the Pseudepigrapha and Gnosticism and related special themes see D.M. Scholer's *Nag Hammadi Bibliography*

---

[33]When we have not been able to locate the work to check on some questionable data we have added the abbreviation "*N.V.*" (*non vidimus*).

[34]For bibliographical details see J.A. Fitzmyer, S.J., *The Dead Sea Scrolls: Major Publications and Tools for Study* ([Sources for Biblical Study 8] Missoula, Mont.: Scholars Press, 1975), pp. 57f.

1948-1969 [Nag Hammadi Studies 1] Leiden: Brill, 1971), which he updates annually in *Novum Testamentum*. Finally, G. Delling has informed me recently that an expanded *Bibliographie*, including publications on the Pseudepigrapha back to the beginning of this century, will appear within the year.[35]

---

[35]After the present monograph was finished I received Delling's thoughtful gift of an advanced copy of his *Bibliographie zur jüdisch-hellenistischen und intertestamentarischen Literatur 1900-1970* ([TU 106.2] Berlin: Akademie, 1975). A cursory comparison of Delling's recent publication with the present work reveals some significant differences, indicating the importance and usefulness of each. Only Delling's *Bibliographie* contains a list of publications on the papyri, Philo, and Josephus. The present work alone contains a bibliographical report of publications that appeared in the years 1970 to 1975, includes documents considered in the inclusive list of the Pseudepigrapha, and supplies introductions to each pseudepigraphon and notices of work in progress.

BIBLIOGRAPHY

General

1 Ackroyd, P.R. and C.F. Evans, eds. "Canonical and Non-
   Canonical," *The Cambridge History of the Bible: From the
   Beginnings to Jerome.* Cambridge: CUP, 1970. Vol. 1,
   pp. 113-59.

2 Aland, K. "Das Problem der Anonymität und Pseudonymität in
   der christlichen Literatur der ersten beiden Jahrhun-
   derte," *Studien zur Überlieferung des Neuen Testaments
   und seines Textes* (Arbeiten zur Neutestamentlichen Text-
   forschung 2) Berlin: Walter de Gruyter, 1967. Pp. 24-34.

3 Andrews, H.T. *An Introduction to the Apocryphal Books of
   the Old and New Testament,* rev. and ed. C.F. Pfeiffer.
   Grand Rapids: Baker, 1964.

4 Artom, E.S. *HSPRYM HḤYṢWNYM.* Yavne, 1965. [This volume apparently contains Hebrew translations of LAE, Tl2P,
   AsMos, Jub, TJob; *N.V.*]

5 Balz, H.R. "Anonymität und Pseudepigraphie im Urchristentum: Überlegungen zum literarischen und theologischen
   Problem der urchristlichen und gemeinantiken Pseudepigraphie," *ZTK* 66 (1969) 403-56.

6 Bauer, J.B., ed. *Index Verborum in Libris Pseudepigraphis
   Usurpatorum,* appended to repr. of C.A. Wahl, *Clavis Li-
   brorum Veteris Testamenti Apocryphorum Philologica.*
   Graz: Akademische Druck- und Verlagsanstalt, 1972.

7 Baumgartner, W. "Pseudepigraphen des AT," *RGG*[3] 5. Cols.
   692f.

8 Botterweck, G. J. "Apokryphen," *LTK*[2] 1. Cols. 712f.

9 Brown, R.E. "Apocrypha; Dead Sea Scrolls; Other Jewish
   Literature," *JBC* 2. Pp. 535-60.

10 Brown, R.E. *The Semitic Background of the Term "Mystery"
   in the New Testament* (FBBS 21) Philadelphia: Fortress,
   1968.

11 Brox, N. "Zum Problemstand in der Erforschung der altchristlichen Pseudepigraphie," *Kairos* 15 (1973) 10-23.

12 Cerulli, E. "Bible, IV (Texts and Versions): Ethiopic Versions," *NCE* 2. Pp. 458f.

13 Charles, R.H. *The Apocrypha and Pseudepigrapha of the Old
   Testament.* 2 vols. Oxford: Clarendon, 1913; repr. 1963
   etc.

14 Charlesworth, J.H. "A Clearing House for the Publication of Jewish Apocryphal Literature," *RQ* 8 (1972) 160.

15 Charlesworth, J.H. "De Pseudepigraphorum Studio," SCS 2. Pp. 129-35.

16 Charlesworth, J.H. "The Renaissance of Pseudepigrapha Studies: The SBL Pseudepigrapha Project," *JSJ* 2 (1971) 107-14.

17 Charlesworth, J.H. "The SBL Pseudepigrapha Project," *Bulletin of the Council on the Study of Religion* 2 (1971) 24f.

18 Charlesworth, J.H. "Some Cognate Studies to the Septuagint," *BIOSCS* 6 (1973) 10f.

19 Charlesworth, J.H. "Some Reflections on Present Work on the Pseudepigrapha," *SBL 1971 Seminar Papers*. Vol. 1, pp. 229-37.

20 Dancy, J.C., *et al. The Shorter Books of the Apocrypha* (The Cambridge Bible Commentary: NEB) Cambridge: CUP, 1972.

21 Delling, G., *et al. Bibliographie zur jüdisch-hellenistischen und intertestamentarischen Literatur 1900-1965* (TU 106) Berlin: Akademie, 1969.

21a Delling, G. "Perspektiven der Erforschung des hellenistischen Judentums," *HUCA* 45 (1974) 133-76.

22 Denis, A.-M. "L'étude des pseudépigraphes: Etat actuel des instruments de travail," *NTS* 16 (1970) 348-53.

23 Denis, A.-M., ed. *Fragmenta pseudepigraphorum quae supersunt graeca* (PVTG 3) Leiden: Brill, 1970. Pp. 47-246.

24 Denis, A.-M. *Introduction aux pseudépigraphes grecs d'Ancien Testament* (SVTP 1) Leiden: Brill, 1970.

25 Denis, A.-M. "Les pseudépigraphes grecs d'Ancien Testament," *NovT* 10 (1968) 313-18.

26 Denis, A.-M. and M. de Jonge. "The Greek Pseudepigrapha of the Old Testament," *NovT* 7 (1965) 319-28.

27 Dimier, C. *The Old Testament Apocrypha*, trans. S.J. Tester. New York: Hawthorn, 1964.

28 Flusser, D. *Hellenistic Pseudepigrapha Concerning the Vision of the End and the Redeemed*, 1966. [in Hebrew; *N.V.*]

29 Foster, R.J. "The Apocrypha of the Old and New Testaments," *NCCHS*. Pp. 109-14.

30 Fritsch, C.T. "Pseudepigrapha," *IDB* 3. Pp. 960-64.

31 Gancho, C. "Apócrifos, Libros," *Enciclopedia de la Biblia* 1. Cols. 589-91.

32 Gancho, C. "Pseudoepigráfico, Libro," *Enciclopedia de la Biblia* 5. Cols. 1325f.

33 Gasque, W.W. "Pseudepigrapha," *ZPEB* 4. Pp. 949-51.

33a Geisler, N.L. "The Extent of the Old Testament Canon," *Current Issues in Biblical and Patristic Interpretation.* M. C. Tenney Festschrift, ed. G.F. Hawthorne. Grand Rapids, Mich.: Eerdmans, 1975. Pp. 31-46.

34 Giversen, S. "Pseudepigrafer," *GDBL* 2. Cols. 551f.

35 Glatzer, N.N. *The Judaic Tradition: Texts Edited and Introduced,* rev. ed. Boston: Beacon, 1969.

36 Grabar, B. "Concerning the Problems in Slavonic Apocrypha," *Kiril Solimski.* Skopje, Yugoslavia, 1970. Vol. 1, pp. 91-97. [in Yugoslavian; *N.V.*]

37 Grelot, P. "Apocalíptica, Literatura," *Enciclopedia de la Biblia* 1. Cols. 585-88.

38 Grintz, Y.M.G. "Apocrypha and Pseudepigrapha," *EncyJud* 3. Pp. 181-87. [See the additional note on "In Medieval Hebrew Literature" by Y. David.]

39 Gross, H. "Apokalypsen, apokryphe. I. des AT," *LTK*[2] 1. Cols. 696-98.

40 Gutman, Y. *The Hellenistic-Jewish Writings.* Bialik Institute, 1963. Vol. 2. [in Hebrew; *N.V.*]

41 Hammershaimb, E., *et al.*, eds. *De Gammeltestamentlige Pseudepigrafer: I Oversaettelse med Inledning og Noter.* Copenhagen: Gads, 1953-.

42 Hengel, M. "Anonymität, Pseudepigraphie und 'Literarische Fälschung' in der jüdisch-hellenistischen Literatur," *Pseud* I. Pp. 229-308. [See the published discussions by K. von Fritz, M. Smith, M. Hengel, W. Speyer, G.J.D. Aalders, H. Thesleff, R. Syme, and W. Burkert, pp. 309-29.]

43 Hurwitz, M.S. "Hellenistic Jewish Literature," *EncyJud* 8. Cols. 303f.

44 James, M.R. *The Lost Apocrypha of the Old Testament* (TED) New York: Macmillan, 1920; repr. with prolegomenon by L. Feldman. New York: KTAV, in press.

45 Kraft, R.A. "Jewish Greek Scriptures and Related Topics: Reports on Recent Discussions," *NTS* 16 (1970) 384-96.

46 Kraft, R.A. "Jewish Greek Scriptures and Related Topics II," *NTS* 17 (1971) 488-90.

47 Kravitz, N. "Apocrypha, Pseudepigrapha, Apocalypse, Apology," *3,000 Years of Hebrew Literature.* Chicago: Swallow, 1972. Pp. 111-17.

48   Krentz, E. "Intertestamental and New Testament Studies,"
      CTM 36 (1965) 430-32.

49   Kümmel, W.G., *et al.*, eds. *Jüdische Schriften aus helleni-
      stisch-römischer Zeit.* Gütersloh: Mohn, 1973-.

50   Lagarde, P.A.de. *Libri Veteris Testamenti Apocryphi Syriace.*
      Leipzig: Brockhaus, 1861; repr. Osnabrück: Zeller, 1972.

51   McNamara, M. *The Apocrypha in the Irish Church.* Dublin:
      Institute for Advanced Studies, 1975.

52   Maier, J. "Frühjüdische Literatur," *Literatur und Religion
      des Frühjudentums.* Pp. 117-22.

53   Mathews, S. "Pseudepigrapha," rev. by B.M. Metzger. Hast-
      ings. Pp. 820-23.

54   Metzger, B.M. "Literary Forgeries and Canonical Pseudepi-
      grapha," *JBL* 91 (1972) 3-24.

55   Metzger, B.M. "Pseudepigraphen," *BHH* 3. Cols. 1529f.

56   Michl, J. "Apocrypha," *Sacramentum Mundi* 1. Pp. 52-66.

57   Mowry, L. "The Intertestamental Literature," *IOCB.* Pp.
      1110-15.

58   Mpratsiōtēs, P.I. "Apocrypha (Old Testament)," *ThEE* 2.
      Cols. 1106-08. [in Greek]

59   Paul, A. "Bulletin de littérature intertestamentaire,"
      RSR 60 (1972) 429-58.

60   Paul, A. "Bulletin de littérature intertestamentaire," *RSR*
      62 (1974) 401-34. See esp. pp. 421-26.

61   Philonenko, M. "La littérature intertestamentaire et le
      Nouveau Testament," *Exégèse biblique et judaïsme.* Pp.
      116-25.

62   Riessler, P. *Altjüdisches Schrifttum ausserhalb der Bibel.*
      Heidelberg: Kerle, 1928; repr. 1966.

63   Rist, M. "Pseudepigraphy and the Early Christians," *Stud-
      ies in New Testament and Early Christian Literature: Es-
      says in Honor of Allen P. Wikgren,* ed. D.E. Aune. Leiden:
      Brill, 1972. Pp. 75-91.

64   Roncaglio, M. "Les apocryphes chrétiens et la gnose," *Les
      origines.* Pp. 65-109.

65   Roncaglio, M. "La 'Praeparatio Evangelica' et les premiers
      contacts avec les idées chrétiennes," *Les origines.*
      Pp. 11-62.

66   Rost, L. *Einleitung in die alttestamentlichen Apokryphen
      und Pseudepigraphen einschliesslich der grossen Qumran-
      Handschriften.* Heidelberg: Quelle & Meyer, 1971.

37

67   Salomonsen, B. "Testamentlitteratur," *GDBL* 2. Col. 960.

68   Sandmel, S. "The Books That Were Left Out," *Keeping Posted* 18 (1973) 19-23. [*N.V.*]

69   Sandmel, S. *The First Christian Century in Judaism and Christianity: Certainties and Uncertainties.* New York: OUP, 1969.

70   Santos Otero, A. de. "Das Problem der kirchen-slavischen Apokryphen," *Zeitschrift für Balkanologie* 1 (1962) 123-32.

71   Schwab, M. *Index of Articles Relative to Jewish History and Literature Published in Periodicals, from 1665-1900.* New York: KTAV, 1971.

72   Sen, F. "Una literatura clava en los estudios bíblicos," *CB* 30 (1973) 229-33.

73   Sint, J. "Pseudonymität," *LTK*^{2} 8. Col. 867.

74   Smith, M. "Pseudepigraphy in the Israelite Literary Tradition," *Pseud* I. Pp. 189-215. [See the published discussions by K. von Fritz, M. Smith, M. Hengel, W. Speyer, R. Syme, H. Thesleff, W. Burkert, and G.J.D. Aalders, pp. 216-27.]

75   Speranskij, M.N. *Concerning the History of Russian-Slavonic Literary Relations: A Collection of Articles.* Moscow, 1960. [in Russian]

76   Speyer, W. "Fälschung, literarische," *RAC* 7. Pp. 236-77.

77   Speyer, W. "Fälschung, pseudepigraphische freie Erfindung und 'echte religiöse Pseudepigraphie,'" *Pseud* I. Pp. 331-66. [See the published discussions by K. von Fritz, W. Speyer, M. Hengel, W. Burkert, and M. Smith, pp. 367-72.]

78   Speyer, W. *Die literarische Fälschung im heidnischen und christlichen Altertum: Ein Versuch ihrer Deutung* (HAW 1.2) Munich: Beck, 1971.

79   Speyer, W. "Religiöse Pseudepigraphie und literarische Fälschung im Altertum," *JAC* 8/9 (1965-1966) 88-125.

80   Stone, M.E. with E. Shefer. *Apocryphal Fragments from Qumran and the Church Fathers.* Jerusalem: Akademon, 1970. [in Hebrew]

81   Stone, M.E. "The Apocryphal Literature in the Armenian Tradition," *Proceedings of the Israel Academy of Sciences and Humanities* 4 (1969) 59-77.

82   Stone, M.E. "Apocryphal Notes and Readings," *Israel Oriental Studies.* [Tel Aviv]: Tel Aviv University, 1971. Vol. 1, pp. 123-31.

83 Stone, M.E. "Methodological Issues in the Study of the Text of the Apocrypha and Pseudepigrapha," *Proceedings of the Fifth World Congress of Jewish Studies,* ed. P. Peli. Jerusalem: World Union of Jewish Studies, 1969. Vol. 1, pp. 211-17.

84 Stone, M.E. "Researches in the Library of the Armenian Patriarchate in Jerusalem, 1967-1970, and Their Importance for Jewish Studies," *Tarbiz* 41 (1972) 157-69. [in Hebrew]

85 Stone, M.E. *The Signs of the Judgement, Onomastica Sacra Armeniaca, the Sons of Noah and the Generations of Adam* (Apocrypha Veteris Testamenti in Lingua Armeniaca Conservata 2) Jerusalem: Israel Academy of Sciences and the St. James Press, in press.

86 Strugnell, J. and H. Attridge. "The Epistles of Heraclitus and the Jewish Pseudepigrapha: A Warning," *HTR* 64 (1971) 411-13.

87 Stuhlmueller, C. "Bible, III (Canon): Apocrypha of the Old Testament," *NCE* 2. Pp. 396-404.

88 Swanson, T.N. *The Closing of the Collection of Holy Scriptures: A Study in the History of the Canonization of the Old Testament.* Vanderbilt Ph.D., 1970.

89 Syme, R. "Fraud and Imposture," *Pseud* I. Pp. 1-17. [See the published discussions by R. Syme, M. Hengel, O. Reverdin, [?]van Berchem, K. von Fritz, M. Smith, W. Speyer, and H. Thesleff, pp. 18-21.]

90 Trenton, R.F. "References to Apocrypha, Pseudepigrapha, and Extrabiblical Literature as Noted in the Outer Margins of the Nestle-Aland New Testament," *CTM* 39 (1968) 328-32.

91 Vriezen, T.C. "Apocriefen en Pseudepigrafen," *De Literatuur van Oud-Israël: Tweede sterk uitgebreide en gewijzigde druk.* Den Haag: Servire, 1961. Pp. 217-23.

92 Wahl, C.A. *Clavis Librorum Veteris Testamenti Apocryphorum Philologica,* ed. J.B. Bauer. Leipzig, 1853; repr. Graz: Akademische Druck- und Verlagsanstalt, 1972.

History

The following section is selective, using as criterion the importance of a publication for understanding the Pseudepigrapha.

93 Anderson, H. "The Intertestamental Period," *The Bible and History,* ed. W. Barclay, New York: Abingdon, 1968. Pp. 153-244.

94 Avi-Yonah, M. *Geschichte der Juden im Zeitalter des Talmud in den Tagen von Rom und Byzanz* (Studia Judaica 2) Berlin: Walter de Gruyter, 1962.

95   Avi-Yonah, M., ed. *The Herodian Period* (The World History of the Jewish People, Ser. 1, vol. 7) New Brunswick, N. J.: Rutgers, 1975.

96   Black, M. "The Development of Judaism in the Greek and Roman Periods (c. 196 B.C.-A.D. 135)," *PCB*. Pp. 693-98.

97   Brandon, S.G.F. *Jesus and the Zealots: A Study of the Political Factor in Primitive Christianity*. Manchester: University of Manchester, 1967.

98   Bruce, F.F. *New Testament History*. Garden City, N.Y.: Doubleday, 1972.

99   Buehler, W.W. *The Pre-Herodian Civil War and Social Debate: Jewish Society in the Period 76-40 B.C. and the Social Factors Contributing to the Rise of the Pharisees and the Sadducees* (Theologische • Dissertationen 11) Basel: Friedrich Reinhardt, 1974.

100 Davies, W.D. "The Jewish State in the Hellenistic World," *PCB*. Pp. 686-92.

101 Filson, F.V. *A New Testament History* (New Testament Library) London: SCM, 1965.

102 Foerster, W. *Neutestamentliche Zeitgeschichte*. Hamburg: Furche, 1968. [ET of 3rd. rev. ed. of Part 1 by G.E. Harris. Edinburgh: Oliver and Boyd; Philadelphia: Fortress, 1964.]

103 Grant, M. *The Jews in the Roman World*. New York: Scribner, 1973.

104 Hengel, M. *Judentum und Hellenismus: Studien zu ihrer Begegnung unter besonderer Berücksichtigung Palästinas bis zur Mitte des 2.Jh. v. Chr.*, 2d. ed. (WUNT 10) Tübingen: Mohr, 1973. [ET by J. Bowden. Philadelphia: Fortress, 1974.]

105 Hruby, K. *Die Synagoge: Geschichtliche Entwicklung einer Institution* (Schriften zur Judentumskunde 3) Zurich: Theologischer Verlag, 1971.

106 Jaubert, A. "Le judaïsme aux abords de l'ère chrétienne," *L'information historique* 27 (1965) 29-32.

107 Kenyon, K.M. *Digging up Jerusalem*. London: Ernest Benn, 1974. [This volume contains a definitive treatment of Jerusalem during the historical period covered by the Pseudepigrapha.]

108 Leipoldt, J. and W. Grundmann. *Umwelt des Urchristentums: Texte zum neutestamentlichen Zeitalter*. Berlin: Evangelische Verlagsanstalt, 1972. Vol. 2.

108a Lieberman, S. "How Much Greek in Jewish Palestine?" *Texts and Studies*. New York: KTAV, 1974. Pp. 216-34; repr. fr. *Biblical and Other Studies*, ed. A. Altmann. Cambridge, Mass.: Harvard University, 1963. Pp. 123-41.

109 Lohse, E. *Umwelt des Neuen Testaments* (GNT 1) Göttingen: Vandenhoeck & Ruprecht, 1971.

110 Michel, O., *et al. Studies on the Jewish Background of the New Testament*. Assen: Van Gorcum, 1969.

111 Negev, A. "The Chronology of the Middle Nabatean Period," *PEQ* 101 (1969) 5-14.

112 Neusner, J. *A History of the Jews in Babylonia: The Parthian Period* (SPB 9) Leiden: Brill, 1969. Vol. 1.

113 Prigent, P. *La fin de Jérusalem*. Paris: Delachaux et Niestlé, 1969.

114 Reicke, B. *The New Testament Era: The World of the Bible from 500 B.C. to A.D. 100*, trans. D.E. Green. Philadelphia: Fortress, 1968.

115 Russell, D.S. *The Jews from Alexander to Herod*. London: OUP, 1967.

116 Safrai, S., *et al.*, eds. *The Jewish People in the First Century: Historical Geography, Political History, Social, Cultural and Religious Life and Institutions*. 2 vols. (Compendia Rerum Iudaicarum ad Novum Testamentum 1) Assen: Van Gorcum, 1974.

117 Schalit, A. "A Clash of Ideologies: Palestine Under the Seleucids and Romans," *Crucible*. Pp. 47-76.

118 Schalit, A., ed. *The Hellenistic Age: Political History of Jewish Palestine from 332 B.C.E. to 67 B.C.E.* (The World History of the Jewish People, Ser. 1, vol. 6) New Brunswick, N.J.: Rutgers University, 1972.

119 Schmitt, J. "Le milieu baptiste de Jean le Précurseur," *Exégèse biblique et judaïsme*. Pp. 237-53.

120 Schürer, E. *The History of the Jewish People in the Age of Jesus Christ*, rev. and ed. G. Vermes, F. Millar, P. Vermes, M. Black. Edinburgh: T. & T. Clark, 1973. Vol. 1.

121 Schürer, E. *The Literature of the Jewish People in the Time of Jesus*, abridged and ed. with intro. by N.N. Glatzer. New York: Schocken, 1972.

122 Schweitzer, F.M. *A History of the Jews Since the First Century A.D.* New York: Macmillan, 1971.

123 Simon, M. *Jewish Sects at the Time of Jesus*, trans. J.H. Farley. Philadelphia: Fortress, 1967.

124 Tcherikover, V. *Hellenistic Civilization and the Jews*, trans. S. Applebaum. New York: Atheneum, 1970.

125 Thoma, C. "Judentum und Hellenismus im Zeitalter Jesu," *Bibel und Leben* 11 (1970) 151-59.

126 Wendland, P. *Die hellenistisch-römische Kultur in ihren*
     Beziehungen zum Judentum und Christentum, 4th ed. rev.
     H. Dörrie (HNT 2) Tübingen: Mohr, 1972.

127 Wirgin, W. "Judah Maccabee's Embassy to Rome and the Jew-
     ish-Roman Treaty," *PEQ* 101 (1969) 15-20.

128 Zeitlin, S. *The Rise and Fall of the Judaean State: A*
     Political, Social and Religious History of the Second
     Commonwealth. 2 vols. Philadelphia: Jewish Publication
     Society of America, 1962-1967.

The Pseudepigrapha and the Dead Sea Scrolls

     This section is extremely selective. See also the entries
below under Dualism, 1 Enoch, Jubilees, Odes of Solomon, 5 Apocryphal Syriac Psalms, and Testaments of the Twelve Patriarchs.
Editions of Qumran fragments of 1 Enoch, Jubilees, and Testaments of the Twelve Patriarchs are listed under the respective
pseudepigraphon. See also nos. 9, 304f., 322, 707, 788, 1207,
1266f.

129 Allegro, J.M. "An Astrological Cryptic Document from Qum-
     ran," *JSS* 9 (1964) 291-94; repr. *DJD* 5. Pp. 88-91
     (Pl. XXXI). [4QCryptic may be related to Enoch cycle.
     See Milik below, no. 159.]

130 Allegro, J.M. "Some Unpublished Fragments of Pseudepigra-
     phical Literature from Qumran's Fourth Cave," *ALUOS* 4
     (1962-1963) 3-5; repr. *DJD* 5. Pp. 77-80 (Pls. XXVII and
     XVIII). [4QAgesCreat is ed. and trans.; although not in
     our list of pseudepigrapha, there are affinities with
     1En 9:6 and 10:8. See Milik below, no. 158.]

131 Baillet, M. "Un apocryphe mentionnant l'Ange de la Pré-
     sence (Pl. XVIII)," *DJD* 3. P. 99. [3Q7 (= Fitzmyer's
     3Q?) may be related, perhaps distantly, to the T12P
     because of restorations that would be close to TJud 24-
     25.]

132 Baillet, M. "Un texte mentionnant un ange de paix (?) (Pl.
     XIX)," *DJD* 3. P. 100. [If fragment 1 reads *ML'K ShLW*[M],
     and if this means "Angel of Peace," then it may possibly
     be related to 1QH 9:10, to some unknown text, or to T12P
     (cf. TDan 6:5, TAsh 6:6, TBenj 6:1).]

133 Beckwith, R.T. "The Modern Attempt to Reconcile the Qumran
     Calendar with the True Solar Year," *RQ* 7 (1970) 379-96.

134 Beckwith, R.T. "The Qumran Calendar and the Sacrifices of
     the Essenes," *RQ* 7 (1971) 587-91.

135 Betz, O. "The Relevance of Some Recently Published Messi-
     anic Fragments from Qumran," *Proceedings of the Fifth*
     World Congress of Jewish Studies, ed. P. Peli. Jerusalem:
     World Union of Jewish Studies, 1969. Vol. 1, pp. 201-10.

136 Black, M. "The Dead Sea Scrolls and Christian Origins,"
     *The Scrolls and Christianity: Historical and Theological
     Significance*, ed. M. Black (Theological Collections 11)
     London: S.P.C.K., 1969. Pp. 97-106.

137 Carmignac, J. "La notion d'eschatologie dans la Bible et
     à Qumrân," *RQ* 7 (1969) 17-31.

138 Charlesworth, J.H. "A Critical Comparison of the Dualism
     in 1QS 3:13-4:26 and the 'Dualism' Contained in the Gos-
     pel of John," *NTS* 15 (1969) 389-418; repr. *John and Qum-
     ran*, ed. J.H. Charlesworth. London: Chapman, 1972. Pp.
     76-106. [The paper touches on the relation of Qumran
     dualism to related concepts in the Pseudepigrapha.]

139 Cross, F.M. Jr. "The Essenes and the Primitive Church,"
     *The Ancient Library of Qumran and Modern Biblical
     Studies*, rev. ed. Garden City, N.Y.: Doubleday, 1961.
     Pp. 195-243. See esp. pp. 198-206.

140 Delcor, M. "Le Testament de Job, la prière de Nabonide et
     les traditions targoumiques," *Bibel und Qumran*. H.
     Bardtke Festschrift, ed. S. Wagner. Berlin: Evangelische
     Haupt-Bibelgesellschaft, 1968. Pp. 57-74.

141 Dequeker, L. "The 'Saints of the Most High' in Qumran and
     Daniel," *Syntax and Meaning: Studies in Hebrew Syntax
     and Biblical Exegesis*, ed. A.S. van der Woude (OTS 18)
     Leiden: Brill, 1973. Pp. 108-87.

142 Driver, G.R. *The Judaean Scrolls: The Problem and a Solu-
     tion*. Oxford: Basil Blackwell, 1965. (*passim*)

143 Eybers, I.H. *Historical Evidence on the Canon of the Old
     Testament with Special Reference to the Qumran Sect*.
     Duke Ph.D., 1965. [Chapter 7, "Other Sacred Books at
     Qumran," is a discussion of the pseudepigrapha at Qum-
     ran.]

144 Fitzmyer, J.A. "The Aramaic 'Elect of God' Text from Qum-
     ran Cave 4," *Essays on the Semitic Background of the New
     Testament*, ed. J.A. Fitzmyer. London: Chapman, 1971.
     Pp. 127-60.

145 Flusser, D. "Qumran and Jewish 'Apotropaic' Prayers,"
     IEJ 16 (1966) 194-205.

146 Geoltrain, P. *Le livre éthiopien d'Hénoch: ses rapports
     avec les manuscrits de Qumrân et le Nouveau Testament*.
     Strasbourg Ph.D., 1960.

147 Geoltrain, P. "Quelques lectures juives et chrétiennes
     des premiers versets de la Genèse de Qoumrân au Nouveau
     Testament," *In Principio: Interprétations des premiers
     versets de la Genèse*. Paris: Etudes Augustiniennes,
     1973. Pp. 47-60.

148 Gnilka, J. "2 Cor. 6:14-7:1 in the Light of the Qumran
     Texts and the Testaments of the Twelve Patriarchs,"
     Paul and Qumran, ed. J. Murphy-O'Connor. London: Chap-
     man, 1968. Pp. 48-68.

149 Grundmann, W. "Die Frage nach der Gottessohnschaft des
     Messias im Lichte von Qumran," *Bibel und Qumran*. H.
     Bardtke Festschrift, ed. S. Wagner. Berlin: Evangelische
     Haupt-Bibelgesellschaft, 1968. Pp. 86-111.

150 Harrison, R.K. "The Rites and Customs of the Qumran Sect,"
     *The Scrolls and Christianity: Historical and Theological
     Significance*, ed. M. Black (Theological Collections 11)
     London: S.P.C.K., 1969. Pp. 26-36.

151 Holm-Nielsen, S. "Erwägungen zu dem Verhältnis zwischen
     den Hodajot und den Psalmen Salomos," *Bibel und Qumran*.
     H. Bardtke Festschrift, ed. S. Wagner. Berlin: Evange-
     lische Haupt-Bibelgesellschaft, 1968. Pp. 112-31.

152 Jaubert, A. "Jésus et le calendrier de Qumrân," *NTS* 7
     (1960) 1-30.

153 Larsson, G. "Is Biblical Chronology Systematic or Not?"
     RQ 6 (1969) 499-515.

154 Laurin, R.B. "The Problem of Two Messiahs in the Qumran
     Scrolls," *RQ* 4 (1963) 39-52. [Includes a discussion of
     T12P.]

155 Licht, J. "The Doctrine of 'Times' According to the Sect
     of Qumran and Other 'Computers of Seasons,'" *Eretz-
     Israel* 8 (1967) 63-70.

156 Lowy, S. "Some Aspects of Normative and Sectarian Inter-
     pretation of the Scriptures (The Contribution of the
     Judean Scrolls Towards Systematization)," *ALUOS* 6 (1966-
     1968) 98-163.

157 Meysing, J. "L'énigme de la chronologie biblique et qum-
     rânienne dans une nouvelle lumière," *RQ* 6 (1967) 229-51.

158 Milik, J.T. "Milkî-ṣedeq et Milkî-rešaʿ dans les anciens
     écrits juifs et chrétiens," *JJS* 23 (1972) 95-144.
     [4QAgesCreat. See Allegro above, no. 130.]

159 Milik, J.T. "Problèmes de la littérature hénochique à la
     lumière des fragments araméens de Qumrân," *HTR* 64 (1971)
     333-78. [4QHenAstr[a-e], 4QCryptic. See Allegro above,
     no. 129.]

160 Milik, J.T. "4Q Visions de ʿAmram et une citation d'Ori-
     gène," *RB* 79 (1972) 77-97. [An apocryphon with parallels
     to TLevi.]

161 Milik, J.T. "Turfan et Qumran: Livre des Géants juif et
     manichéen," Kuhn Festschrift. Pp. 117-27. [1QHenGiants,
     4QHenGiants[a-f].]

162 Nikiprowetzky, V. "Pseudépigraphes de l'Ancien Testament
     et manuscrits de la Mer Morte: Réflexions sur une publi-
     cation récente," *REJ* 128 (1968) 5-40. [See Philonenko
     below, no. 163.]

163 Philonenko, M., *et al*. *Pseudépigraphes de l'Ancien Testa-
     ment et manuscrits de la Mer Morte* (Cahiers de la RHPR
     41) Paris: Presses universitaires de France, 1967. Vol.
     1. [See Nikiprowetzky above, no. 162.]

164 Pryke, E.J. "Some Aspects of Eschatology in the Dead Sea
     Scrolls," *Studia Evangelica*, ed. F.L. Cross (TU 103)
     Berlin: Akademie, 1968. Vol. 5, pp. 296-302. [The note
     also concerns 1En, 2En, SibOr, 4Ezra, AsMos.]

165 Ragot, A. "L'essénisme dans les apocryphes," *Cahiers du
     Cercle Ernest-Renan* 20 (1972) 3-8.

166 Schubert, K. "Pseudepigraphen," *Die Qumran-Essener: Texte
     der Schriftrollen und Lebensbild der Gemeinde* (Uni-
     Taschenbücher 224) Munich: Ernst Reinhardt, 1973. Pp.
     10-19.

167 Smith, M. "The Dead Sea Sect in Relation to Ancient Juda-
     ism," *NTS* 7 (1961) 347-60.

168 Testuz, M. "Deux fragments inédits des manuscrits de la
     Mer Morte," *Sem* 5 (1955) 37f. [4QTestuz ar may be rela-
     ted to the Enoch cycle.]

169 Thorndike, J.P. "The Apocalypse of Weeks and the Qumran
     Sect," *RQ* 3 (1961) 163-84.

170 Villalón, J.R. "Sources vétéro-testamentaires de la doc-
     trine qumrânienne des deux messies," *RQ* 8 (1972) 53-63.
     [Includes T12P.]

171 Winston, D. "The Iranian Component in the Bible, Apocrypha,
     and Qumran: A Review of the Evidence," *History of Reli-
     gions: An International Journal for Comparative Histori-
     cal Studies* 5 (1966) 183-216.

172 Worrell, J.E. *Concepts of Wisdom in the Dead Sea Scrolls*.
     Claremont Ph.D., 1968.

The Pseudepigrapha and Gnosticism

This section is extremely selective; see also below under
Apocalypse of Adam and Odes of Solomon. See also nos. 64,
1486.

173 Bianchi, U. "Gnostizismus und Anthropologie," *Kairos* 11
     (1969) 6-14.

174 Böhlig, A. *Mysterion und Wahrheit: Gesammelte Beiträge zur
     spätantiken Religionsgeschichte* (AGAJU 6) Leiden: Brill,
     1968.

175   Groningen, G. van. *First Century Gnosticism: Its Origin
      and Motifs*. Leiden: Brill, 1967.

176   Gruenwald, I. "Knowledge and Vision: Towards a Clarifica-
      tion of Two 'Gnostic' Concepts in the Light of Their
      Alleged Origins," *Israel Oriental Studies*. [Tel Aviv]:
      Tel Aviv University, 1973. Vol. 3, pp. 63-107.

177   Helmbold, A.K. "Gnostic Elements in the 'Ascension of
      Isaiah,'" *NTS* 18 (1972) 222-27.

178   MacRae, G.W. "The Jewish Background of the Gnostic Sophia
      Myth," *NovT* 12 (1970) 86-101.

179   MacRae, G.W. *Some Elements of Jewish Apocalyptic and Mys-
      tical Tradition and Their Relation to Gnostic Litera-
      ture*. Cambridge Ph.D., 1966.

180   Ménard, J.-E. "Littérature apocalyptique et littérature
      gnostique," *Exégèse biblique et judaïsme*. Pp. 146-49.

181   Pokorný, P. *The Beginnings of Gnosis: The End of the Gnos-
      tic Myth on the Divinity of Man* (Rozpravy Československé
      Akademie Věd 78.9) Prague: Akademie Věd, 1968. [in
      Czechoslovakian; English summary pp. 59-68. In this
      richly documented and brilliant monograph Pokorný argues
      that the immediate source of Gnosticism is neither "the
      pregnostic syncretism nor the heterodox Judaism," but
      only the "combination of the spiritualistic syncretism
      and the misinterpreted Jewish soteriology."]

182   Rudolph, K. "Gnosis und Gnostizismus, ein Forschungsbe-
      richt," *ThRu* 34 (1969) 121-75, 181-231.

183   Schnackenburg, R. "Early Gnosticism," *Jesus in His Time*,
      ed. H.J. Schultz; trans. B. Watchorn. Philadelphia:
      Fortress, 1971. Pp. 132-41.

184   Scholem, G. *Jewish Gnosticism, Merkabah Mysticism and
      Talmudic Tradition*. New York: Jewish Theological Semi-
      nary of America, 1960.

185   Wilcox, M. "Dualism, Gnosticism, and Other Elements in the
      Pre-Pauline Tradition," *The Scrolls and Christianity*,
      ed. M. Black. London: S.P.C.K., 1969. Pp. 83-96.

186   Yamauchi, E.M. *Pre-Christian Gnosticism: A Survey of the
      Proposed Evidences*. Grand Rapids, Mich.: Eerdmans, 1973.

The Pseudepigrapha and the New Testament

The following numbers refer to publications listed herein
that concentrate upon the importance of the Pseudepigrapha for
Christian origins. See esp. nos. 10, 61, 138(Jn), 146, 148
(2Cor), 192, 224, 234 (Mk), 238, 241, 303, 313, 375f., 416,
486, 509 (1Cor), 713 (Lk), 719 (Jude), 721a (Mk), 768 (Jude),

947 (1Cor), 959 (Paul), 981f., 1295 (Jn), 1297 (Jn). Also see nos. 2, 5, 48, 61, 63, 78, 90, 97f., 101, 110, 119, 136, 139, 147, 152, 185, 193, 207f., 225, 238, 241, 247, 251, 275, 282, 306, 324, 327, 329, 347, 359, 377, 380f., 391-94, 404, 407, 428, 433, 448, 464, 837, 1009, 1039, 1110, 1276, 1278, 1281, 1316, 1345.

Apocalyptic

M.E. Stone is contributing to the Compendia Rerum Iudaicarum ad Novum Testamentum the long article on "Apocalyptic Literature."

See works under Messianism and Resurrection and Eschatology. See also nos. 37, 39, 108, 115, 176, 180, 303, 354, 427, 880, 1360, 1451, 1488a, 1489.

187   Aalen, S. "Apokalypsen," *BHH* 1. Cols. 105-07.

188   Aalen, S. "Apokalyptik," *BHH* 1. Cols. 107f.

189   Albrektson, B. *History and the Gods: An Essay on the Idea of Historical Events as Divine Manifestations in the Ancient Near East and in Israel* (Coniectanea Biblica, OT Ser. 1) Lund: Gleerup, 1967. [Albrektson suggests that Jewish apocalyptic may derive from the Babylonian idea of destiny. See W.G. Lambert's review article, cited below, no. 248.]

190   Altizer, T.J.J. "The Dialectic of Ancient and Modern Apocalypticism," *JAAR* 39 (1971) 312-20.

191   Amsler, S. "Zacharie et l'origine de l'apocalyptique," VTSup 22. Pp. 227-31.

192   Audet, L. "L'influence de l'apocalyptique sur le pensée de Jésus et de l'église primitive," *ScEs* 25 (1973) 51-74.

193   Beardslee, W.A. "New Testament Apocalyptic in Recent Interpretation," *Int* 25 (1971) 419-35.

194   Betz, H.D. "Zum Problem des religionsgeschichtlichen Verständnisses der Apokalyptik," *ZTK* 63 (1966) 391-409. [ET by J.W. Leitch. *JThC* 6. Pp. 134-56.]

195   Boyd, W.J.P. "Apocalyptic and Life after Death," *Studia Evangelica*, ed. F.L. Cross (TU 103) Berlin: Akademie, 1968. Vol. 5, pp. 39-56.

196   Braaten, C.E. "The Significance of Apocalypticism for Systematic Theology," *Int* 25 (1971) 480-99.

197   Bruce, F.F. "A Reappraisal of Jewish Apocalyptic Litera-
      ture," *RevExp* 72 (1975) 305-15.

198   Collins, J.J. "Apocalyptic Eschatology as the Transcen-
      dence of Death," *CBQ* 36 (1974) 21-43.

199   Collins, J.J. "Astral Religion and Apocalyptic in Inter-
      testamental Judaism," *JSJ*, in press.

200   Collins, J.J. "The Court-tales in Daniel and the Develop-
      ment of Apocalyptic," *JBL* 94 (1975) 218-34.

201   Collins, J.J. "The Mythology of Holy War in Daniel and the
      Qumran War Scroll: A Point of Transition in Jewish Apoc-
      alyptic," *VT*, in press.

202   Collins, J.J. "The Symbolism of Transcendence in Jewish
      Apocalyptic," *BR* 19 (1974) 1-18.

203   Corsani, B. "L'Apocalittica: fra Antico e Nuovo Testamen-
      to," *Protestantesimo* 27 (1972) 15-22.

204   Cothenet, E. "Survivances du prophétisme dans le bas-
      judaïsme," *DBSup* 8 (1972) 1224-33.

205   Cross, F.M. "Exile and Apocalyptic," *Canaanite Myth and
      Hebrew Epic: Essays in the History of the Religion of
      Israel*. Cambridge, Mass.: Harvard University, 1973.
      Pp. 291-346.

206   Cross, F.M. "New Directions in the Study of Apocalyptic,"
      JThC 6. Pp. 157-65.

207   Daniélou, J. "Apocalyptique juive et messianisme chré-
      tien," *Quatre Fleuves* 2 (1974) 10-21.

208   Daniélou, J. "'That the Scripture Might be Fulfilled':
      Christianity as a Jewish Sect," *Crucible*. Pp. 261-82.

209   Daube, D. "Religious Minorities," *Civil Disobedience in
      Antiquity*. Edinburgh: University of Edinburgh, 1972. Pp.
      81-122.

210   Delcor, M. "Le milieu d'origine et de développement de
      l'apocalyptique juive," *La littérature juive entre
      Tenach et Mishna*, ed. W.C. van Unnik (RechBib 9) Leiden:
      Brill, 1974. [*N.V.*]

211   Eicher, P. "Einsicht in den Gang der Geschichte: Möglich-
      keiten und Grenzen einer sachgerechten Interpretation
      des apokalyptischen Materials," *BiKi* 29 (1974) 126-31.

212   Ellis, D.J. "Biblical Apocalyptic and Prophecy," *Faith
      and Thought* 96, 2 (1967) 27-40.

213   Enslin, M.S. "The Apocalyptic Literature," *IOCB*. Pp.
      1106-09.

214   Erbetta, M. "Apocalissi (Introduzione Generale)," *Apocrifi
      del NT*. Vol. 3, pp. 149-73.

215   Erling, B. "Ezekiel 38-39 and the Origins of Jewish Apoc-
      alyptic," Widengren Festschrift. Vol. 1, pp. 104-14.

216   Flusser, D. "Apocalypse," EncyJud 3. Pp. 179-81.

217   Freedman, D.N. "The Flowering of Apocalyptic," JThC 6.
      Pp. 166-74.

218   Frost, S.B. "Apocalyptic and History," The Bible in Modern
      Scholarship, ed. J.P. Hyatt. Nashville: Abingdon, 1965.
      Pp. 98-113.

219   Funk, R.W., ed. Apocalypticism (JThC 6) New York: Herder,
      1969.

220   Gasque, W.W. "Apocalyptic Literature," ZPEB 1. Pp. 200-04.

221   Gese, H. "Anfang und Ende der Apokalyptik, dargestellt am
      Sacharjabuch," ZTK 70 (1973) 20-49.

222   Grelot, P. "Apocalyptic," Sacramentum Mundi 1. Pp. 48-51.

223   Gruenwald, I. "The Jewish Esoteric Literature in the Time
      of the Mishnah and Talmud," Immanuel 4 (1974) 37-46.

224   Gunther, J.J. St. Paul's Opponents and Their Background:
      A Study of Apocalyptic and Jewish Sectarian Teachings
      (NovTSup 35) Leiden: Brill, 1973.

225   Hadot, J. "Contestation socio-religieuse et apocalyptique
      dans le judéo-christianisme," Archives de sociologie des
      religions 12 (1967) 35-47.

226   Hamerton-Kelly, R.G. "The Temple and the Origins of Jewish
      Apocalyptic," VT 20 (1970) 1-15.

227   Hanhart, R. "The Character of Apocalyptic," Teologinen
      Aikakauskirja 75 (1970) 533-41. [in Finnish]

228   Hanson, P.D. The Dawn of Apocalyptic. Philadelphia: Fort-
      ress, 1975.

229   Hanson, P.D. "Jewish Apocalyptic Against its Near Eastern
      Environment," RB 78 (1971) 31-58.

230   Hanson, P.D. "Old Testament Apocalyptic Reexamined," Int
      25 (1971) 454-79.

231   Hanson, P.D. "Zechariah 9 and the Recapitulation of an
      Ancient Ritual Pattern," JBL 92 (1973) 37-59.

232   Harnisch, W. "Das Geschichtsverständnis der Apokalyptik,"
      BiKi 29 (1974) 121-25.

233   Harrelson, W. "The Celebration of the Feast of Booths
      According to Zech xiv 16:21," Goodenough Festschrift.
      Pp. 88-96.

233a Hartman, L. "The Functions of Some So-Called Apocalyptic
      Timetables," NTS 22 (1975) 1-14.

234 Hartman, L. *Prophecy Interpreted: The Formation of Some Jewish Apocalyptic Texts and of the Eschatological Discourse Mark 13 Par.* (Coniectanea Biblica, NT Ser. 1) Lund: Gleerup, 1966.

235 Harvey, J. "Philosophie de l'histoire et apocalyptique," *ScEs* 25 (1973) 5-15.

236 Hemelsoet, B. "Apokalyptik," $B-L^2$. Cols. 83f.

237 Howard, J.E. *A Critical Evaluation of the Thesis that the Roots of Jewish Apocalyptic are in Israelite Wisdom, Rather than Prophecy.* Baylor University Ph.D., 1971.

238 Hruby, K. "L'influence des apocalypses sur l'eschatologie judéo-chrétienne," *OrSyr* 11 (1966) 291-320.

239 Janssen, E. "Die Apokalypsen," *Gottesvolk.* Pp. 49-96.

240 Janssen, E. "Die Apokalyptiker als Schriftgelehrte," *Gottesvolk.* Pp. 96-100.

241 Kertelge, K. "Apokalyptische Vorstellungs- und Begriffswelt im Neuen Testament," *BiKi* 29 (1974) 116-21.

242 Koch, K. "Die Apokalyptik und ihre Zukunftserwartungen," *Die Zeit Jesu,* ed. H.J. Schultz (Kontexte 3) Stuttgart: Kreuz, 1966. Pp. 51-58. [ET by B. Watchorn. Philadelphia: Fortress, 1971. Pp. 57-65.]

243 Koch, K. *Ratlos vor der Apokalyptik: Eine Streitschrift über ein vernachlässigtes Gebiet der Bibelwissenschaft und die schädlichen Auswirkungen auf Theologie und Philosophie.* Gütersloh: Mohn, 1970. [ET by M. Kohl (SBT, 2d. ser., 22) London: SCM, 1972.]

244 Kocis, E. "Apokalyptik und politisches Interesse im Spätjudentum," *Judaica* (Beiträge zum Verständnis des jüdischen Schicksals in Vergangenheit und Gegenwart 27) Zurich: Theologischer Verlag, 1971. Pp. 71-89.

245 Koole, J.L. "Apocalyptic Literature," *Encyclopedia of Christianity* 1. Pp. 293-306.

246 Ladd, G.E. "Apocalyptic, Apocalypse," *BDT.* Pp. 50-54.

247 Ladd, G.E. "The Apocalyptic Interpretation of the Promise," *Jesus and the Kingdom: The Eschatology of Biblical Realism.* New York: Harper and Row, 1964. Pp. 72-97.

248 Lambert, W.G. "History and the Gods: A Review Article," *Or* n.s. 39 (1970) 170-77. [Lambert rejects Albrektson's thesis (no. 189), arguing that presently there is no connection between the Babylonian predictions and Jewish apocalyptic: 1) the purpose of the Babylonian texts is obscure; 2) the Babylonian predictions do not point to a climax to history.]

249 Lapointe, R. "Actualité de l'apocalyptique," *Eglise et théologie* 4 (1973) 197-211.

250 Limbeck, M. "Apokalyptik oder Pharisäismus? Zu einigen Neuerscheinungen," *TQ* 152 (1972) 145-56.

251 Lohse, E. "Apokalyptik und Christologie," *ZNW* 62 (1971) 48-67; repr. *Die Einheit des Neuen Testaments: Exegetische Studien zur Theologie des Neuen Testaments.* Göttingen: Vandenhoeck & Ruprecht, 1973. Pp. 125-44.

252 Marrow, S.B. "Apocalyptic Genre and Eschatology," *The Word in the World.* F.L. Moriarty Festschrift, eds. R.J. Clifford and G.W. MacRae. Cambridge, Mass.: Weston College, 1973. Pp. 71-81.

253 Martin-Achard, R. "L'apocalyptique d'après trois travaux récents," *RTP* 20 (1970) 310-18.

254 Morris, L. *Apocalyptic.* Grand Rapids, Mich.: Eerdmans, 1972.

255 Mpratsiōtēs, P.I. "Apocalyptic Literature," *ThEE* 2. Cols. 1080f. [in Greek]

256 Müller, H.-P. "Mantische Weisheit und Apokalyptik," VTSup 22. Pp. 268-93.

257 Müller, K. "Die Ansätze der Apokalyptik," *Literatur und Religion des Frühjudentums.* Pp. 31-42.

258 Müller, P.-G. "Entstehung und Anliegen der Apokalyptik," *BiKi* 29 (1974) 110-15.

259 Müller, P.-G. "Ratlos vor der Apokalyptik: Literaturbericht zur Einführung in das Thema 'Apokalyptik,'" *BiKi* 29 (1974) 146-49.

260 Murdock, W.R. "History and Revelation in Jewish Apocalypticism," *Int* 21 (1967) 167-87.

261 Nelis, J.T. "Ausserbiblische Apokalypsen (holl)," *Schrift* 14 (1971) 52-56. [*N.V.*]

262 Neusner, J. "Judaism in a Time of Crisis: Four Responses to the Destruction of the Second Temple," *Judaism* 21 (1972) 313-27.

263 Nielsen, E. "Apokalyptik," *GDBL* 1. Cols. 93-95.

264 North, R. "Prophecy to Apocalyptic via Zechariah," VTSup 22. Pp. 47-71.

265 Osswald, E. "Zum problem der *Vaticinia ex eventu*," *ZAW* 75 (1963) 27-44.

266 Osten-Sacken, P. von der. *Die Apokalyptik in ihrem Verhältnis zu Prophetie und Weisheit* (Theologische Existenz heute 157) Munich: Kaiser, 1969.

267 Prigent, P. "Apocalypse et apocalyptique," *Exégèse biblique et judaïsme.* Pp. 126-45.

268 Rad, G. von. *Wisdom in Israel*. Nashville: Abingdon, 1972.

269 Redditt, P.L. "Postexilic Eschatological Prophecy and the Rise of Apocalyptic Literature," *Ohio Journal of Religious Studies* 2 (1974) 25-39.

270 Reicke, B. "Die jüdische Apokalyptik und die johanneische Tiervision," *RSR* 60 (1972) 173-92.

271 Ringgren, H. "Jüdische Apokalyptik," *RGG*[3] 1. Cols. 464-66.

272 Rist, M. "Apocalypticism," *IDB* 1. Pp. 157-61.

273 Robinson, B. "Koch on Apocalyptic," *New Blackfriars* 53 (1972) 423-28.

274 Rochais, G. "Les origines de l'apocalyptique," *ScEs* 25 (1973) 17-50.

275 Rollins, W.G. "The New Testament and Apocalyptic," *NTS* 17 (1971) 454-76.

276 Rowley, H.H. "Apocalyptic Literature," *PCB*. Pp. 484-88.

277 Russell, D.S. *The Method and Message of Jewish Apocalyptic* (Old Testament Library) Philadelphia: Westminster, 1964.

277a Saldarini, A.J. "Apocalyptic and Rabbinic Literature," *CBQ* 37 (1975) 348-58.

278 Schierse, F.J. "Apokalyptik," *LTK*[2] 1. Cols. 504f.

279 Schmidt, J.M. "Forschung zur jüdischen Apokalyptik," *Verkündigung und Forschung* 14 (1969) 44-69.

280 Schmidt, J.M. *Die jüdische Apokalyptik: Die Geschichte ihrer Erforschung von den Anfängen bis zu den Textfunden von Qumran*. Neukirchen-Vluyn: Neukirchener, 1969.

281 Schmithals, W. *Die Apokalyptik: Einführung und Deutung*. Göttingen: Vandenhoeck & Ruprecht, 1973. [ET by J.E. Steely. New York: Abingdon, 1975.]

282 Schneemelcher, W. "Apocalyptic Prophecy of the Early Church," trans. D. Hill. HSW. Vol. 2, pp. 684-90.

283 Schreiner, J. *Alttestamentlich-jüdische Apokalyptik: Eine Einführung* (Biblische Handbibliothek 6) Munich: Kösel, 1969.

284 Schreiner, J. "Die apokalyptische Bewegung," *Literatur und Religion des Frühjudentums*. Pp. 214-53.

285 Silberman, L.H. "The Human Deed in a Time of Despair: The Ethics of Apocalyptic," *Essays in Old Testament Ethics*. J.P. Hyatt Festschrift, eds. J.L. Crenshaw and J.T. Willis. New York: KTAV, 1974. Pp. 191-202.

286   Stachowiak, L. "Apocalypticism and Eschatology at the
      Threshold of the Christian Era," *Ateneum Kapłańskie* 63
      (1971) 57-68. [in Polish]

287   Strobel, A. "Apokalyptikk, Kristus-åpenbaring og utopi:
      Teologisk vitnesbyrd ved et tideverv," *Tidsskrift for
      Teologi og Kirke* 42 (1971) 1-24.

288   Stuhlmueller, C. "Apocalyptic," *NCE* 1. Pp. 663f.

289   Stuhlmueller, C. "Post-exilic Period: Spirit, Apocalyptic,"
      JBC 1. Pp. 337-43.

289a Testa, P.E., *et al. La distruzione di Gerusalemme del 70
      nei suoi riflessi storico-letterari: Atti del V Conveg-
      no biblico francescano. Roma, 22-27 settembre 1969*
      (Collectio Assisiensis 8) Assisi: Studio Teologico
      "Porziuncola," 1971.

290   Thoma, C. "Jüdische Apokalyptik am Ende des ersten nach-
      christlichen Jahrhunderts: Religionsgeschichtliche
      Bemerkungen zur syrischen Baruchapokalypse und zum
      vierten Esrabuch," *Kairos* 11 (1969) 134-44.

291   Tupper, E.F. "The Revival of Apocalyptic in Biblical and
      Theological Studies," *RevExp* 72 (1975) 279-303.

292   Uffenheimer, B. *The Visions of Zechariah: From Prophecy to
      Apocalyptic.* Jerusalem: Israel Society for Biblical Re-
      search, 1961. [in Hebrew; English summary pp. v-viii.]

293   Vielhauer, P. "Apocalypses and Related Subjects," trans.
      D. Hill. HSW. Vol. 2, pp. 579-607.

294   Wilder, A.N. "The Rhetoric of Ancient and Modern Apocalyp-
      tic," *Int* 25 (1971) 436-53.

295   Wilkinson, T.L. "Doctrine of the Two Ages," *Vox Reformata*
      8 (1967) 1-13.

296   Wypych, S. "'New Heavens and a New Earth': The Development
      of the Biblical Idea of the 'New Creation,'" *Analecta
      Cracoviensia* 3 (1971) 221-43. [in Polish]

Special Themes

Theology

See also nos. 10, 85, 172, 178, 1055, 1205a, 1312, 1489a.

297   Alston, W.M. Jr. *The Concept of the Wilderness in the In-
      tertestamental Period.* Union (Richmond, Va.) Ph.D., 1968.

298   Amir, Y. "The Term *Ioudaismos* on the Self-Understanding of
      Hellenistic Judaism," *Proceedings of the Fifth World
      Congress of Jewish Studies*, ed. A. Shinan. Jerusalem:
      World Union of Jewish Studies, 1972. Vol. 3, pp. 263-68.
      [in Hebrew; English summary pp. 102f.]

299   Baltzer, K. *The Covenant Formulary in Old Testament, Jewish, and Early Christian Writings*, trans. D.E. Green. Philadelphia: Fortress, 1971.

299a Berger, K. *Die Amen-Worte Jesu: Eine Untersuchung zum Problem der Legitimation in apokalyptischer Rede* (BZNW 39) Berlin: Walter de Gruyter, 1970.

300   Black, M. "The Development of Judaism in the Greek and Roman Periods," *PCB*. Pp. 693-98.

301   Brockington, L.H. *Ideas of Mediation Between God and Man in the Apocrypha*. London: Athlone, 1962.

302   Crouch, J.E. "Hellenistic Jewish Lists of Social Duties," *The Origin and Intention of the Colossian Haustafel* (FRLANT 109) Göttingen: Vandenhoeck & Ruprecht, 1972. Pp. 74-83.

303   Daniélou, J. *The Theology of Jewish Christianity*, trans. J.A. Baker (The Development of Christian Doctrine Before the Council of Nicaea 1) London: Darton, Longman and Todd, 1964.

304   Davies, W.D. "The Apocrypha, Pseudepigrapha and Dead Sea Scrolls," *The Setting of the Sermon on the Mount*. Cambridge: CUP, 1966. Pp. 139-56.

305   Davies, W.D. "Contemporary Jewish Religion," *PCB*. Pp. 705-11. [This article emphasizes the variegated nature of first-century Jewish thought.]

306   Davies, W.D. *The Gospel and the Land: Early Christianity and Jewish Territorial Doctrine*. Berkeley, Calif.: University of California, 1974.

307   Davies, W.D. "Paul and Judaism Since Schweitzer," *Paul and Rabbinic Judaism*. New York: Harper and Row, 1967. Pp. vii-xv.

308   Erbetta, M. "La Profezia (200 a.C.-200 d.C.; Introduzione Generale.) Sommario," *Apocrifi del NT*. Vol. 3, pp. 541-57.

309   Evans, J.M. *Paradise Lost and the Genesis Tradition*. Oxford: Clarendon, 1968. See esp. pp. 26-36, 55-58.

310   Falk, Z.W. *Introduction to Jewish Law of the Second Commonwealth* (AGAJU 11) Leiden: Brill, 1972. Vol. 1.

311   Fawcett, T. "Paradise," *Hebrew Myth and Christian Gospel*. London: SCM, 1973. Pp. 253-307.

312   Fiedler, M.J. "*Dikaiosunē* in der diaspora-jüdischen und intertestamentarischen Literatur," *JSJ* 1 (1970) 120-43.

313   Frankel, Z. *Über den Einfluss der palästinischen Exegese auf die alexandrinische Hermeneutik*. Leipzig: J.A. Barth, 1851; repr. Westmead: Gregg International, 1972. [*N.V.*]

54

314   Giblet, J. "Pénitence: Apocryphes et pseudépigraphes,"
      DBSup 7 (1963) 657-59.

315   Goudoever, J. van. "A Study of the Mid-Time," *Bijdragen:
      Tijdschrift voor Filosofie en Theologie* 33 (1972) 262-
      307.

316   Hamerton-Kelly, R.G. *The Idea of Pre-existence in Early
      Judaism: A Study in the Background of New Testament
      Theology.* Union (N.Y.) Ph.D., 1966.

317   Harrelson, W. "The Significance of 'Last Words' for Inter-
      testamental Ethics," *Essays in Old Testament Ethics.* J.
      P. Hyatt Festschrift, eds. J.L. Crenshaw and J.T.
      Willis. New York: KTAV, 1974. Pp. 205-13.

318   Hester, J.D. "The Concept of Inheritance in the Intertes-
      tamental Literature," *Paul's Concept of Inheritance*
      (SJT Occasional Papers 14) Edinburgh: Oliver and Boyd,
      1968. Pp. 29-36.

319   Hruby, K. "Gesetz und Gnade in der rabbinischen Überlie-
      ferung," *Gesetz und Gnade im Alten Testament und im
      jüdischen Denken,* ed. R. Brunner. Zurich: Zwingli, 1969.
      Pp. 30-63.

320   Janssen, E. *Das Gottesvolk und seine Geschichte: Ges-
      chichtsbild und Selbstverständnis im palästinensischen
      Schrifttum von Jesus Sirach bis Jehuda ha-Nasi.* Neukir-
      chen-Vluyn: Neukirchener, 1971. [A survey of the inter-
      pretation of history by the authors of Dan, 1En, T12P,
      ApAb, 4Ezra, 2Bar, Jub, AsMos.]

321   Jeremias, J. "Der Gedanke des 'Heiligen Restes' im Spät-
      judentum und in der Verkündigung Jesu," *Abba* (Studien
      zur neutestamentlichen Theologie und Zeitgeschichte)
      Göttingen: Vandenhoeck & Ruprecht, 1966. Pp. 121-32.
      [This important article was published earlier in *ZNW* 42
      (1949) 184-94.]

322   Johnson, M.D. "The Narrowing of Genealogical Interest in
      Later Judaism," *The Purpose of the Biblical Genealogies*
      (SNTS MS 8) Cambridge: CUP, 1969. Pp. 85-138. [Genea-
      logical interests in the intertestamental books become
      reduced to concerns for the purity and identity of the
      Jewish people and for the ancestry of the Messiah.]

323   Jones, A.H.M. "A Taste for Things Greek: Hellenism in
      Syria and Palestine," *Crucible.* Pp. 99-122.

324   Kraft, R.A. "The Multiform Jewish Heritage of Early
      Christianity," M. Smith Festschrift. Part 3, pp. 175-99.

325   Kraus, H.J. "Zum Gesetzesverständnis der nachprophetischen
      Zeit," *Kairos* 11 (1969) 122-33.

326   Le Déaut, R. "Aspects de l'intercession dans le judaïsme
      ancien," *JSJ* 1 (1970) 35-57.

327 Le Déaut, R. "La tradition juive ancienne et l'exégèse
     chrétienne primitive," *RHPR* 51 (1971) 31-50.

328 Lentzen-Deis, F. "Das Motiv der 'Himmelsöffnung' in ver-
     schiedenen Gattungen der Umweltliteratur des Neuen
     Testaments," *Bib* 50 (1969) 301-27.

329 Levin, A.G. *The Tree of Life: Genesis 2:9 and 3:22-24 in
     Jewish, Gnostic and Early Christian Texts.* Harvard
     Th.D., 1966.

330 Limbeck, M. *Die Ordnung des Heils: Untersuchungen zum
     Gesetzesverständnis des Frühjudentums* (Kommentare und
     Beiträge zum Alten und Neuen Testament) Düsseldorf:
     Patmos, 1971.

331 Lohse, E. "Religiöse Bewegungen und geistige Strömungen
     im Judentum zur Zeit des Neuen Testaments," *Umwelt des
     Neuen Testaments* (GNT 1) Göttingen: Vandenhoeck & Ru-
     precht, 1971. Pp. 37-105.

332 McEleney, N.J. "Orthodoxy in Judaism of the First Christ-
     ian Century," *JSJ* 4 (1973) 19-42.

333 Mack, B.L. *Logos und Sophia: Untersuchungen zur Weis-
     heitstheologie im hellenistischen Judentum* (Studien zur
     Umwelt des Neuen Testaments 10) Göttingen: Vandenhoeck
     & Ruprecht, 1973.

334 Maier, G. *Mensch und freier Wille nach den jüdischen
     Religionsparteien zwischen Ben Sira und Paulus* (WUNT 12)
     Tübingen: Mohr, 1971.

335 Neusner, J. "Judaism in a Time of Crisis: Four Responses
     to the Destruction of the Second Temple," *Judaism* 21
     (1972) 313-27.

336 Neusner, J. "Types and Forms in Ancient Jewish Literature:
     Some Comparisons," *History of Religions: An Internation-
     al Journal for Comparative Historical Studies* 11 (1972)
     354-90.

336a Nikiprowetzky, V. "Le Nouveau Temple: A propos d'un
     ouvrage récent," *REJ* 130 (1971) 5-30. [PssSol, SibOr,
     1En, 2Bar, 4Ezra, TLevi, Jub.]

337 Nissen, A. *Gott und der Nächste im antiken Judentum:
     Untersuchungen zum Doppelgebot der Liebe* (WUNT 15)
     Tübingen: Mohr, 1974.

338 Noack, B. *Spätjudentum und Heilsgeschichte* (Franz
     Delitzsch Vorlesungen 1968) Stuttgart: Kohlhammer, 1971.

339 Pfeifer, G. *Ursprung und Wesen der Hypostasenvorstellungen
     im Judentum* (Arbeiten zur Theologie 1, 31) Stuttgart:
     Calwer, 1967.

340 Powell, C.H. "The Apocrypha and Pseudepigrapha," *The Bib-
     lical Concept of Power.* London: Epworth, 1963. Pp. 44-59.

56

341 Reicke, B. "Da'at and Gnosis in Intertestamental Literature," *Neotestamentica et Semitica*. M. Black Festschrif
eds. E.E. Ellis and M. Wilcox. Edinburgh: T. & T. Clark
1969. Pp. 245-55.

342 Rosenstiehl, J.-M. "Le portrait de l'Antichrist," *Pseudépigraphes*, ed. M. Philonenko. Pp. 45-60.

343 Schäfer, P. "Die Torah der messianischen Zeit," *ZNW* 65
(1974) 27-42.

344 Schubert, K. "A Divided Faith: Jewish Religious Parties
and Sects," *Crucible*. Pp. 77-98.

345 Simon, M. "Remarques sur l'angélolâtrie juive au début de
l'ère chrétienne," *Académie des Inscriptions et Belles-
Lettres, Comptes Rendus des Séances de l'Année* 1 (1971)
120-34.

346 Stone, M.E. "Judaism at the Time of Christ," *Scientific
American* 228 (1973) 80-87; repr. ASOR Newsletter #1
(1973-1974) 1-6.

347 Stuart, S.S. *The Exodus Tradition in Late Jewish and Earl
Christian Literature: A General Survey of the Literatur
and a Particular Analysis of the Wisdom of Solomon, II
Esdras and the Epistle to the Hebrews*. Vanderbilt Ph.D.
1973.

348 Testa, E. "Reazione delle correnti religiose giudaiche e
cristiane sulla distruzione di Gerusalemme (I-II secolo
d.C.)," *RivB* 21 (1973) 301-24.

349 Van den Doel, A. "Blessing and Cursing in the Intertestamental Literature," *Blessing and Cursing in the New
Testament and Related Literature*. Northwestern Ph.D.,
1968. Pp. 79-134.

350 Walters, C.F. *The Immanence and Transcendence of God as
Reflected in Jewish Apocryphal and Pseudepigraphical
Documents Produced Between 200 B.C. and 100 A.D.* Union
(Richmond, Va.) Th.D., 1964.

351 Weiss, H.-F. *Untersuchungen zur Kosmologie des hellenistischen und palästinischen Judentums* (TU 97) Berlin:
Akademie, 1966.

352 Wright, A.G. *The Literary Genre Midrash*. Staten Island,
N.Y.: Alba House, 1967.

353 Wright, R.B. *Sacrifice in the Intertestamental Literature*
Hartford Seminary Ph.D., 1966.

Dualism

Consult works listed under Pseudepigrapha and the Dead Se
Scrolls. See also nos. 138, 185, 1407a.

354   Gammie, J.G. "Spatial and Ethical Dualism in Jewish Wisdom
      and Apocalyptic Literature," *JBL* 93 (1974) 356-85.

355   Stachowiak, L. "The Origin of a Didactic Schema of 'Two
      Ways' in Intertestamental Literature," *Ruch Biblijny i
      Liturgiczny* 22 (1969) 75-85. [in Polish]

356   Stachowiak, L. "The Problem of Anthropological Dualism in
      the Old Testament and Intertestamental Literature,"
      Studia Theologica Varsaviensia 7 (1969) 3-32. [in Polish]

Martyrdom

Consult the numerous related publications listed under
4Mac.

357   Beutler, J. *Martyria: Traditionsgeschichtliche Untersu-
      chungen zum Zeugnisthema bei Johannes* (Frankfurter
      theologische Studien 10) Frankfurt: Josef Knecht, 1972.
      See esp. pp. 119-30, 145-55.

358   Lohse, E. *Märtyrer und Gottesknecht*, 2d. ed. (FRLANT 46)
      Göttingen: Vandenhoeck & Ruprecht, 1963.

359   Winslow, D.F. "The Maccabean Martyrs: Early Christian
      Attitudes," *Judaism* 23 (1974) 78-86.

Messianism

Also consult the publications listed under Apocalyptic and
Resurrection and Eschatology. This section is limited to only
those studies that include significantly the Pseudepigrapha.
See also nos. 154, 322, 1009, 1429.

360   Agourides, S. "The Son of Man in Enoch," *Deltion Biblikon
      Meleton* 2 (1973) 130-47.

361   Amir, Y. "The Concept of the Messiah in Hellenistic Juda-
      ism," *Machanayim* 124 (1970) 54-67. [in Hebrew; English
      summary in *Immanuel* 2 (1973) 58-60.]

362   Arnon, C. "The Messianic Idea in Hellenistic Judaism by J.
      Amir," *Immanuel* 2 (1973) 58-60.

363   Banks, J.S. "Messiah," Hastings. Pp. 646-55.

364   Baumhauer, O. *Messiaserwartungen um das Jahr 1* (Zur Dis-
      kussion gestellt 4) Kevelaer: Butzon und Bercker, 1969.

365   Berger, K. "Die königlichen Messiastraditionen des Neuen
      Testaments," *NTS* 20 (1973) 1-44.

366   Betz, O. "The Relevance of Some Recently Published Messi-
      anic Fragments from Qumran," *Proceedings of the Fifth
      World Congress of Jewish Studies*, ed. P. Peli. Jerusalem:
      World Union of Jewish Studies, 1969. Vol. 1, pp. 201-10.

367 Black, M. "The Son of Man Problem in Recent Research and Debate," *BJRL* 45 (1963) 305-18.

368 Borsch, F.H. *The Son of Man in Myth and History.* London: SCM; Philadelphia: Westminster, 1967.

369 Bruce, F.F. "Preparation for the Messiah," *Jesus and Christian Origins Outside the New Testament.* Grand Rapids, Mich.: Eerdmans, 1974. Pp. 66-81.

370 Bulteau, M.-G. "Le Fils de l'homme dans la littérature apocalyptique," *Jésus? De l'histoire à la foi: Conférences publiques par les professeurs de la section des études bibliques à la Faculté de Théologie de l'Université de Montréal* (Héritage et projet 9) Montreal: Fides, 1974. Pp. 69-81. [*N.V.*]

371 Colpe, C. "Der Begriff 'Menschensohn' und die Methode der Erforschung messianischer Prototypen (I und II)," *Kairos* 11 (1969) 241-63.

372 Coppens. J. *L'espérance messianique: Ses origines et son développement* (ALBO ser. 4, fasc. 9) Bruges-Paris: Desclée de Brouwer, 1963.

373 Coppens, J. "Les origines du symbole 'Fils d'homme,'" *Miscellanées bibliques* (ALBO ser. 4, fasc. 8) Bruges-Paris: Desclée de Brouwer, 1963. Pp. 100-04.

374 Coppens, J. "Le prophète eschatologique: L'annonce de sa venue. Les relectures," *ETL* 49 (1973) 5-35.

375 Duling, D.C. "The Promises to David and Their Entrance into Christianity--Nailing Down a Likely Hypothesis," *NTS* 20 (1973) 55-77.

376 Duling, D.C. *Traditions of the Promises to David and His Sons in Early Judaism and Primitive Christianity.* University of Chicago Ph.D., 1970. [*N.V.*]

377 Flusser, D. "The Son of Man: Jesus in the Context of History," *Crucible.* Pp. 215-34.

378 Grelot, P. "Messiah," *Sacramentum Mundi* 4. Pp. 14-16.

379 Grelot, P. "Le messie dans les apocryphes de l'Ancien Testament: Etat de la question," *La Venue du messie: Messianisme et eschatologie* (RechBib 6) Louvain: Desclée de Brouwer, 1962. Pp. 19-50.

380 Hahn, F. "Menschensohn," *Christologische Hoheitstitel: Ihre Geschichte im frühen Christentum.* Göttingen: Vandenhoeck & Ruprecht, 1963. Pp. 13-53. [ET by H. Knight and G. Ogg. Cleveland, Ohio: World, 1969. Pp. 15-67.]

381 Hengel, M. *Gewalt und Gewaltlosigkeit: Zur politischen Theologie in neutestamentlicher Zeit* (Calwer Hefte zur Förderung biblischen Glaubens und christlichen Lebens 118) Stuttgart: Calwer, 1971. [ET by D.E. Green; intro. R. Scroggs. Philadelphia: Fortress, 1973.]

382   Jaubert, A. "Symboles et figures christologiques dans le judaïsme," *Exégèse biblique et judaïsme*. Pp. 219-36.

383   Jenni, E. "Messiah, Jewish," *IDB* 3. Pp. 360-65.

384   Jocz, J. "Messiah," *ZPEB* 4. Pp. 198-207.

385   Johnson, S.E. "Son of Man," *IDB* 4. Pp. 413-20.

386   Jonge, M. de. "Jewish Expectations About the 'Messiah' According to the Fourth Gospel," *NTS* 19 (1973) 246-70.

387   Jonge, M. de. "The Use of the Word 'Anointed' in the Time of Jesus," *NovT* 8 (1966) 132-48.

388   Kellermann, U. *Messias und Gesetz: Grundlinien einer alttestamentlichen Heilserwartung. Eine traditionsgeschichtliche Einführung* (BibSt 61) Neukirchen-Vluyn: Neukirchener, 1971.

388a Kellermann, U. "Die politische Messias-Hoffnung zwischen den Testamenten," *Pastoraltheologie* 56 (1967) 362-77, 436-47.

389   Klein, R.W. "Aspects of Intertestamental Messianism," *CTM* 43 (1972) 507-17.

390   Koester, W. and J. Schmid. "Messias," *LTK*[2] 7. Cols. 335-42.

391   Leivestad, R. "Der apokalyptische Menschensohn ein theologisches Phantom," *ASTI* 6, eds. H. Kosmala, *et al.* Leiden: Brill, 1968. Pp. 49-105.

392   Leivestad, R. "Exit the Apocalyptic Son of Man," *NTS* 18 (1972) 243-67. [See Lindars below, no. 393a.]

393   Leivestad, R. "Var det noe alternativ til Messias?" *SEA* 37 (1972) 21-34.

393a Lindars, B. "Re-Enter the Apocalyptic Son of Man," *NTS* 22 (1975) 52-72. [See Leivestad above, no. 392.]

394   Longenecker, R.N. *The Christology of Early Jewish Christianity* (SBT, 2d. ser., 17) London: SCM, 1970.

395   Meyer, R. "Messias IV: Im nachbiblischen Judentum," *RGG*[3] 4. Cols. 904-06.

396   Moule, C.F.D. "Neglected Features in the Problem of 'the Son of Man,'" *Neues Testament und Kirche*. R. Schnackenburg Festschrift, ed. J. Gnilka. Freiburg: Herder, 1974. Pp. 413-28.

397   Müller, K. "Beobachtungen zur Entwicklung der Menschensohnvorstellung in den Bilderreden des Henoch und im Buche Daniel," *Wegzeichen*. H.M. Biedermann Festgabe, eds. E.C. Suttner and C. Patock. Würzburg: Augustinus, 1971. Pp. 253-62.

60

398 Müller, M. *Messias og "menneskesøn" i Daniels Bog, Første Enoksbog og Fjerde Ezrabog* (Tekst & Tolkning 3) Copenhagen: Gads, 1972.

399 Müller, U.B. *Messias und Menschensohn in jüdischen Apokalypsen und in der Offenbarung des Johannes* (Studien zum Neuen Testament 6) Gütersloh: Mohn, 1972.

400 Nelis, J. "Menschensohn," *B-L*^{2}. Cols. 1128-34.

401 Nelis, J. "Messiaserwartung," *B-L*^{2}. Cols. 1139-48.

402 Otzen, B. "Messias," *GDBL* 2. Cols. 198-202.

403 Patrōnos, G.P. "The Messianic and Eschatological Expectations of the Intertestamental Period (200 B.C.-A.D. 100)," *Theologia* 43 (1972) 385-401, 692-733. [in Greek]

404 Perrin, N. "The Son of Man in Ancient Judaism and Primitive Christianity: A Suggestion," *A Modern Pilgrimage in New Testament Christology*. Philadelphia: Fortress, 1974. Pp. 23-40.

405 Reicke, B. "Menschensohn," *BHH* 2. Cols. 1191f.

406 Rivkin, E. "The Meaning of Messiah in Jewish Thought," *USQR* 26 (1971) 383-406. See esp. pp. 395-98.

407 Ruppert, L. *Jesus als der leidende Gerechte? Der Weg Jesu im Lichte eines alt- und zwischentestamentlichen Motivs* (SBS 59) Stuttgart: Katholisches Bibelwerk, 1972.

408 Ruppert, L. *Der leidende Gerechte: Eine motivgeschichtliche Untersuchung zum Alten Testament und zwischentestamentlichen Judentum* (Forschung zur Bibel 5) Würzburg: Echter, 1972.

409 Ruppert, L. *Der leidende Gerechte und seine Feinde: Eine Wortfelduntersuchung*. Würzburg: Echter, 1973.

410 Scholem, G. "Die Krise der Tradition im jüdischen Messianismus," *EJ* 37 (1968) 9-42; repr. *Judaica: Studien zur jüdischen Mystik*. Frankfurt: Suhrkamp, 1973. Vol. 3, pp. 152-97.

411 Scholem, G. *The Messianic Idea in Judaism and Other Essays on Jewish Spirituality*. New York: Schocken, 1971.

412 Shemer, B.-A. *The Messianic Idea of the Testaments of the Twelve Patriarchs*. [Tel Aviv]: University of Tel Aviv, 1970. [in Hebrew]

413 Simon, M. and A. Benoit. "Messianisme et apocalyptique," *Le judaïsme et le christianisme antique d'Antiochus Epiphane à Constantin*. Paris: Presses universitaires de France, 1968. Pp. 65-68.

414 Stone, M.E. "The Concept of the Messiah in IV Ezra," Goodenough Festschrift. Pp. 295-312.

415   Tsakonas, V. "The Teaching Concerning·the Messiah in the
      Testaments of the Twelve Patriarchs," *Timetikos tomos V.
      M. Vellas*. Athens, 1969. Pp. 687-93. [in Greek; *N.V.*]

416   Vermes, G. *Jesus the Jew: A Historian's Reading of the
      Gospels*. London: Collins, 1973.

417   Villalón, J.R. "Sources vétéro-testamentaires de la doc-
      trine qumrânienne des deux messies," *RQ* 8 (1972) 53-63.

418   Vögtle, A. "Menschensohn," *LTK*^{2} 7. Cols. 297-300.

419   Wallace, D.H. "Messiah," *BDT*. Pp. 349-51.

420   Weiss, H.-F. "Menschensohn," *RGG*^{3} 4. Cols. 874-76.

421   Woude, A.S. van der. "Messias," *BHH* 2. Cols. 1197-204.

422   Zeitlin, S. "The Origin of the Idea of the Messiah," *In
      the Time of Harvest*. A.H. Silver Festschrift, eds. S.B.
      Freehof, *et al.* New York: Macmillan, 1963. Pp. 447-59;
      repr. *Solomon Zeitlin's Studies in the Early History of
      Judaism*. New York: KTAV, 1974. Vol. 2, pp. 394-406.

Prayer

See the numerous publications on hymns and prayers listed
under the Pseudepigrapha and the Dead Sea Scrolls, Prayer of
Manasses, Joseph and Asenath, Prayer of Joseph, Fragments of
Poetical Works, Philo the Epic Poet, Odes of Solomon, Psalms
of Solomon, and 5 Apocryphal Syriac Psalms.

423   Heinemann, J. *Prayer in the Period of the Tanna'im and the
      Amora'im: Its Nature and Its Patterns*, 2d. ed. Jerusa-
      lem: Magnes, 1966. [in Hebrew]

424   Krupp, M. "Prayer in the Period of the Tanna'im and Amo-
      ra'im by J. Heinemann," *Immanuel* 2 (1973) 23-27.

425   Mayer, G. "Die Funktion der Gebete in den alttestament-
      liche Apokryphen," *Theokratia*. K. H. Rengstorf Fest-
      schrift, eds. W. Dietrich, *et al.* (Jahrbuch des Insti-
      tutum Judaicum Delitzschianum 2) Leiden: Brill, 1973.
      Pp. 16-25.

Old Testament Names Used Pseudonymously

Abraham

Also sée below under Apocalypse of Abraham and Testament
of Abraham.

426   Delcor, M. "La portée chronologique de quelques interpré-
      tations du Targoum Néophyti contenues dans le cycle
      d'Abraham," *JSJ* 1 (1970) 105-19.

427 Dukes, T.F. *Adam, Abraham and Apocalypse.* Philadelphia: Dorrance, 1970. [*N.V.*]

428 Lord, J.R. *Abraham: A Study in Ancient Jewish and Christian Interpretation.* Duke Ph.D., 1968.

429 Martin-Achard, R. "Les traditions juives, néotestamentaires et coraniques sur Abraham," *Actualité d'Abraham.* Neuchâtel: Delachaux et Niestlé, 1969. Pp. 111-79.

430 Mayer, G. "Aspekte des Abrahambildes in der hellenistisch-jüdischen Literatur," *EvT* 32 (1972) 118-227.

431 Stone, M.E. "Abraham, Other Books of," *EncyJud* 2. Cols. 127f.

432 Vermes, G. "The Life of Abraham," *Scripture and Tradition in Judaism: Haggadic Studies* (SPB 4) Leiden: Brill, 1961; repr. with corrections, 1973. Pp. 67-126.

433 Ward, R.B. "Abraham Traditions in Early Christianity," SCS 2. Pp. 165-79.

Adam

Also see below under Apocalypse of Adam, Testament of Adam, Life of Adam and Eve, and Cave of Treasures.

434 Bamberger, B.J. "Adam, Books of," *IDB* 1. Pp. 44f.

435 Denis, A.-M. "L'Apocalypse de Moïse (= Vie d'Adam et Eve) et le cycle d'Adam," *Introduction.* Pp. 3-14.

436 Dingermann, F. "Adambuch," *LTK*[2] 1. Cols. 133f.

437 Dukes, T.F. *Adam, Abraham and Apocalypse.* Philadelphia: Dorrance, 1970. [*N.V.*]

438 Guerin, G.-A. "En marge de la légende d'Adam," *Bulletin du Cercle Ernest-Renan* 142 (1968) 13f.

439 Simon, M. "Adam et la rédemption dans la perspective de l'église ancienne," *Types of Redemption: Contributions to the Theme of the Study-Conference Held at Jerusalem, 14th to 19th July 1968*, eds. R.J.Z. Werblowsky and C.J. Bleeker (Sup *Numen* 18) Leiden: Brill, 1970. Pp. 62-71.

440 Stone, M.E. "Adam, Other Books of," *EncyJud* 2. Cols. 245f.

441 Stone, M.E. "The Death of Adam--An Armenian Adam Book," *HTR* 59 (1966) 283-91.

Asenath

See below under Joseph and Asenath.

Baruch

See below under 2, 3, and 4 Baruch.

Daniel

See below under Lives of the Prophets and Apocalypse of Sedrach.

David

See below under 5 Apocryphal Syriac Psalms.

Eldad

See below under Eldad and Modad.

Elijah

See below under Apocalypse of Elijah.

Enoch

See below under 1, 2, and 3 Enoch.

Eve

See above under Adam.

Ezekiel

See below under Apocryphon of Ezekiel and Lives of the Prophets.

Ezra

See below under 4(4, 5, 6) Ezra, Greek Apocalypse of Ezra, Questions of Ezra, Revelation of Ezra, Vision of Ezra.

Hezekiah

See below under Ascension of Isaiah, part of which contains portions of the Testament of Hezekiah.

Isaac

See below under Testament of Isaac.

Isaiah

See below under Ascension of Isaiah, Martyrdom of Isaiah, and Lives of the Prophets.

Jacob

See below under Ladder of Jacob, Testament of Jacob, Testaments of the Twelve Patriarchs.

Jeremiah

See below under 4 Baruch and Lives of the Prophets.

Job

See below under Testament of Job.

Jonadab

See below under Apocalypse of Zosimus.

Joseph

See below under Joseph and Asenath, Prayer of Joseph, Testament of Joseph, and Testaments of the Twelve Patriarchs.

Manasses

See below under Prayer of Manasses.

Modad

See below under Eldad and Modad.

Moses

See also below under Apocalypse of Moses, Assumption of Moses, Prayer of Moses, and Testament of Moses.

442 Gager, J.G. *Moses in Greco-Roman Paganism* (SBLMS 16) New York: Abingdon, 1972.

443 Haacker, K. and P. Schäfer. "Nachbiblische Traditionen vom Tod des Mose," *Josephus-Studien*. O. Michel Festschrift, eds. O. Betz, *et al*. Göttingen: Vandenhoeck & Ruprecht, 1974. Pp. 147-74.

444 Kastner, P.J.M. "Das Mosesbild des Judentums," *Moses im Neuen Testament: Eine Untersuchung der Mosestraditionen in den neutestamentlichen Schriften.* Munich: Ludwig-Maximilians, 1967. Pp. 44-74.

444a Meeks, W.A. "Moses as God and King," Goodenough Festschrift. Pp. 354-71.

445 Tiede, D.L. "The Figure of Moses in Palestine from 157 B. C. to 70 A.D.," *The Charismatic Figure as Miracle Worker* (SBLDS 1) Missoula, Mont.: SBL, 1972. Pp. 178-206.

446 Turdeanu, E. "La Chronique de Moïse, en russe," *RESl* 46 (1967) 35-64.

447 Wurmbrand, M. "Remarks on the Text of the Falasha 'Death of Moses,'" *BSOAS* 25 (1962) 431-37.

Noah

See below under 1 Enoch and Book of Noah. See also no. 479.

448 Lewis, J.P. *A Study of the Interpretation of Noah and the Flood in Jewish and Christian Literature.* Leiden: Brill, 1968.

449 Stone, M.E. "Noah, Books of," *EncyJud* 12. Col. 1198.

Rechab

See below under Apocalypse of Zosimus.

Shadrach (or Sedrach, the LXX form)

See below under Apocalypse of Sedrach.

Shem

See below under Treatise of Shem.

Solomon

See below under Odes of Solomon, Psalms of Solomon, and Testament of Solomon.

Zephaniah

See below under Apocalypse of Zephaniah.

Resurrection and Eschatology

See the publications listed under Apocalyptic and
Messianism.   See also nos. 137, 518, 625, 1213a.

450   Asmussen, J.P. "Eskatologi," *GDBL* 1. Cols. 452-56.

451   Auer, J. "Auferstehung des Fleisches," *Münchener theolo-
      gische Zeitschrift* 26 (1975) 17-37.

452   Boyd, W.J.P. "Apocalyptic and Life after Death," *Studia
      Evangelica*, ed. F.L. Cross (TU 103) Berlin: Akademie,
      1968. Vol. 5, pp. 39-56.

453   Bright, J. "Eschatology," Hastings. Pp. 265-67.

454   Davenport, G.L. *The Eschatology of the Book of Jubilees*
      (SPB 20) Leiden: Brill, 1971.

455   Drinkwater, F.H. "Jewish Apocalyptic and the Resurrec-
      tion," *Continuum* 6 (1968) 433-36.

456   Filson, F.V. "Resurrection," Hastings. Pp. 843-46.

457   Fohrer, G. "Die Struktur des alttestamentlichen Eschato-
      logie," *TLZ* 85 (1960) cols. 401-20.

458   Freedman, D.N. "History and Eschatology," *Int* 14 (1960)
      143-54.

459   Gaster, T.H. "Resurrection," *IDB* 4. Pp. 39-43.

460   Grelot, P. "L'eschatologie de la Sagesse et les apoca-
      lypses juives," *A la rencontre de Dieu*. A. Gelin Fest-
      schrift (Bibliothèque de la Faculté Catholique de
      Théologie de Lyons 8) Le Puy: Mappus, 1961. Pp. 165-78;
      repr. *De la mort à la vie éternelle: Etudes de théo-
      logie biblique* (LD 67) Paris: Le Cerf, 1971. Pp. 187-99.

461   Jewett, P. "Eschatology," *ZPEB* 2. Pp. 342-58. See esp.
      pp. 346f.

462   Koch, K. "Die Apokalyptik und ihre Zukunftserwartungen,"
      Die Zeit Jesu, ed. H.J. Schultz (Kontexte 3) Stuttgart:
      Kreuz, 1966. Pp. 51-58. [ET by B. Watchorn. Philadel-
      phia: Fortress, 1971. Pp. 57-65.]

463   Kraus, H.J. "Auferstehung III: In Israel," *RGG*[3] 1. Cols.
      692f.

464   Lane, W.L. *Times of Refreshment: A Study of Jewish and
      Christian Eschatological Periodization*. Harvard Ph.D.,
      1962.

465   Larcher, C. "L'immortalité de l'âme et les rétributions
      transcendantes," *Etudes sur le Livre de la Sagesse*
      (EBib) Paris: Lecoffre, 1969. Pp. 237-327.

465a Lieberman, S. "Some Aspects of After Life in Early
     Rabbinic Literature," *Texts and Studies*. New York: KTAV,
     1974. Pp. 235-72; repr. fr. *Harry A. Wolfson Jubilee
     Volume*. Jerusalem: American Academy for Jewish Research,
     1965. Pp. 495-532.

466 Macky, P.W. *The Importance of the Teaching on God, Evil
     and Eschatology for the Dating of the Testaments of the
     Twelve Patriarchs*. Princeton Theological Seminary Ph.D.,
     1969.

467 McNamara, M. "Eschatology," *Targum and Testament; Aramaic
     Paraphrases of the Hebrew Bible: A Light on the New
     Testament*. Shannon: Irish University; Grand Rapids:
     Eerdmans, 1972. Pp. 133-41.

468 Meyer, R. "Eschatologie III: Im Judentum," RGG^3 2. Cols.
     662-65.

469 Moltmann, J. "Der Vergeschichtlichung des Kosmos in apoka-
     lyptischer Eschatologie," *Theologie der Hoffnung: Unter-
     suchungen zur Begründung und zu den Konsequenzen einer
     christlichen Eschatologie* (BEvT, Theologische Abhand-
     lungen 38) Munich: Kaiser, 1964. Pp. 120-24. [ET by J.
     W. Leitch. London: SCM, 1967. Pp. 133-38.]

470 Nelis, J. "Eschatologie," $B-L^2$. Cols. 428-36.

471 Nickelsburg, G.W.E. Jr. *Resurrection, Immortality and
     Eternal Life in Intertestamental Judaism* (HTS 26)
     Cambridge, Mass.: Harvard University, 1972.

472 Pines, S. "Eschatology and the Concept of Time in the Sla-
     vonic Book of Enoch," *Types of Redemption: Contributions
     to the Theme of the Study-Conference Held at Jerusalem,
     14th to 19th July 1968*, eds. R.J.Z. Werblowsky and C.J.
     Bleeker (Sup *Numen* 18) Leiden: Brill, 1970. Pp. 72-87.

473 Plöger, O. *Theocracy and Eschatology*, trans. S. Rudman.
     Oxford: Blackwell, 1968.

474 Pryke, E.J. "Some Aspects of Eschatology in the Dead Sea
     Scrolls," *Studia Evangelica*, ed. F.L. Cross (TU 103)
     Berlin: Akademie, 1968. Vol. 5, pp. 296-302. [The note
     also concerns 1En, 2En, SibOr, 4Ezra, AsMos.]

475 Rigaux, B. "La résurrection des morts dans la pensée juive
     au temps de Jésus," *Dieu l'a ressuscité* (Studii Biblici
     Franciscani Analecta 4) Gemblout: Duculot, 1973. Pp. 3-
     22.

476 Rist, M. "Eschatology of Apoc. and Pseudep.," *IDB* 2. Pp.
     133-35.

477 Seidensticker, P. "Zur Auferstehungshoffnung des Juden-
     tums," *Zeitgenössische Texte zur Osterbotschaft der
     Evangelien* (SBS 27) Stuttgart: Katholisches Bibelwerk,
     1967. Pp. 27-42.

478 Stemberger, G. *Der Leib der Auferstehung: Studien zur*
     Anthropologie und Eschatologie des palästinischen
     Judentums im neutestamentlichen Zeitalter (ca. 170 v.
     Chr.-100 n. Chr.) (AnBib 56) Rome: Biblical Institute
     Press, 1972.

479 Strobel, A. *Untersuchungen zum eschatologischen Verzö-*
     gerungsproblem: Auf Grund der spätjüdisch-urchristlichen
     Geschichte von Habakuk 2, 2ff. Leiden: Brill, 1961.

480 Thraede, K. "Eschatologie," *RAC* 6. Cols. 559-64.

481 Wied, G. *Der Auferstehungsglaube des späten Israel in*
     seiner Bedeutung für das Verhältnis von Apokalyptik und
     Weisheit. Bonn Ph.D., 1967.

Sin

Also see the publications on intercession and penitence
listed above under Theology, esp. nos. 301, 314, 326.

482 Malina, B.J. "Some Observations on the Origin of Sin in
     Judaism and St. Paul," *CBQ* 31 (1969) 18-34.

483 Neusner, J. "The Idea of Purity in Ancient Judaism," *JAAR*
     43 (1975) 15-26.

484 Neusner, J. "Ideas of Purity in the Literature of the
     Period of the Second Temple," *The Idea of Purity in*
     Ancient Judaism: The Haskell Lectures, 1972-1973 (Stud-
     ies in Judaism in Late Antiquity 1) Leiden: Brill, 1973.
     Pp. 32-71.

485 Strobel, A. "Das Zeugnis des Spätjudentums," *Erkenntnis*
     und Bekenntnis der Sünde in neutestamentlicher Zeit
     (Arbeiten zur Theologie 1, 37) Stuttgart: Calwer, 1968.
     Pp. 9-37.

486 Thyen, H. *Studien zur Sündenvergebung im Neuen Testament*
     und seinen alttestamentlichen und jüdischen Vorausset-
     zungen (FRLANT 96) Göttingen: Vandenhoeck & Ruprecht,
     1970.

Apocalypse of Abraham

Extant only in Old Slavic manuscripts, the Apocalypse of
Abraham was edited best by N. Tikhonravov (*Pamiatniki otre-*
chennoĭ russkoĭ literatury. St.Petersburg, 1863. Vol. 1, pp. 32-
53) and translated into English by G.H. Box, assisted by J.I.
Landsman (*The Apocalypse of Abraham.* London: S.P.C.K.; New
York: Macmillan, 1919). This interesting composition, which
has not received the attention it deserves, probably dates
from A.D. 80-100 and was written in a Semitic language. It is

an haggadic midrash upon Genesis 15:9-17, beginning with a
humorous account of Abraham's conversion from idolatry, chapters 1-8, and concluding with the apocalypse itself, 9-32.
One of the most intriguing features is the "Christian" interpolation in chapter 29, which is appreciably different from
the Christianity of the New Testament.

R. Rubinkiewicz is preparing an edition, translation and
commentary, under the direction of R. Le Déaut and J. Olŝr.
M. Philonenko is in charge of a new French translation.

See works above under "Abraham," Old Testament Names Used
Pseudonymously. See also nos. 70, 75, 320, 1490.

487 Bamberger, B.J. "Abraham, Apocalypse of," *IDB* 1. P. 21.

488 Broomall, W. "Abraham, Apocalypse of," *Encyclopedia of
     Christianity* 1. Pp. 29f.

489 Geoltrain, P. *L'Apocalypse d'Abraham*. Strasbourg Ph.D.,
     1960. [*N.V.*]

490 Goodenough, E.R. "Astronomical Symbols," *Jewish Symbols* 8
     (1958) 167-218. See esp. pp. 199, 204-07, 213.

491 Goodenough, E.R. "Birds," *Jewish Symbols* 8 (1958) 22-70.
     See esp. p. 44.

492 Gutiérrez-Larraya, J.A. "Abraham, Apocalipsis de,"
     Enciclopedia de la Biblia 1. Col. 83.

493 Helmbold, A.K. "Abraham, Apocalypse of," *ZPEB* 1. Pp. 26f.

494 Licht, J. "Abraham, Apocalypse of," *EncyJud* 2. Cols. 125-
     27.

495 Meyer, R. "Abraham-Apokalypse," *RGG*[3] 1. Col. 72.

496 [Moustakēs, B.] "Abraham, Apocalypse of," *ThEE* 1. Col. 65.
     [in Greek]

497 Müller, L. and O. Betz. "Apokalypse Abrahams," *JSHRZ* 5,
     in press.

498 Pennington, A. "Apocalypse of Abraham," Clarendon edition.

499 Stempvoort, P.A. van. "Abrahams Apokalypse," *BHH* 1. Col.
     16.

500 Turdeanu, E. *"L'Apocalypse d'Abraham* en slave," *JSJ* 3
     (1972) 153-80.

501 Wernick, N. *A Critical Analysis of the Book of Abraham in
     the Light of Extracanonical Jewish Writings*. Brigham
     Young Ph.D., 1968.

Testament of Abraham

The Testament of Abraham is extant in numerous languages, the texts of which were edited separately by various scholars, viz. the Greek by M.R. James (*The Testament of Abraham: The Greek Text Now First Edited with an Introduction and Notes*. Cambridge: CUP, 1892). The book has been translated into English by G.H. Box (*The Testament of Abraham*. London: S.P.C.K., 1927); M. Gaster (*Transactions of the Society of Biblical Archaeology*. London: Society of Biblical Archaeology, 1887. Vol. 9, pp. 195-226; repr. *Studies and Texts in Folklore, Magic, Medieval Romance, Hebrew Apocrypha and Samaritan Archaeology*. London: Maggs, 1925-1928. Vol. 1, pp. 92-124); W.A. Craigie (*ANF* 10. Pp. 183-201); and M.E. Stone (no. 522 below); also see W. Leslau's *Falasha Anthology*, pp. 92-102. It is unlikely that this composition is either a second-century Jewish-Christian work (James) or a pre-Christian Essene work (K. Kohler, "The Pre-Talmudic Haggada II: The Apocalypse of Abraham and its Kindred," *JQR* 7 [1895] 581-606). It is most likely a Jewish composition from the first century, although the actual date and original language are debatable. In the first nine chapters the archangel Michael vainly seeks to obtain the soul of Abraham, who refuses to die. A deal is arranged by which Abraham agrees to come with Michael if he can first see the created world, a wish that is granted and described in an apocalyptic section that covers chapters 10-14. Upon returning home Abraham refuses to die, but is eventually tricked by Death (chps. 15-20).

I understand that G.W. MacRae, G.W.E. Nickelsburg, Jr., and others are working on the versional materials to the Testament of Abraham. F. Schmidt, under M. Philonenko, has been preparing an edition, introduction and translation, which will appear in Textes et Etudes. J.S. Sibinga is to edit the text for PVTG. Copies of Bodleian MS Canonici Gr. 19, ff. 128v-147v, and Vatican Syr. 199, ff. 21v-45v, are preserved in the Pseudepigrapha Library at Duke University.

See works listed above under "Abraham," Old Testament Names Used Pseudonymously. See also no. 299a.

502 Agourides, S. "*Diathēke Abraam*," *Deltion Biblikon Meleton* 1 (1972) 238-48.

503 Andersen, H.G. "Abraham, Testament of," *ZPEB* 1. Pp. 27f.

504 Bamberger, B.J. "Abraham, Testament of," *IDB* 1. P. 21.

505 Broomall, W. "Abraham, Testament of," *Encyclopedia of Christianity* 1. Pp. 30f.

506 Delcor, M. "De l'origine de quelques traditions contenues dans le Testament d'Abraham," *Proceedings of the Fifth World Congress of Jewish Studies*, ed. P. Peli. Jerusalem: World Union of Jewish Studies, 1969. Vol. 1, pp. 192-200.

507 Delcor, M. *Le Testament d'Abraham: Introduction, traduction du texte grec et commentaire de la recension grecque longue suivie de la traduction des Testaments d'Abraham, d'Isaac et de Jacob d'après les versions orientales* (SVTP 2) Leiden: Brill, 1973.

508 Denis, A.-M. "Le Testament d'Abraham," *Introduction*. Pp. 31-39.

509 Fishburne, C.W. "I Corinthians III. 10-15 and the Testament of Abraham," *NTS* 17 (1970) 109-15.

510 Flusser, D. "Abraham, Testament of," *EncyJud* 2. Col. 129.

511 Gaguine, M. *The Falasha Version of the Testaments of Abraham, Isaac and Jacob*. Manchester, Eng., Ph.D., 1965.

512 Gutiérrez-Larraya, J.A. "Abraham, Testamento de," *Enciclopedia de la Biblia* 1. Cols. 84f.

513 Harrington, D.J. "Abraham Traditions in the Testament of Abraham and in the 'Rewritten Bible' of the Intertestamental Period," SCS 2. Pp. 155-64.

514 Janssen, E. "Testament Abrahams," *JSHRZ* 3 (1975) 193-256.

515 Kolenkow, A.B. "The Angelology of the Testament of Abraham," SCS 2. Pp. 228-45.

515a Kolenkow, A.B. "What is the Role of Testament in the Testament of Abraham?" *HTR* 67 (1974) 182-84.

516 Meyer, R. "Abraham-Testament," $RGG^3$1. Col. 73.

517 [Moustakēs, B.] "Abraham, Testament of," *ThĒE* 1. Col. 66. [in Greek]

518 Nickelsburg, G.W.E. Jr. "Eschatology in the Testament of Abraham: A Study of the Judgment Scenes in the Two Recensions," SCS 2. Pp. 180-227.

519 Piatelli, E. "'Il testamento di Abramo.' (Testo apocallitico del I secolo dell'e.v.)," *Annuario di Studi Ebraici* 2 (1964-1965) 111-22. [*N.V.*]

520 Sanders, E.P. "Testament of Abraham," Doubleday edition.

520a Schmidt, F. *Le Testament d'Abraham*. Strasbourg Ph.D., 1971.

72

521 Stempvoort, P.A. van. "Abrahams Testament," *BHH* 1. Col.17.

522 Stone, M.E. *The Testament of Abraham: The Greek Recensions*
     (T&T 2, Pseudepigrapha Series 2) Missoula, Mont.: SBL,
     1972. [The Greek is reprinted from M.R. James' edition.]

523 Turner, N. "Testament of Abraham," Clarendon edition.

Apocalypse of Adam

The Apocalypse of Adam, which is extant in Coptic and is
one of the Nag Hammadi Codices edited by A. Böhlig and P. Labib
(no. 529), has been translated into English by R. McL. Wilson,
with reference to M. Krause's German (no. 536). While there is
general agreement that the work is non-Christian and dates
either from the first or second century, there is considerable
debate over A. Böhlig's suggestion that the original is a pre-
Christian product of a Syrian-Palestinian baptist sect (no.
528). This attractive hypothesis, which has been supported
with modifications by J. Robinson (no. 542, p. 234), K. Rudolph
(*TLZ* 90 [1965]), G.W. MacRae (no. 539), and R. Kasser (no. 534),
opens the way for the inclusion of the Apocalypse of Adam within the Pseudepigrapha. As 1 Enoch, Jubilees, the Odes of Solomon, and the Testaments of the Twelve Patriarchs disclose the
interrelationships between the Pseudepigrapha and the Dead Sea
Scrolls, the Apocalypse of Adam reveals the rich influence of
the Pseudepigrapha upon the gnostic codices. The Apocalypse
is a revelation by Adam to Seth and includes a lengthy section
on the origin of the Illuminator.

Along with the other Nag Hammadi Codices, the Apocalypse
of Adam is being translated by G.W. MacRae for the Coptic
Gnostic Project of the Institute for Antiquity and Christianity
at Claremont Graduate School. See the reports published intermittently by the director, J.M. Robinson (e.g. no. 541).

See publications listed under the Pseudepigrapha and Gnosticism and "Adam," Old Testament Names Used Pseudonymously.

524 Arai, S. "With Special Reference to the Apocalypse of
     Adam in the Ancient Orient," *Yôroppa Kirisutokyôshi* 1
     (1971) 91-118. [in Japanese; a concept of the Illumina-
     tor in ApAdam.]

525 Beltz, W. *Die Adam-Apokalypse aus Codex V von Nag Hammadi:
     Jüdische Bausteine in gnostischen Systemen.* Berlin (DDR)
     Th.D., 1970.

526 Beltz, W. and P.L. Márton. "The Current Situation of the
     Gnostic 'Search': The Apocalypse of Adam from Nag Hamma-
     di as Presented in Codex V," *Theologiai Szemle* 12 (1969)
     266-70. [in Hungarian]

527 Böhlig, A. "Die Adamapokalypse aus Codex V von Nag Hammadi
     als Zeugnis jüdisch-iranischer Gnosis," *Oriens Christi-
     anus* 48 (1964) 44-49.

528 Böhlig, A. "Jüdisches und iranisches in der Adamapokalypse
     des Codex V von Nag Hammadi," *Mysterion und Wahrheit:
     Gesammelte Beiträge zur spätantiken Religionsgeschichte*
     (AGAJU 6) Leiden: Brill, 1968. Pp. 149-61.

529 Böhlig, A. and P. Labib. *Koptisch-gnostische Apokalypsen
     aus Codex V von Nag Hammadi im Koptischen Museum zu Alt-
     Kairo* (WZHalle Sonderband) Halle: Martin-Luther-Univer-
     sität, 1963.

530 Cardona, G.R. "Sur le gnosticisme en Arménie--les livres
     d'Adam," *Le origini dello gnosticismo: Colloquio di
     Messina, 13-18 aprile 1966*, ed. U. Bianchi (Studies in
     the History of Religions 12) Leiden: Brill, 1967. Pp.
     645-48.

531 Goedicke, H. "An Unexpected Allusion to the Vesuvius
     Eruption in 79 A.D.," *American Journal of Philology* 90
     (1969) 340f.

532 Hedrick, C.W. "The Apocalypse of Adam: A Literary and
     Source Analysis," *SBL 1972 Seminar Papers*. Vol. 2, pp.
     581-90.

533 Kasser, R. "Apocalypse d'Adam," *RTP* 16 (1967) 316-33.

534 Kasser, R. "Bibliothèque gnostique V: Apocalypse d'Adam,"
     RTP 17 (1967) 316-33.

535 Kasser, R. "Textes gnostiques: Remarques à propos des
     éditions récentes du livre secret de Jean et des
     apocalypses de Paul, Jacques, et Adam," *Muséon* 78
     (1965) 71-98. Also see 299-306.

536 Krause, M. "The Apocalypse of Adam," *Gnosis: A Selection
     of Gnostic Texts. Coptic and Mandean Sources*, ed. W.
     Foerster; trans. R. McL. Wilson. Oxford: Clarendon,
     1974. Vol. 2, pp. 13-23.

537 MacRae, G.W. "Apocalypse of Adam," Doubleday edition.

538 MacRae, G. "The Apocalypse of Adam Reconsidered," *SBL 1972
     Seminar Papers*. Vol. 2, pp. 573-79.

539 MacRae, G. "The Coptic Gnostic Apocalypse of Adam," *HeyJ*
     6 (1965) 27-35.

540 Perkins, P. "Apocalyptic Schematization in the Apocalypse
     of Adam and the Gospel of the Egyptians," *SBL 1972 Semi-
     nar Papers*. Vol. 2, pp. 591-99.

74

541   Robinson, J.M. "The Coptic Gnostic Library Today," *NTS* 14
       (1968) 356-401. See esp. pp. 377f.

542   Robinson, J.M. "Jewish Wisdom Literature and the Gattung
       LOGOI SOPHON," *Trajectories Through Early Christianity*.
       Philadelphia: Fortress, 1971. Pp. 103-13.

543   Rudolph, K. "Gnosis und Gnostizismus, ein Forschungs-
       bericht," *ThRu* 34 (1969) 121-75, 181-231. See esp. pp.
       160-69.

544   Schottroff, L. "Animae naturaliter salvandae: Zum Problem
       der himmlischen Herkunft des Gnostikers," *Christentum
       und Gnosis*, ed. W. Eltester (BZNW 37) Berlin: Töpelmann,
       1969. Pp. 65-97.

545   Schwartz, M. "Appendix: I. On the Apocalypse of Adam,"
       *Jewish Gnostic Nag Hammadi Texts: Protocol of the Third
       Colloquy of the Center for Hermeneutical Studies in
       Hellenistic and Modern Culture*. Berkeley, Calif., 1972.
       Pp. 27-30. [*N.V.*]

546   Wilson, R. McL. "Gnostic Apocalypses: The Apocalypse of
       Adam," *Gnosis and the New Testament*. Philadelphia:
       Fortress, 1968. Pp. 130-39.

Testament of Adam

See Cave of Treasures.

*Life of Adam and Eve
(Apocalypse of Moses)*

Of the many books attributed to Adam, the most important
are the *Vita Adae et Evae* and a different recension of the same
book, the misnamed *Apocalypsis Mosis*; the former was edited by
W. Meyer (*Abhandlungen der Bayrischen Akademie der Wissenschaften* 14, 3 [1878] 185-250) and the latter by C. Tischendorf
(no. 1147) and A.M. Ceriani (*Monumenta Sacra et Profana*. Milan:
Bibliotheca Ambrosiana, 1861. Vol. 5, 1, pp. 19-24). English
translations of each recension are respectively by L.S.A. Wells
(*APOT* 2. Pp. 123-54) and M.B. Riddle (*ANF* 8. Pp. 565-70).
There is wide agreement that the original dates from the first
century A.D. and was composed in a Semitic language. This
haggadic midrash on Genesis 1-4 relates in 51 chapters (according to LAE) the life of Adam and Eve, concentrating upon the
problems encountered after the expulsion from Eden and the
cause of their rejection.

See publications listed under "Adam," Old Testament Names
Used Pseudonymously, and Apocalypse of Moses. See also nos.
4, 51, 84, 87, 309, 368.

547   Asmussen, J.P. "Adams og Evas Liv," *GDBL* 1. Col. 14.

548   Bianchi, U. "La rédemption dans les livres d'Adam," *Numen*
      18 (1971) 1-8.

549   Goodenough, E.R. "Psychopomps," *Jewish Symbols* 8 (1958)
      121-66. See esp. p. 141.

550   Goodenough, E.R. "The Tree," *Jewish Symbols* 7 (1958) 87-
      134. See esp. p. 127.

551   Gutiérrez-Larraya, J.A. "Adán y Eva, Libros apócrifos de,"
      Enciclopedia de la Biblia 1. Cols. 154f.

552   Hammershaimb, E. "Adamsbøgerne," *GamPseud* 5 (1970) 525-47.

553   Helmbold, A.K. "Adam, Books of," *ZPEB* 1. P. 56.

554   Johnson, M. "Life of Adam and Eve (Apocalypse of Moses),"
      Doubleday edition.

555   Kʻurcʻikidze, Cʻ. "The Georgian Version of the 'Life of
      Adam,'" *Pʻilologiuri Dziehani* 1 (1964) 97-136. [in
      Georgian]

556   Licht, J. "Adam and Eve, Book of the Life of," *EncyJud* 2.
      Cols. 246f.

557   Liebermann, H. "The Author of 'Ḥayye Adam' and the Gaon of
      Wilnai," *KS* 37 (1962) 413f. [in Hebrew]

558   Meyer, R. "Adambücher," *RGG*[3] 1. Col. 91.

559   Mpratsiōtēs, P.I. "Adam, Apocryphal Books of," *ThEE* 1.
      Cols. 375f. [in Greek]

560   Piatelli, E. ["Life of Adam and Eve"], *Annuario di Studi
      Ebraici* (1968-1969) 9-23. [*N.V.*]

561   Ringgren, H. "Adambücher," *BHH* 1. Col. 25.

562   Stone, M.E., with E. Shefer. *The Books of the Life of
      Adam and Eve and IV Baruch*. Jerusalem: Akademon, 1970.
      [in Hebrew]

563   Whittaker, M. "Life of Adam and Eve (Apocalypse of Moses),"
      Clarendon edition.

Ahiqar

     In the early years of this century at Elephantine, Egypt,
German archaeologists discovered an Aramaic papyrus that dates
from the fifth century B.C. This papyrus reveals both the
antiquity of Ahiqar and the probability that Aramaic is the
original language. Prior to this discovery a convenient edition, based upon six languages, was published by F.C. Conybeare,

J.R. Harris, and A.S. Lewis (*The Story of Aḥiḳar*. London: Clay and Sons, 1898). Recognizing the authority of the Aramaic papyrus, these scholars presented a new translation in 1913 (*APOT* 2. Pp. 715-84), benefiting from the Aramaic text published by E. Sachau (*Aramäische Papyrus und Ostraka aus einer jüdischen Militär-Kolonie zu Elephantine*. 2 vols. Leipzig: Hinrichs, 1911) and A. Ungnad (*Aramäische Papyrus aus Elephantine*. Leipzig: Hinrichs, 1911).

The story of Ahiqar, which influences Tobit 1:21f., is a folktale with a powerful moral: disgrace and punishment are the just results of ingratitude and betrayal. Ahiqar, the exceedingly wise and wealthy Grand-Vizier to Sennacherib, King of Assyria, lacks only a son, so he adopts his sister's son, Nadin, who returns truth with lies and adoption with betrayal. Ahiqar is led to his execution, but is saved by the swordsman, Nabushumishkun, who remembers that the Grand-Vizier had saved his own life. Eventually the need for Ahiqar's wisdom returns him to his former office, from which he executes full revenge upon Nadin. The eight long chapters are divided into four parts: the narrative (1); teaching (2); Nadin's betrayal with Ahiqar's restoration and trip to Egypt (3-7); and the parables of Ahiqar (8).

Ahiqar 8:15 probably influenced the last part of 2 Peter 2:22 and Ahiqar 8:38 (Arabic), the description of Nadin's death, probably has shaped--or been shaped by--the account of the death of another traitor, Judas, in Acts 1:18. Later editorial expansion by Christians is not the only explanation for the impressive parallels between Ahiqar and the sayings of Jesus, e.g. the injunction to be kind to enemies (2:19 [Arabic] cf. Mt 5:44, Lk 6:27, 35); the teaching not to treat your companion by that which seems evil to you (2:88 [Armenian], cf. Mt 7:12, Lk 6:31 [The Golden Rule]); and the parables of the Prodigal Son (8:34 [Syriac], cf. Lk 15:19) and the wicked servant [4:15, cf. Mt 24:45-51, Lk 12:43-48). This folktale is outside the chronological limits represented by the Pseudepigrapha, yet is included in this corpus of literature because it is important for biblical studies but not considered for inclusion by other literary categories.

Dr. James Lindenberger has completed a dissertation on

Ahiqar, under the direction of Delbert R. Hillers. He is preparing a new edition and commentary on the proverbs of Ahiqar.
M. Philonenko is also working on this composition.

See also nos. 22, 471.

564 Altheim, F. and R. Stiehl, "Maṣḥafa falāsfā ṭabībān,"
     In Memoriam Paul Kahḷe, eds. M. Black and G. Fohrer
     (BZAW 103) Berlin: Topelmann, 1968. Pp. 3-9.

565 Andersen, H.G. "Ahikar, Book of," *ZPEB* 1. P. 87.

566 Denis, A.-M. "Les fragments grecs de l'Histoire et des
     Maximes d'Aḥiqar," *Introduction*. Pp. 201-14.

567 Dietrich, M. "Ăḥīqār, Historia de," *Enciclopedia de la
     Biblia* 1. Cols. 264-66.

568 Dumm, D.R. "Ahikar (Achior)," *NCE* 1. Pp. 222f.

569 Greenfield, J.C. "The Background and Parallel to a Proverb
     of Ahiqar," *Hommages à André Dupont-Sommer*, eds. A.
     Caquot and M. Philonenko. Paris: Adrien- Maisonneuve,
     1971. Pp. 49-60.

570 Gutman, Y. "Ahikar, Book of," *EncyJud* 2. Cols. 460f.

571 Kraeling, E.G. "Ahikar, Book of," *IDB* 1. Pp. 68f.

572 Lindenberger, J.M. "Ahiqar," Doubleday edition.

572a McKane, W. "Ahikar," *Proverbs: A New Approach*. Philadel-
     phia: Westminster, 1970. Pp. 156-82.

573 Stone, M.E. "Ahikar," *EncyJud* 2. Cols. 461f.

574 Termes, P. "Ăḥīqār y el Libro de Tobías," *Enciclopedia de
     la Biblia* 1. Cols. 266-68.

*An Anonymous Samaritan Text
(Pseudo-Eupolemus)*

Of this text, called by B.Z. Wacholder (no. 574e) and N.
Walter (no. 574f) Pseudo-Eupolemus and by P. Riessler (no. 62)
simply "Anonymous," only sixteen verses are preserved in quotations of Alexander Polyhistor (80-35 B.C.) by Eusebius in his
Praeparatio Evangelica (9.17-18), which was translated by E.H.
Gifford (Eusebius. *Preparation for the Gospel*. Oxford: Clarendon, 1903). Alexander Polyhistor mentions two fragments of
the Anonymous Samaritan, calling the first "an anonymous writing" (*Pr. ev.* 9.18, 2), but incorrectly attributing the second
to Eupolemus (*Pr. ev.* 9.17, 2-9). The Greek text of these two
excerpts has been republished by A.-M. Denis in his *Fragmenta*

pseudepigraphorum quae supersunt graeca (no. 23, pp. 197f.).
This Samaritan text was probably composed between 200 and 150
B.C., and was written by a Samaritan because Mt. Gerazim is
called "the mountain of the Most High."

574a Denis, A.-M. "Historien anonyme," *Introduction.* Pp. 261f.

574b Hengel, M. "Der samaritanische Anonymus," *Judentum und
    Hellenismus: Studien zu ihrer Begegnung unter besonderer
    Berücksichtigung Palästinas bis zur Mitte des 2. Jh. v.
    Chr.* (WUNT 10) Tübingen: Mohr, 1969. Pp. 162-69. [ET of
    2d. ed. by J. Bowden. Philadelphia: Fortress, 1974. Pp.
    88-92.]

574c Kippenberg, H.G. *Garizim und Synagoge: Traditionsge-
    schichtliche Untersuchungen zur samaritanischen Religion
    der aramäischen Periode* (Religionsgeschichtliche Ver-
    suche und Vorarbeiten 30) Berlin: Walter de Gruyter,
    1971. See esp. pp. 80-85.

574d Wacholder, B.Z. "Biblical Chronology in the Hellenistic
    World Chronicles," *HTR* 61 (1968) 451-81. See esp. pp.
    458-62.

574e Wacholder, B.Z. "Pseudo-Eupolemus' Two Greek Fragments on
    the Life of Abraham," *HUCA* 34 (1963) 83-113.

574f Walter, N. "Zu Pseudo-Eupolemos," *Klio: Beiträge zur alten
    Geschichten* 43-45 (1965) 282-90.

Letter of Aristeas

Extant only in Greek, albeit in at least twenty-three
known manuscripts, the Letter of Aristeas has been re-edited
recently by A. Pelletier (no. 595). English translations have
been published by H.St.J. Thackeray (*The Letter of Aristeas*
[TED 2] London: S.P.C.K., 1917; which is a revision of his
translation published in *JQR* 15 [1903] 337-91); H.T. Andrews
(*APOT* 2. Pp. 83-122); and M. Hadas (*Aristeas to Philocrates*
[Dropsie Coll. Ed. Jew. Apoc. Lit.] New York: Harper, 1951).
The original composition dates from the early decades of the
second century B.C. The author presents an apology for Judaism, defending the Septuagint and the Jerusalem Temple. S.
Jellicoe suggested that Aristeas is directed against a rival
Greek translation of the Old Testament developed at Leontopolis
(see no. 586, p. 50).

Aristeas, a member of Ptolemy Philadelphus' court, relates
the circumstances that preceded and accompanied the translation
of the Law from the Hebrew into the Septuagint. With repeated

digressions the story unfolds in four parts: the preparation
for the translation (1-82); a description of Palestine (83-
120); an emphasis upon the unparalleled quality of the translation (121-311); and the return to Jerusalem of the Jewish
scribes who are burdened with gifts (312-322).

See also nos. 88, 289a, 302, 465, 1480.

575 Altheim, F. and R. Stiehl. "Alexander und das Avesta,"
     Geschichte Mittelasiens im Altertum. Berlin: Walter de
     Gruyter, 1970. Pp. 248-63.

576 Brock, S.P. "The Phenomenon of the Septuagint," *The Wit-
     ness of Tradition*, ed. A.S. van der Woude (OTS 18)
     Leiden: Brill, 1972. Pp. 11-36.

577 Denis, A.-M. "La Lettre d'Aristée," *Introduction*. Pp. 105-
     10.

578 Gasque, W.W. "Aristeas," *ZPEB* 1. P. 302.

579 Goodenough, E.R. "Birds," *Jewish Symbols* 8 (1958) 22-70.
     See esp. p. 45.

580 Goodenough, E.R. "The Relevance of Rabbinic Evidence,"
     Jewish Symbols 4 (1954) 3-24. See esp. p. 12.

581 Goodenough, E.R. "Wine in Jewish Cult and Observance,"
     Jewish Symbols 6 (1956) 126-217. See esp. p. 135.

582 Gutiérrez-Larraya, J.A. "Aristeas, Carta de," *Enciclopedia
     de la Biblia* 1. Cols. 713f.

583 Hegermann, H. "Das griechischsprechende Judentum," *Litera-
     tur und Religion des Frühjudentums*. Pp. 328-52.

584 Howard, G. "The Letter of Aristeas and Diaspora Judaism,"
     JTS n.s. 22 (1971) 337-48.

585 Isserlin, B.S.J. "The Names of the 72 Translators of the
     Septuagint (Aristeas, 47-50)," [Gaster Festschrift]
     *Journal of the Ancient Near Eastern Society of Columbia
     University* 5 (1973) 191-97.

585a Jellicoe, S. "St. Luke and the 'Seventy(-Two),'" *NTS* 6
     (1960) 319-21.

586 Jellicoe, S. "Septuagint Origins: *The Letter of Aristeas*,"
     The Septuagint and Modern Study. Oxford: Clarendon,
     1968. Pp. 29-58.

586a Jellicoe, S. *Studies in the Septuagint: Origins, Recen-
     sions, and Interpretations*. New York: KTAV, 1974. See
     esp. pp. 158-225.

587 Lewis, J.J. "The Table-Talk Section in the Letter of
     Aristeas," *NTS* 13 (1966) 53-56.

588   Meisner, N. "Aristeas ief," *JSHRZ* 2 (1973) 35-87.

589   Meisner, N. *Untersuchungen zum Aristeasbrief.* 2 vols. Berlin: Kirchliche Hochschule, 1972.

590   Michaelis, W. "Aristeasbrief," *RGG*³ 1. Col. 596.

591   Mpratsiotēs, "Aristeas, Letter of," *ThEE* 3. Col. 137. [in Greek]

592   Munck, J. "Aristeas," *GamPseud* 4 (1963) 381-440.

593   Murray, O. "Aristeas and Ptolemaic Kingship," *JTS* 18 (1967) 337-71.

594   Parente, F. "La Lettera di Aristea come fonte per la storia del Giudaismo alessandrino durante la prima metà del I secolo A.C.," *Annali della scuola normale superiore di Pisa* 2 (1972) 177-237, 517-67. [*N.V.*]

595   Pelletier, A. *Flavius Josèphe adapteur de la Lettre d'Aristée: une réaction atticisante contre la koinè.* Paris: Klincksieck, 1962.

596   Rappaport, U. "When Was the Letter of Aristeas Written?" *Studies in the History of the Jewish People and the Land of Israel in Memory of Zvi Avneri*, eds. A. Gilboa, *et al.* Haifa: University of Haifa, 1970. Pp. 37-50.

597   Shutt, R.J.H. "Letter of Aristeas," Doubleday edition.

598   Skehan, P.W. "Aristeas, Letter of," *NCE* 1. Pp. 797f.

599   Søndergård, S.M. "Aristeas," *GDBL* 1. Col. 119.

600   Stambaugh, J.E. "Aristeas of Argos in Alexandria," *Aegyptus* 47 (1967) 69-74.

601   Stendahl, K. "Aristeasbrief," *BHH* 1. Cols. 127f.

602   Tcherikover, A., *et al.* "Aristeas, Letter of," *EncyJud* 3. Cols. 439f.

603   Ziegler, J. "Aristeasbrief," *LTK*² 1. Col. 852.

604   Zuntz, G. "Aristeas," *IDB* 1. Pp. 219-21.

Aristeas the Exegete

Aristeas the Exegete is known only through a quotation of about sixteen lines from Alexander Polyhistor that is preserved in Eusebius' *Praeparatio Evangelica* (9.25), which was translated into English by E.H. Gifford (Eusebius. *Preparation for the Gospel.* Oxford: Clarendon, 1903). The Greek is reprinted in A.-M. Denis' *Fragmenta pseudepigraphorum quae supersunt graeca* (no. 23, pp. 195f.). The fragment concerns Job, called

"Jobab," and reveals dependence upon the Septuagint (see N. Walter, no. 607, p. 293; B.Z. Wacholder, no. 605, col. 438); hence Aristeas the Exegete lived in the period between the completion of the Septuagint and the time of Alexander Polyhistor (80-35 B.C.), perhaps around 100 B.C. He may have lived in Palestine or Egypt, but the data will not permit us to decide which country is more probable.

See Fragments of Historical Works.

604a Denis, A.-M. "Aristée," *Introduction*. Pp. 258f.

605   Wacholder, B.Z. "Aristeas," *EncyJud* 3. Cols. 438f.

606   Wacholder, B.Z. "Aristeas the Exegete," Doubleday edition.

607   Walter, N. "Fragmente jüdisch-hellenistischer Exegeten: Aristobulos, Demetrios, Aristeas," *JSHRZ* 3 (1975) 257-96. See esp. pp. 293-96.

Aristobulus

Aristobulus' work is extant only fragmentarily in Clement of Alexandria (*Strom.* 6.3, 1.22, 5.14, 6.16) and Eusebius (*Pr. ev.* 8.10, 13.12, 7.14. *H.E.* 7.32). The Greek excerpts are re-edited by A.-M. Denis in his *Fragmenta pseudepigraphorum quae supersunt graeca* (no. 23, pp. 217-28). Recommended English translations are by W. Wilson (*The Writings of Clement of Alexandria* [Anti-Nicene Chr. Lib., 4 and 12] Edinburgh: Clark, 1867-1869; repr. *ANF* 2. Pp. 299-567); E.H. Gifford (Eusebius. *Preparation for the Gospel*. Oxford: Clarendon, 1903); and J.E. L. Oulton (Eusebius. *The Ecclesiastical History* [LCL] London: Heinemann; Cambridge, Mass.: Harvard, 1938).

Aristobulus, according to 2 Maccabees 1:10, belonged to a priestly family and was a teacher of Ptolemy in Egypt. He lived around the middle of the second century B.C. (Hengel suggests 175-170 B.C.; see no. 610, p. 164). An eclectic Jewish philosopher, he combined Pythagorean, Platonic, and Stoic thought with Jewish ideas, especially those characteristic of Proverbs, Ben Sira, the Wisdom of Solomon, Pseudo-Phocylides, and 4 Maccabees. It is, therefore, inaccurate to follow Clement of Alexandria (*Strom.* 1.72) and categorize him as a Peripatetic (see N. Walter, *Der Thoraausleger Aristobulos: Untersuchungen zu seinen Fragmenten und zu pseudepigraphischen*

Resten der jüdisch-hellenistischen Literatur [TU 86] Berlin:
Akademie, 1964; esp. pp. 10-13).

The extant fragments contain an allegorical interpretation
of Genesis with an apologetic goal: the Mosaic law is the
true philosophy; and Pythagoras, Socrates, and Plato heard the
voice of God. Wisdom seems identified with seven, the cosmic
principle.

Consult Fragments of Poetical Works.

608   Barabas, S. "Aristobulus," *ZPEB* 1. Pp. 303f.

609   Gutman, Y., *et al.* "Aristobulus of Paneas," *EncyJud* 3.
      Cols. 443-45.

610   Hengel, M. "Schöpfung und Weisheit bei Aristobul, dem
      ersten jüdischen 'Philosophen' in Alexandrien," *Judentum
      und Hellenismus: Studien zu ihrer Begegnung unter
      besonderer Berücksichtigung Palästinas bis zur Mitte
      des 2. Jh. v. Chr.* (WUNT 10) Tübingen: Mohr, 1969. Pp.
      295-307. [ET by J. Bowden. Philadelphia: Fortress, 1974
      Vol. 1, pp. 163-69.]

611   [Ioannidēs, B. Ch.] "Aristobulus," *ThEE* 3. Col. 140 [in
      Greek]

612   Walter, N. "Fragmente jüdisch-hellenistischer Exegeten:
      Aristobulos, Demetrios, Aristeas," *JSHRZ* 3 (1975) 257-
      96. See esp. pp. 261-79.

Artapanus

Artapanus' writings are preserved in three quotations
found in Eusebius' *Praeparatio Evangelica* (9.18, 9.23, 9.27);
the third is also extant in part in Clement of Alexandria's
Stromata (1.23).   These Greek excerpts are conveniently reprinted in A.-M. Denis' *Fragmenta pseudepigraphorum quae
supersunt graeca* (no. 23, pp. 186-95). English translations
of Eusebius and Clement were mentioned above under Aristobulus

Although it is impossible to specify Artapanus' dates, it
is evident he lived in the second century B.C., probably in
Egypt. The fragments contain the claim that Egyptian culture,
including idolatry and polytheism, was shaped by Abraham,
Joseph and Moses. The last is even deified. These liberal
ideas scarcely warrant the conclusion that Artapanus was a
"heathen" (so J. Freudenthal, *Alexander Polyhistor*. Breslau:
Skutsch, 1875; pp. 146-48); they reveal how far a syncretistic

hellenistic Jew can veer away from the biblical tradition (so
E. Schürer, *History*, 2d Div., vol. 3, p. 208; P. Dalbert,
Missionsliteratur, pp. 42-52). It is probable that Artapanus
was forced into hyperbole because he was composing a pro-Jewish
apology against an Egyptian anti-Semitic Moses legend (so M.
Braun, *History and Romance in Graeco- Oriental Literature*. Oxford: Blackwell, 1938; pp. 26-31).

The first fragment, an extract of one section from his *En
tois Ioudaikois*, contains both an explanation of *Hermioth*, the
name of the Jews before Abraham called them *Hebraious*, and a
report that Abraham taught astrology to Pharaoh. The second,
a quotation of four sections from his *Peri Ioudaiōn*, notes that
Joseph was master (*despotēs*) of the Egyptians. The third, a
narrative of 37 sections also taken from *Peri Ioudaiōn*, contains a story of Moses, who is identified with Musaeus, described as the teacher of Orpheus, and called Hermes. *Inter
alia* Moses divided the state (*tēn polin*) into 36 sections and
assigned to each a god (*kai hekastō tōn nomōn apotaxai ton
theon sephthēsesthai*), invented hieroglyphics, and was military
commander of a war against the Ethiopians.

See Fragments of Historical Works. See also no. 819.

612a Denis, A.-M. "Artapan," *Introduction*. Pp. 255-57.

613 Hanhart, R. "Artapanus," *BHH* 1. Cols. 131f.

614 [Merentitēs, K.I.] "Artapanus," *ThEE* 3. Cols. 257f. [in
    Greek]

615 Schalit, A. "Artapanus," *EncyJud* 3. Cols. 645f.

616 Wacholder, B.Z. "Artapanus," Doubleday edition.

617 Walter, N. "Artapanos," *JSHRZ* 1, in press.

2 (Syriac) Baruch

Except for a Greek fragment, re-edited by A.-M. Denis in
Fragmenta pseudepigraphorum quae supersunt graeca (no. 23, pp.
118-20), 2 Baruch is extant entirely in only one Syriac manuscript (Bibliotheca Ambrosiana B. 21 Inf., ff. 257a-265b). It
has been re-edited recently by S. Dedering (no. 623) and translated earlier into English by R.H. Charles (*APOT* 2. Pp. 481-
526, based upon his *Apocalypse of Baruch*. London: Black, 1896;

repr. [TED 1.9] London: S.P.C.K., 1917 [repr. 1929]). While
there is a consensus that 2 Baruch was composed during the
last decades of the first century A.D., there is considerable
debate concerning its original language. P.-M. Bogaert, for
example, concludes that Greek and Hebrew are equally possible
(no. 619, vol. 1, p. 380). It is possible that it was composed
in Palestine.

Most scholars have divided the book into seven sections,
with some disagreement regarding borderline verses: an account
of the destruction of Jerusalem (1-12); the impending judgment
(13-20); the time of retribution and the subsequent messianic
era (21-34); Baruch's lament and an allegory of the vine and
the cedar (35-46); terrors of the last time, nature of the
resurrected body, and the features of Paradise and Sheol (47-
52); Baruch's vision of a cloud (53-76); Baruch's letters to
the nine and a half tribes and to the two and a half tribes
(77-87). The pseudepigraphon is important for numerous theological concepts, e.g. the explanation that Jerusalem was
destroyed not by enemies but by angels (7:1-8:5); the pre-
occupation with the origin of sin (15:5f., 23:4f., 48:42,
54:15, 19; cf. 4Ezra 7:116-31); pessimism for the present
(85:10); the contention that the end will not come until the
number of those to be born is fulfilled (23:4-7; cf. 4Ezra
4:35-37); the description of the resurrected body (49:1-51:6);
and the varied messianic concepts.

R.Y. Ebied is editing an Arabic text that apparently contains a version of Syriac Baruch. Some interesting variants
have been noted already, signifying that the Arabic represents
a tradition distinct from the extant Syriac (see P.Sj. van
Koningsveld, no. 642a).

See also nos. 10, 23, 50, 87, 175f., 234, 289a, 297, 309,
320, 330, 407-09, 471, 477-79.

618 Baars, W. "Neue Textzeugen der syrischen Baruchapokalypse,"
     VT 13 (1963) 476-78.

619 Bogaert, P.-M. *L'Apocalypse de Baruch: introduction,
     traduction du syriaque et commentaire* (SC 144, 145)
     Paris: Le Cerf, 1969. [See J. Strugnell's review in
     JBL 89 (1970) 484f.]

620 Bogaert, P.-M. "Le nom de Baruch dans la littérature pseudépigraphique: l'apocalypse syriaque et le livre deutérocanonique," *La littérature juive entre Tenach et Mishna*, ed. W.C. van Unnik (RechBib 9) Leiden: Brill, 1974. [*N.V.*]

621 Bogaert, P.-M. "Le personnage de Baruch et l'histoire du livre de Jérémie: Aux origines du livre de Baruch," *BIOSCS* 7 (1974) 19-21.

622 Brockington, L.H. "2 (Syriac) Baruch," Clarendon edition.

623 Dedering, S., ed. "Apocalypse of Baruch," *Peshiṭta*. Part 4, fasc. 3 (1973) i-iv, 1-50.

624 Denis, A.-M. "Les fragments grecs de l'Apocalypse syriaque de Baruch," *Introduction*. Pp. 182-86.

625 Fàbrega, V. *Das Endgericht in der syrischen Baruchapokalypse*. Innsbruck Ph.D., 1969.

626 Glatzer, N.N. "The Consolation of Zion," *Judaic Tradition*. Pp. 173-75.

627 Goodenough, E.R. "Astronomical Symbols," *Jewish Symbols* 8 (1958) 167-218. See esp. p. 204.

628 Goodenough, E.R. "Psychopomps," *Jewish Symbols* 8 (1958) 121-66. See esp. p. 137.

629 Goodenough, E.R. "The Reredos," *Jewish Symbols* 9 (1964) 78-123. See esp. p. 117.

630 Goodenough, E.R. "The Symbolic Value of the Fish in Judaism," *Jewish Symbols* 5 (1956) 31-61. See esp. p. 37.

631 Grintz, Y.M. "Baruch, Apocalypse of (Syriac)," *EncyJud* 4. Cols. 270-72.

632 Gutiérrez-Larraya, J.A. "Bārūk, Apocalipsis siríaco de," *Enciclopedia de la Biblia* 1. Cols. 1063f.

633 Hadot, J. "La datation de l'Apocalypse syriaque de Baruch," *Sem* 15 (1965) 79-95.

634 Hadot, J. "Le problème de l'Apocalypse syriaque de Baruch d'après un ouvrage récent," *Sem* 20 (1970) 59-76.

635 Hammershaimb, E. [in] *GamPseud* 7. [*N.V.*]

636 Harnisch, W. *Verhängnis und Verheissung der Geschichte: Untersuchungen zum Zeit- und Geschichtsverständnis im 4. Buch Esra und in der syr. Baruchapokalypse* (FRLANT 97) Göttingen: Vandenhoeck & Ruprecht, 1969.

637 Hercigonya, E. "The Apocalypse of Baruch According to Codex Petris, Dated A.D. 1468," *Zbornik za filologiju i lingvistiku Matice Srpske* 7 (1964) 63-69. [in Czechoslovakian; *N.V.*]

638 Ioannidēs, B. Ch. "Baruch (Apocalypse of)," *ThĒE* 3. Cols. 650f. [in Greek]

639 Klijn, A.F.J. "2 (Syriac) Baruch," Doubleday edition.

640 Klijn, A.F.J. "The Sources and the Redaction of the Syriac Apocalypse of Baruch," *JSJ* 1 (1970) 65-76.

641 Klijn, A.F.J. "Syrische Baruch-Apokalypse," *JSHRZ* 5, in press.

642 Kolenkow, A.C.B. *An Introduction to II Bar. 53, 56-74: Structure and Substance.* Harvard Ph.D., 1972.

642a Koningsveld, P.Sj. van. "An Arabic Manuscript of the Apocalypse of Baruch," *JSJ* 6 (1975) 205-07.

643 Nickelsburg, G.W.E. Jr. "Narrative Traditions in the Paralipomena of Jeremiah and 2 Baruch," *CBQ* 35 (1973) 60-68.

644 Noack, B. "Baruks apokalypser," *GDBL* 1. Cols. 186f.

645 Rist, M. "Baruch, Apocalypse of," *IDB* 1. Pp. 361f.

646 Thoma, C. "Jüdische Apokalyptik am Ende des ersten nach-christlichen Jahrhunderts: Religionsgeschichtliche Bemerkungen zur syrischen Baruchapokalypse und zum vierten Esrabuch," *Kairos* 11 (1969) 134-44.

647 Weise, M. "Baruchschriften," *BHH* 1. Cols. 202f.

648 Werbeck, W. "Baruchschriften, apokryphe," *RGG*[3] 1. Cols. 900-03.

649 White, W. Jr. "Baruch, Apocalypse of," *ZPEB* 1. Pp. 482f.

3 (Greek) Baruch

Except for the existence of two Slavonic versions (see J.-C. Picard, no. 659, pp. 69-71), 3 Baruch is extant in only two Greek manuscripts that have been edited recently by J.-C. Picard (no. 659). English translations were published from the Slavonic by W.R. Morfill (*Apocrypha Anecdota II*, ed. M.R. James [T&S 5.1] Cambridge: CUP, 1897. Pp. 95-102) and from the Slavonic and Greek by H.M. Hughes (*APOT* 2. Pp. 533-41). The pseudepigraphon was composed in the beginning of the second century A.D., but it is difficult to discover whether it was written in Greek, Hebrew, or Aramaic.

The chapters are internally divided according to the pro-gression of Baruch through five heavens: prologue (1); first (2), second (3), third (4-9), fourth (10), and fifth heaven

(11-17). Except for intermittent Christian additions (4:15, 13:4, 15:4), the Jewish character of chapters 1-17 is now wide-ly accepted.

H.E. Gaylord, Jr., is preparing a critical edition of the Slavic versions under the direction of D. Flusser, M.E. Stone, and M. Altbauer.

See also no. 87.

650 Denis, A.-M. "L'Apocalypse grecque de Baruch," *Introduction*. Pp. 79-84.

651 Denis, A.-M. with Y. Janssens. *Concordance de l'Apocalypse grecque de Baruch* (PIOL 1) Louvain: Institut Orienta-liste, 1970.

652 Gaylord, H.E. "3 (Greek) Baruch," Doubleday edition.

653 Goodenough, E.R. "Birds," *Jewish Symbols* 8 (1958) 22-70. See esp. pp. 42, 69f.

654 Goodenough, E.R. "Wine in Jewish Cult and Observance," *Jewish Symbols* 6 (1956) 126-217. See esp. p. 131.

655 Guggenheim, J.Y. "Baruch, Greek Apocalypse of," *EncyJud* 4. Cols. 273f.

656 Hage, W.   "Griechische Baruch-Apokalypse," *JSHRZ* 5, in press.

657 Hammershaimb, E. "Den Graeske Baruksapokalypse," *GamPseud* 6 (1972) 659-76.

658 Noack, B. "Baruks apokalypser," *GDBL* 1. Cols. 186f.

658a Picard, J.-C. *L'Apocalypse grecque de Baruch*. University of Strasbourg thesis, 1966.

659 Picard, J.-C., ed. *Apocalypsis Baruchi Graece* (PVTG 2) Leiden: Brill, 1967. Pp. 61-96.

660 Picard, J.-C. "Observations sur l'Apocalypse grecque de Baruch I: Cadre historique fictif et efficacité sym-bolique," *Sem* 20 (1970) 77-103.

661 Thanhill, R. "3 (Greek) Baruch," Clarendon edition.

662 Weise, M. "Baruchschriften," *BHH* 1. Cols. 202f.

663 Werbeck, W. "Baruchschriften, apokryphe," *RGG*^{3} 1. Cols. 900-03.

4 Baruch [and Jeremiah (Baruch) Cycle]
(Paraleipomena Jeremiou, *sometimes called the Rest of the*
Words of Baruch, 2 Baruch, 3 Baruch, Christian Baruch)

4 Baruch is extant in numerous languages; the Greek has
been re-edited recently by R.A. Kraft and A.-E. Purintun (no.
670). English translations are from the Armenian by J.
Issaverdens (*UWOT.* Pp. 190-204) and from the Greek by Kraft
and Purintun (no. 670). The original composition dates from
the first half of the second century A.D., perhaps after the
destruction of Jerusalem following the Simeon bar Kosiba
(Kochba) revolt (132-135; so J.R. Harris, *The Rest of the Words*
of Baruch [Haverford Coll. St. 2] Cambridge: CUP, 1889; pp. 7-
26; J. Licht, "The Book of the Sayings of Jeremiah from the
Hidden Books," Pinkhos Churgin Memorial Volume of the *Annual of*
Bar-Ilan University 1 [1963] 66-72 [in Hebrew]; P. Bogaert, no.
619; and M.E. Stone, no. 678). The author lived probably in or
near Jerusalem and wrote in a Semitic language (G. Delling, no.
665; J.D. Kilpatrick, "Acts vii. 52: *Eleusis*," *JTS* 46 [1945]
136-45; and Licht in the publication cited above). The heated
debate over the Jewish or Christian character of the pseudepigraphon has now resided; most scholars conclude it is a Jewish
composition reworked by a Jewish-Christian (Delling, no. 665;
O. Wintermute in *CBQ* 30 [1968] 442-45; Bogaert, no. 619; A.-M.
Denis, no. 24; Stone, no. 678). 4 Baruch is dependent upon 2
Baruch and may be influenced by 4 Ezra.

The Greek text contains nine chapters: the Lord tells
Jeremiah he is about to destroy Jerusalem (1); Jeremiah and
Baruch lament in the Temple (2); the holy vessels are buried
(3); angels open the gates of Jerusalem to the Chaldeans and
'Jeremiah and the people are taken to Babylon (4); Abimelech
sleeps 66 years and awakens to find his "figs dripping milk"
(5); Baruch prays, receives a response from an angel of the
Lord, and writes a letter to Jeremiah (6); the eagle carries
the letter to Jeremiah, who reads it to the people; Jeremiah
writes Baruch a letter which is carried by the eagle (7); "the
people" return from Babylon to Jerusalem, and "half" of them
(the Samaritans) are rejected (8); Jeremiah prays and is
eventually martyred (9).

Related to 4 Baruch and indicating the extent of the
Jeremiah (Baruch) cycle are three dissimilar Jeremiah

apocrypha. A later modification of 4 Baruch is found in "A
Jeremiah Apocryphon," that was edited and translated from two
Karshuni manuscripts by A. Mingana and discussed by J.R. Harris
(*Woodbrooke Studies*. Cambridge: Heffer, 1927. Vol. 1, pp. 125-
38, 148-233; see the facsimiles on pp. 192-233; cf. L. Leroy
and P. Dib, "Un apocryphe carchouni sur la captivité de Baby-
lone," *Revue de l'orient chrétien* 15 [1910] 255-74, 398-409;
16 [1911] 128-54). Second, also influenced by , but more independent of, 4 Baruch is the Coptic text recently edited and
translated by K.H. Kuhn (no. 671).

Third, W. Leslau draws attention to a work which he calls
5 Baruch or the Ethiopic Apocalypse of Baruch (*Falasha Anthology*, p. 58). This writing is extant only in Ethiopic, was
edited by J. Halévy (*Tĕ'ĕzâza Sanbat*. Paris: [Leroux], 1902),
and translated into English by Leslau (pp. 64-76). The pseudepigraphon appears to be a medieval reworking of 4 Baruch with
significant influence from the Hebrew Apocalypse of Elijah (2
Elijah), and the Apocalypse of the Virgin. The composition has
two divisions: the angel Sutu'ēl takes Baruch to the heavenly
Jerusalem from which he sees rewards and punishments (64:1-75:
8); the future is revealed with the times of the Messiah, the
false Messiah (Antichrist), and the resurrection of the righteous (75:9-76:31).

For additional information on the Jeremiah (Baruch) cycle,
see M.R. James' *LAOT* (pp. 62-64); L. Ginzberg's *Legends* (see
esp. vol. 4, pp. 294-326 and vol. 6, pp. 384-413); and the
works cited in A.-M. Denis' *Introduction* (no. 24, esp. pp.
74-76).

To be distinguished from these Jewish and Jewish-Christian
compositions is the so-called Book of Baruch written by the
gnostic Justin near the end of the second century A.D. It is
preserved only in quotations by Hippolytus (*Refutation of All
Heresies* 5.24-27; see the bibliography and English translation
in R.M. Grant's *Gnosticism* [New York: Harper, 1961; pp. 93-
100]). In this gnostic text Baruch is not the scribe of Jeremiah but one of the paternal angels and the tree of life [*sic*].

A.-E. Purintun is writing a Ph.D. dissertation on 4 Baruch
at the University of Pennsylvania, under Professor R.A. Kraft.

See also nos. 399, 636, 646, 1188.

664   Argyle, A.W. "4 Baruch (Paralipomena Jeremiou)," Clarendon edition.

665   Delling, G. *Jüdische Lehre und Frömmigkeit in den Paralipomena Jeremiae* (BZAW 100) Berlin: Töpelmann, 1967. [See the important reviews by O. Wintermute in *CBQ* 30 (1968) 442-45; and W. Baars in *VT* 17 (1967) 487f.]

666   Denis, A.-M. "Les Paralipomènes de Jérémie," *Introduction*. Pp. 70-78.

667   Gablenz, C. von. "Paralipomena Jeremiae," *BHH* 3. Col. 1387.

668   Goodenough, E.R. "Psychopomps," *Jewish Symbols* 8 (1958) 121-66. See esp. pp. 138-40.

669   Gutiérrez-Larraya, J.A. "Jeremías, Paralipómenos de," *Enciclopedia de la Biblia* 4. Col. 334.

670   Kraft, R.A. and A.-E. Purintun, eds. *Paraleipomena Jeremiou* (T&T 1, Pseudepigrapha Series 1) Missoula, Mont.: SBL, 1972.

671   Kuhn, K.H. "A Coptic Jeremiah Apocryphon," *Muséon* 83 (1970) 95-135, 291-350. [This text is not 4Bar but a related work from the Jeremiah tradition.]

672   Meyer, R. "Paralipomena Jeremiae," *RGG*[3] 5. Cols. 102f.

673   Moutzoures, I. "Paraleipomena Jeremiou," *ThEE* 6. Col. 779. [in Greek]

674   Nickelsburg, G.W.E. Jr. "Narrative Traditions in the Paralipomena of Jeremiah and 2 Baruch," *CBQ* 35 (1973) 60-68.

675   Noack, B. "Baruks apokalypser," *GDBL* 1. Cols. 186f.

675a   Purintun, A.-E. "4 Baruch," Doubleday edition.

676   Purintun, A.-E. and R.A. Kraft. "Paraleipomena Jeremiou: English Translation Made From the Editors' Own Greek Text," *SBL 1971 Seminar Papers*. Vol. 2, pp. 327-46.

677   Schaller, B. "Paralipomena Jeremiae," *JSHRZ* 1, in press.

678   Stone, M.E. "Baruch, Rest of the Words of," *EncyJud* 4. Cols. 276f.

679   Stone, M.E. "Some Observations on the Armenian Version of the Paralipomena of Jeremiah," *CBQ* 35 (1973) 47-59.

680   Stone, M.E., with E. Shefer. *The Books of the Life of Adam and Eve and IV Baruch*. Jerusalem: Akademon, 1970. [in Hebrew]

681   Turdeanu, E. "L'Apocalypse de Baruch en slave," *RESl* 48 (1969) 23-48.

682   Weise, M. "Baruchschriften," *BHH* 1. Cols. 202f.

683   Werbeck, W. "Baruchschriften, apokryphe," *RGG*[3] 1. Cols.
      900-03.

Cave of Treasures

The Syriac and Arabic texts were edited, with critical
notes to the Ethiopic, by C. Bezold (*Die Schatzhöhle*. 2 vols.
Leipzig: Hinrichs, 1883-1888), and the Syriac text of B.M. Add.
25875 was translated into English by E.A. Wallis Budge (*The
Book of the Cave of Treasures*. London: Religious Tract Society,
1927). Two Arabic manuscripts of a different recension of the
Cave of Treasures, one on Mt. Sinai and the other in Cambridge,
were brought to the attention of scholars by M.D. Gibson. She
edited and translated the former and appended a description of
the latter (*Apocrypha Arabica* [Studia Sinaitica 8] London:
CUP, 1901).

The present form of the work dates from the sixth century
A.D. (Budge, pp. xi, 21f.), but the original is from about the
fourth century, and was written somewhere near Edessa in Syriac
because of the exalted concept of that language (see Budge, pp.
22f., 132, 230; Gibson, p. 34).

For specialists on the Pseudepigrapha the main question is
not how later sources, like the Book of the Bee, were dependent
on the Cave of Treasures (see E.A. Wallis Budge, *The Book of
the Bee*. Oxford: Clarendon, 1886), but how it used and preserved earlier Jewish and Jewish-Christian writings, e.g.
Jubilees and Life of Adam and Eve.

Worthy of special note is a text often appended to the
Cave of Treasures (contrast Gibson's text), the Testament of
Adam, which was edited from the Syriac by M. Kmosko ("Testamentum Patris Nostri Adam," *Patrologia Syriaca*, ed. R. Graffin.
Paris: Firmin-Didot, 1907. Vol. 2, pp. 1306-60), and from a
different recension in Arabic by Gibson (pp. 12-17 [in Arabic
numbering]). An English translation is found in Budge's *The
Book of the Cave of Treasures* (cf. the different recension
translated by Gibson, pp. 13-17). This pseudepigraphon evi-
dences many features that suggest a date of composition in the
late second century A.D. The rewriting of tradition in the
second half in which Cain slays his brother because of jealousy

over Lud, their sister (cf. Budge, *Cave of Treasures*, p. 70;
Gibson, p. 17) may reflect early Syrian asceticism, perhaps
that of the Encratites. Even earlier is the first half, because of the conspicuous absence of Christian elements and the
general early Jewish tone (cf. the ending with 4Q Morgen- und
Abendgebete). Significantly, the Greek portions preserve only
this first section (see the editions mentioned by A.-M. Denis,
no. 24, p. 11, n. 37).

   The Testament of Adam is a good candidate for inclusion
within the Pseudepigrapha because of its date and apparent Jewish character. The Cave of Treasures should not be so included, because it is beyond the chronological limits and is per-
meated with relatively late Christian ideas (e.g., "Eden is
the Holy Church;" Budge, *Cave of Treasures*, p. 62; Gibson, p.
8).

   The purpose of the Cave of Treasures is to relate the
"succession of families from Adam to Christ." After the expulsion from Eden, Adam and Eve dwell in a cave on the top of one
of the mountains near Paradise, which has been shut. The cave
is called "Cave of Treasures" because Adam places therein gold,
myrrh, and frankincense "from the skirts of the mountain of
Paradise."

   Copies of Vatican Arabic MS 165 and B.M. Syr. MS O.M.P.
5394, Add. 25875, are preserved in the Pseudepigrapha Library
at Duke University.

   See the publications listed above under "Adam," Old Testament Names Used Pseudonymously, and Life of Adam and Eve. See
also nos. 448, 1188.

684   Ebied, R.Y. "Some Syriac Manuscripts from the Collection
      of Sir E.A. Wallis Budge," *Orient. Christ. Analecta* 197
      (1974) 509-39. See esp. pp. 524f.

685   Knippenberg, R. "Schatzhöhle," *BHH* 3. Pp. 168f.

Cleodemus Malchus

   Cleodemus Malchus wrote a history of the Jews which is
extant only in citations by Eusebius (*Pr. ev.* 9.20) and Josephus (*Ant.* 1.15). Eusebius cites Josephus, who credits Alexander Polyhistor with the tradition. For an edition and translation of Eusebius' work see above under Aristobulus. For

Josephus, see the Loeb Classical Library edition by H.St.J.
Thackeray (Josephus. *Jewish Antiquities, Books I-IV*. New York:
Putnam; London: Heinemann, 1930; p. 119. The Greek of Josephus
is also found in A.-M. Denis' *Fragmenta pseudepigraphorum quae
supersunt graeca* [no. 23, pp. 196f.].).

Cleodemus Malchus probably lived sometime in the second
century B.C. The odd mixture of Jewish and Greek ideas and
loyalties leads some authorities either to affirm that he was
a Samaritan (J. Freudenthal, *Alexander Polyhistor*. Breslau:
Skutsch, 1875; p. 133) or to deny that he was a Jew (B.Z.
Wacholder, no. 688; cf. no. 819). However, the extreme varie-
ties we are now perceiving within Judaism, especially in the
second century B.C., should preclude us from denying that he
was a Jew.

In the preserved fragment we find the idea that Abraham's
sons Apheras and Japhras gave their names to the city Aphras
and the continent Africa, while another son, Sures, gave his
name to Assyria. The first two join Heracles in a battle
against Libya and Antaeus.

See Fragments of Historical Works. See also no. 819.

685a Denis, A.-M. "Cléodème-Malchâs," *Introduction*. Pp. 259-61.

686 Müller-Bardorff, J. "Kleodemos," *BHH* 2. Col. 969.

687 Wacholder, B.Z. "Cleodemus Malchus," Doubleday edition.

688 Wacholder, B.Z. "Cleodemus Malchus," *EncyJud* 5. Col. 603.

Demetrius

Demetrius' chronological history of the Jews is extant in
six fragmentary citations: five by Eusebius (*Pr. ev.* 9.19, 4;
9.21, 1-19; 9.29, 1-3; 9.29, 15; 9.29, 16. Only the second,
third, and fourth are clearly attributed to Demetrius; the
others are now considered probable [cf. A.-M. Denis, no. 689a,
and N. Walter, no. 692, pp. 280-92].), and the sixth by Clement
of Alexandria (*Strom.* 1.21, 141, 1-2). The Greek fragments are
conveniently assembled in Denis' *Fragmenta pseudepigraphorum
quae supersunt graeca* (no. 23, pp. 175-79). English translations of Eusebius' and Clement of Alexandria's works just
mentioned are reported above under Aristobulus.

It is evident from fragment six, which extends the chronological history up to Ptolemy IV Philopator (221-204 B.C.; *heōs Ptolemaiou tetartou*), that this hellenistic-Jewish exegete wrote his history in Alexandria in the last two decades of the third century B.C. B.Z. Wacholder suggests correctly that Demetrius represents an exegetical and chronographical school (no. 819, p. 99).

Fragment one, of one line, contains a short account of Abraham's offering of Isaac. Fragment two, of nineteen lines, is a redundant retelling of Jacob's life with interwoven chronological notes. Fragment three, of three lines, contains a summary of Demetrius in which it is argued that Moses' father-in-law, *Iothōr*, is a descendant of Abraham. Fragment four, of one line, is a short account of the bitter water Moses found at Marah (Ex 15:22-25). Fragment five, of one line, explains that the Israelites' weapons used after the Exodus were obtained from the drowning Egyptians. Fragment six, of two lines, explains that the tribes of Judah, Benjamin, and Levi may not have been taken into exile by Sennacherib, and concludes with a chronological summary up to Ptolemy IV. Throughout these fragments we find dependence upon the Septuagint (see esp. Wacholder, no. 321, and no. 819, pp. 99-104) and an apologetical exegesis that moves from difficulties to explanations (*aporiai kai luseis*). [Walter's numbering of fragments has been followed; see no. 692.]

See Fragments of Historical Works.

689   Bickerman, E.J. "The Jewish Historian Demetrios," M. Smith Festschrift. Part 3, pp. 72-84.

689a Denis, A.-M. "Démétrius," *Introduction*. Pp. 248-51.

690   Wacholder, B.Z. "Demetrius," Doubleday edition.

691   Wacholder, B.Z. "Demetrius," *EncyJud* 5. Cols. 1490f.

692   Walter, N. "Fragmente jüdisch-hellenistischer Exegeten: Aristobulos, Demetrios, Aristeas," *JSHRZ* 3 (1975) 257-96. See esp. pp. 280-92.

Eldad and Modad

The pseudepigraphon Eldad and Modad (LXX; Medad in MT) is lost except for one explicit quotation in the Shepherd of

Hermas (*Vis.* 2.3, 4). The Greek is republished by A.-M. Denis
(no. 23, p. 68), and the Greek and English are conveniently
juxtaposed by K. Lake (*The Apostolic Fathers* [LCL] Cambridge,
Mass.: Harvard University; London: Heinemann, 1913 [repr.
1965]. Vol. 2, pp. 22f.).

According to Numbers 11:24-30, Eldad and Modad (Medad) are
two of the seventy elders who received the spirit and prophesied while the Israelites were wandering in the wilderness under the leadership of Moses. The Stichometry of Nicephorus
indicates that the book contained 400 lines, but only the
following is extant:

> "The Lord is near those that turn to him," as it
> is written in the book of Eldad and Modat, who proph-
> esied to the people in the wilderness. [ET by Lake]

693 Aberbach, M. "Eldad and Medad," *EncyJud* 6. Cols. 575f.

694 Chrēstou, P.K. "Eldad and Modad," *ThEE* 5. Cols. 551f.
     [in Greek]

695 Denis, A.-M. "Les fragments du Livre d'Eldad et Modad,"
     Introduction. Pp. 142-45.

696 Wallis, G. "Eldad und Medad," *BHH* 1. Col. 390.

697 White, W. Jr. "Eldad and Medad, Book of," *ZPEB* 2. P. 266.

Apocalypse of Elijah [and Elijah Cycle]

Two works bear this name and should be distinguished as
1 Elijah and 2 Elijah. The first is extant in Coptic fragments
which were edited by G. Steindorff (*Die Apokalypse des Elias*
[TU 17] Leipzig: Hinrichs, 1899) and translated into English by
H.P. Houghton ("The Coptic Apocalypse. Part III, Akhmîmice:
'The Apocalypse of Elias,'" *Aegyptus* 39 [1959] 179-210). There
are also a few minor excerpts and fragments in Greek which are
reprinted by A.-M. Denis (no. 23, pp. 103f.).

In its present form the pseudepigraphon is Christian and
dates from the third century. Most scholars concur that it
derives from an earlier Jewish work, and J.-M. Rosenstiehl
(no. 706, pp. 9, 75f.) concludes that the *Grundschrift* was composed in Egypt during the first century B.C.

The work consists of three large chapters: a parenetic
section (1:1-26); an apocalyptic timetable (2:1-44); and

legends about the Antichrist (3:1-99).

The second, 2 Elijah, is extant in rabbinic Hebrew; this was edited and translated into German by M. Buttenwieser (*Die hebräische Elias-Apokalypse*. Leipzig: Pfeiffer, 1897). As far as I know an English translation has not yet been published. Scholars have generally rejected Buttenwieser's claim that this work is as early as A.D. 260, although there are earlier Jewish traditions preserved in it.

2 Elijah purports to be a revelation by Michael to Elijah on Mt. Carmel. Elijah receives a description of Antichrist, perceives how punishment is suffered according to the sin, and sees a revelation concerning the end.

Regarding the common origin of these two apocalypses, little advance has been achieved beyond the position of M.R. James: "But neither of the extant Apocalypses can be supposed to represent the old book faithfully. The Coptic has been Christianized, the Hebrew abridged, and additions made to both." (*LAOT*, p. 61). Such an early Jewish apocryphon existed, since it is mentioned as the source of 1 Corinthians 2:9 by Origen (*Comm. Mt.* 27.9); and is listed in the Apostolic Constitutions, the List of Sixty Books, the Synopsis of Pseudo-Athanasius, the Stichometry of Nicephorus, and the Armenian list by Mechithar. Clement of Rome and Clement of Alexandria may have quoted from the early Jewish composition (see the Greek texts reprinted in Denis, no. 23, p. 103).

A Latin apocryphal text entitled *Epistula Titi Discipuli Pauli* contains a vision of punishments in Gehenna which is attributed to the prophet Elijah. This quotation was edited by D. de Bruyne ("Nouveaux fragments des Actes de Pierre, de Paul, de Jean, d'André, et de l'Apocalypse d'Elie," *RBen* 25 [1908] 149-60), and translated into English by M.R. James (*LAOT*, p. 55). De Bruyne (pp. 153-55), James (p. 54), and F. Maass (no. 702) contend that the excerpt comes from the original Apocalypse of Elijah. It is wise to be hesitant in identifying this quotation with the Apocalypse of Elijah since it is not found in the Coptic or Hebrew texts, and because there were other compositions pseudonymously attributed to Elijah, although some are now lost.

Some of these still extant, at least partially, are a
Sahidic fragment in the British Museum (Or. 3581B[6]), which
preserves a story on the assumption of Elijah (see W.E. Crum,
Catalogue of the Coptic Manuscripts in the British Museum. London: British Museum, 1905; p. 128, no. 291); a late medieval
Armenian text entitled "A Short History of the Prophet Elias"
(see J. Issaverdens, *UWOT*, pp. 149-61); and a Falasha composition named "Abba Elijah" (see Leslau's *Falasha Anthology*, pp.
40-49). Also note the numerous rabbinic legends about Elijah
that are mentioned by L. Ginzberg (*Legends*, vol. 4, pp. 195-
235; vol. 6, pp. 316-42).

Concerning the Prophecy of Elijah, which Eupolemus apparently cites according to Eusebius, see below under Eupolemus.
Also see the comments below under the Apocalypse of Zephaniah.

G. MacRae, M.E. Stone, E. Isaac and J. Strugnell have been
working on texts related to the Apocalypse of Elijah and Elijah
material generally which will be published in T&T. A. Pietersma
and S. Turner are editing the fourth-century Chester Beatty
manuscript of the Apocalypse of Elijah, which is in Sahidic.

698   Cots, C. "Elías, Apocalipsis de," *Enciclopedia de la
        Biblia* 2. Cols. 1213f.

699   Denis, A.-M. "Les fragments grecs de l'Apocalypse d'Elie,"
        Introduction. Pp. 163-69.

700   Kuhn, K.H. "Elia-Apokalypse," *BHH* 1. Col. 398.

701   Lacau, P. "Remarques sur le manuscrit akhmimique des
        Apocalypses de Sophonie et d'Elie," *JA* 254 (1966) 169-
        95.

702   Maass, F. "Eliasapokalypse," *RGG*[3] 2. Col. 427.

703   Oikonomidēs, D.B. "Elijah (Apocalypse of)," *ThEE* 6. Cols.
        22-24. [in Greek]

704   Pietersma, A. "Greek and Coptic Inedita of the Chester
        Beatty Library," *BIOSCS* 7 (1974) 10-18. See esp. pp. 17f.

705   Rist, M. "Elijah, Apocalypse of," *IDB* 2. P. 88.

706   Rosenstiehl, J.-M. *L'Apocalypse d'Elie* (Textes et études
        pour servir à l'histoire du judaïsme intertestamentaire
        1) Paris: Geuthner, 1972.

707   Rosenstiehl, J.-M. "Un sobriquet essénien dans l'Apoca-
        lypse copte d'Elie," *Sem* 15 (1965) 97-99.

708   Schneemelcher, W. "Apocalypse of Elijah," trans. E. Best.
        HSW. Vol. 2, p. 752.

709 Schrage, W. "Apokalypse Elias," *JSHRZ* 5, in press.

710 Stone, M.E. "Elijah, Apocalypse of," *EncyJud* 6. Col. 643.
     [Stone contributed this material, although it is attri-
     buted to the editor, C. Roth.]

711 White, W. Jr. "Elijah, Apocalypse of," *ZPEB* 2. Pp. 287f.

712 Wintermute, O.S. "Apocalypse of Elijah," Doubleday edition.

1 (Ethiopic) Enoch [and Enoch Cycle]

One of the most important pseudepigrapha is entirely extant only in Ethiopic manuscripts. These were edited and
translated into English by R.H. Charles (*The Ethiopic Version
of the Book of Enoch* [Anecdota Oxoniensia, Sem. Ser. 11] Oxford: Clarendon, 1906; *APOT* 2. Pp. 163-281; *The Book of Enoch
or 1 Enoch*, 2d. ed. Oxford: Clarendon, 1912; translation repr.
in TED with intro. by W.O.E. Oesterley. *The Book of Enoch*. London: S.P.C.K., 1917 [repr. 1972]). The extensive Greek portions are re-edited by M. Black (no. 717), and a Syriac fragment has been published by S.P. Brock (no. 722).

This pseudepigraphon has evoked divergent opinions; but
today there is a consensus that the book is a composite, portions of which are clearly pre-Christian as demonstrated by
the discovery of Aramaic and Hebrew fragments from four of the
five sections of the book among the Dead Sea Scrolls. One of
these fragments, moreover, Hen[a], was copied in the second half
of the second century B.C. The main question concerns the
date of the second section, chapters 37-71, which contains the
Son of Man sayings. J.T. Milik (esp. no. 755) has shown that
this section, which is not represented among the early fragments, is probably a later addition to 1 Enoch; but his contention that it was composed around A.D. 270 (no. 755), p. 377)
is very speculative. If, as most specialists concur, the early
portions of 1 Enoch date from the first half of the second century B.C., chapters 37-71 could have been added in the first
century B.C. or first century A.D. The original language of
1 Enoch appears to be Aramaic, except for the Noah traditions,
which were probably composed in Hebrew. The earliest portions
display impressive parallels with the nascent thoughts of the
Jewish sect which eventually settled at Qumran.

1 Enoch, i.e. Ethiopic Enoch, contains five sections:

Enoch's journey (1-36); the Similitudes (37-71); an astronomical section (72-82); dream visions (83-90); and admonitions of Enoch (91-105). Chapters 106-108 are an addendum taken from a book of Noah (cf. Jub 10:13, 21:10).

The existence of an Enoch cycle is obvious from the composite nature of 1 Enoch itself, and by the existence of 2 and 3 Enoch. Other Enoch traditions are preserved in the Coptic papyri edited by W.E. Crum (*Theological Texts from Coptic Papyri* [Anecdota Oxoniensia, Sem. Ser. 12] Oxford: Clarendon, 1913. Pp. 3-11); the three Coptic fragments which mention Enoch that were edited by H. Munier ("Mélanges de littérature copte, 3, Livre d'Enoch (?)," *Annales du service des antiquités de l'Egypte* 23 [1923] 212-15); the Book of the Giants (see Milik, nos. 755, pp. 366-72; 756); the Armenian text entitled the Vision of Enoch the Just (trans. by J. Issaverdens, *UWOT*, pp. 209-18); the borrowed portions of the Falasha composition called the Commandments of the Sabbath (see W. Leslau's *Falasha Anthology*, pp. 3-39); and *Peri tēs prophēteias Enōch* preserved in *Chronicon Paschale* 21 (ed. L. Dindorf in PG 92). Consult A.-M. Denis' *Introduction* (no. 24, pp. 15-30) and L. Ginzberg's *Legends* (vol. 1, pp. 124-40; vol. 5, pp. 153-64).

E. Ullendorff and M. Knibb have prepared for Clarendon a new Ethiopic edition, in the light of the Aramaic material. G.W.E. Nickelsburg, Jr., is preparing a commentary for *Hermeneia*. R.T. Lutz is completing a dissertation on "Biblical Forms and Traditions in 1 Enoch 12-36," and D. Suter has almost completed one on the myth of the fallen angels in 1 Enoch. J. T. Milik and M. Black have been working on a monograph to be entitled, perhaps, *The Books of Enoch: Aramaic Fragments of Qumrân Cave 4*. E. Turdeanu is preparing a book on "Les apocryphes du cycle d'Hénoch."

Consult the publications listed under the Pseudepigrapha and the Dead Sea Scrolls, 2 Enoch, and 3 Enoch, and those listed under "Enoch" and "Noah," Old Testament Names Used Pseudonymously. See also the numerous discussions on the Son of Man listed above under Messianism. See also nos. 10, 87, 108, 115, 176, 184, 234, 309, 320, 330, 403, 407-09, 465, 471, 477-79, 1295, 1480.

713   Aalen, S. "St. Luke's Gospel and the Last Chapters of
      I Enoch," *NTS* 13 (1967) 1-13.

714   Agourides, S. "Enoch," *ThEE* 5. Cols. 706-08. [in Greek]

715   Agourides, S. "The Son of Man in Enoch," *Deltion Biblikon
      Meleton* 2 (1973) 130-47.

716   Andersen, H.G. "Enoch, Books of," *ZPEB* 2. Pp. 309-12.

717   Black, M., ed. *Apocalypsis Henochi Graece* (PVTG 3) Leiden:
      Brill, 1970. Pp. 5-44.

718   Black, M. "The Fragments of the Aramaic Enoch from Qum-
      ran," *La littérature juive entre Tenach et Mishna*, ed.
      W.C. van Unnik (RechBib 9) Leiden: Brill, 1974. Pp. 15-
      28. [*N.V.*]

719   Black, M. "The Maranatha Invocation and Jude 14, 15
      (1 Enoch 1:9)," *Christ and Spirit in the New Testament*.
      C.F.D. Moule Festschrift, eds. B. Lindars and S.S.
      Smalley. Cambridge: CUP, 1973. Pp. 189-96.

720   Bonner, C. with H.C. Youtie, eds. *The Last Chapters of
      Enoch in Greek*. London: Christopher, 1937; repr. Darm-
      stadt: Wissenschaftliche Buchgesellschaft, 1968.

721   Borger, R. "Die Beschwörungsserie *bīt mēseri* und die Him-
      melfahrt Henochs," [*From Assurbanipal's Library: Stud-
      ies in Memory of F.W. Geers*, Part 1] *JNES* 33 (1974)
      183-96.

721a Borsch, F.H. "Mark XIV.62 and 1 Enoch LXII.5," *NTS* 14
      (1968) 565-67.

722   Brock, S.P. "A Fragment of Enoch in Syriac," *JTS* n.s. 19
      (1968) 626-31.

723   Caquot, A. and P. Geoltrain. "Notes sur le texte éthiopien
      des 'Paraboles' d'Hénoch," *Sem* 13 (1963) 39-54.

724   Coughenour, R.A. *Enoch and Wisdom: A Study of the Wisdom
      Elements in the Book of Enoch*. Case Western Reserve
      University Ph.D., 1972.

725   Denis, A.-M. "Le Livre grec d'Hénoch (éthiopien)," *Intro-
      duction*. Pp. 15-30.

726   Donadoni, S. "Un frammento della versione copta del 'Libro
      di Enoch,'" *AcOr* 25 (1960) 197-202.

727   Ettisch, E.E. "Das Buch Henoch und die vier Kardinalpunkte
      des Sonnenlaufes," *VT* 11 (1961) 444f.

728   Evans, J.M. "Microcosmic Adam," *Medium Aevum* 31 (1966)
      38-42.

729   Geoltrain, P. *Le Livre éthiopien d'Hénoch: ses rapports
      avec les manuscrits de Qumrân et le Nouveau Testament*.
      Strasbourg Ph.D., 1960.

730 Gil, M. "Enoch in the Land of the Living," *Tarbiz* 38 (1969) 322-37. [in Hebrew]

731 Glatzer, N.N. "The Hope for a New Age," *Judaic Tradition*. Pp. 62-66.

732 Goodenough, E.R. "Astronomical Symbols," *Jewish Symbols* 8 (1958) 167-218. See esp. pp. 199, 203f.

733 Goodenough, E.R. "The Bull," *Jewish Symbols* 7 (1958) 3-28. See esp. pp. 24f.

734 Goodenough, E.R. "Miscellaneous Fertility Symbols," *Jewish Symbols* 8 (1958) 71-118. See esp. p. 112.

735 Goodenough, E.R. "Moses Leads the Migration from Egypt," *Jewish Symbols* 10 (1964) 105-39. See esp. p. 136.

736 Goodenough, E.R. "The North Wall," *Jewish Symbols* 10 (1964) 166-96. See esp. p. 174.

737 Goodenough, E.R. "The Reredos," *Jewish Symbols* 9 (1964) 78-123. See esp. p. 89.

738 Goodenough, E.R. "The Symbolic Value of the Fish in Judaism," *Jewish Symbols* 5 (1956) 31-61. See esp. pp. 35f.

739 Goodenough, E.R. "Symbolism of Dress," *Jewish Symbols* 9 (1964) 124-74. See esp. p. 169.

740 Goodenough, E.R. "The Tree," *Jewish Symbols* 7 (1958) 87-134. See esp. pp. 126-29.

741 Goodenough, E.R. "Two Fragmentary Scenes," *Jewish Symbols* 10 (1964) 98-104. See esp. p. 101.

742 Goodenough, E.R. "Wine in Jewish Cult and Observance," *Jewish Symbols* 6 (1956) 126-217. See esp. p. 195.

743 Grintz, Y.M. "Enoch, Ethiopic Book of," *EncyJud* 6. Cols. 795-97.

744 Hammershaimb, E. "Første Enoksbog," *GamPseud* 2 (1956) 69-174.

745 Hindley, J.C. "Towards a Date for the Similitudes of Enoch: An Historical Approach," *NTS* 14 (1968) 551-65. [See J. Jeremias, *New Testament Theology*. New York: Scribner, 1971; p. 269, n. 5.]

746 Isaac, E. "1 (Ethiopic) Enoch," Doubleday edition.

747 Kam, J. vander. "The Theophany of Enoch I 3b-7, 9," *VT* 23 (1973) 129-50.

748 Kaske, R.E. "*Beowulf* and the Book of Enoch," *Speculum* 46 (1971) 421-31.

749 Knibb, M.A. "1 (Ethiopic) Enoch," Clarendon edition.

750   Kutsch, E. "Die Solstitien im Kalender des Jubiläenbuches und in äth. Henoch 72," *VT* 12 (1962) 205-07.

751   Limbeck, M. "Der Lobpreis Gottes als Sinn des Daseins," *TQ* 150 (1970) 349-57.

752   Lührmann, D. "Henoch und die Metanoia," *ZNW* 66 (1975) 103-16.

753   Milik, J.T. "Hénoch au pays des aromates (ch. xxvii à xxxii): Fragments araméens de la grotte 4 de Qumran," *RB* 65 (1958) 70-77. [4QHen^{c,e}]

754   Milik, J.T. "Livre de Noé (Pl. XVI)," *DJD* 1. Pp. 84-86. [1QNoah is related to 1En 8:4-9:4, 106:9f.]

755   Milik, J.T. "Problèmes de la littérature hénochique à la lumière des fragments araméens de Qumrân," *HTR* 64 (1971) 333-78. [4QHenAstr^{a-e}, 4QCryptic. See Allegro above, no. 129.]

756   Milik, J.T. "Turfan et Qumran: Livre des Géants juif et manichéen," Kuhn Festschrift. Pp. 117-27. [1QHenGiants, 4QHenGiants^{a-f}]

757   Müller, K. "Beobachtungen zur Entwicklung der Menschen-sohnvorstellung in den Bilderreden des Henoch und im Buche Daniel," *Wegzeichen*. H.M. Biedermann Festgabe, eds. E.C. Suttner and C. Patock. Würzburg: Augustinus, 1971. Pp. 253-62.

758   Müller, M. *Messias og "menneskesøn" i Daniels Bog, Første Enoksbog og Fjerde Ezrabog* (Tekst & Tolkning 3) Copenhagen: Gads, 1972.

758a Nibley, H. "A Strange Thing in the Land: The Return of the Book of Enoch, Part I," *Ensign* 5 (1975) 78-84.

759   Nikitina, V.B., E.V. Paevskaiâ, L.D. Pozdneeva, and D.G. Reder. *Literature of the Ancient East*. Moscow, 1962. [in Russian]

760   Noack, B. "Enoksbøgerne," *GDBL* 1. Cols. 441f.

761   Philonenko, M. "Une allusion de l'*Asclepius* au livre d'*Hénoch*," M. Smith Festschrift. Part 2, pp. 161-63.

762   Philonenko, M. "Une citation manichéenne du livre d'Hénoch," *RHPR* 52 (1972) 337-40.

763   Plöger, O. "Henochbücher," *RGG*^{3} 3. Cols. 222-25.

764   Rau, [?]. "Äthiopisches Henochbuch," *JSHRZ* 5, in press.

765   Reese, G. *Die Geschichte Israels in der Auffassung des frühen Judentums: Eine Untersuchung der Tiervision und der Zehnwochenapokalypse des äthiopischen Henochbuches, der Geschichtdarstellung der Assumptio Mosis und des 4. Esrabuches*. Heidelberg Ph.D., 1967.

766 Reicke, B. "Henochbücher," *BHH* 2. Pp. 692f.

767 Romano, D. "Enok, Libro etíope de," *Enciclopedia de la Biblia* 3. Cols. 36f.

768 Rowston, D.J. "The Most Neglected Book in the New Testament," *NTS* 21 (1975) 554-63. [A discussion of the use of lEn and AsMos by Jude, a "Jewish-Christian apocalyptic" book.]

769 Schmitt, A. "Die Angaben über Henoch Gen 5, 21-24 in der LXX," *Wort, Lied und Gottespruch: Beiträge zur Septuaginta*. J. Ziegler Festschrift, ed. J. Schreiner (Forschung zur Bibel 1) Würzburg: Echter, 1972. Pp. 161-69.

769a Theisohn, J. *Der auserwählte Richter: Untersuchungen zum traditionsgeschichtlichen Ort der Menschensohngestalt der Bilderreden des Äthiopischen Henoch* (Studien zur Umwelt des Neuen Testaments 12) Göttingen: Vandenhoeck & Ruprecht, 1975.

770 Theocharēs, A. "The Concept of Wisdom in the Ethiopic Book of Enoch," *Deltion Biblikon Meleton* 1 (1972) 287-311.

771 Thorndike, J.P. "The Apocalypse of Weeks and the Qumran Sect," *RQ* 3 (1961) 163-84.

772 Trever, J.C. "Completion of the Publication of Some Fragments from Qumran Cave I," *RQ* 5 (1965) 323-44, pls. IV, VII. [lQNoah 2]

773 Ullendorff, E. "An Aramaic 'Vorlage' of the Ethiopic Text of Enoch?" *Atti del Convegno Internazionale di Studi Etiopici*. Rome: Accademia Nazionale dei Lincei, 1960. Pp. 259-67.

774 Vida, G.L. della. "Discussione sulla Relazione del prof. E. Ullendorff," *Atti del Convegno Internazionale di Studi Etiopici*. Rome: Accademia Nazionale dei Lincei, 1960. P. 268.

775 Widengren, G. "Iran and Israel in Parthian Times with Special Regard to the Ethiopic Book of Enoch," *Temenos* 2 (1966) 139-77.

2 (Slavonic) Enoch
(Book of the Secrets of Enoch)

2 Enoch is extant in Slavonic manuscripts, which were edited by A. Vaillant (*Le Livre des Secrets d'Hénoch: texte slave et traduction française*. Paris: Institut d'études slaves, 1952), and translated into English from an earlier edition by W.R. Morfill (*The Book of the Secrets of Enoch*. Oxford: [Clarendon], 1896) and N. Forbes (*APOT* 2. Pp. 431-69).

Specialists date the original, which was probably in
Greek, in the decades prior to the destruction of the Temple
in A.D. 70. While most scholars have followed R.H. Charles'
suggestion that the provenance is Egyptian (*APOT* 2, p. 429),
there is some evidence that the short recension is Palestinian
(N. Schmidt, "The Two Recensions of Slavonic Enoch," *JAOS* 41
[1921] 307-12).

The pseudepigraphon is preserved in a long and a short
recension, both of which, especially the former, have been reworked by later scribes. As with 1 Enoch there appear to be
five divisions: Enoch informs his sons about his imminent
ascension (1-2); he ascends through seven (expanded to ten by
a later editor) heavens (3-21); Enoch meets the Lord and records His revelations (22-38); he returns to the earth in order
to instruct and admonish his sons (39-66); Enoch is taken by
angels to the highest heaven (67; the long recension adds how
the people praised God for the sign delivered through Enoch,
68).

F.I. Andersen is collating the Slavonic manuscripts for
a new edition.

See the publications listed above under "Enoch," Old Testament Names Used Pseudonymously, 1 Enoch, and 3 Enoch. See
also nos. 70, 75, 87, 108, 171, 175, 184, 303, 309, 368.

776 Agourides, S. "Enoch," *ThĒE* 5. Cols. 706-08. [in Greek]

777 Andersen, F. "2 (Slavonic) Enoch," Doubleday edition.

778 Andersen, H.G. "Enoch, Books of," *ZPEB* 2. Pp. 309-12.

779 Goodenough, E.R. "Astronomical Symbols," *Jewish Symbols* 8
    (1958) 167-218. See esp. pp. 204-07.

780 Goodenough, E.R. "Birds," *Jewish Symbols* 8 (1958) 22-70.
    See esp. p. 69.

781 Goodenough, E.R. "Miscellaneous Fertility Symbols," *Jewish
    Symbols* 8 (1958) 71-118. See esp. p. 84.

782 Goodenough, E.R. "Symbolism of Dress," *Jewish Symbols* 9
    (1964) 124-74. See esp. p. 169.

783 Goodenough, E.R. "The Tree," *Jewish Symbols* 7 (1958) 87-
    134. See esp. pp. 126f.

784 Goodenough, E.R. "Wine in Jewish Cult and Observance,"
    Jewish Symbols 6 (1956) 126-217. See esp. p. 195.

785 Lilienfeld, F. von. "Slawisches Henochbuch," *JSHRZ* 5, in press.

786 Meščerskij, N.A. "Concerning the History of the Text of the Book of Slavonic Enoch," *Bizantijskij Bremennik* 24 (1964) 91-108. [in Russian]

787 Meščerskij, N.A. "Concerning the Problem of the Sources of the Book of Slavonic Enoch," *Short Reports of the Institute of the Peoples of Asia* 86 (1965) 72-78. [in Russian]

788 Meščerskij, N.A. "Qumran Manuscripts and the Problem of Sources in Old Slavic and Old Russian Apocryphal Literature, With Special Reference to Slavonic Enoch," *Trudy otdela Drevnerusskoj Literatury* 19 (1963) 130-43. [in Russian; *N.V.*]

789 Nikitina, V.B., E.V. Paevskaiâ, L.D. Pozdneeva, and D.G. Reder. *Literature of the Ancient East*. Moscow, 1962. [in Russian]

790 Noack, B. "Enoksbøgerne," *GDBL* 1. Cols. 441f.

791 Pennington, A. "2 (Slavonic) Enoch," Clarendon edition.

792 Philonenko, M. "La cosmogonie du 'Livre des Secrets d'Hénoch,'" *Religions en Egypte hellénistique et romaine: Colloque de Strasbourg, 16-18 mai 1967*. Paris: Presses universitaires de France, 1969. Pp. 109-16.

793 Pines, S. "Enoch, Slavonic Book of," *EncyJud* 6. Cols. 797-99.

794 Pines, S. "Eschatology and the Concept of Time in the Slavonic Book of Enoch," *Types of Redemption: Contributions to the Theme of the Study-Conference Held at Jerusalem, 14th to 19th July 1968*, eds. R.J.Z. Werblowsky and C.J. Bleeker (Sup *Numen* 18) Leiden: Brill, 1970. Pp. 72-87.

795 Plöger, O. "Henochbücher," *RGG*[3] 3. Cols. 222-25.

796 Potter, C.F. *Did Jesus Write This Book?* New York: University Books, 1965. [The author wishes his readers to believe that Jesus wrote 2En: "it may well be that he wrote it, or part of it." (p. 27) Of interest for scholars is the list of parallels between 2En and the NT, pp. 80-91.]

797 Reicke, B. "Henochbücher," *BHH* 2. Pp. 692f.

798 Repp, F. "Textkritische Untersuchungen zum Henoch-Apokryph des cod. slav. 125 der Österreichischen Nationalbibliothek," *Wiener Slavistisches Jahrbuch* 10 (1963) 58-68.

799 Rist, M. "Enoch, Book of," *IDB* 2. Pp. 103-05.

800 Romano, D. "Enok, Libro eslavo de," *Enciclopedia de la Biblia* 3. Col. 36.

801   Tikhomirov, M.N. *"A Pious Rule" According to a Fourteenth-Century Manuscript.* Moscow, 1961. [in Russian; a facsimile of a mid-fourteenth century MS; for the Enoch material see ff. 36-38.]

3 (Hebrew) Enoch
(Sepher Heikhalot)

Extant in Hebrew is a pseudepigraphon called 3 Enoch, which was edited and translated into English by H. Odeberg (no. 808; see the favorable review by R. Bultmann in *TLZ* 62 [1937] cols. 449-53). He concludes that while the main body (chps. 3-48A) and its redaction date from the second half of the third century (p. 41), some portions (48B and C, 1 and 2) are later, and others (3-15) go back to the second or first century A.D. (pp. 42, 79, 83, 188).

3 Enoch contains 48 chapters: R. Ishmael ben Elisha's ascension and vision of the Merkabah (1-2); concerning Metatron, the Prince of the Presence, who is also Enoch (3-16); angelology (17-28:6); divine judgment and the heavenly tribunal (28:7-33:2); the Merkabah phenomena (33:3-40); Metatron reveals secrets to R. Ishmael (41-48A); divine names (48B); an Enoch-Metatron section (48C); names of Metatron (48D).

This pseudepigraphon should be considered for inclusion within the Pseudepigrapha. The work is Jewish, and at least portions of it predate A.D. 200. The form and content are related, at least intermittently, to the Old Testament, and the book is heavily influenced by the apocalyptic genre, showing impressive relationships with 1 and 2 Enoch. It is attributed pseudonymously to an Old Testament figure.

See the works listed under "Enoch," Old Testament Names Used Pseudonymously, and under 1 Enoch and 2 Enoch. See also nos. 87, 176.

802   Alexander, P. "3 (Hebrew) Enoch," Doubleday edition.

803   Andersen, H.G. "Enoch, Books of," *ZPEB* 2. Pp. 309-12.

804   Goodenough, E.R. "Astronomical Secrets," *Jewish Symbols* 8 (1958) 167-218. See esp. p. 189.

805   Goodenough, E.R. "The Tree," *Jewish Symbols* 7 (1958) 87-134. See esp. p. 130.

806 Goodenough, E.R. "Victory and Her Crown," *Jewish Symbols* 7 (1958) 135-71. See esp. p. 170.

807 Noack, B. "Enoksbøgerne," *GDBL* 1. Cols. 441f.

808 Odeberg, H. *3 Enoch or the Hebrew Book of Enoch*. Cambridge: CUP, 1928; repr. with prolegomenon by J.C. Greenfield. New York: KTAV, 1973.

809 Plöger, O. "Henochbücher," *RGG*³ 3. Cols. 222-25.

810 Reicke, B. "Henochbücher," *BHH* 2. Pp. 692f.

811 Romano, D. "Enok, Libro hebreo de," *Enciclopedia de la Biblia* 3. Col. 37.

812 Scholem, G. "Kabbalah," *EncyJud* 10. Cols. 489-653.

813 Scholem, G. "Metatron (Matatron)," *EncyJud* 11. Cols. 1443-46.

814 Scholem, G. *Les origines de la Kabbale*, trans. J. Loewenson. Paris: Editions Montaigne, 1966.

815 Scholem, G. "Some Remarks on Metatron and Akatriel," *Jewish Gnosticism, Merkabah Mysticism and Talmudic Tradition*. New York: Jewish Theological Seminary of America, 1960. Pp. 43-55.

Eupolemus

Five quotations in the Fathers have been attributed to Eupolemus. One of these, in Eusebius' *Praeparatio Evangelica* (9.17, 2-9), was falsely attributed to him and belongs to an anonymous Samaritan (see above, *ad loc. cit.*). Four of them, three by Eusebius (*Pr. ev.* 9.26, 1 [cf. Clem. Alex., *Strom.* 1.23, 153, 4]; 9.30, 1-34, 18 [cf. Clem. Alex., *Strom.* 1.21, 130, 3; and *Chronicon Paschale* 91, ed. L. Dindorf in PG 92, col. 253]; 9.34, 20) and one by Clement of Alexandria (*Strom.* 1.21, 141, 4-5), are now judged to be from Eupolemus. Another fragment cited by Eusebius (*Pr. ev.* 9.39, 2-5) is anonymous, but is now recognized as probably derived from Eupolemus' work, receiving the attribution "fragment four." These five Greek fragments are re-edited by A.-M. Denis (no. 23, pp. 179-86), and retranslated into English by B.Z. Wacholder (no. 819, pp. 307-12).

There is a growing consensus that the Eupolemus of the fragments is to be identified with "Eupolemus the son of John, son of Accos," whom Judas Maccabeus sent to Rome as ambassador

108

in 161 B.C. (1Mac 8:17, 2Mac 4:11; Josephus, *Ant.* 12.415).

The first fragment states that Moses taught writing to
the Jews, who gave it to the Phoenicians, who passed it on to
the Greeks. The second, apparently taken from the "Prophecy
of Elijah," purports to contain letters sent and received by
Solomon; these concern the construction of the Temple. It
also describes the magnificence of the completed Temple. The
third records that Solomon made 1,000 shields of gold and lived
52 years. The fourth contains an account of Jonachim's attempt
to burn Jeremiah alive, and of the destruction of Jerusalem by
Nebuchadnezzar. The fifth shows a concern for the chronology
from Adam until the time of Gnaius Dometian and Asinius, the
consuls in Rome.

See Fragments of Historical Works.

816   Denis, A.-M. "Eupolémos," *Introduction*. Pp. 252-55.

816a [Georgoulēs, K.D.] "Eupolemus," *ThĒE* 5. Col. 1069.
      [in Greek]

816b Giblet, J. "Eupolème et l'historiographie du judaïsme
      hellénistique," *ETL* 39 (1963) 539-54.

817   Hanhart, R. "Eupolemus," *BHH* 1. Cols. 448f.

818   Wacholder, B.Z. "Eupolemus," Doubleday edition.

818a Wacholder, B.Z. "Eupolemus," *EncyJud* 6. Cols. 964f.

819   Wacholder, B.Z. *Eupolemus: A Study of Judaeo-Greek Liter-
      ature* (Monographs of the Hebrew Union College 3) New
      York: Hebrew Union College-Jewish Institute of Religion,
      1974.

820   Walter, N. "Eupolemos," *JSHRZ* 1, in press.

Pseudo-Eupolemus
(An Anonymous Samaritan Text)

It is widely recognized that the quotation in Eusebius'
Praeparatio Evangelica 9.17, 2-9 is incorrectly attributed to
Eupolemus. There is some doubt whether Pseudo-Eupolemus should
be identified with the "anonymous" writer quoted later by Eusebius at 9.18, 2. N. Walter (no. 574f) questions the identification, B.Z. Wacholder (nos. 574e and 819) affirms it.

A new English translation has been published by Wacholder
(no. 819, pp. 313f.). See the comments above under An Anonymous Samaritan Text.

Aprocryphon of Ezekiel
(Apocalypse of Ezekiel, Legends of Ezekiel)

Extant only in quotations by the Fathers and in three fourth-century fragments of Chester Beatty Papyrus 185 are remnants of one or more apocryphal compositions attributed to Ezekiel. Four of these quotations--two by Epiphanius (*Haer.* 64.70, 6-17; 30.30, 3), and one each by Clement of Rome (*1 Clem* 8.3) and Clement of Alexandria (*Quis dives salv.* 40.2 and parallel citations)--and the text of Chester Beatty Papyrus 185 are republished by A.-M. Denis (no. 23, pp. 121-28). An English translation of these quotations was published by M.R. James (*LAOT*. Pp. 64-68).

At least one pseudepigraphon is as early as the first century A.D., because Josephus mentions two books of Ezekiel (*Ant.* 10.5, 1). The extant fragments are certainly Jewish; but some of them, especially number two, reveal that somewhere in the transmission there may have been editing by a Jewish Christian (see the similar idea expressed by C. Bonner, *The Homily on the Passion by Melito Bishop of Sardis with Some Fragments of the Apocryphal Ezekiel* [St. and Doc. 12] Philadelphia: University of Pennsylvania, 1940; p. 185; see pl. II for one side of the papyrus fragments). A date of composition somewhere between 50 B.C. and A.D. 50 was suggested by K. Holl ("Das Apokryphon Ezekiel," *Gesammelte Aufsätze zur Kirchengeschichte.* Tübingen: Mohr, 1928. Vol. 2, p. 39), and this proposal has met with wide approval (e.g., J.B. Frey in *DBSup* 1, col. 460; E. Kutsch, no. 826; A.-M. Denis, no. 24, p. 190; E.B. Oikonomos, no. 827, col. 750).

The first fragment is a relatively long excerpt preserving a parable about a blind and a lame man who combined abilities to destroy the king's garden because they had not been invited to the son's marriage feast. The just judge perceives how the act had been accomplished and hears each culprit blame the other. The purpose of the parable is to illustrate that the body and soul are joined together, sharing a common fate. (A similar story is found in rabbinic sources; cf. Sanh. 91 a-b, Mekh. Shirata 2; Lev. R. 4.5.) The second is very short and has been linked with the virgin birth of Jesus: "and the heifer shall bear and they shall say, 'she has not born.'"

The third fragment contains a plea for Israel to repent, and
the fourth contains an idea concerning judgment.

A T&T fascicle on Ezekiel material is projected under the
editorship of J. Strugnell and M.E. Stone.

821   Baker, A. "Justin's Agraphon in the Dialogue with Trypho,
      JBL 87 (1968) 277-87.

822   Denis, A.-M. "Les fragments de l'Apocryphe grec
      d'Ezéchiel," *Introduction*. Pp. 187-91.

823   Duensing, H. "Apocalypse of Paul," trans. E. Best. HSW.
      Vol. 2, pp. 755-98. See esp. p. 792, which contains
      ApPaul 49, in which ApocEzek may be quoted.

824   Eckart, K.G. "Apokalypse Ezechiels," *JSHRZ* 5, in press.

825   Gutiérrez-Larraya, J.A. "Ezequiel, Apócrifo de,"
      Enciclopedia de la Biblia 2. Col. 406.

826   Kutsch, E. "Ezechiel, Apokryphon," *RGG*³ 2. Col. 844.

827   Oikonomos, E̅.B. "Ezekiel," *ThE̅E* 6. Cols. 746-50. [in
      Greek; see esp. col. 750.]

828   Stone, M.E. "Ezekiel, Apocryphal Books of," *EncyJud* 6.
      Col. 1099.

Ezekiel the Tragedian
(Ezekiel the Poet)

Ezekiel the Tragediañ's *Exagōgē* is preserved only in quotations by Eusebius (*Pr. ev.* 9.28, 2-4; 9.29, 5-14; 9.29, 16;
cf. Clem. Alex.'s *Strom.* 1.23, 155 and 156; 5.14, 131) and
Epiphanius (*Haer.* 64.29, 6). These Greek excerpts are republished by A.-M. Denis (no. 23, pp. 207-16); those found in
Eusebius were translated into English by E.H. Gifford (Eusebius. *Preparation for the Gospel*. Oxford: Clarendon, 1903).
No English translation of Epiphanius' work has yet been published, except for Ptolemaeus' letter to Flora, *Haer.* 33.3-7,
which is translated by R.M. Grant (*Second-Century Christianity*
London: S.P.C.K., 1946. Pp. 30-37).

Since Ezekiel the Tragedian was quoted by Alexander Polyhistor and was influenced by the Septuagint, he wrote sometime
in the second century B.C., possibly in Alexandria (P. Dalbert
*Die Theologie der hellenistisch-jüdischen Missionsliteratur
unter Ausschluss von Philo und Josephus*. Hamburg: Reich, 1954;
p. 55) or in Samaria (Denis, no. 24, pp. 276f.). J. Strugnell

(no. 300, p. 450, n. 5) demonstrates that Ezekiel the Tragedian
followed the strict norms of Greek tragical metrics. The extant 269 verses of *Exagōgē* are in iambic trimeters and suggest
influence from Euripides (M.S. Hurwitz, no. 829, col. 1103).

Ezekiel's drama, as the title indicates, concerns the exodus from Egypt under the leadership of the hero Moses. The
first quotation, of 67 verses, is an account by Moses of the
oppression of Jacob's descendants, and of his life from the
rescue by Pharaoh's daughter from "the thick rushes" of the
Nile to his marriage to Zipporah. The second, of 175 verses,
contains four parts: a dialogue between Moses and his father-
in-law concerning Moses' dream in which he is offered a throne
(22 vss.; *Pr. ev.* 9.29, 4-6); a dialogue between God and Moses
concerning the latter's mission (42 vss.; *Pr. ev.* 9.29, 7-11);
God's command to Moses regarding the plagues and the celebration of the feast of Passover (61 vss.; *Pr. ev.* 9.29, 12f.);
and an Egyptian's description of his nation's defeat by the
Most High through the waves of "the deep sea" (30 vss.; *Pr. ev.*
9.29, 14). The third, of 27 verses, is a speech to Moses by
someone who describes the beauty of the oasis Elim (Ex 15:27)
and the grandeur of a bird of unparalleled size and beauty.

Consult Fragments of Poetical Works. See also no. 65.

829 Hurwitz, M.S. "Ezekiel the Poet," *EncyJud* 6. Cols. 1102f.

830 Lohse, E. "Ezechiel, Tragiker," *RGG*[3] 2. Col. 847.

831 Strugnell, J. "Notes on the Text and Metre of Ezekiel the
       Tragedian's Exagôgê," *HTR* 60 (1967) 449-57.

832 Vogt, [E.] "Tragiker Ezechiel," *JSHRZ* 4, in press.

833 Ziegler, J. "Ezechiel der Tragiker," *LTK*[2] 3. Col. 1328.

4 Ezra [and Ezra Cycle]
(4,5,6 Ezra; 2 Esdras, 4 Esdras, Apocalypse of Ezra)

4 Ezra, one of the most brilliant and original of the
apocryphal compositions, is extant in numerous versions, of
which the most important are the Syriac (recently re-edited by
R.J. Bidawid, no. 834) and the Latin (most recently edited by
L. Gry, *Les dires prophétiques d'Esdras.* 2 vols. Paris:
Geuthner, 1938). It has been translated into English frequently, from the Armenian by J. Issaverdens (*UWOT*. Pp. 326-452);

from the Latin, earlier by G.H. Box (*The Ezra-Apocalypse*. London: Pitman, 1912; repr. *APOT* 2. Pp. 561-624), and more recently by B.M. Metzger and the Committee for the Oxford Annotated
Apocrypha (no. 859; also see the translations in the NEB, no.
856, and the Jerusalem Bible); and from the Syriac by G.H. Box
(*The Apocalypse of Ezra*. London: S.P.C.K., 1917).

The pseudepigraphon was composed in the last decades of
the first century A.D., perhaps in Palestine. The original
language is Semitic, but it is difficult to decide whether it
is Hebrew or Aramaic. Most scholars now affirm the structural
unity of the Jewish core, chapters 3-14.

Eventually added to the core were two later Christian compositions in Greek, now sometimes called 5 (chps. 1-2) and 6
Ezra (chps. 15-16). The central section contains seven revelations to Ezra, called Salathiel, by Uriel, in which *inter alia*
the writer confronts the problem of theodicy, and speculates
about the coming of the Messiah and the end of this age. The
prefixed chapters, probably added in the second century, de-
lineate God's faithfulness and Israel's apostasy with subsequent exhortations. The suffixed chapters, probably added in
the third century, contain prophecies of woe, followed by exhortations and promises of deliverance for the elect.

Numerous writings circulated under the name of Ezra during
the early centuries of the present era. Discussed below are
the Apocalypse of Ezra, the Questions of Ezra, the Revelation
of Ezra, the Vision of Ezra, and the Apocalypse of Sedrach
which is related to the Ezra cycle. Medieval compositions
were sometimes attributed to Ezra; most of these are conveniently summarized by A.-M. Denis (no. 24, pp. 93-96; also see
M.R. James' comments in *LAOT*, pp. 79-81). Most important of
these late compositions attributed to Ezra is one which mentions the expansion of Islam. It has received various names
such as the Vision of Ezra, the Apocalypse of Ezra, the Question of Ezra, the Prayer of Ezra, and Syriac Ezra. The Syriac
text and a French translation was published by J.-B. Chabot
("L'Apocalypse d'Esdras touchant le royaume des arabes," *Revue
sémitique d'épigraphie et d'histoire ancienne* 2 [1894] 242-50
[text], 333-46 [transl. and commentary]). Another Syriac text
among Wallis Budge's Collection has been announced recently by

R.Y. Ebied (no. 840a). Ezra's life and accomplishments are, as expected, given prominence in rabbinic writings, many of which preserve early traditions (see L. Ginzberg, *Legends*, vol. 4, pp. 354-59; vol. 6, pp. 441-47).

M.E. Stone is preparing a commentary on 4 Ezra for *Hermeneia*. Dr. R. Rubinkiewicz has found a new Greek text of 4 Ezra which will be discussed in a forthcoming issue of *Le Muséon*. Dr. A. Thompson has completed a Ph.D. dissertation at the University of Edinburgh on *Responsibility for Evil in the Theodicy of IV Ezra: A Study Illustrating the Significance of Form and Structure for the Meaning of the Book*.

4 Ezra is often included in publications on the Apocrypha of the Old Testament. These are noted below only when they are deemed significant according to the guidelines of the present bibliography.

See the numerous publications listed above under Messianism. Also consult the works listed below under (Greek) Apocalypse of Ezra, Questions of Ezra, Revelation of Ezra, and Vision of Ezra. See also nos. 1, 10, 23, 51, 82, 87f. 108, 147, 162, 176, 234, 249, 289a, 297, 309, 320, 330, 347, 471, 477-79, 1491.

834 Bidawid, R.J., ed. "4 Ezra," *Peshiṭta*, sample ed. (1966) i-ii, 1-51; repr. with corrections: "4 Esdras," *Peshiṭta*. Part 4, fasc. 3 (1973) i-iv, 1-50.

835 Boyarin, D. "Penitential Liturgy in 4 Ezra," *JSJ* 3 (1972) 30-34.

836 Breech, E. "These Fragments I Have Shored Against My Ruins: The Form and Function of 4 Ezra," *JBL* 92 (1973) 267-74.

837 Daniélou, J. "Le Ve Esdras et le judéo-christianisme latin au second siècle," Widengren Festschrift. Vol. 1, pp. 162-71.

838 Denis, A.-M. "Les fragments grecs de l'Apocalypse 4 Esdras," *Introduction*. Pp. 194-200.

839 Duensing, H. "The Fifth and Sixth Books of Esra," trans. D. Hill. HSW. Vol. 2, pp. 689-703.

840 Dunnett, W.M. "Esdras, Second (2)," *ZPEB* 2. Pp. 362-64.

840a Ebied, R.Y. "Some Syriac Manuscripts from the Collection of Sir E.A. Wallis Budge," *Orient. Christ. Analecta* 197 (1974) 509-39. [See esp. p. 525 which contains a discussion of another manuscript of the Syriac "Apocalypse of Ezra."]

841 Erbetta, M. "5-6 Esdras," *Apocrifi del NT.* Vol. 3, pp. 317-31.

842 Glatzer, N.N. "After the Fall of Jerusalem," *Judaic Tradition.* Pp. 159-72.

843 Goodenough, E.R. "Astronomical Symbols," *Jewish Symbols* 8 (1958) 167-218. See esp. pp. 203f.

844 Goodenough, E.R. "Birds," *Jewish Symbols* 8 (1958) 22-70. See esp. p. 43.

845 Goodenough, E.R. "The Lion and Other Felines," *Jewish Symbols* 7 (1958) 29-86. See esp. pp. 79f.

846 Goodenough, E.R. "Psychopomps," *Jewish Symbols* 8 (1958) 121-66. See esp. p. 136.

847 Goodenough, E.R. "The Symbolic Value of the Fish in Judaism," *Jewish Symbols* 5 (1956) 31-61. See esp. p. 37.

848 Goodenough, E.R. "The Tree," *Jewish Symbols* 7 (1958) 87-134. See esp. p. 126.

849 Goodenough, E.R. "Victory and Her Crown," *Jewish Symbols* 7 (1958) 135-71. See esp. pp. 163, 170.

850 Goodenough, E.R. "Wine in Jewish Cult and Observance," *Jewish Symbols* 6 (1956) 126-217. See esp. p. 195.

851 Gutiérrez-Larraya, J. A. "Esdras, Cuarto libro de," *Enciclopedia de la Biblia* 3. Cols. 124f.

852 Gutiérrez-Larraya, J.A. "Esdras, Quinto y sexto libros de," *Enciclopedia de la Biblia* 3. Col. 126.

853 Harnisch, W. *Verhängnis und Verheissung der Geschichte: Untersuchungen zum Zeit- und Geschichtsverständnis im 4. Buch Esra und in der syrischen Baruchapokalypse* (FRLANT 97) Göttingen: Vandenhoeck & Ruprecht, 1969.

853a Hayman, A.P. "The Problem of Pseudonymity in the Ezra Apocalypse," *JSJ* 6 (1975) 47-56.

854 Lane, W.L. "Apocrypha," *Encyclopedia of Christianity* 1. Pp. 307-64. See esp. pp. 330-32.

854a Licht, J.S. *The Book of the Apocalypse of Ezra* (Sifriyat Dovot 6) Jerusalem: Bialik Institute, 1968. [in Hebrew]

855 Licht, J.S. "Ezra, 4 Ezra, Apocalypse of Ezra," *Encyclopedia Mikra'ith* 6 (1971) 155-60. [in Hebrew]

856　McHardy, W.D., *et al.* "The Second Book of Esdras," *The New English Bible with the Apocrypha.* New York: OUP, 1971. Pp. 19-53.

857　Mehlmann, D.J. *Os Livros 3 e 4 de Esdras e Livro do Eclesiastico em Tertuliano* (Atualidades bíblicas) Petrópolis: Vozes, 1973. Pp. 115-28.

858　Metzger, B.M. "The 'Lost' Section of II Esdras (=IV Ezra)," *Historical and Literary Studies: Pagan, Jewish and Christian* (NTTS) 8) Grand Rapids, Mich.: Eerdmans, 1968. Pp. 48-51.

859　Metzger, B.M. "The Second Book of Esdras," *The Apocrypha of the Old Testament: Revised Standard Version,* ed. B. M. Metzger. New York: OUP, 1965. Pp. 23-62.

860　Müller, M. *Messias og "menneskesøn" i Daniels Bog, Første Enoksbog og Fjerde Ezrabog* (Tekst & Tolkning 3) Copenhagen: Gads, 1972.

861　Myers, J.M. *I and II Esdras* (Anchor Bible) Garden City, N.Y.: Doubleday, 1974. See esp. pp. 131-34 for Ezra cycle.

862　Noack, B. "Ezrabøgerne," *GDBL* 1. Cols. 482f.

863　Noack, B. "Fjerde Ezrabog," *GamPseud* 1 (1953) 1-68.

864　Oikonomos, Ē.B. "Esdras," *ThĒE* 5. Cols. 899-905. [in Greek]

865　Philonenko, M. "L'âme à l'étroit," *Hommages à André Dupont-Sommer,* eds. A. Caquot and M. Philonenko. Paris: Adrien-Maisonneuve, 1971. Pp. 421-28.

866　Reese, G. *Die Geschichte Israels in der Auffassung des frühen Judentums: Eine Untersuchung der Tiervision, der Zehnwochenapokalypse des äthiopischen Henochs, der Geschichtsdarstellung der Assumptio Mosis und des 4. Esrabuches.* Heidelberg Ph.D., 1967.

867　Schneider, H. "Esdras," *LTK*[2] 3. Cols. 1101-03.

868　Schreiner, [?]. "4. Esra-Buch," *JSHRZ* 5, in press.

869　Silberman, L.H. "Esrabücher, nichtkanonische," *BHH* 1. Cols. 442f.

870　Sixdenier, G.-D. "Le IIIe livre d'Esdras et la 'Vulgate' de Stuttgart," *Revue des études anciennes* 71 (1969) 390-401.

871　Stegemann, H. "5. und 6. Esra-Buch," *JSHRZ* 3, in press.

872　Stone, M.E. "The Concept of the Messiah in IV Ezra," *Goodenough Festschrift.* Pp. 295-312.

873 Stone, M.E. *Concordance and Texts of the Armenian Version of IV Ezra* (Oriental Notes and Studies 11) Jerusalem: Israel Oriental Society, 1971.

874 Stone, M.E. "Ezra, Apocalypse of," *EncyJud* 6. Cols. 1108f.

875 Stone, M.E. *Features of the Eschatology of IV Ezra.* Harvard Ph.D., 1965.

876 Stone, M.E. "Manuscripts and Readings of Armenian IV Ezra," *Textus* 6 (1968) 48-61.

877 Stone, M.E. "Paradise in IV Ezra iv:8 and vii:36, viii: 52," *JJS* 17 (1966) 85-88.

878 Stone, M.E. "Some Features of the Armenian Version of IV Ezra," *Muséon* 79 (1966) 387-400.

879 Stone, M.E. "Some Remarks on the Textual Criticism of IV Ezra," *HTR* 60 (1967) 107-15.

880 Thoma, C. "Jüdische Apokalyptik am Ende des ersten nach- christlichen Jahrhunderts: Religionsgeschichtliche Bemerkungen zur syrischen Baruchapokalypse und zum vierten Esrabuch," *Kairos* 11 (1969) 134-44.

881 Weber, R., *et al.*, eds. "Liber Ezrae IIII," *Biblia Sacra.* Vol. 2, pp. 1931-74.

882 Zink, J.K. "IV Ezra," *The Use of the Old Testament in the Apocrypha.* Duke Ph.D., 1963. Pp. 20-39.

Apocalypse of Ezra
(Greek Esdras)

This apocalypse is extant in only two manuscripts, Paris. gr. 929, ff. 510-32 and Paris. gr. 390, ff. 50-59 (according to R.P.J. Noret; see A.-M. Denis, no. 24, pp. 4, 91); the for- mer was edited by K. von Tischendorf (no. 888) and translated into English by A. Walker (*ANF* 8. Pp. 571-74).

The pseudepigraphon is a rather late imitation of 4 Ezra and is frequently similar to the Apocalypse of Sedrach. The work, however, is not so late as the ninth century, as M.R. James suggested (*Apocrypha Anecdota* [T&S 2.3] Cambridge: CUP, 1893; p. 113).

Most scholars have concluded that the work is Christian (e.g., E. Schürer, *History*, 2d. Div., vol. 3, p. 110; H. Gunkel in *APAT* 2, p. 352; H. Weinel in the Gunkel Festschrift, pp. 157f.), but P. Riessler argued that there is a Jewish *Grund- stock* which has been reworked by a Christian (no. 62, p. 1273).

The work has not yet been assigned chapters, but it is divided internally into four parts. First, Ezra ascends to heaven and pleads with God for mercy upon sinners. Second, led by Michael and Gabriel he descends into Tartarus, where he views the punishment of Herod and other sinners, one of whom is described as the Antichrist. Third, he ascends into the heavens and witnesses more punishments, even in Paradise, where he sees Enoch, Elijah, Moses, Peter, Paul, Luke, and Matthew. Fourth, he descends again deeper into Tartarus where he witnesses more torments, and eventually wins blessings for those who revere his book (*to biblion touto*) and curses for those who do not believe it. He dies, giving up his soul; his body is buried.

O. Wahl is editing the Apocalypse (Greek) of Ezra for PVTG.

Consult the list of works under 4 Ezra [and Ezra Cycle].

883 Denis, A.-M. "L'Apocalypse grecque d'Esdras," *Introduction*. Pp. 91-96.

884 Licht, J.S. "Ezra, 4 Ezra, Apocalypse of Ezra," *Encyclopedia Mikra'ith* 6 (1971) 155-60. [in Hebrew]

885 Müller, U. "Apokalypse Esras," *JSHRZ* 5, in press.

886 Shutt, R.J.H. "Apocalypse of Ezra," Clarendon edition.

887 Stone, M.E. "Apocalypse of Ezra," Doubleday edition.

888 Tischendorf, K. von. "Apocalypsis Esdrae," *Apocalypses Apocryphae Mosis, Esdrae, Pauli, item Mariae dormitio: Additis Evangeliorum et actuum apocryphorum supplementis.* Leipzig, 1866; repr. Hildesheim: Olms, 1966. Pp. 24-33.

Questions of Ezra

The one extant Armenian manuscript of the Questions of Ezra has not been edited, but parts of it were translated into English by J. Issaverdens (*UWOT*. Pp. 457-61).

The work is Christian, rather late, and apparently influenced by traditions recorded in 1 Enoch, 2 Enoch, the Apocalypse of Abraham, and the Apocalypse of Zosimus. Issaverdens translates six of the questions Ezra asks "the Angel of God"; these can be paraphrased as follows:

1. What has God prepared for the righteous and
    sinners?
    Ans. For the righteous are prepared rejoicing
          and light, for sinners darkness and fire.

2. If all men living are sinners and hence deserve
    condemnation, are not beasts more blessed?
    Ans. Do not repeat these words to "Him who
          is above you."

3. Where does the soul go after death?
    Ans. A good angel comes to a good soul, and a
          wicked one to a bad soul (cf. ApAb). The
          soul is taken eastward.

4. What is that way like?
    Ans. There are seven steps to the Divinity; the
          righteous soul passes through four steps
          of terror, one of enlightenment, and two
          of blessing.

5. Why do you not take the soul to the Divinity?
    Ans. Ezra is called a vain man (cf. ApZos) who
          thinks according to human nature. No man
          or angel can see the face of God, but only
          the place of God's throne, which is fiery
          (cf. 1En 14:18-23, 2En 20).

6. What shall become of "us [sic] sinners"?
    Ans. When you die you will obtain mercy and
          rest if a Christian prays or performs
          some act of devotion for you.

Consult the list under 4 Ezra [and Ezra Cycle].

889 Stone, M.E. "Questions of Ezra," Doubleday edition.

Revelation of Ezra

Extant in full only in Latin, this work was edited and
discussed by G. Mercati (*Note di letteratura biblica e christiana antica* [Studi e Testi 5] Rome: Vatican, 1901. Pp. 74-79).
No English translation has appeared.

No research has been published regarding the date,
provenance, or original language of the writing. The work is
a kalandologion, describing the characteristics of a year according to the day upon which it begins. Recension A, of the
ninth century, which is the earliest of the three recensions,
begins as follows: *Revelatio quae facta est Esdrae et filiis
Israhel de qualitatibus anni per introitum Ianuarii.* The work
is relatively short; Recension A contains 248 words.

This kalandologion shows few similarities to the one

attributed to Shem (see below).

890   Denis, A.-M. "L'Apocalypse grecque d'Esdras," *Introduction*. Pp. 91-96. See esp. pp. 94f.

Vision of Ezra

Preserved only in Latin, this pseudepigraphon was edited and discussed by G. Mercati (*Note di letteratura biblica e christiana antica* [Studi e Testi 5] Rome: Vatican, 1901. Pp. 61-73). An English translation has not been published.

This work, like the Apocalypse of Ezra and the Apocalypse of Sedrach, is dependent upon 4 Ezra. A.-M. Denis thinks that the Vision of Ezra, the Apocalypse of Ezra, and the Apocalypse of Sedrach are three recensions of the same work (no. 24, p. 93). As with the Revelation of Ezra, no critical research has been published regarding the date, provenance, and original language of the Vision of Ezra.

In sixty-six verses, according to P. Riessler's divisions (no. 62, pp. 350-54), Ezra sees the punishments suffered by sinners (*omnia iudicia peccatorum*). Then at the end of his journey Michael and Gabriel take him into Paradise, where he sees the blessed manner of life of the righteous (*et habitaciones eorum erant splendidissimae omni tempore*).

Consult the list under 4 Ezra [and Ezra Cycle].

891   Denis, A.-M. "L'Apocalypse grecque d'Esdras," *Introduction*. Pp. 91-96. See esp. p. 93.

892   Shutt, R.J.H. "Vision of Ezra," Clarendon edition.

Hecataeus of Abdera

Hecataeus of Abdera lived in the fourth century B.C. and was a prolific historian and ethnographer. Preserved are only portions from two works, *Aiguptiaka* which is quoted by Diodorus Siculus (*Bibliotheca Historica* 40.3), and *Peri Ioudaiōn* which is quoted by Josephus (*Contr. Ap.* 1.22, 183-204 and 2.4, 42-43; cf. LetAris 31). The Greek texts and English translations of the first two, reprinted from the Loeb Classical Library, are conveniently assembled by M. Stern (no. 894). The Greek from Josephus' *Contra Apionem* is also reprinted by A.-M. Denis (no. 23, pp. 199-202). J.G. Gager, Jr. (no. 892b, pp. 26-28) published an idiomatic translation of *Aiguptiaka.*

In the *Aiguptiaka* Hecataeus reports that the Egyptians perceive a pestilence is caused by the failure to honor the gods; hence they dismiss the foreigners from their land. Those who settled in Judaea were led by Moses, who was outstanding in wisdom and courage.

In *Peri Ioudaiōn* Hecataeus mentions the victory by Ptolemy at Gaza and describes those who followed him to Egypt, among whom was Ezechias, a chief priest (see the coin bearing that name discussed by Gager, no. 892c). The reverence and readiness to suffer for "our laws" is lauded. The vastness of the Jewish population and fertileness of the Judaean soil are praised. The excerpt, which is intermittently quoted or paraphrased by Josephus, concludes with an account of how Mosollamus, a Jew, shot a bird, which had been circling above the caravan and delaying a march towards the Red Sea, because a seer had claimed the bird was gifted with divination. Later Josephus notes that Hecataeus wrote that Alexander, in recognition of the Jews' loyalty to him, added Samaria to their territory.

See Fragments of Historical Works and Pseudo-Hecataeus.

892a Denis, A.-M. "Hécatée," *Introduction.* Pp. 262-67.

892b Gager, J.G. Jr. "Hecataeus of Abdera," *Moses in Greco-Roman Paganism* (SBLMS 16) New York: Abingdon, 1972. Pp. 26-37.

892c Gager, J.G. Jr. "Pseudo-Hecataeus Again," *ZNW* 60 (1969) 130-39.

893 Schmid, J. "Hekataios v. Abdera," *LTK*^{2} 5. Col. 206.

894 Stern, M., ed. "Hecataeus of Abdera," *GLAJJ.* Pp. 20-44.

895 Wacholder, B.Z. "Hecataeus of Abdera," Doubleday edition.

896 Wacholder, B.Z. "Hecataeus of Abdera," *EncyJud* 8. Cols. 236f.

Pseudo-Hecataeus

Three phases in work upon so-called Pseudo-Hecataeus can be discerned. Nineteenth- and early twentieth-century scholars concurred that *Peri Ioudaiōn* was also called *Peri Abramou* (Jos. *Ant.* 1.7, 2; cf. Clem. Alex. *Strom.* 5.14, 113 and *Protr.* 7.74,

2; and Eus. *Pr. ev.* 13.13, 40), and was written in the third
century B.C. by a Jewish pseudographer, founded perhaps on
selections from Hecataeus (viz. E. Schürer, *History*, 2d. Div.,
vol. 3, pp. 304f.; J. Freudenthal, *Alexander Polyhistor*.
Breslau: Skutsch, 1875; pp. 165f; P. Dalbert, *Missionsliteratur*, pp. 65-67).

The second phase began with H. Lewy's critical analysis
of the traditions preserved in Josephus ("Hekataios von Abdera
Peri Ioudaiōn," *ZNW* 31 [1932] 117-32). Lewy's conclusion that
Peri Ioudaiōn is not pseudepigraphical but authentically from
Hecataeus has influenced the judgment of several specialists,
notably V. Tcherikover (no. 124, pp. 426f.), Y. Gutman (no.
40, pp. 39ff.), and J.G. Gager, Jr. (no. 892c).

Today we are in a third phase; while subtle distinctions
are perceived, two contrary conclusions are affirmed. Thirty
years after Lewy's publication B. Schaller claimed that much of
the material attributed to Hecataeus was spurious (no. 898c;
cf. also A.-M. Denis, no. 24, pp. 262-67). N. Walter (no.
899a) and B.Z. Wacholder (no. 898) are now arguing that all of
Josephus' material is derived from a pseudographer. They distinguish between a Pseudo-Hecataeus 1, who wrote *Peri Ioudaiōn*
in the first half of the second century B.C., and a Pseudo-
Hecataeus 2, who wrote *Peri Abramou* sometime later but before
Josephus.

M. Stern (no. 894) would agree with Walter and Wacholder
that *Peri Ioudaiōn* and *Peri Abramou* must be distinguished and
that the latter is a pseudonymous product of Jewish religious
propaganda. But he would reject the claim that there is
anachronistic material in *Peri Ioudaiōn*, and that the tone in
this text is dissimilar to that in the Diodorus material.
Peri Ioudaiōn, therefore, is a Jewish revision of a genuine
Hecataeus composition.

Gager published many arguments similar to those by Stern,
but seems to be in even greater disagreement with Walter and
Wacholder. In 1969 he presented an impressive argument in
favor of the authenticity of many passages that had been considered spurious (no. 892c).

The main question is whether some traditions which

criticize the Jews for not mixing with other nations can be identified with other traditions which sound like an apology for Judaism. The issue is clarified but not completely resolved by a recognition that "pagans" could speak favorably about the Jews.

See Fragments of Historical Works and the publications just cited under Hecataeus.

897 Barr, J. "Philo of Byblos and his 'Phoenician History,'" *BJRULM* 57 (1974) 17-68. See esp. pp. 31f. [Philo of Byblos questioned the authenticity of *Peri Ioudaiōn*.]

897a Denis, A.-M. "Interpolations juives d'auteurs païens," *Introduction*. Pp. 223-38.

897b Schaller, B. "Hekataios von Abdera über die Juden," *ZNW* 54 (1963) 15-31. [Schaller argued against H. Lewy and in favor of a Pseudo-Hecataeus. J.G. Gager, Jr. (no. 892c) responded to him.]

898 Wacholder, B.Z. "Hecataeus of Abdera," *EncyJud* 8. Cols. 236f.

899 Walter, N. "Pseudo-Hekataios," *JSHRZ* 1, in press.

899a Walter, N. "Zur Frage des Zusammenhanges der jüdischen Fälschungen auf Namen griechischer Dichter untereinander und mit Pseudo-Hekataios," *Der Thoraausleger Aristobulos* (TU 86) Berlin: Akademie, 1964. Pp. 172-201.

Testament of Hezekiah

This Christian composition was written around the end of the second century A.D. It apparently was a work that circulated independently, but now it is incorporated within the Ascension of Isaiah. Georgius Cedrenus in the twelfth century in his *Compendium Historiarum* 120 (PG 121, col. 152C) quotes the so-called Ascension of Isaiah 4:12 under the title "The Testament of Hezekiah" (*Diathēkē Ezekiou*).

See the discussion and the publications cited under the Ascension of Isaiah.

Fragments of Historical Works

This category is ill-defined in recent research and needs polishing. Included herein because their dates are related to those of the early pseudepigrapha and because of the exclusiveness of other categories are some writings, which are noted under the following headings:

> Anonymous Samaritan (=Pseudo-Eupolemus)
>
> Aristeas the Exegete
>
> Artapanus
>
> Cleodemus Malchus
>
> Demetrius
>
> Eupolemus
>
> Hecataeus of Abdera and Pseudo-Hecataeus
>
> Pseudo-Menander
>
> Thallus
>
> See also nos. 23, 430, 1205a.

900   Denis, A.-M. "Les historiens juifs hellénistiques,"
       Introduction. Pp. 241-69.

901   Wacholder, B.Z. "Biblical Chronology in the Hellenistic
       World Chronicles," *HTR* 61 (1968) 451-81.

>   *Testament of Isaac*
>   *(The Testaments of Abraham, Isaac and Jacob*
>   *are called sometimes the Testaments of the*
>   *Three Patriarchs; cf.* Apostolicae Constitu-
>   tiones *6.16)*

While this writing is extant in Ethiopic and Arabic (see
M.R. James, *The Testament of Abraham* [T&S 2] Cambridge: CUP,
1892; pp. 6f., 157), the major version is the Coptic, extant
in Bohairic and Sahidic. The latter dialect is the most important and was edited recently by K.H. Kuhn ("The Sahidic Version
of the Testament of Isaac," *JTS* n.s. 8 [1957] 226-39). English
translations of the Arabic and both dialects of the Coptic have
been published: of the Arabic by W.E. Barnes (extracts only
in an appendix to James' *The Testament of Abraham*, pp. 140-51);
of the Bohairic by S. Gaselee (in an appendix to G.H. Box's
The Testament of Abraham [TED] London: S.P.C.K., 1927; pp. 57-
75); and of the Sahidic by K.H. Kuhn (no. 904).

There is agreement that the Testament of Isaac, which is
not mentioned in ancient lists of Old Testament apocryphal
works, is dependent upon the Testament of Abraham, but the
exact date is difficult to discern. P. Nagel (no. 907) thinks
it was written around A.D. 400 and M. Delcor (no. 507, p. 83)
affirms its earliness, suggesting because of affinities with
the Dead Sea Scrolls that it may come from approximately the

same milieu and date as the Testament of Abraham. Kuhn
cautions, however, that there is really no convincing evidence
for a precise dating of the Testament of Isaac (no. 904).
Nagel (no. 907) argues that the Sahidic version, the earliest,
is translated from Greek. Kuhn (no. 904) responds that Nagel's
published argument is questionable.

The most intriguing question concerns the Christian elements in the text. Some of these, I am convinced, are interpolated because they are not grammatically linked to the con-
tiguous sentences and appear to disrupt the flow of thought
(viz. 14v, first sentence; from 16r, last sentence, to 17r,
first sentence; 24v, second sentence; 25v, concluding state-
ment). Other passages (e.g. 15r, third sentence) are similar
to traditions in the New Testament, but it is difficult to
trace the direction of influence, if any.

The Sahidic text covers 27 pages of about 80 words per
page. The setting for the narrative is the events immediately
before Isaac's death and the separation of his soul from the
body. Isaac converses with angels, Jacob, a crowd, and a
priest within the crowd, to whom he presents a series of ethical exhortations. He ascends to heaven under the guidance of
"the angel of Abraham." He sees torments and tormentors,
especially Abdemerouchos, who is in charge of punishments.
Isaac is taken higher where he sees and worships Abraham, who
receives from the Lord two conditions for becoming "a son in
my kingdom." These requirements are provision for Isaac with
reverence for his testament, and compassionate deeds. Excep-
tions are allowed, by the mercy and love of the Lord, for those
who cannot fulfill these requirements; the most important provision is the offering of a sacrifice in the name of Isaac.
The Lord commands Michael to assemble the angels and saints
before Isaac, who then sees "the face of our Lord" (*epho
mpenδoeis*). Jacob embraces his father and receives a blessing
from the Lord, who then takes Isaac's soul from the body with
his chariot and ascends into the heavens.

A copy of Vatican Syr. 199, ff. 21v-45v, which contains
the Testaments of Abraham, Isaac, and Jacob, is preserved in
the Pseudepigrapha Library at Duke University.

See some of the publications listed under the Testament

of Abraham.   See also no. 507.

902   Estelrich, P. "Isaac, Testamento de," *Enciclopedia de la Biblia* 4. Col. 220.

903   Gaguine, M. *The Falasha Version of the Testaments of Abraham, Isaac and Jacob.* Manchester, Eng., Ph.D., 1965.

904   Kuhn, K.H. "An English Translation of the Sahidic Version of the Testament of Isaac," *JTS* 18 (1967) 325-36.,

905   Kuhn, K.H. "Testament of Isaac," Clarendon edition.

906   Müller, W. "Testament Isaaks," *JSHRZ* 3, in press.

907   Nagel, P. "Zur sahidischen Version des Testamentes Isaaks," *WZHalle* 12 (1963) 259-63. [*N.V.*]

908   Papadopoulos, S.G. "Isaac, Testament of," *ThĒE* 6. Col. 1003. [in Greek]

909   Philonenko, M. "Isaaks Testament," *BHH* 2. Col. 776.

910   Stinespring, W.F. "Testament of Isaac," Doubleday edition.

911   Stone, M.E. "Isaac, Testament of," *EncyJud* 9. Cols. 10f.

Ascension of Isaiah [and Isaiah Cycle]
(Martyrdom of Isaiah, Testament of Hezekiah, Vision of Isaiah)

Fragmentarily extant in Greek (see A.-M. Denis, no. 23, pp. 105-14), Slavonic, Coptic, and Latin, the entire work is preserved only in Ethiopic, which was edited by R.H. Charles (*The Ascension of Isaiah, Translated from the Ethiopic Version, Which, Together with the New Greek Fragment, the Latin Versions and the Latin Translation of the Slavonic, is Here Published in Full.* London: Black, 1900). An English translation of the Martyrdom of Isaiah was published by Charles (*APOT* 2. Pp. 155-62) and two English translations of the entire work have appeared, one by Charles (*The Ascension of Isaiah* [1900]; repr. Charles, *The Ascension of Isaiah*, intro. by G.H. Box [TED] London, New York: S.P.C.K., 1919), and one by D. Hill, based upon the German of J. Flemming and H. Duensing (no. 920).

The Martyrdom and Ascension of Isaiah, like many pseudepigrapha (especially 1 Enoch) is composite, comprising three separate sections: the Martyrdom of Isaiah (basically chps. 1-5, except for THez); the Testament of Hezekiah (3:13-4:18); and the Vision of Isaiah (chps. 6-11). Some specialists see only two sections, chapters 1-5 and 6-11, but argue for the

existence of extraneous material in each section (viz. Flemming
and Duensing, no. 920, pp. 642f.; A. Vaillant, no. 943). Two
or three of the writings originally may have circulated independently (see Box in Charles' *The Ascension of Isaiah*, p. vii;
M. Philonenko, no. 231, p. 2; contrast C.C. Torrey, *Apoc. Lit.*,
esp. pp. 133-35). The first writing is Jewish, dating from
around the second century B.C., and the other two are Christian, having been composed around the end of the second century
A.D. A few scholars think that all three compositions already
existed in the first century (Charles in *APOT* 2, pp. 157f.;
Box in Charles' *The Ascension of Isaiah*, pp. x, xiii; E. Hammershaimb, no. 914, p. 19), and it is conceivable that the
author of the Epistle to the Hebrews knew the Martyrdom of
Isaiah (see Heb 11:37), but it should not be forgotten that
Isaiah's martyrdom is also recorded in the Lives of the
Prophets (see below). The probable original language of the
Martyrdom of Isaiah is Semitic, perhaps Hebrew (cf. Hammer-
shaimb, no. 927, p. 19; Philonenko, no. 231, p. 2), that of
the other sections Greek (cf. Hammershaimb, no. 927, p. 19).
Some scholars (D. Flusser, "The Apocryphal Book of *Ascensio
Isaiae* and the Dead Sea Sect," *IEJ* 3 [1953] 30-47; J. van der
Ploeg, "Les manuscrits du désert de Juda: Etudes et découvertes
récentes (Planches IV-V)," *BO* 11 [1954] 145-60, see esp. pp.
154f.; R. Meyer, no. 934a; L. Rost, no. 66, p. 114; Philonenko,
no. 231, p. 10) have been persuaded that the Martyrdom of
Isaiah is related to the Dead Sea Scrolls. Some parallels are
interesting, especially the denigration of Jerusalem and the
retreat from Jerusalem to the desert; but noticeably absent
are peculiarly Qumranic *termini technici*, the light-darkness
paradigm, mention of the Teacher of Righteousness, an eschatological emphasis, and the general Qumranic *Zeitgeist* (see V.
Nikiprowetzky, no. 162; Hammershaimb, no. 927, p. 19; A.
Caquot, no. 914, p. 93). A Palestinian provenance, however,
is probable (A.-M. Denis, no. 917, p. 175; L. Rost, no. 66,
p. 114).

The Ascension of Isaiah contains eleven chapters:

1a) Martyrdom of Isaiah (1:1-3:12): With Isaiah present
Hezekiah summons Manasseh, his only son, in order to deliver
words of righteousness. After Hezekiah dies Manasseh causes
Israel to apostatize; Isaiah leaves Jerusalem for Bethlehem,

and eventually retreats to a mountain in the desert, where he
is soon joined by other prophets who lead with him an ascetic
existence. Belchira, a Samaritan and false prophet, speaks
against Isaiah and persuades Manasseh to seize him.

2) Testament of Hezekiah (3:13-4:18): Beliar is angry
about Isaiah's vision in which he saw the descent of the
Beloved, the twelve disciples, the crucifixion, the resurrection, the establishment of the Church, and the subsequent
corruption and apostasy from the teaching, faith, love, and
purity of the Twelve. Beliar will descend and persecute the
plant planted by the Twelve, then the Lord will come with his
angels from the seventh heaven and drag Beliar into Gehenna.
The godly will receive rest, the ungodly will be consumed by
fire.

1b) Martyrdom of Isaiah (5:1-14): Manasseh, influenced
by Beliar, saws Isaiah in two with a wooden saw, but Isaiah
continues to speak under the influence of the Holy Spirit.

3) Vision of Isaiah (6:1-11:4): When Isaiah comes from
Galgala to Hezekiah forty prophets come to be with him. While
they are praying Isaiah's mind leaves his body, and an angel
from the seventh heaven descends in order to explain to him
his vision.

Isaiah ascends to the firmament, where Sammael and his
hosts are fighting. He passes consecutively through six
heavens in which the quality of light, glory, and praise in-
creases. In the sixth heaven Isaiah receives garments of
glory and is given power; he then joins in praise to the pri-
mal Father, His Beloved (Christ), and the Holy Spirit.

In the seventh heaven he is amazed at the unparalleled
quality of the light, and sees innumerable angels and all the
righteous, especially Abel and Enoch. After he sees the book
of the deeds of the children of Israel his transformation is
complete, for he is like an angel.

From the seventh heaven Isaiah watches the descent of
Christ through the seven heavens and the firmament and the pro-
gressive emptying of his glory until he is born through Mary.
Both the Virgin and Joseph are descendants of David. Jesus'
life is summarized and his ascent through all levels, without

128

any need for retransformation, is described, until he sits down on the right hand of the Great Glory.

Numerous writings early were attributed to Isaiah. The major impulse for pseudepigraphical composition would be the mention in canonical Isaiah that the prophet "saw the Lord sitting upon a throne, high and lifted up; and his train filled the temple." (RSV, Isa 6:1). Besides the two just mentioned there are probably some compositions attributed to him that are now lost. Probably Origen's *Apokruphon Hēsaiou* is the Ascension of Isaiah, as R.H. Charles suggested (*APOT* 2, p. 155). It may represent another work, since it is impossible to know the precise contents (so Hammershaimb, no. 927, p. 17). The same situation applies to the apocryphal book of Isaiah mentioned in the fourth-century *Apostolicae Constitutiones* (6.16, 3). Also see the chapter on Isaiah in the Lives of the Prophets.

M.A. Knibb has found recently an unexamined Ethiopic manuscript of the Ascension of Isaiah.

See also nos. 23, 87, 162, 175, 270, 297, 303.

912 Barton, J.M.T. "Ascension of Isaiah," Clarendon edition.

913 Buck, F. "Are the 'Ascension of Isaiah' and the 'Odes of Solomon' Witnesses to an Early Cult of Mary?" *De primordiis cultus mariani*. Rome: Pontificia Academia Mariana Internationalis, 1970. Vol. 4, pp. 371-99. [*N.V.*]

914 Caquot, A. "Bref commentaire du 'Martyre d'Isaïe,'" *Sem* 23 (1973) 65-93.

915 Cothenet, E. "Isaïe (L'Ascension de)," *Catholicisme* 6 (1963) 144-46.

916 Delcor, M. "L' 'Ascension d'Isaïe' à travers la prédication d'un évêque cathare en Catalogne au quatorzième siècle," *RHR* 184 (1973) 157-78.

917 Denis, A.-M. "Les fragments grecs du Martyre d'Isaïe," *Introduction*. Pp. 170-76.

918 Erbetta, M. "Ascensione di Isaia 4, 3 è la testimonianza più antica del martirio di Pietro," *Euntes Docete* 19 (1966) 427-36. [*N.V.*]

919 Erbetta, M. "L'Ascensione d'Isaia," *Apocrifi del NT*. Vol. 3, pp. 175-204.

920 Flemming, J. and H. Duensing. "The Ascension of Isaiah," trans. D. Hill. HSW. Vol. 2, pp. 642f.

921 Flusser, D. "Isaiah, Ascension of," *EncyJud* 9. Col. 71.

922   Goodenough, E.R. "Astronomical Symbols," *Jewish Symbols*
      8 (1958) 167-218. See esp. p. 205.

923   Goodenough, E.R. "Two Fragmentary Scenes," *Jewish Symbols*
      10 (1964) 98-104. See esp. p. 101.

924   Goodenough, E.R. "Victory and Her Crown," *Jewish Symbols*
      7 (1958) 135-71. See esp. p. 170.

925   Gutiérrez-Larraya, J.A. "Isaías, Ascensión de," *Enciclo-
      pedia de la Biblia* 4. Cols. 241-43.

926   Hammershaimb, E. "Esajas' Martyrium," *GamPseud* 3 (1958)
      303-15.

927   Hammershaimb, E. "Das Martyrium Jesajas," *JSHRZ* 2 (1973)
      15-34.

928   Helmbold, A.K. "Ascension of Isaiah," *ZPEB* 1. Pp. 348-50.

929   Helmbold, A.K. "Gnostic Elements in the 'Ascension of
      Isaiah,'" *NTS* 18 (1972) 222-27.

930   Heussi, K. "Die Ascensio Isaiae und ihr vermeintliches
      Zeugnis für ein römisches Martyrium des Apostels
      Petrus," *WZJena* 12 (1963) 269-74.

931   Kalokyrēs, K.D. "The Ascension of Isaiah," *ThĒE* 6. Cols.
      76f. [in Greek]

932   Katz, E. "Das Martyrium Isaias," *Communio Viatorum* 11
      (1968) 169-74. [*N.V.*]

933   Knibb, M.A. "Martyrdom and Ascension of Isaiah," Doubleday
      edition.

934   Meslin, M. "L'Ascension d'Isaïe," *Les ariens d'occident
      335-430* (Patristica Sorbonensia 8) Paris: Seuil, 1967.
      Pp. 242f.

934a Meyer, R. "Himmelfahrt und Martyrium des Jesaja," *RGG*[3] 3.
      Cols. 336f.

935   Moraldi, L. "Recenti scoperte archeologiche e letterarie
      in Palestina," *RevistB* 20 (1972) 187-202.

936   Noack, B. "Esajas' Himmelfart, Esajas' Martyrium," *GDBL* 1.
      Cols. 450f.

937   Philonenko, M. "Le Martyre d'Esaïe et l'histoire de la
      secte de Qoumrân," *Pseudépigraphes*, ed. M. Philonenko.
      Pp. 1-10.

938   Reicke, B. "Jesajas Martyrium und Himmelfahrt," *BHH* 2.
      Col. 857.

939   Rist, M. "Isaiah, Ascension of," *IDB* 2. Pp. 744-46.

940 Sánchez, J.M.C. "San José en los libros apócrifos del
     Nuevo Testamento," *Cahiers de Joséphologie* 19 (1971)
     123-49.

941 Stead, C. "The Origins of the Doctrine of the Trinity, 1,"
     Theology 77 (1974) 508-17. [Discusses AncenIs.]

942 Stone, M.E. "Isaiah, Martyrdom of," *EncyJud* 9. Pp. 71f.

943 Vaillant, A. "Un apocryphe pseudo-bogomile: La Vision
     d'Isaïe," *RESl* 42 (1963) 109-21.

Martyrdom of Isaiah

See the discussion and the publications listed under the
Ascension of Isaiah.

Ladder of Jacob

This writing is preserved in two recensions in Old Church
Slavonic which were edited by N.S. Tikhonravov (*Pamĭatniki
otrechennoĭ russkoĭ literatury*. St. Petersburg, 1863. Vol. 1,
pp. 91-95) and I. Porfirijev (*Apokrificheskiĭa skazaniĭa o
vetkhozavĭetnykh litsakh*. St. Petersburg, 1877. Pp. 138-49).
An English translation has been published by M.R. James (*LAOT*.
Pp. 96-103), but James' translation was incomplete and apparently taken from the German translation by N. Bonwetsch ("Die
apokryphe 'Leiter Jakobs,'" *Göttinger Nachrichten, philol.-
histor. Klasse* [1900] 77-85).

The date, provenance, and original language of this work
have not been researched. The Jewish character and similarities to the Apocalypse of Abraham, the Odes of Solomon, the
Gospel of Thomas, and the Epistle of Barnabas raise the possibility that it is not a medieval composition by Slavs but
rather a pseudepigraphon from the second century A.D. Moreover, chapters four and five may refer respectively to the
destruction of Jerusalem and the persecution under Domitian.
A Palestinian provenance might be reflected in the emphasis
upon the land (chp. 1) and the choice of a base text (esp.
Gen 28:13-15). It is improbable (see James, *LAOT*, pp. 102f.;
contrast A. Vassiliev, *Anecdota Graeco-Byzantina*. Moscow: Uni-
versitatis Caesareae, 1893. Vol. 1, pp. xxixf.; and H. Weinel
in Gunkel Festschrift, pp. 172f.) that the Ladder of Jacob is
identical with the Ascents of Jacob (*anabathmoi Jakōbou*)

which Epiphanius (*Haer*. 30.16) reported was used by the Ebionites. H. Weinel argued that the work is a combination of Jewish, gnostic, and Christian traditions (p. 173).

A haggadic midrash with an apocalyptic emphasis based on Genesis 28:10-17, this pseudepigraphon describes Jacob's vision of the ladder that extended into heaven. Eight small chapters are preserved, but the latter two are Christian additions that are not found in the oldest manuscript.

R. Rubinkiewicz has discovered some unexamined manuscripts of the Ladder of Jacob. The texts are similar to those published by Tikhonravov.

See works cited under Joseph and Asenath [and Joseph Cycle], especially the "Prayer of Jacob." See also nos. 70, 75.

944 Pennington, A. "Ladder of Jacob," Clarendon edition.

945 Rubinkiewicz, R. "Ladder of Jacob," Doubleday edition.

Testament of Jacob
(The Testaments of Abraham, Isaac and Jacob are
called sometimes the Testaments of the Three
Patriarchs; cf. Apostolicae Constitutiones *6.16)*

This composition is extant in Ethiopic, Arabic, and Bohairic Coptic; the latter is the most important version and was edited by I. Guidi ("Il Testamento di Isacco e il Testamento di Giaccobo," *Rendiconti della Reale Accademia dei Lincei, Classe di scienze morali, storiche e filologiche.* Ser. 5, vol. 9 [1900] 157-80, 223-64). S. Gaselee (in G.H. Box, *The Testament of Abraham* [TED] London: S.P.C.K., 1927; pp. 76-89) translated the Coptic into English. W.E. Barnes (in M.R. James, *The Testament of Abraham* [T&S 2] Cambridge: CUP, 1892; pp. 152-54) rendered selections from the Arabic into English.

The work is later than the Testament of Isaac, and is a series of excerpts from Genesis 47:29-50:26, with expansions that intermittently reflect influence from the Testament of Isaac, and with a Christian ending (ff. 187a-189b).

M.E. Stone (nos. 951 and 952) has discovered in Armenian MS 939 of the Armenian Convent of St. James in Jerusalem a text, which precedes the Testaments of the Twelve Patriarchs, entitled *Ktakkʿ Yakobay nahapetin*, "The Testament of the

Patriarch Jacob." This text should be distinguished from the apocryphal Testament of Jacob; it is not apocryphal but contains the last chapters of Genesis, beginning with the end of chapter 47. This excerpt from the Old Testament is similar to three other works: an extract from Genesis 49 called the "Testament of Jacob" in a Greek manuscript (Coislin 296) in Paris, noted earlier by M.R. James (*The Testament of Abraham*, p. 1507; *LAOT*, p. 18); the "Testament of Jacob," which is in modern Greek and contains Genesis 47:29-49:27, and precedes the Testaments of the Twelve Patriarchs in MS Gr. 580 (341) in the Academy Library in Bucharest; and the "Blessing of Jacob" (*Eulogia Jakōb*), which is Genesis 48:8-50:26 and follows the Testaments of the Twelve Patriarchs, in MS 39, Koutloumous, on Mt. Athos (see Stone, no. 952).

The Coptic text of the Testament of Jacob is shorter than the Testament of Isaac and appears to be a midrashic expansion of Genesis 47:29-50:26. The Lord sends Michael the archangel to Jacob in order to instruct him to prepare his testament for his sons. Jacob accepts God's will, in contrast to the Testament of Abraham, and prays. The angel returns to heaven; Jacob calls his sons, and then ascends to heaven and meets a multitude of tormentors. Jacob ascends higher and sees Abraham and Isaac, who are full of life and joy, and the good things prepared for the righteous.

Beginning with folio 184b a second tradition repeats the preceding account. Jacob is with his sons, when the Lord, Michael and Gabriel come from heaven and receive his soul. Jacob's life is summarized and it is declared that he was "perfect in every virtue and spiritual grace." Joseph kisses his father and embalms the body "after the manner of the Egyptians." Joseph and a train of attendants take Jacob's body to Mamre for burial, and mourn seven days. The testament concludes with exhortations and a few Christian passages.

A copy of Vatican Syr. 199, ff. 21v-45v, which contains the Testaments of Abraham, Isaac, and Jacob, is preserved in the Pseudepigrapha Library at Duke University.

See some of the publications listed under the Testament of Abraham. See also no. 507.

946 Gaguine, M. *The Falasha Version of the Testaments of Abraham, Isaac and Jacob.* Manchester, Eng., Ph.D., 1965.

947 Hofius, O. "Das Zitat 1 Kor 2:9 und das koptische Testament des Jakob," *ZNW* 66 (1975) 140-42.

948 Kuhn, K.H. "Testament of Jacob," Clarendon edition.

949 Stinespring, W.F. "Testament of Jacob," Doubleday edition.

950 Stone, M.E. "Jacob, Testament of," *EncyJud* 9. Col. 1213.

951 Stone, M.E. "The Testament of Jacob," *Revue des études arméniennes* n.s. 5 (1968) 261-70.

952 Stone, M.E. "Two Additional Notes on the Testament of Jacob," *Revue des études arméniennes* n.s. 6 (1969) 103f.

Jannes and Jambres
(Jannes and Mambres)

This apocryphal composition is lost except for fragments in Greek, recently discovered (see below), and in Latin, which were edited by M. Förster ("Das lateinisch-altenglische Fragment der Apokryphe von Jamnes und Mambres," *Archiv für das Studium der neueren Sprachen und Litteraturen* 108 [1902] 15-28) and translated into English by M.R. James (*LAOT*. pp. 32f.).

The *Decretum Gelasianum* in the sixth century condemns an apocryphal book entitled the Penitence of Jamnes and Mambres (*liber qui appellatur Poenitentia Ianne et Mambre apocryphus*). This apocryphon is as early as the first century A.D., because the author of 2 Timothy 3:8 refers to it, and appears to be much older, because it--or at least the legend naming Jannes and Jambres--is mentioned in the Damascus Document (5:17f.). K. Koch (no. 957) argued for a pre-Maccabean date for the work, but C. Burchard (no. 954) rejected Koch's thesis.

Many early writers--pagan, Christian (esp. Origen, *Comm. Mt.* 23:37, 27:9), and Jewish (see L. Ginzberg, *Legends*, esp. vol. 2, pp. 283-89, 331-36; vol. 3, pp. 28f.; Strack-Billerbeck, *Kommentar*, vol. 3, pp. 660-64)--mention Jannes and Jambres (see A.-M. Denis, no. 24, pp. 146-49). M. McNamara argues that the author of 2 Timothy is dependent on the passage concerning Jannes and Jambres in the Targum of Pseudo-Jonathan (no. 959).

Jannes and Jambres are the names eventually given to the anonymous Egyptian magicians who compete against Moses and

Aaron (cf. Ex 7). In the Latin fragment "Mambres," using correctly his brother Jannes' books, brings back the shade
(*indolum*) of his departed brother. The soul (*anima*) of Jannes
tells him that his death and judgment are just, and that hell
is full of sadness and darkness.

H. Chadwick is working on fragmentary Greek texts from
the Rainer collection. A. Pietersma and T. Lutz are collabo-
rating on an edition of the Chester Beatty Greek fragments (see
no. 962). See also nos. 23, 442.

953   Arrabal, M.V. "Yannés y Yambrés," *Enciclopedia de la
      Biblia* 6. Col. 1306.

954   Burchard, C. "Das Lamm in der Waagschale," *ZNW* 57 (1966)
      219-28.

955   Colpe, C. "Jannes und Jambres," *BHH* 2. Col. 802.

956   Denis, A.-M. "Les fragments du Livre de la Pénitence des
      Jannès et Mambré," *Introduction*. Pp. 146-49.

957   Koch, K. "Das Lamm, das Ägypten vernichet, ein Fragment
      aus Jannes und Jambres und sein geschichtlicher Hinter-
      grund," *ZNW* 57-58 (1966) 79-93.

958   Lohse, E. "Jannes und Jambres," *RGG*[3] 3. Col. 530.

959   NcNamara, M. "Traditions Relating to Moses, Jannes and
      Jambres, in the Palestinian Targum and in St Paul,"
      *The New Testament and the Palestinian Targum to the
      Pentateuch*. Rome: Pontifical Biblical Institute, 1966.
      Pp. 70-96.

960   Mare, W.H. "Jannes and Jambres," *ZPEB* 3. Pp. 403f.

961   [Oikonomidēs, D.B.] "Jannes," *ThEE* 6. Col. 660. [in Greek]

962   Pietersma, A. "Greek and Coptic Inedita of the Chester
      Beatty Library," *BIOSCS* 7 (1974) 10-18. See esp. pp.
      15-17.

963   Salomonsen, B. "Jannes og Jambres," *GDBL* 1. Col. 909.

964   Schmid, J. "Jannes u. Jambres," *LTK*[2] 5. Col. 865.

965   Stern, M. "Jannes and Jambres," *EncyJud* 9. Col. 1277.

966   Wikgren, A. "Jannes and Jambres," *IDB* 2. Pp. 800f.

Testament of Job

The most important version of the Testament of Job is the
Greek, which has been re-edited recently by S.P. Brock (no.
968) and R.A. Kraft, *et al*. (no. 977). English translations

have been published by K. Kohler ("The Testament of Job: An Essene Midrash on the Book of Job: Reëdited and Translated with Introductory and Exegetical Notes," *Semitic Studies in Memory of Rev. Dr. Alexander Kohut*, ed. G.A. Kohut. Berlin: Calvary, 1897. Pp. 314-38) and R.A. Kraft, *et al.* (no. 977).

Some scholars date the work to the first century B.C. (C. C. Torrey, *Apoc. Lit.*, p. 145; R.H. Pfeiffer, *IB* 1 [1952] 425); M. Delcor (no. 971) thinks that 17:12-18 is a clear allusion to the Parthian invasion into Palestine around 40 B.C. M. Philonenko (no. 980), however, concludes that this pseudepigraphon comes from the first century A.D., perhaps from the Therapeutae in Egypt. H.C. Kee (no. 976) also dates the composition to the first century A.D., but argues that it is clearly related to Merkabah mysticism.

The original language may be Semitic, perhaps Aramaic (Torrey, *Apoc. Lit.*, p. 143; Pfeiffer, *IB* 1 [1952] 425). Delcor (no. 971), Philonenko (no. 980; similarly J.B. Frey in *DBSup* 1, col. 455), and Kee (no. 976), however, think the work was composed in Greek. Chapter 43, the hymn of Eliphaz, may be an exception, having been translated from Hebrew.

The Greek text of the Testament of Job, which contains 53 chapters, is a midrash in the form of a testament on the canonical book (see J.J. Collins, no. 969). Job not only freely gives to the poor and needy in his own city but also sends caravans to other regions. He destroys idols, causing Satan, with God's permission, to test him with afflictions. Job suffers; his wife, Sitidos, provides for him by means of hard labor, finally being forced to cut her hair to buy three loaves for herself and her husband. Before she dies near a manger, she sees her children wearing crowns in heaven. Job, restored physically, becomes wealthy, marries Dinah, and has seven sons and three daughters. He dies, his spirit goes to heaven in a chariot, and his body is taken to the grave.

M. Weber is in charge of editing the Cologne Coptic Manuscript of the Testament of Job.

See also nos. 4, 1492.

967 [Bontöf, B.] "Job (Testament of)," *ThEE* 7. Col. 87. [in Greek]

968 Brock, S.P., ed. *Testamentum Iobi* (PVTG 2) Leiden: Brill, 1967. Pp. 1-59.

969 Collins, J.J. "Structure and Meaning in the Testament of Job," *SBL 1974 Seminar Papers*. Vol. 1, pp. 35-52.

970 Datz, G. *Die Gestalt Hiobs in der kirchlichen Exegese und der "Arme Heinrich" Hartmanns von Aue* (Göppinger Arbeiten zur Germanistik 108) Göppingen: Alfred Kümmerle, 1973. See esp. pp. 34-39.

971 Delcor, M. "Le Testament de Job, la Prière de Nabonide et les traditions targoumiques," *Bibel und Qumran*. H. Bardtke Festschrift, ed. S. Wagner. Berlin: Evangelische Haupt-Bibelgesellschaft, 1968. Pp. 57-74.

972 Denis, A.-M. "Le Testament de Job," *Introduction*. Pp. 100-04.

973 Glatzer, N.N. "Rereading a Biblical Work," *Judaic Tradition*. Pp. 100-14.

974 Gutiérrez-Larraya, J.A. "Job, Testamento de," *Enciclopedia de la Biblia* 4. Col. 577.

975 Jacobs, I. "Literary Motifs in the *Testament of Job*," *JJS* 21 (1970) 1-10.

976 Kee, H.C. "Satan, Magic, and Salvation in the Testament of Job," *SBL 1974 Seminar Papers*. Vol. 1, pp. 53-76.

977 Kraft, R.A., *et al.*, eds. *The Testament of Job* (T&T 5, Pseudepigrapha Series 4) Missoula, Mont.: SBL, 1974.

978 Meyer, R. "Hiobtestament," *RGG³* 3. Col. 361.

979 Philonenko, M. "Hiobs Testament," *BHH* 2. Cols. 726f.

980 Philonenko, M. *Le Testament de Job: Introduction, traduction et notes* (*Sem* 18) Paris: Adrien-Maisonneuve, 1968.

981 Rahnenführer, D. *Das Testament des Hiob in seinem Verhältnis zum Neuen Testament*. Halle Dissertation, 1967.

982 Rahnenführer, D. "Das Testament des Hiob und das Neue Testament," *ZNW* 62 (1971) 68-93.

983 Schaller, B. "Testament Hiobs," *JSHRZ* 3, in press.

984 Spittler, R.P. *The Testament of Job: Introduction, Translation, and Notes*. Harvard Ph.D., 1971.

984a Spittler, R.P. "Testament of Job," Doubleday edition.

985 Thanhill, R. "Testament of Job," Clarendon edition.

986 Wacholder, B.Z. "Job, Testament of," *EncyJud* 10. Cols. 129f.

Joseph and Asenath [and Joseph Cycle]
(Book of the Prayer of Asenath, Life and
Confession of Asenath, History of Assaneth)

This work is preserved in numerous languages, of which the most important is Greek. The text was re-edited recently by M. Philonenko (no. 1003) and translated earlier into English by E.W. Brooks (*Joseph and Asenath* [TED] London: S.P.C.K., 1918). An English translation of the Armenian version was published by J. Issaverdens (*UWOT*. Pp. 67-107).

That Joseph and Asenath is a fifth-century Christian work, based upon a Jewish writing, is a dated conclusion (P. Batiffol, *Le Livre de la Prière d'Asénath* [Studia Patristica 1-2] Paris: Leroux, 1889-1890). That it is an early, perhaps late first-century A.D., Jewish composition is a contemporary perspective (cf. C. Burchard, *Untersuchungen zu Joseph und Aseneth* [WUNT 8] Tübingen: Mohr, 1965; see esp. pp. 148-51; Philonenko, no. 1003; A.-M. Denis, no. 24, pp. 40-48). Most scholars now contend that the original language is Greek (Burchard, *Untersuch.*, pp. 91-99; Philonenko, no. 1003, pp. 27-32). The parallels with the Dead Sea Scrolls have raised the possibility of influence from the Essenes, or more probably from the Therapeutae; some scholars affirm a relationship (P. Riessler, no. 62, p. 1303; K.G. Kuhn in *The Scrolls and the New Testament*, ed. K. Stendhal. New York: Harper, 1957; pp. 75f.; M. Delcor, "Un roman d'amour d'origine thérapeute: le livre de Joseph et Asénath," *BLE* 63 [1962] 3-27); others deny it (Philonenko, no. 1003, p. 105; Burchard, *Untersuch.*, pp. 107-12).

This haggadic midrash on Genesis 41:45 consists of twenty-nine chapters that contain *inter alia* polemics against retribution for wrongdoers and idol worshippers, and propaganda for the Jewish religion. It centers upon the romance between Joseph and Asenath. Joseph, on a trip to gather corn during the time of plenty, is received by Pentephres, priest of Heliopolis. Pentephres' daughter, Asenath, refuses her father's offer to marry Joseph, because he is a lowly son of a shepherd and has slept with another (chps. 1-5). When Asenath sees Joseph, however, she repents of her earlier judgment, because of Joseph's beauty as "the son of God" (*ho huios tou theou*); but he refuses her because she does not acknowledge the God of the Hebrews, but is a worshipper of idols (chps. 6-8).

Joseph leaves; Asenath does penitence, breaks her idols, and prays to God for forgiveness for her sins, asking to become Joseph's handmaid. An angel comes to her and announces that she has been forgiven and been given to Joseph in marriage (chps. 9-17).

Asenath prepares for the return of Joseph, who now kisses her and plans to ask Pharaoh for her hand in marriage. The wedding feast lasts seven days; the marriage is consummated and Asenath gives birth to Manasses and Ephraim (chps. 18-21). The couple visits Jacob; but the firstborn son of Pharaoh, who sees them on their journey, plots the death of Joseph, so that he can marry Asenath. He fails to elicit the aid of Levi and Simeon; but by lying he persuades Dan and Gad to kill Joseph, while he will slay his own father. The conspiracy fails. Asenath forgives Dan and Gad, and Levi dissuades Benjamin from giving Pharaoh's son the *coup de grâce*; but the latter dies three days later from the stone Benjamin had hurled (chps. 22-29).

Joseph's life was so colorful and important that many legends circulated about him, and some of these must have been collected into apocryphal compositions that are now lost. Besides the pseudepigrapha discussed herein--Joseph and Asenath, the Prayer of Joseph, and the Testament of Joseph--some writings about Joseph are particularly interesting and worth noting.

Preserved in Greek on two papyrus fragments from the sixth or seventh century is a Jewish midrash on Genesis 42-47, which has been called a "History of Joseph" (H.J.M. Milne, *Catalogue of the Literary Papyri in the British Museum*. London: British Museum, 1927; pp. 187-90). Preserved in Arabic are two interesting works: a "History of Joseph, the Son of Jacob" (G. Graf, *Geschichte*, vol. 1, pp. 205f.); and a poem on Joseph and his brothers (R.Y. Ebied and M.J.L. Young, no. 994a). The Syriac composition falsely attributed to Ephrem entitled ʿ*al ywsp k'n*ʾ, James of Sarough's "History of Joseph," and "Banni's" poem on Joseph may preserve ancient legends and portions of apocryphal works. G. Oppenheim (*Fabula Josephi et Asenethae Apocrypha e Libro Syriaco Latine Vertit*. Berlin: [?], 1886; cf. Denis, no. 24, pp. 43, 48; Burchard, *Untersuch.*, p. 96, n. 6) noted some Syriac manuscripts in the collection of E. Sachau that concern

Joseph. One of these is similar to an Armenian tale which mentions that Dinah's daughter, Asenath, was transported to Egypt by an eagle (see Issaverdens, *UWOT*, pp. 64-66; Burchard, *Untersuch.*, p. 96). Origen mentions an apocryphon that describes Joseph's life in Egypt (*In Genesim* 41.45, 46; PG 12, col. 136). L. Ginzberg gathered together the rabbinic legends about Joseph (*Legends*, vol. 2, pp. 1-184).

Especially important for the Prayer of Joseph (see below) is the so-called "Prayer of Jacob," which seems Jewish and early, and which E.R. Goodenough translated from K. Preisendanz's edition (*Papyri Graecae Magicae: Die griechischen Zauberpapyri*. Leipzig-Berlin: Teubner, 1931. Vol. 2, pp. 148f.), suggesting it was a product of hellenized Judaism (*Jewish Symbols* 2 [1953] 203f.). The perennial religious stimulus evoked by Joseph is placarded by J. MacGowan's *The Life of Joseph, the Son of Israel: Chiefly Designed to Allure Young Minds to a Love of the Sacred Scriptures* (Halifax: W. Milner, 1840).

Dr. G. Vikan is completing an extensive study of the pictorial additions to the texts concerning the Life of Joseph and the Romance of Joseph and Asenath. These pictures represent 110 scenes and are extant in three post-Byzantine manuscripts. Ebied and Young are preparing a critical edition with English translation of the Arabic manuscript described above. Dr. E.W. Smith, Jr., has just completed a Ph.D. dissertation, under the direction of H.D. Betz, entitled *"Joseph and Asenath" and Early Christian Literature: A Contribution to the Corpus Hellenisticum Novi Testamenti*. C. Burchard is preparing a new Greek edition of Joseph and Asenath for the PVTG series.

Consult the entries under Prayer of Joseph and Testament of Joseph. See also nos. 752, 1484.

987 Burchard, C. "Joseph and Asenath," Doubleday edition.

988 Burchard, C. "Joseph et Asénath: questions actuelles," *La littérature juive entre Tenach et Mishna*, ed. W.C. van Unnik (RechBib 9) Leiden: Brill, 1974. Pp. 77-100.

989 Burchard, C. "Joseph und Asenath," *JSHRZ* 2, in press.

990 Burchard, C. "Zum Text von 'Joseph und Asenath,'" *JSJ* 1 (1970) 3-34.

991 Cook, D. "Joseph and Asenath," Clarendon edition.

992 Delcor, M. "José y Asénet, Historia de," *Enciclopedia de la Biblia* 4. Col. 638.

993 Denis, A.-M. "Le Livre de la Prière d'Asénath," *Introduction*. Pp. 40-48.

994 Dwyer, R.A. "Asenath of Egypt in Middle English," *Medium Aevum* 39 (1970) 118-22.

994a Ebied, R.Y. and M.J.L. Young. "An Unknown Arabic Poem on Joseph and His Brethren," *JRAS* 1 (1974) 2-7.

995 Glatzer, N.N. "I Take Refuge," *Judaic Tradition*. Pp. 135f.

996 Gutman, Y. "Joseph Legends in the Vienna Genesis," *Proceedings of the Fifth World Congress of Jewish Studies*, ed. A. Shinan. Jerusalem: World Union of Jewish Studies, 1973. Vol. 4, pp. 181-84.

997 Holtz, T. "Christliche Interpolationen in 'Joseph und Aseneth,'" *NTS* 14 (1968) 482-97.

998 Levin, M.D. "Some Jewish Sources for the Vienna Genesis," *Art Bulletin* 54 (1972) 241-44.

999 Lohse, E. "Joseph und Aseneth," *RGG*^{3} 3. Col. 864.

1000 Mpratsiōtēs, P.I. "Aseneth," *ThĒE* 3. Col. 360. [in Greek]

1001 Noack, B. "Josef og Asenat," *GDBL* 1. Col. 1021.

1002 Philonenko, M. "Joseph and Asenath," *EncyJud* 10. Col. 223f.

1003 Philonenko, M. *Joseph et Asénath: Introduction, texte critique, traduction et notes* (SPB 13) Leiden: Brill, 1968.

1004 Philonenko, M. "Joseph et Asénath: questions actuelles," *La littérature juive entre Tenach et Mishna*, ed. W.C. van Unnik (RechBib 9) Leiden: Brill, 1974. [*N.V.*]

1005 Philonenko, M. "Joseph und Asenath," *BHH* 2. Cols. 889f.

1006 Pines, S. "From Darkness into Great Light," *Immanuel* 4 (1974) 47-51.

1006a Smith, E.W. Jr. "Joseph Material in Joseph and Asenath and Josephus Relating to the Testament of Joseph," *SCS* 5. Pp. 133-37.

1007 West, S. "*Joseph and Asenath*: A Neglected Greek Romance," *Classical Quarterly* 24 (1974) 70-81.

Prayer of Joseph

This pseudepigraphon, which is noted in the lists by Pseudo-Athanasius, Mechithar of Arivank, Nicephorus, and in

the list of "Sixty Canonical Books," is lost. It is quoted by
Origen (frag. 1: *Comm. in Joh.* 2.31, 25; frag. 2: *Comm. in Gen.*
3.9, *Philoc.* 23.15; cf. Eusebius, *Pr. ev.* 6.11, 64). These
Greek excerpts are assembled conveniently by A.-M. Denis (no.
23, pp. 61f.). The first fragment was translated into English
by A. Menzies (*ANF* 10. P. 341; cf. L. Ginzberg, *Legends*, vol.
5, p. 273; R.M. Grant, *Gnosticism and Early Christianity*, 2d.
ed. New York, London: Columbia, 1966; pp. 18f.); both were
translated by M.R. James (*LAOT*. Pp. 22f.), and are now translated and discussed by J.Z. Smith (no. 1012).

It is difficult to date the original composition because
of the paucity of the preserved fragments, a mere sixteen lines
out of an original 1100, according to Nicephorus; and because
of the ambiguous character of the extant data. Attempts to explain the thought have produced an amazing number of mutually
exclusive hypotheses; for example, some scholars conclude that
it is Jewish-Christian (viz., A. Resch, *Agrapha* [1906]; pp.
295-97; J. Daniélou, *The Theology of Jewish Christianity*,
trans. J.A. Baker. London: Darton, Longman & Todd, 1964; p. 16;
contrast Daniélou's comments in *The First Six Hundred Years*,
trans. V. Cronin [The Christian Centuries 1] London: Darton,
Longman & Todd; New York: McGraw-Hill, 1964; p. 76); others
claim it is Jewish (viz., E. Schürer, *History*, 2d. Div., vol.
3, pp. 127f.; Grant, *Gnosticism and Early Christianity*, 2d.
ed., pp. 18f.; E. Schweizer, "Die Kirche als Leib Christi,"
TLZ 86 [1961] col. 167; J.Z. Smith, no. 1012, pp. 259, 271,
291). One scholar even claimed to detect an anti-Jewish character (V. Burch, "The Literary Unity of the *Ascensio Isaiae*,"
JTS 20 [1919] 17-23, esp. pp. 20f.), but this hypothesis is
highly improbable because, among other reasons, Origen called
it one "of the apocrypha popular among the Hebrews" (*tōn par
Hebraiois pheromenōn apokruphōn*). Numerous scholars have expressed the opinion that the pseudepigraphon is an anti-Christ-
ian Jewish writing (viz., J.T. Marshall, "Joseph, Prayer of,"
Dictionary of the Bible, ed. J.R. Hastings. New York: Scribner,
1899. Vol. 2, col. 778b; R.H. Charles, *The Ascension of Isaiah.*
London: Black, 1900; p. 39; James, *LAOT*, pp. 30f.; D.S.
Russell, *The Method and Message of Jewish Apocalyptic*. Philadelphia: Westminster, 1964; p. 67), but this hypothesis is
unlikely if we take literally Origen's comment that it is a

142

respectable writing (*ouk eukataphronēton graphēn*). Smith (no. 1012) may be correct in suggesting that the Prayer of Joseph is a first or second century A.D. product of mystical hellenistic Judaism.

The original may have taken the literary form of a testament by Jacob to his sons, and of a midrash on Genesis 32: 24-31. Jacob identifies himself as "Israel, an angel of God (*angelos theou*) and a ruling spirit...the firstborn (*prōtogonos*) of every living thing." Uriel, who informed him he had "descended to earth," wrestles with him, desiring to have his own name above Jacob's. Jacob clarifies that Uriel is "the eighth after me" (*ogdoos emou*), and that he is "the archangel of the power of the Lord and the chief captain among the sons of God" (*archangelos dunameōs kuriou kai archichiliarchos eimi en huiois theou*).

See the works listed above under Joseph and Asenath [and Joseph Cycle]. See also no. 303.

1008 Denis, A.-M. "Les fragments de la Prière de Joseph," *Introduction*. Pp. 125-27.

1009 Nock, A.D. "'Son of God' in Pauline and Hellenistic Thought," *Essays on Religion and the Ancient World*, ed. Z. Stewart. Oxford: Clarendon, 1972. Vol. 2, pp. 928-39.

1010 Schultz, A.C. "Joseph, Prayer of," *ZPEB* 3. P. 696.

1011 Smith, J.Z. "Prayer of Joseph," Doubleday edition.

1012 Smith, J.Z. "The Prayer of Joseph," Goodenough Festschrift. Pp. 253-94.

1013 Turner, N. "Joseph, Prayer of," *IDB* 2. P. 979.

Testament of Joseph

Preserved now within the Testaments of the Twelve Patriarchs is a Testament of Joseph, which itself contains two narratives (1:1-10:4, 10:5-20:6). There are good reasons to think that the second of these is earlier and may have been a stimulus for the composition of the other testaments attributed to the sons of Jacob.

See the publications listed under the Testaments of the Twelve Patriarchs, especially the SBL seminar papers edited by G.W.E. Nickelsburg, Jr. (no. 1443a). The two-day discussions

in this seminar are recorded by J.H. Charlesworth in Pseudepigrapha Newsletter 8.

Jubilees
(Little Genesis, Leptē Genesis, Book of the Division)

Jubilees is preserved in numerous languages (for the Greek
see A.-M. Denis, no. 23, pp. 70-102). It is, however, extant
in full only in Ethiopic, which was edited from four manuscripts by R.H. Charles (*The Ethiopic Version of the Hebrew
Book of Jubilees*. Oxford: Clarendon, 1895), and translated by
him into English (*APOT* 2. Pp. 1-82; repr. *The Book of Jubilees,
or The Little Genesis*, intr. G.H. Box [TED] London: S.P.C.K.,
1927).

Jubilees is one of the most important pseudepigrapha, and
dates from the second century B.C. The discovery of fragments
from about ten Hebrew manuscripts among the so-called Dead Sea
Scrolls has strengthened the probability that the original
language is Hebrew. Parallels with some thoughts in the Dead
Sea Scrolls indicate that Jubilees represents the type of
Judaism out of which Essenism evolved.

Jubilees contains 50 chapters and claims to be a revelation to Moses by the Angel of the Presence (1:29-2:1). This
midrash on Genesis 1:1 through Exodus 12:50 depicts the episodes from creation with the celebration of the Sabbath by the
angels to the Exodus from Egypt with the strict observance of
the Sabbath, as written in the heavenly tablets, by the children of Israel. As the biblical account is rewritten the author
takes considerable liberty with the text: supplying names for
persons and places, explaining problems within the text, and
whitewashing some acts (viz., Rebecca is commanded by Abraham,
who saw Esau's deeds and knew Jacob was the true heir, to love
and cherish Jacob more than Esau [19:16-31]). The patriarchs
are perceived as the innovators of culture; writing, medicine,
and plowing originated respectively with Enoch, Noah, and
Abraham. There is a clear polemic against the lunar calendar
(6:36-38), and a possible polemic against the idea that an
angel protects Israel, since angels rule other nations but God
Himself guides Israel (15:31f.; contrast 1QS 3:13ff.). The
emphasis of the writing is upon the exclusiveness of the Jews

(no intermarriage, no eating with the Gentiles, and a special
heavenly calendar), and upon the blessed joy of the Law.

Two additional Ethiopic manuscripts on parchment have been
found in Ethiopia, each of which is now photographed and recorded in the Monastic Manuscript Microfilm Library at Saint
John's University. EMML Pr. No. 101 is of the eighteenth century; EMML Pr. No. 207 is dated A.D. 1919-1920 according to
the colophon on folio 179b. See W.F. Macomber, *A Catalogue of
Ethiopian Manuscripts Microfilmed for the Ethiopian Manuscript
Library, Addis Ababa, and for the Monastic Manuscript Microfilm
Library, Collegeville* (Vol. 1: *Project Numbers 1-300*. Collegeville, Minn.: MMML, 1975; see esp. pp. 106 and 218).

W. Baars and R. Zuurmond are preparing a new edition of
the Ethiopic (cf. *JSS* 9 [1964] 67-74). Copies of the following
Ethiopic manuscripts are preserved in the Pseudepigrapha
Library at Duke University: Bibliothèque Nationale Eth. ancien
fonds 51, ff. 1-110; Bibliothèque Nationale Eth. 117, ff. 128r-
161r; British Museum Or. 485, ff. 1-190.

Consult the publications listed under the Pseudepigrapha
and the Dead Sea Scrolls. See also nos. 4, 23, 51, 82, 87,
108, 115, 234, 297, 299, 309, 315, 320, 330, 429f., 432, 445,
448f., 465, 471, 477, 1295, 1427, 1480.

1014   Agourides, S. "The Book of Jubilees," *Theologia* 43 (1972)
        550-83. [in Greek]

1015   Baillet, M. "Livre des Jubilés (i) (Pl. XV)," *DJD* 3. Pp.
        77f. [2QJub^a = Jub 23:7-8 (cf. Gen 25:9, 7-8)]

1016   Baillet, M. "Livre des Jubilés (ii) (Pl. XV)," *DJD* 3. Pp.
        78f. [2QJub^b = Jub 46:1-3 (cf. Ex 1:7 and Gen 50:26,
        22 plus fragments of uncertain relation)]

1017   Baillet, M. "Remarques sur le manuscrit du livre des
        Jubilés de la grotte 3 de Qumrân," *RQ* 5 (1965) 423-33.

1018   Baumgarten, J.M. "The Calendar of the Book of Jubilees
        and the Bible," *Tarbiz* 32 (1963) 317-28. [in Hebrew]

1019   Berger, [K.] "Buch der Jubiläen," *JSHRZ* 2, in press.

1020   Caquot, A. "Les enfants aux cheveux blancs (Remarques sur
        Jubilés 23, 25)," *RHR* 177 (1970) 131f.

1021   Cazelles, H. "Sur les origines du calendrier des Ju-
        bilés," *Bib* 43 (1962) 202-12.

1022　[Chrēstou, P.K.] "Jubilees," *ThĒĒ* 7. Cols. 91-93. [in Greek]

1023　Cothenet, E. "Jubilés (Le livre des)," *Catholicisme* 6 (1965) 1123-28.

1024　Davenport, G.L. *The Eschatology of the Book of Jubilees* (SPB 20) Leiden: Brill, 1971.

1025　Deichgräber, R. "Fragmente einer Jubiläen-Handschrift aus Höhle 3 von Qumran," *RQ* 5 (1965) 415-22. [3QJub. See Rofé below, no. 1050.]

1026　Delcor, M. "Jubileos, Libro de los," *Enciclopedia de la Biblia* 4. Cols. 711f.

1027　Denis, A.-M. *Concordance Latine du Liber Jubilaeorum sive Parva Genesis* (Informatique et étude de textes, collection dirigée par Paul Tombeur 4) Louvain: CETEDOC, 1973.

1028　Denis, A.-M. "Les fragments grecs du livre des Jubilés," *Introduction.* Pp. 150-62.

1029　Ellis, E.E. "Midrash, Targum and New Testament Quotations," *Neotestamentica et Semitica: Studies in Honour of Matthew Black,* eds. E.E. Ellis and M. Wilcox. Edinburgh: T.&T. Clark, 1969. Pp. 61-69.

1030　Goodenough, E.R. "The Contents of Jewish Tombs in Palestine," *Jewish Symbols* 1 (1953) 103-77. See esp. p. 107.

1031　Goodenough, E.R. "The Lulab and Ethrog," *Jewish Symbols* 4 (1954) 145-66. See esp. pp. 149, 157.

1032　Goodenough, E.R. "The Relevance of Rabbinic Evidence," *Jewish Symbols* 4 (1954) 3-24. See esp. p. 12.

1033　Goodenough, E.R. "The Shofar," *Jewish Symbols* 4 (1954) 167-94. See esp. pp. 175-77.

1034　Goodenough, E.R. "Victory and Her Crown," *Jewish Symbols* 7 (1958) 135-71. See esp. p. 164.

1035　Goodenough, E.R. "Wine in Jewish Cult and Observance," *Jewish Symbols* 6 (1956) 126-217. See esp. p. 170.

1036　Grintz, Y.M. "Jubilees, Book of," *EncyJud* 10. Cols. 324-26.

1037　Jaubert, A. "The Calendar of *Jubilees,*" *The Date of the Last Supper,* trans. I. Rafferty. Staten Island, N.Y.: Alba House, 1965. Pp. 15-30.

1038　Jaubert, A. "The Date of *Jubilees* and the Figure of Juda, Son of Jacob," *The Date of the Last Supper,* trans. I. Rafferty. Staten Island, N.Y.: Alba House, 1965. Pp. 125-28.

1039　Kutsch, E. "Der Kalender des Jubiläenbuches und das Alte und das Neue Testament," *VT* 11 (1961) 39-47.

1040 Kutsch, E. "Die Solstitien im Kalender des Jubiläenbuches und in äth. Henoch 72," *VT* 12 (1962) 205-07.

1041 Lach, J. "The Liturgical Calendar of the Book of Jubilees in the Light of the Latest Discussions," *Ruch Biblijny i Liturgiczny* 16 (1963) 98-105. [in Polish]

1042 Milik, J.T. "A propos de 11QJub," *Bib* 54 (1973) 77f. [See van der Woude below, no. 1060.]

1043 Milik, J.T. "Fragment d'une source du Psautier et fragments des Jubilés, du Document de Damas, d'un phylactère dans la grotte 4 de Qumrân," *RB* 73 (1966) 94-106, pls. I-III. [4QJub^f]

1044 Milik, J.T. "Livre des Jubilés (Pl. XVI)," *DJD* 1. Pp. 82-84. [1QJub^a = Jub 27:19-21; 1QJub^b = Jub 35:8-10 plus fragments, perhaps from Jub 36:12]

1045 Milik, J.T. "Orthographe et langue," *DJD* 3. Pp. 221-35. [On p. 226 a reference is given to 4QJub^e which is from Jub 25:12.]

1046 Milik, J.T. "Recherches sur la version grecque du livre des Jubilés," *RB* 78 (1971) 545-57.

1047 Noack, B. "Jubilaeerbogen," *GamPseud* 3 (1958) 175-301.

1048 Rabin, C. "Jubilees," Clarendon edition.

1049 Rönsch, H. *Das Buch der Jubiläen.* Leipzig, 1874; repr. Amsterdam: Rodopi, 1970.

1050 Rofé, A. "Further Manuscript Fragments of Jubilees in Qumran Cave 3," *Tarbiz* 34 (1965) 333-36. [in Hebrew; Rofé claims correctly that 3QJub (cf. *DJD* 3, pl. XVIII, the 7 fragments under "5") is from Jub 23:6f., 12f., 23. See Deichgräber above, no. 1025.]

1051 Rost, L. "Jubiläenbuch," *RGG*^{3} 3. Col. 960.

1052 Salomonsen, B. "Jubilaeerbogen," *GDBL* 1. Cols. 1030f.

1052a Skehan, P.W. "*Jubilees* and the Qumran Psalter," *CBQ* 37 (1975) 343-47.

1053 Strothotte, G. "Jubilees, Book of," *ZPEB* 3. Pp. 716f.

1054 Tedesche, S. "Jubilees, Book of," *IDB* 2. Pp. 1002f.

1055 Testuz, M. *Les idées religieuses du livre des Jubilés.* Genève: E. Droz, 1960.

1056 Vogt, E. "Jubiläenbuch," *LTK*^{2} 5. Cols. 1148f.

1057 Weise, K. "Jubiläen," *BHH* 2. Cols. 897f.

1058 Wintermute, O.S. "Jubilees," Doubleday edition.

1059 Wirgin, W. *The Book of Jubilees and the Maccabean Era of Shmittah Cycles* (LUOS MS 7) Leeds: Leeds University Oriental Society, 1964.

1060 Woude, A.S. van der. "Fragmente des Buches Jubiläen aus Qumran Höhle XI (11QJub)," *Kuhn Festschrift*. Pp. 140-46, pl. VIII. [See Milik above, no. 1042.]

1061 Zeitlin, S. "The Judaean Calendar During the Second Commonwealth and the Scrolls," *Solomon Zeitlin's Studies in the Early History of Judaism*. New York: KTAV, 1973. Vol. 1, pp. 194-211; repr. fr. *JQR* n.s. 57 (1966) 28-45.

Liber Antiquitatum Biblicarum

See Pseudo-Philo.

The Lost Tribes
(The Story Concerning the Nine and a Half Tribes)

This apocryphon is not extant, but appears to be preserved in part by the Christian Latin poet Commodian and by the author of the Ethiopic Acts of St. Matthew. Commodian's writings were re-edited recently by J. Martin (*Commodiani Carmina* [Corp. Christ. Ser. Lat. 128] Turin: Brepolis, 1960; cf. A. Salvatore, *Instructiones: Libro Secondo; Testo Critico, Traduzione, e Note Esegetiche* [Coll. di Stud. Lat. 17] Naples: Libreria Scientifica Editrice, 1968), and the Acts of St. Matthew were edited and translated by E.A.W. Budge (*The Contendings of the Apostles*. 2 vols. London: Frowde, 1889-1901. Vol. 1 contains the Ethiopic text, pp. 101-03; vol. 2 an English translation, pp. 111-14.). Some of these selections were translated into English by M.R. James, who concluded that both writers preserved a common tradition, which was apocalyptic and Jewish (*LAOT*. Pp. 103-06). Later Jewish writings preserve a debate between Rabbi Akiba, who claimed the ten tribes will not return, and Rabbi Eliezer, who said they shall move from darkness to light (viz., Sanh. 10:3; see L.I. Rabinowitz, no. 1063, for a discussion of the influence of this story on later Jews).

During the early centuries of this era legends circulated about the manner of life of the nine and a half tribes of Israel taken into exile by the king of Assyria. It is possible that a midrash was written based upon 2 Kings 17:23 (cf. 1Chr 5:26, Isa 11:11, Jer 31:8, and esp. Ezek 37:19-28). It is significant that three compositions from the last quarter of

the first century A.D. apparently refer to this legend or
apocryphon, namely 4 Ezra (13:34-51), 2 Baruch (77:17-26), and
Josephus' *Antiquities* (11.5). Add to this apparent literary
relationship the probability that the conclusion to Commodian's
Instructiones refers to the capture of Jerusalem in A.D. 70,
and it begins to appear that the apocryphon dates from the last
quarter of the first century A.D.

The clearest description of this legend or apocryphon is
by Commodian, who apparently lived in Africa during the third
century (J. Martin, *Commodiani Carmina*, pp. x-xiii). Beginning
with line 941 of the *Carmen* he notes that the nine and a half
tribes are cut off by a river (called Sambatyon in later Jewish
literature, viz. Pseudo-Jonathan [Ex 34:10]; cf. A. Rothkoff,
no. 1064) beyond Persia, in a place in which there is no lying
or hating, where a son does not die before his parents, and
where there is no mourning the dead because of the resurrection
to come. The inhabitants are vegetarians, full of righteousness, with unblemished bodies, free from the evil influences
from the stars, free from fevers or colds, and purely obedient
to the Law. These people will return to the land of Judah.

In Book 1, section 42 (=2.1) of the *Instructiones* Commodian describes the state of the nine and a half tribes.
Christ descends to his elect (cf. 2En 8:3), who live in this
place, where a son does not die before his father, and where
the body has no pains or sores, but dies in full age while at
rest. These true heavenly people fulfill the Law and are hidden beyond a river; they will return in order "to rescue their
captured mother" (*Hic tamen festinat matrem defendere captam*).

An impressively similar description of a hidden mysterious
place, related to the legend or apocryphon of the lost tribes,
is found in the Ethiopic Acts of St. Matthew. According to
this source Matthew tells Peter and Andrew that he is returning
from the country Prokumenos ("those who rejoice"; Budge, *Contendings*, vol. 2, pp. 111f.), where the Lord frequently visits
the inhabitants (some of whom are Christian). These asked him,
"Hast thou not heard the story concerning the nine tribes and
the half tribe whom God Almighty brought into the land of
inheritance? We are they!" (p. 112) The people in that country have no desire for gold and silver and partake of neither

flesh nor wine, but are nourished by honey and dew. There is no lust, and the firstborn is offered to God. They drink water that flows from paradise; their garments are "the leaves of trees." They do not lie, each man has one wife, the son does not die before his father, and youths do not speak in the presence of the elderly. They live peacefully with lions, and smell the pleasant scents of paradise. The country is not cold but pleasant.

See the discussion below on the Apocalypse of Zosimus, the core of which describes the abode of the Rechabites.

1062 Godbey, A.H. *The Lost Tribes: A Myth*. Durham: Duke, 1930; repr. with prolegomenon by M. Epstein. New York: KTAV, 1973.

1063 Rabinowitz, L.I. "Ten Lost Tribes," *EncyJud* 15. Cols. 1003-06.

1064 Rothkoff, A. "Sambatyon," *EncyJud* 14. Cols. 762-64.

1065 Schoeps, H.J. "Zehn verlorene Stämme Israels," *RGG*[3] 6. Cols. 1876f.

1066 Shochat, A. "Eldad Ha-Dani," *EncyJud* 6. Cols. 576-78.

1067 Tamar, D. "An Epistle from Safed, Dated 1525 or 1625, Dealing with the Ten Tribes," *Sefunot* 6 (1962) 303-10. [in Hebrew; English summary pp. 20f.]

3 Maccabees
(Ptolemaika)

The Greek text has been edited recently by R. Hanhart *(Maccabaeorum Liber III* [Sept. Gott. 9.3] Göttingen: Vandenhoeck & Ruprecht, 1960; see also A. Rahlfs, no. 1084). An English translation was published by C.W. Emmet *(APOT* 1. Pp. 155-73; repr. *The Third and Fourth Books of Maccabees* [TED] London: S.P.C.K.,1918), and by M. Hadas *(The Third and Fourth Books of Maccabees* [JAL] New York: Harper, 1953. Pp. 31-85; cf. pp. 30-84 for a reprint of Rahlfs' Greek text of 1935).

There is wide agreement today that 3 Maccabees was composed in the first century B.C. or A.D. in Egypt, probably in Alexandria, in Greek.

The theme of the seven chapters is that Israel cannot be conquered because God Himself, not merely an angel (with Jubilees; contrast 1QS 3:13ff.), is her Deliverer *(ho rustēs)*.

150

Saved by the Jew Dositheus, Ptolemy IV Philopator defeats
Antiochus III, the Great, at Raphia (in 217 B.C.); then he
attempts to enter the Jerusalem Temple, but is prohibited when
God paralyzes him (1:1-2:24). He returns to Alexandria and
launches futile, even ridiculous, persecutions against the
Jews (2:25-6:21). The triumphant Jews receive from Ptolemy
due respect and the permission to slay apostates; they resolve
to celebrate annually the victory (6:22-7:23).

In the John Rylands University Library of Manchester, in
Syriac MS 3, on folios *sg* rev. to *ᶜd* rev. there is an unexamined version of 3 Maccabees. A microfilm copy of the entire
manuscript is preserved in the Pseudepigrapha Library at Duke
University.

Under B.M. Metzger the RSV Committee is preparing a new
translation.

See the publications listed above under "Martyrdom." See
also nos. 50f., 65, 82, 87, 297, 465, 471, 475, 478, 594.

1068 Amir, Y. "Maccabees, Third Book of," *EncyJud* 11. Cols.
660f.

1069 Anderson, H. "3 Maccabees," Doubleday edition.

1070 Arrabal, M.V. "Macabeos, Apócrifos de los," *Enciclopedia
de la Biblia* 4. Col. 1137.

1071 Baars, W. "Eine neue griechische Handschrift des 3.
Makkabäerbuches," *VT* 13 (1963) 82-87.

1072 Brownlee, W.H. "Maccabees, Books of," *IDB* 3. Pp. 201-15.

1073 Goodenough, E.R. "The Relevance of Rabbinic Evidence,"
Jewish Symbols 4 (1954) 3-24. See esp. p. 12.

1074 Goodenough, E.R. "Victory and Her Crown," *Jewish Symbols*
7 (1958) 135-71. See esp. p. 164.

1075 Hanhart, R. "Makkabäerbücher," *BHH* 2. Cols. 1126-30.

1076 Hyldahl, N. "Tredie Makkabaeerbog," *GamPseud* 5 (1970)
596-623.

1077 Jellicoe, S. "3 Maccabees," *The Septuagint and Modern
Study*. Oxford: Clarendon, 1968. Pp. 304f.

1078 Luck, U. "Makkabäerbücher," *RGG*³ 4. Cols. 622f.

1079 Moore, C.A. "On the Origins of the LXX Additions to the
Book of Esther," *JBL* 92 (1973) 382-93. [3Mac may have
influenced Greek Esther.]

1080 Müller, K. "3. Makkabäerbuch," *JSHRZ* 1, in press.

1081 Munk, A. "Makkabaeerbøgerne," *GDBL* 2. Cols. 121f.

1082 Nock, A.D. "*Isopoliteia* and the Jews," *Essays on Religion and the Ancient World*, ed. Z. Stewart. Oxford: Clarendon, 1972. Vol. 2, pp. 960f.

1083 Oikonomos, Ē.B. "Maccabees," *ThĒE* 8. Cols. 507-11. [in Greek; see esp. cols. 510f.]

1084 Rahlfs, A., ed. "Machabaeorum III," *Septuaginta* 1. Pp. 1139-56.

1085 Schötz, D. "Makkabäer III. Apokr. M.-Bücher," *LTK*^{2} 6. Cols. 1318f.

1086 Wolf, H. "Maccabees, Books of," *ZPEB* 4. Pp. 8-22.

4 Maccabees
(Concerning the Supreme Power of Reason)

The Greek text has been re-edited by A. Rahlfs (no. 1106; for a reprint of Rahlfs' 1935 text cf. M. Hadas, *The Third and Fourth Books of Maccabees* [JAL] New York: Harper, 1953). English translations are available by R.B. Townshend (*APOT* 2. Pp. 653-85), C.W. Emmet (*The Third and Fourth Books of Maccabees* [TED] London: S.P.C.K., 1918), and Hadas (pp. 145-243).

4 Maccabees, most critics concur, was composed in Greek sometime between A.D. 40 and 118, either in Egypt, perhaps in Alexandria, or in Syrian Antioch.

The composition is a diatribe (see J.C.H. Lebram, no. 1101) with Stoic influences by a Jew who had mastered Greek thought and language. The theme is clarified in the prologue (1:1-12): inspired reason is the supreme ruler over passions (pleasures and pains). After a definition of reason and passion, Joseph, Moses, Jacob, and David are chosen as examples of how reason can rule the passions (1:13-3:19). Following an historical note regarding the cultural and religious innovations by Antiochus Epiphanes and Jason (3:20-4:26), "the demonstration of the story of the self-controlled reason" (*tēn apodeixin tēs historias tou sōphronos logismou*, 3:19), the heart of the book, unfolds with an account of the courageous words and actions of Eleazar (cf. 2Mac 6:18-31), and of the seven young men and their mother (cf. 2Mac 7:1-42), with appropriate concluding summaries (5:1-17:24). The work ends

152

with an exhortation to the Israelites to obey the Law, be righteous, and recognize "that inspired reason is lord over passion" (*hoti tōn pathōn estin despotēs ho eusebēs logismos*, 18:2), and with a speech by the mother (18:1-24). There are tensions and inconsistencies, since the motive for martyrdom is not reason but obedience to Torah (cf. 5:16, 9:1-8, 16:17-22).

Under B.M. Metzger the RSV Committee is preparing a new translation.

Consult the publications listed above under "Martyrdom." See also nos. 51, 65, 82, 87f., 302, 407-09, 429, 465, 471, 475, 477f.

1087   Amir, Y. "Maccabees, Fourth Book of," *EncyJud* 11. Cols. 661f.

1088   Anderson, H. "4 Maccabees," Doubleday edition.

1089   Arrabal, M.V. "Macabeos, Apócrifos de los," *Enciclopedia de la Biblia* 4. Col. 1137.

1090   Brownlee, W.H. "Maccabees, Books of," *IDB* 3. Pp. 201-15.

1091   Eizenhöfer, L. "Stellen aus der *Passio S.S. Machabaeorum* in der westgotisch-mozarabischen *Inlatio* ihres Festes," *Archiv für Liturgiewissenschaft* 7 (1961) 416-22. [*N.V.*]

1092   Glatzer, N.N. "Inspired Reason," *Judaic Tradition*. Pp. 136-38.

1093   Goodenough, E.R. "Astronomical Symbols," *Jewish Symbols* 8 (1958) 167-218. See esp. p. 207.

1094   Goodenough, E.R. "Cosmic Judaism: The Temple of Aaron," *Jewish Symbols* 10 (1964) 3-26. See esp. p. 26.

1095   Goodenough, E.R. "Judaism in the Inscriptions," *Jewish Symbols* 2 (1953) 121-50. See esp. p. 134.

1096   Goodenough, E.R. "The North Wall," *Jewish Symbols* 10 (1964) 166-96. See esp. p. 193.

1097   Goodenough, E.R. "The Shofar," *Jewish Symbols* 4 (1954) 167-94. See esp. p. 176.

1098   Goodenough, E.R. "Victory and Her Crown," *Jewish Symbols* 7 (1958) 135-71. See esp. p. 169.

1099   Hanhart, R. "Makkabäerbücher," *BHH* 2. Cols. 1126-30.

1100   Hyldahl, N. "Fjerde Makkabaeerbog," *GamPseud* 6 (1972) 625-58.

1101 Lebram, J.C.H. "Die literarische Form des vierten Makka-
       bäerbuches," *VC* 28 (1974) 81-96.

1102 Luck, U. "Makkabäerbücher," *RGG*[3] 4. Cols. 622f.

1103 Munk, A. "Makkabaeerbøgerne," *GDBL* 2. Cols. 121f.

1104 O'Hagan, A. "The Martyr in the Fourth Book of Maccabees,"
       SBFLA 24 (1974) 94-120.

1105 Oikonomos, Ē.B. "Maccabees," *ThĒE* 8. Cols. 507-11. [in
       Greek; see esp. col. 511.]

1106 Rahlfs, A., ed. "Machabaeorum IV," *Septuaginta* 1. Pp.
       1157-84.

1107 Renehan, R. "The Greek Philosophic Background of Fourth
       Maccabees," *Rheinisches Museum für Philologie* 115
       (1972) 223-38.

1108 Schatkin, M. "The Maccabean Martyrs," *VC* 28 (1974) 97-
       113.

1109 Schötz, D. "Makkabäer III. Apokr. M.-Bücher," *LTK*[2] 6.
       Cols. 1318f.

1110 Staples, P. "The Unused Lever? A Study on the Possible
       Literary Influence of the Greek Maccabean Literature
       in the New Testament," *Modern Churchman* 9 (1966) 218-
       24.

1111 Wickert, [?]. "4. Makkabäerbuch," *JSHRZ* 3, in press.

1112 Wolf, H. "Maccabees, Book of," *ZPEB* 4. Pp. 8-22.

5. Maccabees [and Maccabean Cycle]
(The Arabic Maccabean Book, Second Book of the Maccabees)

This book is extant in unedited Karshuni (Borg. syr. 28,
ff. 412v-482v of A.D. 1581; Par. syr. 3, ff. 92v-116v [?] of
A.D. 1695; Vien. or.1548, ff. 20r-199r of A.D. 1729 [Karshuni
or Syriac?]) and Arabic manuscripts (Vat. ar. 468, ff. 718v-
759v of A.D. 1579; Vat. syr. 461, ff. 831-888 of A.D. 1667;
Leningrad, Collection of Gregory IV. Nr. 3 [?]; and Leningrad,
Collection of Gregory IV. Nr. 18, ff. 69-78 of A.D. 1642).
The Arabic manuscript listed first was probably (so G. Graf,
Geschichte, vol. 1, p. 223) the text behind G. Sionita's edition (in Le Jay's Polyglotte de Paris, 1645. Vol. 9, pp. 1-76
at the end; repr. in Walton's London Polyglotta, 1657. Vol. 4,
pp. 112-59). An English translation, unfortunately made "from
the Latin version of the Arabic text printed in the Poly-
glotts," was published by H. Cotton (*The Five Books of Macca-*

bees. Oxford: OUP, 1832; see esp. pp. xxx-xxxv, 227-446).

The crucial question regarding this work, which is virtually unknown to scholars, is its date. While Graf (*Geschichte*, vol. 1, p. 223) suggested it originated in early Melchite circles, Cotton (p. xxxii) and E. Beurlier ("Machabées [Livres apocryphes des]," *DB* 4, col. 502) concluded that the book was written in the latter part of the first century.

A date in the early Middle Ages appeared likely until the lack of later tendencies and ideas became noticeable, along with the recognition of early expressions (viz., "the third carrying into captivity," 9:5; "in the time of the second house," 22:9), the mention of the destruction of Jerusalem (9: 5, 21:30), and the impossibility of concluding that it is a pasticcio of 1, 2, 3, and 4 Maccabees and Josephus' *Antiquities* and *Wars*. It is wise to remain skeptical about the possibility of a late first century A.D. date for the work, although the intrinsic evidence presently appears to point in that direction.

The author of 5 Maccabees used other sources besides the works attributed to the Maccabees and Josephus' writings. Is it possible that this document preserves portions of the books written by Jason of Cyrene, Justus of Tiberias, or Nicolaus of Damascus? This question needs examination along with another: what is the relation between 5 Maccabees and the medieval Hebrew chronicle of Jewish history called Josippon? D. Flusser has completed a critical edition of the Hebrew text, which is now with the printer.

An important link between 5 Maccabees and Nicolaus of Damascus is that both, against Josephus (*Wars* 1.6, 2) and others (e.g. Hegesippus), claim that Antipater, Herod's father, was not an Idumaean, but a Jew who had come from Babylonia with Ezra (cf. 5Mac 35:1 with Josippon 37).

Is 5 Maccabees an epitome of the Josippon, as Graf contended (p. 223)? It is tempting to dismiss so-called 5 Maccabees from the Pseudepigrapha and assume it is derived from the late Jewish Josippon. This attribution would solve some problems and explain why specialists of the Pseudepigrapha and of Josippon do not discuss or mention 5 Maccabees (e.g. it is mentioned neither in J. Strugnell's "Josippon," *NCE* 7, p. 1124,

nor in A.A. Neuman's "Josippon and the Apocrypha," *Landmarks
and Goals*. Philadelphia: Dropsie, 1953; pp. 35-59). The acid
test is always the sources themselves, and the manuscripts of
5 Maccabees and of Josippon resist a simple explanation of
their relationship. 5 Maccabees, moreover, is dissimilar from
the Arabic epitomes of Josippon (it is extremely different
from the text edited and translated by M. Sanders and H.
Nahmad; cf. their "A Judeo-Arabic Epitome of the Yosippon,"
Essays in Honor of Solomon B. Freehof, eds. W. Jacob, *et al.*
Pittsburgh: Rodef Shalom Congregation, 1964; pp. 275-99).
Since neither the Arabic of 5 Maccabees nor the Hebrew of
Josippon was available, Cotton's translation of 5 Maccabees
was juxtaposed with J. Wellhausen's translation of Josippon
(*Der arabische Josippus* [Abhand. der Königl. Gesell. d. Wiss.
z. Göttingen, Philol.-Hist. Klasse, n.F. 1, 4] Berlin: Weidmann, 1897). The comparison did not suggest that 5 Maccabees
derives from Josippon. Any conclusion, however, must be un-
usually cautious since no reliable edition exists of either
text. It is also difficult to conclude that 5 Maccabees is an
abbreviated version of Josippon, because it is a longer text
yet covers only a portion of the history represented in Josippon, which begins with Alexander the Great and concludes with
the capture of Masada in A.D. 73.

Additional evidence that a relationship exists between
5 Maccabees and Josippon is that both interrupt, though with
substantial differences, the chronology from Heliodorus to
Antiochus IV by inserting an account of the translation of the
Septuagint for Ptolemy. A significantly shared feature is the
identification of the famous martyr Eleazar as one of the
·seventy translators.

Without having completed a detailed research on the relationships of 5 Maccabees with the other Maccabean books, with
Josephus' two works, and with Josippon, one should not suggest
a theory. A tentative hypothesis, which is similar to those
suggested by Wellhausen (p. 47) and Beurlier (cols. 502f.),
may be proposed: perhaps 5 Maccabees is a late first-century
A.D. compilation of early documents, some now lost, and of a
few new sections; this compilation was later epitomized along
with other texts by the author of the Josippon.

Beurlier (col. 502) thought that the original language of the book is Hebrew. This possibility is enhanced by numerous Semitisms that suggest a Hebrew *Vorlage*. It is difficult to prove this hypothesis since some of the Semitisms could have been introduced in the transmission of the Karshuni and Arabic texts. A note in some Arabic manuscripts at the end of the first sixteen chapters, however, reports that this section had been translated from Hebrew.

5 Maccabees is a chronicle of Jewish history from Heliodorus' attempt to rob the Temple treasury in the early decades of the second century B.C. to the death of Herod the Great's two sons about 6 B.C.--with an interpolation relating Eleazar's role in translating the Septuagint, as well as other interesting expansions (viz. the futile prayer of Antiochus Epiphanes, chp. 8). The work is bifurcated internally: the first section, 1:1-16:26, relates the history from Heliodorus to the death of Nicanor which is called "The Second Book of Maccabees According to the Translation of the Hebrews"; 17:1-59:96, the second section, is the history from the war between the Roman Scipio and the Carthaginian King Hannibal to the murder of the sons Alexander and Aristobulus, which is called "The Second Book of Maccabees" (cf. the preface in the Polyglotte de Paris).

Not to be confused with 5 Maccabees is the so-called "Fifth Book of Maccabees" in the Peshiṭta manuscript in the Bibliotheca Ambrosiana. The latter text is an excerpt of the sixth book of Josephus' *Wars*.

The work entitled "Maccabees" in B.M. Add. 16188 (Ethiopic) is not one of the apocryphal or pseudepigraphical works by that name. J.M. Harden describes the book as "a romance" about the martyrdom of three Jews during the reign of King Ṣiruṣâyadân (Tyre and Sidon), accompanied by passages that concern the immortality of the soul, the resurrection, and the history of the Jews (*An Introduction to Ethiopic Christian Literature*. London: S.P.C.K., 1926; p. 38).

Prayer of Manasses

This pseudepigraphon is extant in several languages; the most important of these are the Greek, which is conveniently edited in numerous collections (viz., A. Rahlfs, no. 1125a;

A.-M. Denis, no. 23, pp. 115f.); and the Syriac, which has
been re-edited recently by W. Baars and H. Schneider (no. 1113).
English translations have appeared in some of the standard collections of the Apocrypha (see B.M. Metzger, no. 1123 [RSV];
and W.D. McHardy, *et al.*, no. 1121 [NEB]), and H.E. Ryle published a critical translation with notes in R.H. Charles'
famous collection (*APOT* 1. Pp. 612-24).

Because of its brevity and the lack of any links with historical events or dated literature, it is impossible to date
the Prayer of Manasses. It appears that it may have been written between 200 B.C. and A.D. 70. It is quite possible that
the work was composed in Palestine (B.M. Metzger, *Intr. to the
Apoc.*, p. 125; R.H. Pfeiffer, *History*, p. 459). It may have
been written in Greek (Ryle, *APOT* 1, pp. 612, 614f., but cf.
Charles' footnote on pp. 614f.; V. Ryssel, *APAT* 1, p. 166; W.
Baumgartner, no. 1114; Denis, no. 1117, p. 181) or Hebrew (C.
C. Torrey, *Apoc. Lit.*, pp. 68f.; Pfeiffer, p. 459).

This pseudepigraphon attributed to the wickedest King of
Judah (cf. 2Kgs 21:1-18, and esp. 2Chr 33:1-20; cf. 2Bar 64:8)
preserves one of the most beautifully conceived penitential
prayers and confessions of personal sin (cf. A. Strobel, no.
485, pp. 15f.). M. Luther called it *"pulcherrima oratio"* (cf.
the important article by H. Volz, "Zur Überlieferung des
Gebetes Manasse," *ZKG* 70 [1959] 293-307). The fifteen verses
can be divided into five sections (so Metzger, *Intr. to the
Apoc.*, p. 127): an ascription of praise to the Lord (1-4);
acknowledgment of God's mercy (5-8); a personal confession
(9-10); supplication for pardon (11-13); and a petition for
grace and a doxology (14-15). The poetic image of contrition
is pictured in verse eleven: "And now I bend the knee of my
heart...."

Many scholars place the Prayer of Manasses in the Apocrypha, hence see the publications on that literature. Consult
the section above on Prayer. See also nos. 20, 23, 65, 82, 87.

1113 Baars, W. and H. Schneider, eds. "Prayer of Manasseh,"
      Peshitta. Part 4, fasc. 6 (1972) i-vii, 1-9.

1114 Baumgartner, W. "Manasse-Gebet," *RGG*[3] 4. Col. 708.

1115 Charlesworth, J.H. "Prayer of Manasseh," Doubleday edi-
      tion.

1116   Dancy, J.C., *et al*. "The Prayer of Manasseh," *The Shorter Books of the Apocrypha* (The Cambridge Bible Commentary: NEB) Cambridge: CUP, 1972. Pp. 242-48.

1117   Denis, A.-M. "La Prière de Manassé," *Introduction*. Pp. 177-81.

1118   Gutiérrez-Larraya, J.A. "Manasés, Oración de," *Enciclopedia de la Biblia* 4. Cols. 1235f.

1119   Hagner, D.A. "Manasses, Prayer of," *ZPEB* 4. Pp. 65f.

1120   Lane, W.L. "Apocrypha," *Encyclopedia of Christianity* 1. Pp. 307-64. See esp. pp. 325f.

1121   McHardy, W.D., *et al*. "The Prayer of Manasseh," *The New English Bible with the Apocrypha*. New York: OUP, 1971. Pp. 208f.

1122   Metzger, B.M. "Manasseh, Prayer of," *EncyJud* 11. Cols. 854f.

1123   Metzger, B.M. "The Prayer of Manasseh," *The Apocrypha of the Old Testament: Revised Standard Version*, ed. B.M. Metzger. New York: OUP, 1965. Pp. 219f.

1124   Mpratsiotēs, P.I. "Manasses," *ThEE* 8. Cols. 547f. [in Greek]

1125   Osswald, E. "Das Gebet Manasses," *JSHRZ* 4 (1974) 15-27.

1125a   Rahlfs, A., ed. "Prayer of Manasses," *Septuaginta* 2. Pp. 180f.

1126   Salomonsen, B. "Manasses bøn," *GDBL* 2. Cols. 128f.

1127   Schilling, O. "Manasse, Gebet des M." *LTK*[2] 6. Col. 1342.

1128   Schneider, H. "Der Vulgata-Text der Oratio Manasse eine Rezension des Robertus Stephanus," *BZ* n.F. 4 (1960) 227-82.

1129   Weber, R., *et al*. "Oratio Manasse," *Biblia Sacra*. Vol. 2, pp. 1909f.

1130   Westermann, C. "Manasse, Gebet des," *BHH* 2. Cols. 1137f.

1131   Wikgren, A. "Manasseh, Prayer of," *IDB* 3. Pp. 255f.

1132   Zink, J.K. "The Prayer of Manasseh," *The Use of the Old Testament in the Apocrypha*. Duke Ph.D., 1963. Pp. 128-32.

Pseudo-Menander
(Meander of Ephesus, Menander the Ephesian, Menander, Menander of Pergamum)

The writings of this early second-century B.C. historian are lost. He apparently was one of the students of

Eratosthenes (276/5-195/4 B.C.). Theophilus of Antioch in his
Ad Autolycum extracted a substantial quotation from Pseudo-
Menander (*Ad Autol.* 22, 23; for the Greek and English, cf.
Theophilus of Antioch. *Ad Autolycum*, ed. R.M. Grant. Oxford:
Clarendon, 1970; pp. 130-35). Josephus (*Contr. Ap.* 1.112-26;
Ant. 8.144-49) referred to him, reporting that he wrote a his-
tory of Phoenicia, in which Hiram of Tyre's relationships with
Solomon are described. Particular attention is given to
Hiram's construction of Zeus' golden pillars for the Jerusalem
Temple. Josephus claimed Pseudo-Menander translated some of
the royal Tyrian archives from Phoenician into Greek (*Ant.*
8.144).

R. Dalven (no. 1133) correctly suggests that Pseudo-
Menander may be identical with Menander of Pergamum, who was
quoted by Clement of Alexandria (*Strom.* 1.114). B.Z. Wacholder
(no. 819, p. 110) argues that Eupolemus borrowed from Pseudo-
Menander.

See Fragments of Historical Works. See also nos. 23, 65.

1133   Dalven, R. "Menander of Ephesus," *EncyJud* 7. Col. 895.

1134   Meister, C. "Menander von Ephesus," *BHH* 2. Col. 1188.

1135   Stern, M., ed. "Menander of Ephesus," *GLAJJ*. Pp. 119-22.

1136   Ullmann, M. *Die arabische Überlieferung der sogenannten
       Menandersentenzen* (Abhandlungen für die Kunde des
       Morgenlandes 34) Wiesbaden: F. Steiner, 1961.

1137   Wacholder, B.Z. "Pseudo-Menander," Doubleday edition.

Apocalypse of Moses

"The Apocalypse of Moses" served as a title for three different writings. It was infrequently used to designate "the
Little Genesis" (= Jubilees; e.g. by George Syncellus; cf. the
notes in A.-M. Denis, no. 24, pp. 152, 159f.). J. Leipoldt
edited a Coptic fragment which he claimed was from an Apocalypse of Moses (cf. *Ägyptische Urkunden aus den kön. Museen zu
Berlin, Koptische Urkunden* 1 [1904] 171f.; *N.V.*, but cf. Denis,
no. 24, p. 13). This text has defied identification with extant pseudepigrapha.

The Apocalypse of Moses as a title is usually reserved by
modern scholars for the Greek recension of the Life of Adam

and Eve, because of the preface added to this recension which
describes the book as revealed to Moses (*Diēgēsis kai politeia
Adam kai Euas tōn prōtoplastōn, apokaluphtheisa para theou
Mōusē tō theraponti autou*).

M. Nagel is preparing a Greek edition for PVTG.

Consult the list above under "Moses," Old Testament Names
Used Pseudonymously, and publications listed under the Life of
Adam and Eve. See also nos. 67, 75, 82.

1138 Bianchi, U. "Gnostizismus und Anthropologie," *Kairos* 11
(1969) 6-14.

1139 Denis, A.-M. "L'Apocalypse de Moïse (= Vie d'Adam et Eve)
et le cycle d'Adam," *Introduction*. Pp. 3-14.

1140 Giannopoulos, B.N. "Moses (Apocalypse of)," *ThEE* 9. Cols.
284f. [in Greek]

1141 Giversen, S. "Moses' Apokalypse," *GDBL* 2. Col. 245.

1142 Goodenough, E.R. "The Tree," *Jewish Symbols* 7 (1958) 87-
134. See esp. pp. 126f.

1143 Nagel, M. *La Vie grecque d'Adam et d'Eve (Apocalypse de
Moïse)*. Strasbourg Ph.D., 1972.

1144 Sharpe, J.L. *Prolegomena to the Establishment of a Critical Text of the Apocalypse of Moses*. Duke Ph.D., 1969.

1145 Sharpe, J.L. "The Second Adam in the Apocalypse of
Moses," *CBQ* 35 (1973) 35-46.

1146 Sirat, C. "Un midraš juif en habit musulman: la vision de
Moïse sur le mont Sinaï," *RHR* 168 (1965) 15-28.

1147 Tischendorf, K. von. "Apocalypsis Mosis," *Apocalypses
Apocryphae Mosis, Esdrae, Pauli, Ioannis, item Mariae
dormitio: Additis Evangeliorum et actuum apocryphorum
supplementis*. Leipzig, 1866; repr. Hildesheim: Olms,
1966. Pp. 1-23.

*Assumption of Moses [and Moses Cycle]
(Ascension of Moses, Testament of Moses)*

The Assumption of Moses is lost except for some quotations
in the Fathers (cf. A.-M. Denis, no. 23, pp. 63-67; *idem*, no.
24, pp. 128-41; for the Latin fragments, along with the Greek,
see R.H. Charles' *The Assumption of Moses*. London: Black, 1897;
pp. 105-10). The "Testament of Moses" (see separate entry
below) is extant only in a Latin text that begins as follows:
qui est bis millesimus et quingentesimus annus a creatura orbis

terrae... (note that the opening lines in English translations
are R.H. Charles' hypothetical restorations). It is generally
agreed today that this Latin manuscript preserves portions of
the Testament of Moses, which probably was written before the
Assumption of Moses. If so, it once circulated independently of
the Assumption of Moses; but there is abundant evidence that
they soon circulated together. It is probable that the Assumption of Moses was contained in the lost ending of the Latin
manuscript. It is significant that in the List of Sixty Books,
the list by Pseudo-Athanasius, the Stichometry of Nicephorus,
and in the Slavic lists, the order of these two pseudepigrapha
is with the Testament of Moses immediately before the Assumption of Moses. Nicephorus also reported that each had respectively 1100 and 1400 lines. When these two pseudepigrapha were
linked, they frequently were called the Assumption of Moses.

It is virtually certain that Jude 9 alludes to the Assumption of Moses, as stated by numerous Fathers, especially
Clement of Alexandria (*Frag. in Ep. Jud.* 9) and Origen (*De
Principiis* 3.2, 1). Jude 16 seems influenced by the Testament
of Moses (5:5, 7:7, 9; cf. Charles, *The Assumption of Moses*,
ad loc. cit.; Charles in *APOT* 2, p. 412).

Moses, especially the account of his death as recorded in
Deuteronomy 34, stirred the imagination and evoked many pseudepigraphical compositions. It is impossible, given the focus
of this monograph, to do more than merely point to some of the
numerous pseudepigrapha that bear his name (for discussions
see esp. A.F. Gfroerer, "De Vita et Morte Mosis," *Prophetae
Veteres Pseudepigraphi.* Stuttgart: Krabbe, 1840; pp. 303-62;
Charles, *The Assumption of Moses*, pp. xiv-xvii; M.R. James,
LAOT, pp. 42-51; L. Ginzberg, *Legends*, vols. 2 and 3 plus
notes; and A.-M. Denis, no. 24, pp. 128-41).

In the fragments of historical and poetical works Moses
looms prominent (see the authors noted under these headings).
Forty-nine fragments from a Moses apocryphon (1QDM; ed. J.T.
Milik, *DJD* 1, pp. 91-97, pls. XVIII, XIX) were recovered from
Qumran Cave 1; these preserve a tradition reminiscent of the
Testament of Moses. Two fragments from a possible Moses
apocryphon (2QapMoses; ed. M. Baillet, *DJD* 3, pp. 79-81, pl.
XV)--in contrast to the former fragments, Moses' name is not

present--were found in Qumran Cave 2.

J. Issaverdens translated into English from Armenian "The History of Moses" (*UWOT*. Pp. 111-18), the latter part of which has been retranslated by M.E. Stone (no. 1178), along with two other Armenian texts concerning Moses. While these Armenian texts are late, there are sections that appear fairly early. The same situation appertains to the Ethiopic material translated by W. Leslau (*Falasha Anthology*, pp. 103-11) and E. Ullendorff (no. 1181).

Moses pseudepigrapha were compiled from ancient sources by Christians, Samaritans, Rabbinic Jews, and Muslims. Denis (no. 24, p. 138) draws attention to a Christian writing in Ethiopic which was edited and translated by A. Goldschmidt (*Die abessinischen Handschriften der Stadtbibliothek zu Frankfurt am Main*. Berlin: [?], 1897 [*N.V.*]). J.D. Purvis (no. 1172) has discussed recently the important traditions concerning the death of Moses that are preserved in Samaritan sources. H.W. Attridge (no. 1149) has translated into English the haggadic midrash on Moses' ascension that is preserved in *Bereshit Rabbati* (*Midrashe Ge'ulah*, 2d. ed., ed. J. Ebn-Shmuel. Jerusalem: Bialik, 1954. Pp. 14-22 [*N.V.*]). The Muslims, of course, preserved ancient traditions as they compiled works about Moses, and the text mentioned above that was translated by Issaverdens clearly derives from a Muslim source (cf. also G. Graf, *Geschichte*, vol. 1, pp. 207f.; Denis, no. 24, p. 140).

It is difficult to define the contents of the Apocryphon of Moses mentioned by Euthalius in the middle of the fourth century A.D. and Photius in the ninth century A.D. (cf. Denis, no. 24, pp. 76f., 137f.). The Apostolic Constitutions from the latter part of the fourth century notes among the apocryphal writings related in the Old Testament a book of Moses. These notices may denote texts or a text that is lost, or may represent one of the texts discussed herein. All of these ambiguous references may refer to the combined Testament and Assumption of Moses.

A copy of the extant Latin manuscript of the Assumption of Moses is preserved in the Pseudepigrapha Library at Duke University.

See the publications listed under "Moses," Old Testament
Names Used Pseudonymously; Apocalypse of Moses, Prayer of
Moses, and Testament of Moses.

Prayer of Moses

In 1893 M.R. James (*Apocrypha Anecdota* [T&S 2.3] Cambridge: CUP, 1893. Pp. 164-73) discussed a Latin text called
the Prayer of Moses and suggested it derived from the last
portion of the Assumption of Moses. It is now recognized that
this prayer is from *Liber Antiquitatum Biblicarum* (19:14-16).

See Pseudo-Philo.

Testament of Moses
(Assumption of Moses)

Except for some Greek fragments, which have been re-edited
recently by A.-M. Denis (no. 23, pp. 63-67), the Testament of
Moses is extant only in a frequently illegible fifth-century
text which is beneath an imperfect sixth-century Latin palimp-
sest preserved in the Bibliotheca Ambrosiana in Milan. The
text was most recently edited by R.H. Charles (*The Assumption
of Moses Translated from the Latin Sixth Century MS., The Un-
emended Text of Which is Published Herewith, Together with the
Text in Its Restored and Critically Emended Form*. London:
Black, 1897), and translated into English by him on two different occasions (in the work just mentioned and in *APOT* 2,
pp. 414-24). It has also been translated into English by W.
J. Ferrar (*The Assumption of Moses* [TED] London: S.P.C.K.,
1917; repr. with corr. 1929).

The date of the composition has been a subject of considerable controversy. Most critics today correctly place the
original sometime in the opening decades of the first century
A.D. (cf. J.J. Collins, no. 1151); but J. Licht ("Taxo, or the
Apocalyptic Doctrine of Vengeance," *JJS* 12 [1961] 95-103) and
G.W.E. Nickelsburg, Jr. (no. 471, pp. 28-31, 43-45, 97; no.
1168; cf. 1169, p. 6) have argued for a date during the early
stages of the Maccabean revolt, allowing for interpolations
and re-editing in the Herodian period. Given the incomplete,
often illegible state of the extant text and our fragmentary
knowledge of early Judaism it has been impossible to reach a

scholarly consensus regarding the text's provenance or relationship to a Jewish sect, if any. Scholars have generally
concluded that the original language is Hebrew (Charles, *APOT*
2, p. 410; Ferrar, *Assumption of Moses*, p. 8; D.H. Wallace,
"The Semitic Origin of the Assumption of Moses," *TZ* 11 [1955]
321-28; cf. *idem*, no. 1182).

The extant text can be divided into twelve chapters.
Moses instructs and encourages Joshua regarding his ministry
to the Israelites, service in the tabernacle, and role as con-
queror (chp. 1). Moses continues by predicting the entrance
"into the land," civil war, apostasy of "the ten tribes" (chp.
2), and the conquest and deportation of the ten tribes and of
the two tribes (chp. 3). In captivity "one who is over them"
unus qui supra eos =Daniel) utters a prayer for compassion;
"some portions" of the two tribes return "to their land and
country" (chp. 4). Foretold is the idolatry and unfaithfulness
of the Jews during the Greek period (chp. 5), the degenerations
of the Hasmoneans, and Herod's reign (chp. 6). The rule of
destructive and impious men is prophesied (chp. 7), followed
by the persecution of the faithful, especially the crucifixions
of those who have been circumcized (chp. 8). Taxo and his
seven sons shall enter a cave and die, refusing to transgress
the commands of the Lord (chp. 9). God's kingdom shall come,
Satan shall pass away, and the Most High will arise in order to
punish the Gentiles (chp. 10). When Joshua hears Moses' words
he laments and despairs for the Jews (chp. 11). Moses comforts
Joshua by revealing that God knows what is to happen and is in
control of creation, and that his "covenant has been established and by the oath which..." [the remainder of the text is
lost] (chp. 12).

A beautiful collection of photographs of the Latin palimp-
sest is preserved in the Pseudepigrapha Library at Duke University.

A. Schalit is preparing for Brill a German translation of
the extant Latin manuscript with introduction and commentary.

Consult the list on "Moses," under Old Testament Names
Used Pseudonymously. See also nos. 4, 23, 234, 249, 317, 320,
330, 471.

1148 Andersen, H.G. "Moses, Assumption of," *ZPEB* 4. Pp. 295f.

1149   Attridge, H.W. "The Ascension of Moses and the Heavenly
       Jerusalem," SCS 4. Pp. 122-25.

1150   Brandenburger, E. "Himmelfahrt Moses," JSHRZ 5, in press.

1151   Collins, J.J. "The Date and Provenance of the Testament
       of Moses," SCS 4. Pp. 15-32.

1152   Collins, J.J. "Some Remaining Traditio-Historical Prob-
       lems in the Testament of Moses," SCS 4. Pp. 38-43.

1153   Denis, A.-M. "Les fragments grecs de l'Assomption de
       Moïse," Introduction. Pp. 128-41.

1154   Giannopoulos, B.N. "Moses (Assumption of)," ThĒE 9. Col.
       285. [in Greek]

1155   Giversen, S. "Moses' Himmelfart," GDBL 2. Cols. 245f.

1156   Goldstein, J.A. "The Testament of Moses: Its Content, Its
       Origin, and Its Attestation in Josephus," SCS 4. Pp.
       44-52.

1157   Goodenough, E.R. "The Reredos," Jewish Symbols 9 (1964)
       78-123. See esp. p. 116.

1158   Gutiérrez-Larraya, J.A. "Moisés, Asunción de," Enciclo-
       pedia de la Biblia 5. Col. 269.

1159   Haacker, K. "Assumptio Mosis-eine samaritanische
       Schrift?" TZ 25 (1969) 385-405.

1160   Harrington, D.J. "Interpreting Israel's History: The
       Testament of Moses as a Rewriting of Deut 31-34,"
       SCS 4. Pp. 59-68.

1161   Harrington, D.J. "Summary of Günther Reese, Die Geschich-
       te Israels in der Auffassung des frühen Judentums, Ch
       III," SCS 4. Pp. 69-71.

1162   Isenberg, S.R. "On the Non-Relationship of the Testament
       of Moses to the Targumim," SCS 4. Pp. 79-85.

1163   Janssen, E. "Die Himmelfahrt Moses," Gottesvolk. Pp. 101-
       08.

1164   Klein, R.W. "The Text of Deuteronomy Employed in the Tes-
       tament of Moses," SCS 4. P. 78.

1165   Kolenkow, A.B. "The Assumption of Moses as a Testament,"
       SCS 4. Pp. 71-77.

1166   Laperrousaz, E.-M. Le Testament de Moïse (généralement
       appelé 'Assomption de Moïse'): Traduction avec intro-
       duction et notes (Sem 19) Paris: Adrien-Maisonneuve,
       1970.

1166a Meyer, R. "Himmelfahrt Moses," RGG[3] 3. Col. 337.

1167   Michaelis, W., *et al.* "Moses, Assumption of," *EncyJud* 12. Cols. 411f.

1168   Nickelsburg, G.W.E. Jr. "An Antiochan Date for the Testament of Moses," SCS 4. Pp. 33-37.

1169   Nickelsburg, G.W.E. Jr., ed. *Studies on the Testament of Moses: Seminar Papers* (SCS 4) Cambridge, Mass.: SBL, 1973.

1170   Noack, B. "Moses's Himmelfahrt," *GamPseud* 4 (1963) 317-40.

1171   Priest, J. "Assumption of Moses," Doubleday edition.

1172   Purvis, J.D. "Samaritan Traditions on the Death of Moses," SCS 4. Pp. 93-117.

1173   Reese, G. *Die Geschichte Israels in der Auffassung des frühen Judentums: Eine Untersuchung der Tiervision und der Zehnwochenapokalypse des äthiopischen Henochbuches, der Geschichtdarstellung der Assumptio Mosis und des 4 Esrabuches.* Heidelberg Ph.D., 1967.

1174   Rhoads, D.M. "The Assumption of Moses and Jewish History: 4 B.C.-A.D. 48," SCS 4. Pp. 53-58.

1175   Rist, M. "Moses, Assumption of," *IDB* 3. Pp. 450f.

1176   Rowston, D.J. "The Most Neglected Book in the New Testament," *NTS* 21 (1975) 554-63. [A discussion of the use of 1En and AsMos by Jude, a "Jewish-Christian apocalyptic" book.]

1177   Schultz, J.P. "Angelic Opposition to the Ascension of Moses and the Revelation of the Law," *JQR* 61 (1971) 282-307.

1178   Stone, M.E. "Three Armenian Accounts of the Death of Moses," SCS 4. Pp. 118-21.

1179   Sweet, J.P.M. "Assumption of Moses," Clarendon edition.

1180   Tiede, D.L. "The Figure of Moses in the Testament of Moses," SCS 4. Pp. 86-92.

1181   Ullendorff, E. "The 'Death of Moses' in the Literature of the Falashas," *BSOAS* 24 (1961) 419-43.

1182   Wallace, D.H. "Moses Himmelfahrt," *BHH* 2. Cols. 1243f.

Book of Noah

During the early parts of the second century B.C. a pseudepigraphon circulated that contained considerable material concerning Noah. The tradition was not merely oral but had been written down, since the author of Jubilees (*SPR NḤ*, 10:13;

cf. 21:10) and of an interpolation in the Testament of Levi
18:2 (*en tē graphē tēs biblou tou Nōe*, vs. 57 in Greek MS e;
cf. R.H. Charles, *The Greek Versions of the Testaments of the
Twelve Patriarchs*. Oxford: OUP, 1908 [repr. 1960]; pp. liii-
lvii, 252; *APOT* 2, pp. 364-67) refer to a "Book of Noah" (J.P.
Lewis, no. 448, questions the existence of a book of Noah.).
The work is now lost except for excerpts preserved in 1 Enoch
(viz., 6:1-11:2, 54:7-55:2, 60:1-24, 65:1-69:25, 106:1-107:3)
and Jubilees (viz., 7:20-39, 10:1-15, 20:7, 21:10), for 21
fragments preserved in Qumran Cave 1 (1QNoah, cf. *DJD* 1, pp.
84-86, 152, pl. XVI), and for two large fragments found in
Cave 4 that are not yet published (cf. J. Starcky, "Cave 4 of
Qumran," *BA* 19 [1956] 94-96). The work disappeared early;
Noah's name does not appear in the numerous lists of apocryphal
books.

It is possible that the so-called Genesis Apocryphon was
sometimes called a book of Noah since this work, which has
been published only partially (cf. N. Avigad and Y. Yadin, *A
Genesis Apocryphon: A Scroll from the Wilderness of Judaea.
Description and Contents of the Scroll: Facsimiles, Transcrip-
tion and Translation of Columns II, XIX-XXII*. Jerusalem:
Magnes, 1956), centers upon Noah, especially his miraculous
birth, the flood, and the division of the earth among Noah's
sons.

See the works listed under the Pseudepigrapha and the
Dead Sea Scrolls, Old Testament Names Used Pseudonymously, 1
Enoch, and Jubilees.

Pseudo-Orpheus
(Diathēkai, *Testament of Orpheus*)

During the second or first century B.C. some Jewish poems
falsely attributed to Orpheus were composed that bear resem-
blances to the Jewish pseudepigraphical testaments (cf. N.
Walter, no. 1183a, p. 260), because the setting is Orpheus'
parting testament to his son Musaeus (*en tō diathēkai epigra-
phomenō bibliō*; Ps-Just, *de Mon. 2*). These poems are now lost
except for quotations preserved by Pseudo-Justin, Clement of
Alexandria, Eusebius, and others. The Greek fragments have
been reprinted by A.-M. Denis (no. 23, pp. 163-67; cf. O. Kern,

Orphicorum Fragmenta. Berlin: Weidmann, 1922; esp. pp. 255-66).
The major questions remain unanswered due to the lack of data
and published research. It is possible, however, that these
poems reflect the missionary efforts of Alexandrian Jews, since
the effort to have Orpheus reject his polytheistic ideas and
proclaim one true God, perhaps "one of the boldest forgeries
ever attempted" (E. Schürer, *History*, 2d. Div., vol. 3, p.
300), may be an example of hellenistic Jewish propaganda (A.
Hausrath claimed the Alexandrian Aristobulus composed these
Orphic verses; *History...The Time of the Apostles*, 2d. ed.,
vol. 1, pp. 110-13.   Schürer claimed that the poems were composed by Pseudo-Hecataeus; cf. his *History*, 2d. Div., vol. 3,
p. 296. P. Dalbert's silence on this claim is disappointing;
cf. his *Missionsliteratur*, esp. pp. 18-20, 102-06. Also see
the comments by F. Münzer in Pauly-Wissowa n.B. 18.1 [1939]
cols. 1313-16; and by K. Ziegler in Pauly-Wissowa n.B. 18.1
(= 18.2) [1942] cols. 1398-1400.).

These remnants of Pseudo-Orpheus should be included with
the Jewish poems masquerading under the names of Sophocles,
Euripides, Aeschylus, Pythagoras, Diphilus, Homer, Hesiod, and
Heraclitus (cf. J. Strugnell and H. Attridge, no. 86). They
could perhaps be subsumed under the Pseudepigrapha, even though
they are not attributed to an Old Testament figure and are not
related to the poetic style of the biblical Psalms, as are most
of the psalms and hymns preserved in the Pseudepigrapha.

See the discussions and publications listed under Aristobulus, Pseudo-Hecataeus, and the Sibylline Oracles.

1183   Walter, N. "Pseudo-Orpheus und andere gefälschte Verse,"
         JSHRZ 4, in press.

1183a Walter, N. "Zur Entwicklungsgeschichte des jüdisch-
         orphischen Gedichts," *Der Thoraausleger Aristobulos*
         (TU 86) Berlin: Akademie, 1964. Pp. 202-61.

Paraleipomena Jeremiou

See the publications listed under 4 Baruch.

Philo the Epic Poet
(Philo the Ancient, Philo the Elder)

The extensive composition of at least four books by Philo

the Epic Poet is lost except for excerpts derived from Alexander Polyhistor by Eusebius (*Pr. ev.* 9.20, 1; 9.24, 1; 9.37,
1-3; cf. Josephus, *Contr. Ap.* 1.23, 218; Clement of Alexandria,
Strom. 1.21, 141, 3). The Greek has been republished by A.-M.
Denis (no. 23, pp. 203f.), and was partly translated into English by E.H. Gifford (Eusebius. *Preparation for the Gospel.*
Oxford: Clarendon, 1903. The first fragment is left in Greek
because it is "unintelligible," the second is translated, the
third is translated except for the beginning.).

Philo the Epic Poet was a Jew who wrote in the second
century B.C., probably in the second quarter (cf. Y. Gutman,
"Philo the Epic Poet," *Scripta Hierosolymitana* 1 [1954] 36-63;
E. Lohse, no. 1183a; R. Laqueur in Pauly-Wissowa n.B. 20.1
[1941] cols. 51f.), and may have lived in Jerusalem (so also
J. Freudenthal, *Alexander Polyhistor.* Breslau: Skutsch, 1875;
p. 129; P. Dalbert, *Missionsliteratur*, p. 34; B.Z. Wacholder,
no. 1184; and A.-M. Denis, no. 24, p. 271. M. Hengel sur-
prisingly claims this assumption is "pure speculation," and
opts for an Egyptian provenance [no. 104, ET, vol. 2, p. 71].
See, however, his discussion of "Jewish literature in Greek in
Palestine" [no. 104, ET, vol. 1, pp. 88-102].). He composed
his verses in Greek, demonstrating ability with the hexameters
of the Greek epics.

Eusebius preserved three fragments which total 24 hexameters from Philo the Epic Poet's *Concerning Jerusalem (Peri
ta Ierosoluma).* Ten verses concern the sacrifice of Isaac
(*Pr. ev.* 9.20, 1; Gutman rejects this interpretation of the
fragment, claiming the text has been emended incorrectly.
Wacholder, however, dismisses Gutman's conjectures, and claims
that at least six lines "appear clearly to deal with the bind-
ing of Isaac" [no. 1184, col. 407].), five portray Joseph's
accomplishments in Egypt (*Pr. ev.* 9.24, 1), and nine describe
the water system in Jerusalem (*Pr. ev.* 9.37, 1-3).

Consult Fragments of Poetical Works and Sibylline Oracles.
See also no. 65.

1183b Lohse, E. "Philo," *RGG*[3] 5. Col. 347.

1184 Wacholder, B.Z. "Philo (The Elder)," *EncyJud* 13. Cols.
407f.

1185 Walter, N. "Epiker Philon," *JSHRZ* 4, in press.

Pseudo-Philo
(Pseudo-Philo's Biblical Antiquities, Liber
Antiquitatum Biblicarum, Historia *of Philo)*

Pseudo-Philo is extant primarily in two recensions, one
in Latin and the other in late Hebrew. The *Liber Antiquitatum
Biblicarum* is the more important version, and was edited by G.
Kisch (*Pseudo-Philo's Liber Antiquitatum Biblicarum* [Publ. in
Mediaeval Stud. 10] Notre Dame, Ind.: University of Notre Dame,
1949), and recently re-edited by D.J. Harrington, *et al.* (no.
1204a). An English translation was published by M.R. James
(no. 1205). The Hebrew fragments, which are medieval retro-
versions from Latin, have been edited and retranslated recently
by Harrington (no. 1199).

It is becoming clear that Pseudo-Philo is not so late as
earlier scholars concluded. The traditions recorded therein
are ancient (cf. G. Vermes, *Scripture and Tradition in Judaism:
Haggadic Studies*, 2d. ed. [SPB 4] Leiden: Brill, 1973; *passim*),
and the work itself is rather early, dating probably from
around A.D. 100 (G. Delling, nos. 1190, 1191; C. Dietzfelbinger
dates Ps-Philo between A.D. 70 and 135; cf. his *Pseudo-Philo,
Liber Antiquitatum Biblicarum*. Göttingen Ph.D., 1964; pp. 191-
94 [*N.V.*], and his no. 1192, p. 95; also see L.H. Feldman's
caveat, no. 1205, pp. xxviii-xxxi) and possibly before A.D. 70
(P.-M. Bogaert, no. 619, vol. 1, p. 246; Harrington, nos. 1198,
1202, 1203). The author probably lived in Palestine (cf. Delling, nos. 1190, 1191; Dietzfelbinger, no. 1192, p. 96; Harrington, no. 1200) and wrote in Hebrew (J. Strugnell, no. 1391d,
esp. p. 207; Harrington, nos. 1198, 1202, 1203; Dietzfelbinger,
no. 1192, pp. 92f.; but cf. Feldman's caution regarding the
possibility of Greek, no. 1205, pp. xxv-xxvii). Some scholars
have argued for a relationship with the Dead Sea Scrolls (e.g.
M. Philonenko, "Remarques sur un hymne essénien de caractère
gnostique," *Sem* 11 [1961] 43-54; *idem*, "Une paraphrase du
cantique d'Anne," *RHPR* 42 [1962] 157-68; *idem*, nos. 1207, 1208;
cf. Feldman, no. 1205, pp. xxxviii-xliii).

Liber Antiquitatum Biblicarum contains 65 chapters and is
a haggadic midrash on Genesis through 2 Samuel, comprising
events from the beginning of the world to the death of Saul.
Of particular interest for us are the legendary expansions,
especially the lengthy apocryphal description of Kenaz (cf.

Judg 3:9-11) culminating with his vision (28:6-10); the
"prayer" of Moses and response (19:14-16); the moving lament
of Seila, the daughter of Jephthah (Judg 11:30-40), when she
perceived that her father was bound by his vow to sacrifice
her (40:5-8); and the song of David (60:2f.).

Pseudo-Philo clearly belongs among the Pseudepigrapha.
It is ignored unfortunately in numerous studies (viz. D. Patte,
Early Jewish Hermeneutic in Palestine [SBLDS 22] Missoula,
Mont.: SBL, 1975).

Other Pseudo-Philonic materials exist. H. Lewy's translation of and commentary upon *De Jona* was lost during the
Second World War. An incomplete draft of this work has been
recovered in Lewy's archives at the Hebrew University of Jerusalem. The Israel Academy of Sciences is preparing this work
for publication. Chana Safrai is writing a dissertation on
De Sampsane, which will include an introduction, text, and
translation.

See also nos. 147, 297, 330, 352, 432, 445f., 448, 478f.,
1492a.

1186 Bogaert, P.-M. "Les 'Antiquités Bibliques' du Pseudo-
        Philon: Quelques observations sur les chapitres 39 et
        40 à l'occasion d'une réimpression," *Revue théologique
        de Louvain* 3 (1972) 334-44.

1187 Bowker, J. "The Biblical Antiquities of Philo: A Trans-
        lation of the Passages Related to Genesis," *The Targums
        and Rabbinic Literature*. Cambridge: CUP, 1969. Pp.
        301-14.

1188 Collins, M.F. "The Hidden Vessels in Samaritan Tradi-
        tions," *JSJ* 3 (1972) 97-116.

1189 Delcor, M. "Philo (Pseudo-)," *DBSup* 41 (1966) 1354-75.

1190 Delling, G. "Von Morija zum Sinai (Pseudo-Philo Liber
        Antiquitatum Biblicarum 32, 1-10)," *JSJ* 2 (1971) 1-18.

1191 Delling, G. "Die Weise, von der Zeit zu Reden, im Liber
        Antiquitatum Biblicarum," *NovT* 13 (1971) 305-21.

1192 Dietzfelbinger, C. "Pseudo-Philo: Antiquitates Biblicae
        (Liber Antiquitatum Biblicarum)," *JSHRZ* 2 (1975).

1192a Feldman, L.H. "Epilegomenon to Pseudo-Philo's *Liber An-
        tiquitatum Biblicarum* (LAB)," *JJS* 25 (1974) 305-12.

1193 Goodenough, E.R. "Birds," *Jewish Symbols* 8 (1958) 22-70.
        See esp. pp. 43f.

1194   Goodenough, E.R. "Cosmic Judaism: The Well of the Wilder ness," *Jewish Symbols* 10 (1964) 27-41. See esp. p. 34.

1195   Goodenough, E.R. "Jewish Royalty," *Jewish Symbols* 9 (1964) 177-96. See esp. p. 190.

1196   Goodenough, E.R. "Psychopomps," *Jewish Symbols* 8 (1958) 121-66. See esp. p. 136.

1197   Goodenough, E.R. "Symbolism of Dress," *Jewish Symbols* 9 (1964) 124-74. See esp. p. 170.

1198   Harrington, D.J. "The Biblical Text of Pseudo-Philo's *Liber Antiquitatum Biblicarum*," *CBQ* 33 (1971) 1-17.

1199   Harrington, D.J. *The Hebrew Fragments of Pseudo-Philo's* Liber Antiquitatum Biblicarum *Preserved in the* Chronicles of Jerahmeel (T&T 3, Pseudepigrapha Series 3) Missoula, Mont.: SBL, 1974.

1199a Harrington, D.J. "Joseph in the Testament of Joseph, Pseudo-Philo, and Philo," *SCS* 5. Pp. 127-31.

1200   Harrington, D.J. "*Liber Antiquitatum Biblicarum*," Doubleday edition.

1201   Harrington, D.J. "Liber Antiquitatum Biblicarum," *NCE* 16 Sup. (1974) 251.

1202   Harrington, D.J. "The Original Language of Pseudo-Philo' *Liber Antiquitatum Biblicarum*," *HTR* 63 (1970) 503-14.

1203   Harrington, D.J. *Text and Biblical Text in Pseudo-Philo' Liber Antiquitatum Biblicarum*. Harvard Ph.D., 1969.

1204   Harrington, D.J. "The Text-Critical Situation of Pseudo- Philo's 'Liber Antiquitatum Biblicarum,'" *RBen* 83 (1973) 383-88.

1204a Harrington, D.J., J. Cazeaux, C. Perrot, and P.-M. Bogaert. *Pseudo-Philon, Les Antiquités Bibliques* (SC 229-230) Paris: Cerf, 1976.

1205   James, M.R. *The Biblical Antiquities of Philo Now First Translated from the Old Latin Version* [TED] New York: Macmillan, 1917; repr. with prolegomenon by L.H. Feld- man. New York: KTAV, 1971.

1205a Loewenstamm, S.E. "The Splitting of the Red Sea in Extra Biblical Sources," *The Tradition of the Exodus in its Development*. Jerusalem: Magnes, 1965. Pp. 120-29. [in Hebrew; English summary pp. viii-x.]

1206   Merino, L.D. "Jewish Piety Outside the Gospels in Galile After A.D. 70," *TBT* 50 (1970) 81-85.

1207   Philonenko, M. "Essénisme et gnose chez le Pseudo-Philor Le symbolisme de la lumière dans le *Liber Antiquitatum Biblicarum*," *Le Origini dello Gnosticismo*, ed. U. Bianchi. Leiden: Brill, 1967. Pp. 401-10.

1208   Philonenko, M. "Iphigénie et Sheila," *Les syncrétismes dans les religions grecque et romaine*. Vendôme: Presses universitaires de France, 1973. Pp. 165-77.

1209   Reicke, B. "Philo," *BHH* 3. Cols. 1458-61.

1210   Silkin, J. "Philo (Pseudo-) or *Liber Antiquitatum Biblicarum*," *EncyJud* 13. Cols. 408f.

1211   Winter, P. "Philo, Biblical Antiquities of," *IDB* 3. Pp. 795f.

1212   Zeron, A. "Einige Bemerkungen zu M.F. Collins 'The Hidden Vessels in Samaritan Tradition,'" *JSJ* 4 (1973) 165-68.

1213   Zeron, A. "Lacrimatorio and Pseudo-Philo's Biblical Antiquities," *IEJ* 23 (1973) 238.

Pseudo-Phocylides
(Poiēma Nouthetikon)

Extant in Greek, which has been reprinted by D. Young (*Theognis, Ps.-Pythagoras, Ps.-Phocylides, Chares, Anonymi Avlodia, Fragmentvm Teliambicvm*. Leipzig: Teubner, 1961) and excerpted from this edition by A.-M. Denis (no. 23, pp. 149-56), Pseudo-Phocylides was translated into English by B.S. Easton ("Pseudo-Phocylides," *ATR* 14 [1932] 222-28). This work was attributed falsely to the Greek poet Phocylides who lived in the sixth century B.C.

The work was written probably by a Jew--or possibly by a Christian or pagan--sometime in the first two centuries of this era (cf. Easton, p. 222; W. Kroll in Pauly-Wissowa n.B. 20.1 [1941] cols. 509f.; Denis, no. 24, p. 219); M.S. Hurwitz (no. 1216) suggests sometime between the second century B.C. and the first century A.D. It was written in Greek, probably somewhere in Egypt.

Pseudo-Phocylides appears to be an example of Jewish missionary literature (cf. P. Dalbert, *Missionsliteratur*, pp. 9-12; M. Guttmann, *Das Judentum und seine Umwelt*. Berlin: Philo, 1927; p. 112; J.E. Crouch, no. 1213a). Although A. Harnack claimed Pseudo-Phocylides was Christian (*Dogmengeschichte*[4], vol. 1, p. 172) or Jewish with a Christian interpolation (*Geschichte der altchristlichen Literatur bis Eusebius*, 2d. ed. with a foreword by K. Aland. Leipzig: Hinrichs, 1958. Teil 1, Bd. 2, pp. 863f.; Teil 2, Bd. 1, p. 589), scholars today conclude that the work is not Christian (Easton, p. 222; Denis,

no. 24, p. 218). We must be cautious in denying this possibil
ity (so also E. Lohse, no. 1216a), since we know very little
about earliest Christianity. E. Schürer's argument (*History*,
2d. Div., vol. 3, p. 314), for example, that Pseudo-Phocylides
cannot be Christian because its moral claims are based only on
the Old Testament and not upon Christ, "as we have it in the
synoptists," overlooks both the early limited areas of influence and acceptance of the first three canonical gospels, and
the fact that the author of the Letter of James uses as a para
digm the suffering and patience of the prophets and not that o
Jesus of Nazareth (5:10; cf. 5:11, 17). In summary, it is onl
possible that a Christian, but probable that a Jew, wrote
Pseudo-Phocylides to win "heathens" not so much to his own religion as to the high ethical norms and values it professed.
Note, for example, the opening: "These are the counsels of God
designed for both sinners and righteous..." (ET by Easton).
If this hypothesis is sound, the work belongs in the Pseudepigrapha.

The 230 hexameters of Pseudo-Phocylides reflect similarities with Philo's *Hypothetica* (7.1-9) and Josephus' *Contra
Apionem* (2.190-219), as Crouch has demonstrated (no. 1213b).
The influences from Aristotelianism and Stoicism are not as
determinative as those from 4 Maccabees, Deuteronomy, Exodus,
and Jewish Wisdom Literature. These eclectic poems contain
moral exhortations. Notable passages are as follows (ET by
Easton): "If thou drawest thy sword, use it to shield, not to
slaughter." (vs. 32); "If thou harmest thy neighbor/ Not by
intent, thou art guiltless; guilt lies in the intention." (vss
51f.); "Death never touches the soul, which lives though the
body is sleeping..." (vs. 105).

P.W. van der Horst is preparing a new edition with introduction and commentary.

See Sibylline Oracles, because Book 2, lines 56-148 contain Pseudo-Phocylides, lines 5-79; and Letter of Aristeas,
since J.J. Lewis (no. 587) claims it also borrowed from Pseudo
Phocylides. See also no. 302.

1213a Christ, F. "Das Leben nach dem Tode bei Pseudo-
        Phokylides," *TZ* 31 (1975) 140-49.

213b Crouch, J.E. "The *Sitz im Leben* of the Stoic Schema in
      Judaism," *The Origin and Intention of the Colossian
      Haustafel*. Göttingen: Vandenhoeck & Ruprecht, 1972.
      Pp. 84-101.

214 Denis, A.-M. "Les Sentences du Pseudo-Phocylide,"
      Introduction. Pp. 215-19.

215 Horst, P.W. van der. "Pseudo-Phocylides," Doubleday
      edition.

216 Hurwitz, M.S. "Pseudo-Phocylides," *EncyJud* 13. Cols.
      1335f.

217 Lohse, E. "Phokylides," *RGG*[3] 5. Col. 362.

218 Schmid, J. "Pseudo-Phokylides," *LTK*[2] 8. Cols. 867f.

219 Schneider, C. "Phokylides," *BHH* 3. Cols. 1463f.

220 Walter, N. "Pseudo-Phokylides," *JSHRZ* 4, in press.

Fragments of Poetical Works

This category is ill-defined in contemporary research and
needs clarification. Included herein because their dates are
similar to those of the major pseudepigrapha, and because they
are not considered by other categories, are some compositions,
which are noted under the following headings:

     Aristobulus
     Ezekiel the Tragedian
     Pseudo-Orpheus
     Philo the Epic Poet
     Theodotus

See also no. 1205a.

221 Denis, A.-M. "Les auteurs littéraires juifs hellénis-
      tiques," *Introduction*. Pp. 270-83.

Lives of the Prophets
(Deaths of the Prophets, Triumphs of
the Prophets, Pseudo-Epiphanius)

The Lives of the Prophets is preserved in numerous versions, of which the most important are the Syriac, Armenian,
and Greek. The Syriac was edited from one recension by J.-B.
Chabot (*Chronique de Michel le Syrien*. Paris: Culture et Civi-
lisation, 1910 [repr. 1963]. Vol. 4, pp. 38-64) and from
another by E. Nestle (*Syriac Grammar with Bibliography*,

176

*Chrestomathy and Glossary, Second Enlarged and Improved Editic
of the Brevis Linguae Syriacae Grammatica*, trans. from German
by R.S. Kennedy [Porta Ling. Or. 5] New York: B. Westermann,
1889). The Armenian was edited by S. Hovsepean (*Non-Canonical
Books of the Old Testament*. Venice: Armenian Press of St.
Lazarus, 1896 [in Armenian; *N.V.*]). The Greek, which is the
most important, was edited in five consecutive recensions by
T. Schermann (*Prophetarum Vitae Fabulosae, Indices Apostolorum
Discipulorumque Domini: Dorotheo, Epiphanio, Hippolyto,
Aliisque Vindicata*. Leipzig: Teubner, 1907. Pp. xxxiii-106)
and edited in an eclectic text, based on Schermann's recensior
D, by C.C. Torrey (*The Lives of the Prophets* [JBLMS 1] Phila-
delphia: SBL, 1946). English translations have been published
from a Syriac manuscript at Union Theological Seminary in New
York by I.H. Hall ("The Lives of the Prophets," *JBL* 7 [1887]
28-40), from the Armenian by J. Issaverdens ("Concerning the
Deaths of the Prophets," *UWOT*. Pp. 119-33), and from the Greek
by Torrey (*Lives*, pp. 34-48). Inserted into the Book of the
Bee at chapter 32 is a Syriac version "Of the Death of the
Prophets"; this text was edited (pp. ʿD to ʿṬ) and translated
into English (pp. 69-73) by E.A.W. Budge (*The Book of the Bee*
[Anecdota Oxoniensia Sem. Ser. 1. 2] Oxford: Clarendon, 1886).

The original text was probably composed from diverse and
ancient oral traditions sometime just prior to or in the first
century A.D. (T. Schermann, *Propheten- und Apostellegenden
nebst Jüngerkatalogen des Dorotheus und verwandter Texte* [TU
31.3] Leipzig: Hinrichs, 1907; pp. 119, 126; Torrey, *Lives*,
p. 11; *idem, Apoc. Lit.*, p. 135; R.H. Pfeiffer, *IB* 1 [1952]
425). The original language is probably Hebrew (Schermann in
TU 31.3, pp. 130-33; Torrey, *Lives*, pp. 1, 7, 16f.; *idem,
Apoc. Lit.*, pp. 135-40; Pfeiffer in *IB* 1 [1952] 425.
Schermann noted it might be Syriac and Hall argued for a
Syriac original, *JBL* 7 [1887] 38f.), or possibly Greek (cf.
A.-M. Denis, no. 24, p. 89; M.E. Stone, no. 1229). The author
who was apparently more a compiler of legends--some of which
he missed (cf. L. Ginzberg, *Legends, ad loc. cit.*)--probably
lived in Jerusalem, since there is convincing evidence that he
was intimately familiar with Jerusalem, Judaean, and Palestinian topography and geography. The Jeremiah legends, however,
betray an Egyptian provenance. Christian additions abound in

he various recensions, but the only ancient ones are in the
life of Jeremiah, verses 7-8 and 10 (cf. only vaguely possible
Christian interpolations in Hosea, vs. 2, and in Habakkuk,
vss. 11-14).

Since the list of the prophets in the numerous recensions
and versions varies markedly, both in order and in those names
included or deleted, it is best to limit our summary to the
text edited by Torrey. Ranging in length from one verse with
Joel to twenty-two verses with Daniel, this text summarizes
the lives and deaths of twenty-three prophets. Significant are
the notices of violent deaths: Isaiah was sawn in two by
Manasseh in Jerusalem; Jeremiah was stoned by a mob (Syriac =
"a Jewish mob") in Egypt; Ezekiel was slain by the leader of
the Israelite exiles in Babylonia; Micah was thrown from a
cliff by Joram, son of Ahab, in Israel; Amos was clubbed by
the son of Amaziah at or near Bethel but managed to return to
Tekoa before he died; Joed was slain by a lion; and Zechariah
was slain by Joash, king of Judah, in the Jerusalem Temple.

This work should be included among the Pseudepigrapha.

M.E. Stone has made this pseudepigraphon a subject of
special concern and research over the last two years. He is
responsible for the reproduction of T. Schermann's *Die Vitae
Prophetarum*.

See also nos. 51, 84, 87, 1188.

222 Denis, A.-M. "Les Vies des Prophètes," *Introduction*. Pp.
    85-90.

223 Ebied, R.Y. "Some Syriac Manuscripts from the Collection
    of Sir E.A. Wallis Budge," *Orient. Christ. Analecta*
    197 (1974) 509-39. See esp. pp. 523f.

224 Elze, [?]. "Vitae Prophetarum," *JSHRZ* 1, in press.

225 Hare, D.R.A. "Lives of the Prophets," Doubleday edition.

226 Michl, J. "Prophetarum Vitae," *LTK*[2] 8. Col. 794.

227 Negoiță, A. "The Lives of the Prophets According to the
    Synaxarion of the Greek Church," *Festschrift J. Bakoš*.
    Bratislava, 1965. Pp. 173-92. [This article is not in
    English, but I have been unable to locate this book.]

228 Philonenko, M. "Prophetenleben," *BHH* 3. Cols. 1512f.

229 Stone, M.E. "Prophets, Lives of the," *EncyJud* 13. Cols.
    1149f.

Apocalypse of Sedrach [*and Daniel Cycle*]

This pseudepigraphon is extant only in a fifteenth-centur
Greek manuscript preserved in the Bodleian Library (Cod. Misc.
Gr. 56, ff. 92-100). It was partially edited by M.R. James
(*Apocrypha Anecdota* [T&S 2.3] Cambridge: CUP, 1893 [repr. 1967
Pp. 130-37), and this edition was translated into English by
A. Rutherfurd (*ANF* 10. Pp. 175-80).

Very little critical work has been published on this
pseudepigraphon. It is probably neither a Jewish work as C.C.
Torrey intimated ("Apocalypse," *The Jewish Encyclopedia* 1
[1901] col. 674) nor a Christian redaction of a Jewish writing
as P. Riessler suggested (no. 62, p. 1274). It appears to be
a late Christian farrago of Jewish traditions (cf. A.-M. Denis
no. 24, pp. 97-99; and R. Meyer, no. 1233). Although extremel
difficult to date, it may have been compiled sometime in the
third or fourth century A.D. (contrast H. Weinel in Gunkel
Festschrift, pp. 158-60). The author borrows directly from
Job, Paul, John, the Testament of Abraham (cf. M.R. James, *The
Testament of Abraham* [T&S 2.2] Cambridge: CUP, 1892 [repr.
1967]; pp. 31-33, 66), the Apocalypse of Ezra (cf. the compar-
isons outlined by James in *Apocrypha Anecdota*, p. 128), 2
Baruch, and 4 Ezra (cf. the parallels outlined by James in
Apocrypha Anecdota, p. 129). The Christian elements are pervasive: "concerning...orthodox Christians, and the second
coming of our Lord Jesus Christ" (preface); "his only begotten
(*monogenē*) Son" (chp. 9); "and they obeyed neither apostles
nor my word in the Gospels" (chp. 14).

It is difficult to follow James' suggestion (*Testament of
Abraham*, p. 32; *Apocrypha Anecdota*, p. 129) that this pseudepigraphon embodies two separate documents, one a homily on lov
and the other an apocalypse. The connection between these two
which James missed, is that God's actions are motivated mainly
by love (chp. 8; cf. outline below). The work was probably
compiled from diverse writings by one person who prefaced the
whole compilation as follows: "The word of the holy and blesse
Sedrach concerning love, repentance, orthodox Christians, and
the second coming of our Lord Jesus Christ." It is not incon-
ceivable, however, that two independent compositions, with som
similar ideas, when combined were introduced by the preface.

James divided the text into sixteen chapters. Apparently under the influence of Paul and John the author praises "love" (*agapē*; 1). With a rough transition typical of the compiler, Sedrach is introduced as one who aspired to talk with God. "A voice [*sic*]" (*hē phōnē*) takes him up into the third heaven (2). Sedrach converses with the Lord and receives answers to his questions; for example, he asks why God made the earth and is told "for the sake of man" (*dia ton anthrōpon*; 3). Sedrach laments man's condition (4), and wonders why God, if he loves (*ēgapēsas*) man, willed Adam's deceitfulness (*sou thelēmatos ēpatēthē, despota mou, ho Adam*; 5). God replies that Adam, although he was given everything, became a sinner (6). Sedrach repeats his opinion that man failed because of God's will (*sou thelēmatos hēmarten*), and pleads for God to save man and protect him from sin (7). God's answer is eloquent: "But I have permitted him to have (his own) will because I loved (*ēgapēsa*) him."

God now asks Sedrach a few questions, similar to those in Job, forcing him to confess that only God knows such things (8). God sends his son to take Sedrach's soul, but Sedrach, as Abraham in the Testament of Abraham, refuses to do so (9). Sedrach asks God from whence he will take the soul, and receives the answer that, although it is scattered throughout the body, it comes out through the lungs, heart, throat, and mouth (10). Sedrach, weeping, catalogues the physical qualities of his body that will soon be interred (11), and asks Christ about the forgiveness of sinners. He receives the assurance that repentance "for three years" will erase the memory of all (*pasas*) his sins (12). Sedrach succeeds in reducing the three years to forty days (13), and then beseeches Michael to help him attain God's mercy for the world, but is told of man's continuous failures (14). Sedrach again pleads for God's compassion (15) and sympathy for sinners, moving God to reduce the forty days to twenty. God takes Sedrach's soul and places him in Paradise with all the saints (16). Running throughout the entire work, despite rough transitions and tensions sometimes caused by employing numerous disrelated sources, is the love motif and the appeal for God's forgiveness.

A very few comments should be appended to draw attention to the Daniel cycle, which in the early centuries of the present era received influences from the Ezra cycle. Long before that time, however, works related to Daniel had been composed. Aramaic fragments of the Prayer of Nabonidus were recovered from Qumran Cave 4, and these date from the second half of the first century B.C. (cf. J.T. Milik, "'Prière de Nabonide' et autres écrits d'un cycle de Daniel: Fragments araméens de Qumrân 4," *RB* 63 [1956] 407-15, with plates and transcriptions).

Considerably later and beyond the chronological limits of the Pseudepigrapha are two medieval compositions: the Apocalypse of Daniel, and the Seventh Vision of Daniel. The Apocalypse of Daniel is extant in Greek and was edited numerous times during the nineteenth century (cf. E. Klostermann, "Die Apokalypse des Propheten Daniel," *Analecta zur Septuaginta, Hexapla und Patristik*. Leipzig: Deichert, 1895; pp. 113-23; also see *idem*, "Zur Apokalypse Daniels," *ZAW* 15 [1895] 147-50; cf. Denis, no. 1231a). This apocalypse, as extant, is very late, dating from the Byzantine Empire, perhaps sometime between the seventh and the thirteenth centuries (cf. H. Weinel in Gunkel Festschrift, pp. 160f.; Denis, no. 24, pp. 309-14; and L. Ginzberg, *Legends*, vol. 4, p. 334; vol. 6, pp. 393-97, 423f., 436). It apparently was never translated into English. The Seventh Vision of Daniel is extant only in Armenian, and also dates from the seventh century (see Kalemkiar, cited below, p. 114). It was edited by P.Gr. Kalemkiar ("Die siebente Vision Daniels," *WZKM* 6 [1892] 109-36 [intr., text], 227-40 [transl.]; for a discussion of the Daniel cycle see pp. 109-11) and S. Hovsepean (*Non-Canonical Books of the Old Testament*. Venice: Armenian Press of St. Lazarus, 1896 [in Armenian; *N.V.*]). It was translated from the latter edition into English by J. Issaverdens (*UWOT*. Pp. 207f. [intr.], 219-34 [transl.]). This vision, in its present form, also dates from Byzantine times; perhaps it was composed sometime between the fifth and seventh centuries (cf. Issaverdens, p. 208; Denis, no. 1231a, p. 312).

Five other apocryphal compositions attributed to Daniel are even later than the two just mentioned. Except for the Arabic Apocalypse of Daniel, which seems to date from the ninth century, the earliest date for the other four would be the twelfth century. These four are the Fourteenth Vision of Daniel, extant in Coptic; the History of Daniel, preserved in Persian; the Visions of Daniel, contained in Russian and Serbian texts; and the Revelation to Daniel, found in medieval Hebrew manuscripts (ed. L. Ginzberg, "*Ḥzwn Dny'l*," *Genizah Studies: In Memory of Doctor Solomon Schechter*. New York: Hermon, 1928 [repr. 1969]; pp. 313-23). These compositions are beyond the scope of our present concerns, so it is sufficient to refer to a recent summary of them by Denis (no. 24, pp. 309-14; M.R. James, *LAOT*, p. 70, refers also to a Passion of Daniel and a Dreambook of Daniel).

As we have seen, Daniel's name was given to different apocryphal compositions for over a millennium. It is probable that during the first century A.D. an apocryphon of Daniel was circulating. James (*LAOT*, p. 70) offered the opinion that the Seventh Vision of Daniel, which he tended to equate with the Apocalypse of Daniel, in an earlier form is the Daniel pseudepigraphon listed by Pseudo-Athanasius and Nicephorus. Although this equation is possible we should be cautious. More than one composition attributed to Daniel was circulating early (cf. Ginzberg, *Legends*, vol. 6, p. 436; James, *LAOT*, p. 70). The Daniel pseudepigraphon mentioned by these Fathers may refer to one of them, and the Seventh Vision should not be confused or equated with the Apocalypse. James, who identified the Seventh Vision with the Daniel pseudepigraphon noted by the Greek Fathers, failed to perceive that it was the Armenian Mechithar who included in his list of apocryphal writings the Seventh Vision of Daniel, which is the Daniel pseudepigraphon extant in Armenian.

Concluding evidence that several Daniel pseudepigrapha were extant by the first century A.D. is Josephus' witness. In his *Antiquities*, which was written near the end of the first century A.D., he reports the existence of "books" (*ta gar biblia, hosa dē sungrapsamenos kataleloipen, anaginōsketai par' hēmin eti kai nun*) written by Daniel (*Ant.* 10.11, 7).

Photographs of the extant manuscript of the Apocalypse of Sedrach are preserved in the Pseudepigrapha Library at Duke University.

O. Wahl is editing this text for PVTG.

1230   Agourides, S. "Apocalypse of Sedrach," Doubleday edition.

1231   Denis, A.-M. "L'Apocalypse de Sédrach," *Introduction*.
        Pp. 97-99.

1231a   Denis, A.-M. "Les apocalypses de Daniel," *Introduction*.
        Pp. 309-14.

1232   Knippenberg, R. "Sedrachapokalypse," *BHH* 3. Col. 1754.

1233   Meyer, R. "Sedrach-Apokalypse," *RGG*³ 5. Col. 1631.

1234   Porten, B. "Shadrach, Meshach, Abed-Nego," *EncyJud* 14.
        Cols. 1255f.

1234a   Schüpphaus, J. "Das Verhältnis von LXX- und Theodotion-
        Text in den apokryphen Zusätzen zum Danielbuch," *ZAW*
        83 (1971) 49-72.

1235   Shutt, R.J.H. "Apocalypse of Sedrach," Clarendon edition.

1235a   Stone, M.E. "An Armenian Tradition Relating to the Death
        of the Three Companions of Daniel," *Muséon* 86 (1973)
        111-23.

Treatise of Shem
(Book of Shem)

This pseudepigraphon is extant only in an unbound
fifteenth-century Syriac manuscript in the John Rylands University Library of Manchester (Syriac MS 44, ff. 81b-83b). It was
edited and translated into English by A. Mingana (*Some Early
Judaeo-Christian Documents in the John Rylands Library: Syriac
Texts*. Manchester: University of Manchester, 1917. Pp. 52-59
[text], 24-29 [transl.]; repr. from *BJRL* 4 [1917] 59-118).

Only Mingana has published research on this composition.
He suggested that the original text could have been written in
the Roman period, perhaps after the ravaging of Palestine by
Vespasian or Hadrian, because of the mention of emigration from
Palestine. The provenance, according to him, is probably
Egyptian or Palestinian.

In favor of an early date is the internal evidence. The
Roman king will move about (chp. 1). The Romans will defeat
the [Persians] in a severe war (chp. 2). The Romans will find
it difficult to subdue the pirates (*leṣṭānê*, Gk. loan word)
from Palestine.

External data tend to resist the assumption of an early date. The work is not cited by the Fathers, the genre (see below) is typical of later writings (cf. G. Furlani, "Astrologisches aus syrischen Handschriften," *ZDMG* 75 [1921] 122-28; A. Baumstark, *Geschichte*, pp. 230, 352f.; G. Graf, *Geschichte*, p. 216), and brontologia, selenodromia, and calendologia are listed by Nicephorus with later writings such as the Apocalypse of Ezra and the Apocalypse of Zosimus (cf. M.R. James' comments in R.L. Bensly's *The Fourth Book of Ezra* [T&S 3.2] Cambridge: CUP, 1895; pp. xxivf.).

Generally speaking internal evidence takes precedence over external; moreover, the latter in this case is not impressive. First, numerous early works, such as the Odes of Solomon, are not quoted by the Fathers; others, such as Jubilees, are not mentioned in the famous lists of apocryphal works. Second, medieval kalandologia could be modeled upon earlier examples: Jewish horoscopes and astrological documents are not always late, since examples of them have been found at Qumran (4QCryptic; cf. J.M. Allegro, no. 129; 4Q186; cf. J. Carmignac, "Les horoscopes de Qumran," *RQ* 5 [1965] 199-217). Jewish interest in the Zodiac is clearly much earlier than we once envisioned (cf. SibOr 5:512-31). Third, Nicephorus' order of listing works is of no consequence, since there is no evidence that he followed a chronological order; moreover, the Apocalypse of Zosimus appears to contain early traditions (see the entry below).

Indicative of an Egyptian, perhaps Alexandrian, provenance is the mention of the Nile (chps. 1, 2, 3, 4, 5, [6], 7, 8, 12), Egypt (chps. 1, 2, 7, 8, 9, 12), and Alexandria (chps. 4, 6). The numerous realia are typical of Egypt, but there is no mention of beer or crocodiles. Probably reflecting an Egyptian provenance, since only Egypt and Palestine (chps. [1], 11, 12) are likely, is the note of pirates who come "from Palestine." The original language is Semitic, with Greek loan words, since there are abundant Semitisms and personal names are defined in terms of the Semitic alphabet (chps. 2, 6, 7, 8, 9, 10, 11, 12). Future research might indicate that the Treatise of Shem was composed by one of the Therapeutae. It will be interesting to see if there is any relation between

the Treatise of Shem and the unpublished Nag Hammadi Codex
entitled the Paraphrase of Shem (cf. J.M. Robinson, no. 541,
esp. pp. 378-80).

The work is a Jewish calendologion, of which other examples are attributed to Ezra (cf. James, *LAOT*, pp. 80f.),
describing the features of a year when it begins in a particular sign of the Zodiac. The composition can be divided into
twelve chapters, following the twelve signs running counter-
clockwise from Aries to Capricorn, but reversing the order of
the last two so that Pisces precedes Aquarius. The worst year
apparently begins in Aries, the first, and the best in Pisces
(the eschatological peace and harmony noted at the end prompts
the question whether this section was copied inadvertently,
due to parablepsis and the confusion between rubrics, before
the one which is now last).

If the pseudepigraphon dates from the Roman period, as
indicated above, it should be included within the Pseudepigrapha.

J.H. Charlesworth is preparing a new edition for the
BJRL (= *BJRULM*). A copy of John Rylands Library Syriac MS   42
is preserved in the Pseudepigrapha Library at Duke University.

1236   Charlesworth, J.H. "Book of Shem," Doubleday edition.

Sibylline Oracles

The Sibylline Oracles are extant primarily in Greek. The
text was edited by J. Geffcken (no. 1251) and A. Kurfess
(*Sibyllinische Weissagungen*. Berlin: Heimeran, 1951; for the
three Greek fragments, that probably belong at the beginning
of Book 3, cf. Theophilus of Antioch. *Ad Autolycum*, ed. and
trans. R.M. Grant. Oxford: Clarendon, 1970; *ad loc.*) and translated into English by three scholars: from Books 3-5, plus the
three fragments, by H.C.O. Lanchester (*APOT* 2. Pp. 377-406);
from Books 3-5 by H.N. Bate (*The Sibylline Oracles: Books III-
V* [TED] London: S.P.C.K., 1918 [repr. 1937]); and selectively
from Books 1, 2, 6, 7, and 8, as well as from the Latin
Prophetia Sibillae Magae, by R.McL. Wilson, based upon A.
Kurfess' German translation (no. 1262).

Only Books 3-5 appear to be Jewish; the others are Christian. Book 3 is the oldest, being a composite of heterogeneous

sources. V. Nikiprowetzky (no. 1265) has attempted to show
that it is a unity, except for two later additions (3:63-74,
736), and that it was written in the first century B.C. Most
scholars agree, however, that the corpus of this book dates
from the middle of the second century B.C. (viz. J.J. Collins,
nos. 1242; 1244, p. 33), and Collins (no. 1244, pp. 57-71)
isolates three passages (3:46-62, 75-92, 350-80) which may be
first-century B.C. additions. Book 4 is later, and should be
dated to c. A.D. 80, because verses 115-18 and 125-27 describe
the destruction of Jerusalem, verses 119-22 and 138f. refer
to Nero, and verses 130-36 mirror the eruption of Vesuvius in
A.D. 79. Book 5 probably was written in the first third of the
second century A.D.; verses 46-50 refer favorably [!] to
Hadrian. The Jewish Sibyllines eventually received Christian
interpolations (cf. 3:62-96 [no], 372 [?], 776; 5:68, 256-59 [!]).

The so-called Christian Sibyllines--some scholars think
they may be partly Jewish--are later. Books 1 and 2 seem to
date from around the middle of the second century A.D., since
they presuppose the Gospel of John and Revelation and since
Books 6 and 7 depend upon them. Book 8 dates from around A.D.
180. Book 6 dates from the latter part of the second century
and was used by Book 7 before the end of that century. Additions were made intermittently by Christian scribes until
around the sixth century A.D. when these heterogeneous oracles
were collected into fifteen books, of which only twelve are
preserved (1-8, 11-14).

Books 3 and 5 were written in Egypt, probably Alexandria
(Collins, no. 1244, thinks Book 3 comes from the region in
which the Leontopolis temple was soon to be built). Book 4
could have been written in Egypt, Asia Minor, or Palestine.
It is practically impossible to be convinced of the provenance
for the other books. Greek is usually considered the original
language.

A. Peretti argued for a direct relationship between the
Jewish Sibyllines and the Dead Sea Scrolls (cf. "Echi di
dottrine esseniche negli Oracoli Sibillini giudaici," *La Parola
del Passato* 85 [1962] 247-95). V. Nikiprowetzky (no. 1265)
and B. Noack (nos. 1266, 1267, 1268, 1269) independently demonstrated the weakness in this hypothesis. M. Roncaglia has

argued for contacts between Books 6 and 7 and the Dead Sea
Scrolls (no. 1270).

Since only Books 3, 4, and 5 are clearly among the Pseudepigrapha, the summary shall be limited to them. Book 3 consists of three long sections. The first (1-294), after an
argument regarding God's omnipotence and invisibility, found
in the fragments, and a brief introduction regarding the
Sibyl's compulsion to prophesy (1-7), presents affirmations of
the sovereignty, ineffableness, and remoteness of the only God
(8-45). Following this passage are an eschatological passage
(46-62); a prediction regarding God's destruction of Beliar
(63-96); and an excerpt from the Erythraean Sibyllines regarding the Tower of Babel, Titans, and the birth of Zeus, followed
by a history of the Israelites from Moses to the return from
the Babylonian exile (97-294). The second section (294-488)
contains general oracles regarding crises between and within
the major nations. The third section (489-829) prophesies
God's wrath upon countries, especially Greece, with an inter-
ruption (652-795) concerning the messianic kingdom.

Book 4 has four main sections. The first is a description
of God's invisibility but involvement with men (1-23). The
second mentions the eschatological rewards and punishments
(24-48). The third is a history of two generations of the
world, followed by oracles against countries and towns, because
God is no longer merciful (49-161). The fourth is an eschatological passage (162-92) which is introduced by an exhortation
to repentance (162-78).

Book 5 contains two main sections. The first is a history up to Hadrian, with a later interpolation that brings it
up to Marcus Aurelius (1-51). The second contains woes against
Rome and numerous countries, notably Egypt, Asia, Greece, and
Babylon (52-511). The second section has five self-contained
passages: an ode concerning the Fates (228-46), a description
of the messianic kingdom prefaced by a vision of the destruction of Judaea and followed by eschatological predictions
(247-360), a condemnation of Roman sexual perversions (386-
402), a prophecy regarding the destruction of Jerusalem by
Titus and its restoration by a heavenly man (403-33), and a
warning of cosmic phenomena which are described in terms of

the Zodiac (512-31).

See also nos. 59, 64, 87, 234, 265, 270, 303, 308, 330, 361, 403, 465, 471, 594.

1237 Amir, Y. "Sibyl and Sibylline Oracles," *EncyJud* 14. Cols. 1489-91.

1238 Arnon, C. "The Messianic Idea in Hellenistic Judaism by J. Amir," *Immanuel* 2 (1973) 58-60. [See J. Amir in *Machanayim* 124 (1970) 54-67.]

1239 Bertrand, D.A. "Les *Oracles Sibyllins*," *Le baptême de Jésus: Histoire de l'exégèse aux deux premiers siècles.* Tübingen: Mohr, 1973. Pp. 52-55.

1240 Bischoff, B. "Die lateinischen Übersetzungen und Bearbei-tungen aus den Oracula Sibyllina," *Mittelalterliche Studien.* Stuttgart: Hiersemann, 1967. Vol. 1, pp. 150-71.

1241 Collins, J.J. "The Place of the Fourth Sibyl in the Development of the Jewish Sibyllina," *JJS* 25 (1974) 365-80.

1242 Collins, J.J. "The Provenance and Date of the Third Sibyl," *Bulletin of the Institute of Jewish Studies* 2 (1974) 1-18.

1243 Collins, J.J. "Sibylline Oracles," Doubleday edition.

1244 Collins, J.J. *The Sibylline Oracles of Egyptian Judaism* (SBLDS 13) Missoula, Mont.: SBL, 1974.

1245 Denis, A.-M. "Les Oracles Sibyllins," *Introduction.* Pp. 111-22.

1246 Dornseiff, F. "Die sibyllinischen Orakel in der august-eischen Dichtung," *Römische Dichtung der augusteischen Zeit.* Berlin: Akademie, 1960. Pp. 43-51. [*N.V.*]

1247 Erbetta, M. "Gli Oracoli Sibillini Cristiani," *Apocrifi del NT.* Vol. 3, pp. 485-540.

1248 Flusser, D. "A Quotation from the Ghathas in a Christian Sibylline Oracle," Widengren Festschrift. Vol. 1, pp. 172-75.

1249 Gager, J.G. "Some Attempts to Label the *Oracula Sibyl-lina*, Book 7," *HTR* 65 (1972) 91-97.

1250 Gancho, C. "Oráculos Sibilinos," *Enciclopedia de la Biblia* 5. Cols. 667f.

1251 Geffcken, J. *Die Oracula Sibyllina* (GCS) Leipzig, 1902; repr. Amsterdam: A.M. Hakkert, 1970.

1252 Geoltrain, P. "Sibyllinische Orakel," *BHH* 3. Cols. 1779f.

1253   Giversen, S. "Sibyllinske Orakler," *GDBL* 2. Col. 743.

1254   Goodenough, E.R. "Astronomical Symbols," *Jewish Symbols*
       8 (1958) 167-218. See esp. p. 203.

1255   Goodenough, E.R. "The Relevance of Rabbinic Evidence,"
       Jewish Symbols 4 (1954) 3-24. See esp. p. 12.

1256   Goodenough, E.R. "The Reredos," *Jewish Symbols* 9 (1964)
       78-123. See esp. p. 99.

1257   Goodenough, E.R. "Victory and Her Crown," *Jewish Symbols*
       7 (1958) 135-71. See esp. p. 163.

1258   Goodenough, E.R. "Wine in Jewish Cult and Observance,"
       Jewish Symbols 6 (1956) 126-217. See esp. p. 135.

1259   Grant, F.C. "Sibyllinen," *RGG*^{3} 6. Cols. 14f.

1260   Helmbold, A.K. "Sibylline Oracles," *ZPEB* 5. P. 425.

1261   Knox, J. "Sibylline Oracles," *IDB* 4. P. 343.

1262   Kurfess, A. "Christian Sibyllines," trans. R.McL. Wilson.
       HSW. Vol. 2, pp. 703-45.

1263   Michl, J. "Sibyllinen, Sibyllinische Orakel oder Bücher,"
       LTK^2 9. Cols. 728f.

1264   Nikiprowetzky, V. "Réflexions sur quelques problèmes du
       quatrième et du cinquième livre des Oracles Sibyllins,"
       HUCA 43 (1972) 29-76.

1265   Nikiprowetzky, V. *La troisième Sibylle* (Etudes juives 9)
       Paris-La Haye: Mouton, 1970.

1266   Noack, B. "Are the Essenes Referred to in the Sibylline
       Oracles?" *Studia Theologica* 17 (1963) 90-102.

1267   Noack, B. "Er Essaeerne omtalt i de Sibyllinske
       Orakler?" *DTT* 25 (1962) 176-89.

1268   Noack, B. "De Sibyllinske Oraklers baggrund," *SEA* 31
       (1966) 64-79.

1269   Noack, B. "Sibyllinske Orakler," *GamPseud* 4 (1963) 441-
       508.

1270   Roncaglia, M. "Les 'Oracles Sybillins' judéo-chrétiens,"
       Les origines. Pp. 76-78.

1271   Rosenstiehl, J.M. and J.G. Heintz. "De Šibtu, la reine
       de Mari, à Sambéthé, la Sibylle chaldéene?" *RHPR* 52
       (1972) 13-15.

1272   Schwark, [?]. "Sibyllinen," *JSHRZ* 5, in press.

1273   Stomfohl, H. "Zur Psychologie der Sibylle," *ZRGG* 13
       (1971) 84-103.

Odes of Solomon

Forty of the forty-two Odes of Solomon are extant in Syriac, five are preserved in Coptic, and one in Greek. An eclectic text has been edited and translated into English by J.H. Charlesworth (no. 1292). Other translations into English were published by J.R. Harris and A. Mingana (*The Odes and Psalms of Solomon*. 2 vols. Manchester: University of Manchester; London, New York: Longmans, Green & Co., 1916-1920. Vol. 1, text and facsimile; vol. 2, transl.), by J.H. Bernard (*The Odes of Solomon* [T&S 8.3] Cambridge: CUP, 1912), and by M. MarYosip (*The Oldest Christian Hymn-book*, foreword by M. Sprengling. Temple, Tex.: M. MarYosip, 1948).

The date of the Odes of Solomon is no longer as puzzling as it was at the beginning of the century. Most scholars now think they are from the years A.D. 70-125; the similarities to the Dead Sea Scrolls and the Gospel of John indicate for some that they were written near the end of the first century A.D. (cf. Charlesworth, nos. 1297, 1295, 1290).

A few scholars claim that the original language is Greek (M. Testuz, ed., *Papyrus Bodmer X-XII*. Geneva: Bibliotheca Bodmeriana, 1959; p. 57; A.F.J. Klijn, nos. 1312, 1313; M. Philonenko, no. 1325; contrast A. Adam, no. 1275; K. Rudolph, no. 1329), and J. Carmignac (nos. 1284, 1286) argues for Hebrew. The most detailed research, published independently, concludes that it is Syriac (cf. J.A. Emerton, no. 1302; Charlesworth, nos. 1288, 1289, 1292; A. Vööbus, *Celibacy: A Requirement for Admission to Baptism in the Early Syrian Church* [PETSE 1] Stockholm: Estonian Theological Society in Exile, 1951; p. 21; *idem*, *History of Asceticism in the Syrian Orient* [CSCO 14] Louvain: CSCO, 1958; p. 63; *idem*, no. 1337; J.C.L. Gibson, no. 1305a). Some specialists, especially in Germany, connect the Odes with second-century Gnosticism (viz. Rudolph, nos. 1328, 1329), but others deny this attribution (cf. Charlesworth, no. 1293; H. Chadwick, no. 1287; R. Murray, nos. 1320, 1321, 1321a; E.M. Yamauchi, no. 1338). A relationship with, and perhaps even direct influence from (cf. Carmignac, nos. 1284, 1285; Charlesworth, nos. 1290, 1295), the ideas peculiar to the Dead Sea Scrolls is widely acknowledged (viz. J. Licht, no. 1317; H. Nibley, no. 1323a); but the Odes are not Essene as M. Testuz (*Papyrus Bodmer X-XII*, p. 58) stated.

The original language, Syriac, and the affinities with the Dead Sea Scrolls, the Johannine literature, and Ignatius of Antioch indicate that the Odes may have been composed in or near Syrian Antioch.

The forty-one extant odes are not Jewish but Jewish-Christian. The poetical style is not that of the Qumranic Hodayoth nor the Sibylline Oracles, but akin to and based upon the Davidic Psalter. Baptismal motifs abound, and two features from the life of Jesus of Nazareth given special attention are the walking on the water (Ode 39) and the baptism (Ode 24; cf. Charlesworth, no. 1296; E.E. Fabbri, no. 1303). Other prominent features are the pervasive present joy of salvation, the image of the cross (esp. Odes 17, 42), and the virginal birth of the Son (Ode 19).

These Odes clearly belong in the Pseudepigrapha, even though they are Jewish-Christian, because of their strong Jewishness, early date, and attribution to Solomon.

J.H. Charlesworth is preparing an edition of the Greek for the SBL T&T Series. A.T. Morrison is writing a Ph.D. dissertation under Prof. C.K. Barrett, on a literary and theological comparison between the Johannine literature and the Odes of Solomon. Glossy photographs of all extant manuscripts are preserved in the Pseudepigrapha Library at Duke University.

See the publications listed under the Pseudepigrapha and the Dead Sea Scrolls, the Pseudepigrapha and Gnosticism, and Prayer. See also nos. 87, 108, 368, 935, 940, 1493. For a full bibliography of older publications see J.H. Charlesworth, no. 1292.

1274   Adam, A. "Die Salomo-Oden," *Lehrbuch der Dogmengeschichte*. Gütersloh: Mohn, 1965. Vol. 1, pp. 142-46.

1275   Adam, A. "Die ursprüngliche Sprache der Salomo-Oden," *ZNW* 52 (1961) 141-56.

1276   Aune, D.E. *The Cultic Setting of Realized Eschatology in Early Christianity* (NovTSup 28) Leiden: Brill, 1972. Pp. 166-94.

1277   Baars, W. "A Note on Ode of Salomon xi 14," *VT* 12 (1962) 196.

1278 Barnard, L.W. "The Origins and Emergence of the Church
     in Edessa During the First Two Centuries A.D.," *VC* 22
     (1968) 161-75.

1279 Bauer, W. "Die Oden Salomos," *Neutestamentliche Apokry-
     phen in deutscher Übersetzung*, 3rd ed., eds. E.
     Hennecke and W. Schneemelcher. Tübingen: Mohr, 1964.
     Vol. 2, pp. 576-625.

1280 Bertrand, D.A. "Les Odes de Salomon," *Le baptême de
     Jésus: Histoire de l'exégèse aux deux premiers siècles*.
     Tübingen: Mohr, 1973. Pp. 23-26.

1281 Boesse, J. "La mystique du christianisme primitif,"
     Encyclopédie des mystiques, ed. M.-M. Davy. [Paris]:
     Robert Laffont, 1972. Pp. 157-60. [It is unfortunate
     that no place is given in this volume to the Jewish
     apocryphal works, but see R. Weil's "Les origines de
     la Kabbale," pp. 99-105.]

1282 Borig, R. "Oden Salomos," *Der Wahre Weinstock: Untersu-
     chungen zu Jo 15, 1-10* (StANT 16) Munich: Kösel, 1967.
     P. 190.

1283 Buck, F. "Are the 'Ascension of Isaiah' and the 'Odes of
     Solomon' Witnesses to an Early Cult of Mary?" *De pri-
     mordiis cultus mariani*. Rome: Pontificia Academia
     Mariana Internationalis, 1970. Vol. 4, pp. 371-99.
     [*N.V.*]

1284 Carmignac, J. "Les affinités qumrâniennes de la onzième
     Ode de Salomon," *RQ* 3 (1961) 71-102.

1285 Carmignac, J. "Un qumrânien converti au christianisme:
     l'auteur des Odes de Salomon," *Qumran-Probleme*, ed. H.
     Bardtke (Deutsche Akademie der Wissenschaften zu Berlin
     42) Berlin: Akademie, 1963. Pp. 75-108.

1286 Carmignac, J. "Recherches sur la langue originelle des
     Odes de Salomon," *RQ* 4 (1963) 429-32.

1287 Chadwick, H. "Some Reflections on the Character and The-
     ology of the Odes of Solomon,"*Kyriakon*. J. Quasten
     Festschrift, eds. P. Granfield and J.A. Jungmann.
     Münster: Aschendorff, 1970. Vol. 1, pp. 266-70.

1288 Charlesworth, J.H. "*B'WT'* in Earliest Christianity,"
     *The Use of the Old Testament in the New and Other
     Essays: Studies in Honor of William Franklin Stine-
     spring*, ed. J.M. Efird. Durham, N.C.: Duke, 1972. Pp.
     271-79.

1289 Charlesworth, J.H. *A Critical Examination of the Odes of
     Solomon: Identification, Text, Original Language, Date*.
     Duke Ph.D., 1967.

1290 Charlesworth, J.H. "Les Odes de Salomon et les manuscrits
     de la Mer Morte," *RB* 77 (1970) 522-49.

1291 Charlesworth, J.H. "Odes of Solomon," Doubleday edition.

1292 Charlesworth, J.H. *The Odes of Solomon*. Oxford: Clarendon, 1973.

1293 Charlesworth, J.H. "The Odes of Solomon--Not Gnostic,"
CBQ 31 (1969) 357-69.

1294 Charlesworth, J.H. "Paronomasia and Assonance in the
Syriac Text of the Odes of Solomon," *Semitics* 1 (1970)
12-26.

1295 Charlesworth, J.H. "Qumran, John and the Odes of Solomon,
John and Qumran, ed. J.H. Charlesworth. London: Chap-
man, 1972. Pp. 107-36.

1296 Charlesworth, J.H. "Tatian's Dependence upon Apocryphal
Traditions," *HeyJ* 15 (1974) 5-17.

1297 Charlesworth, J.H. and R.A. Culpepper. "The Odes of
Solomon and the Gospel of John," *CBQ* 35 (1973) 298-322.

1298 Drijvers, H.J.W. "Edessa und das jüdische Christentum,"
VC 24 (1970) 4-33.

1299 Drijvers, H.J.W. "The Other Works Ascribed to Bardaiṣan,"
Bardaiṣan of Edessa, trans. G.E. van Baaren-Pape
(Studia Semitica Neerlandica 6) Assen: Van Gorcum,
1966. Pp. 209-12.

1300 Driver, G.R. "Notes on Two Passages in the Odes of
Solomon," *JTS* 25 (1974) 434-37.

1301 Emerton, J.A. "Odes of Solomon," Clarendon edition.

1302 Emerton, J.A. "Some Problems of Text and Language in the
Odes of Solomon," *JTS* n.s. 18 (1967) 372-406.

1303 Fabbri, E.E. "El Enigma de la 24ª Oda de Salomón,"
Ciencia y Fe 16 (1960) 383-98.

1304 Fabbri, E.E. "El Simbolo de la Leche en las Odas de
Salomón," *Ciencia y Fe* 17 (1961) 273-87.

1305 Gamber, K. "Die Oden Salomos als frühchristliche Gesänge
beim heiligen Mahl," *Ostkirchliche Studien* 15 (1966)
182-95.

1305a Gibson, J.C.L. "From Qumran to Edessa: *or* The Aramaic
Speaking Church Before and After 70 A.D.," *New College
Bulletin* 2 (1965) 9-19; repr. *ALUOS* 5 (1963-1965) 24-39

1306 Giversen, S. "Salomos Oder," *GDBL* 2. Col. 678.

1307 Goodenough, E.R. "Cosmic Judaism: The Temple of Aaron,"
Jewish Symbols 10 (1964) 3-26. See esp. p. 26.

1308 Goodenough, E.R. "The Divine Fluid in the Late Syncre-
tism," *Jewish Symbols* 6 (1956) 94-125. See esp. p. 121.

1309 Goodenough, E.R. "Wine in Jewish Cult and Observance,"
Jewish Symbols 6 (1956) 126-217. See esp. pp. 195-98.

1310 Hill, D. "On the Evidence for the Creative Role of Christian Prophets," *NTS* 20 (1974) 262-74.

1311 Klijn, A.F.J. "Christianity in Edessa and the Gospel of Thomas: On Barbara Ehlers, Kann das Thomasevangelium aus Edessa stammen?" *NovT* 14 (1972) 70-77.

1312 Klijn, A.F.J. "The Influence of Jewish Theology on the Odes of Solomon and the Acts of Thomas," *Aspects du judéo-christianisme: Colloque de Strasbourg 23-25 avril 1964.* Paris: Presses universitaires de France, 1965. Pp. 167-77. [See also the discussion of Klijn's paper, pp. 177-79.]

1313 Klijn, A.F.J. "Die Oden Salomos," *Edessa, Die Stadt des Apostels Thomas,* trans. M. Hornschuh (Neukirchener Studienbücher 4) Giessen: Neukirchener, 1965. Pp. 45-64.

1314 Kragerud, A. *Die Hymnen der Pistis Sophia.* Oslo: Universitetsforlaget, 1967.

1315 Kuhl, J. "Die Oden Salomons," *Die Sendung Jesu und der Kirche nach dem Johannes-Evangelium* (Studia Instituti Missiologici Soc. Verbi Divini 11) St. Augustin, Siegburg: Steyler, 1967. Pp. 36-38.

1316 Lampe, G.W.H. *The Seal of the Spirit: A Study in the Doctrine of Baptism and Confirmation in the New Testament and the Fathers,* 2d. ed. London: S.P.C.K., 1967. See esp. pp. 111-14.

1317 Licht, J. "Solomon, Odes of," *EncyJud* 15. Cols. 114f.

1318 Ménard, J. "Le 'Descensus ad Inferos,'" Widengren Festschrift. Vol. 2, pp. 296-306.

1319 Merrill, E.H. "The Odes of Solomon and the Acts of Thomas: A Comparative Study," *Journal of the Evangelical Theological Society* 17 (1974) 231-34.

1320 Murray, R. "The Exhortation to Candidates for Ascetical Vows at Baptism in the Ancient Syriac Church," *NTS* 21 (1974) 59-80. See esp. pp. 72-74.

1321 Murray, R. "Recent Studies in Early Symbolic Theology," *HeyJ* 6 (1965) 412-33.

1321a Murray, R. *Symbols of Church and Kingdom: A Study in Early Syriac Tradition.* Cambridge: CUP, 1975.

1322 Musurillo, H. "The Odes of Salomon 17, 42, 30," *Classical Folia* 18 (1964) 54-56.

1323 Nauck, W. "Oden Salomos," *BHH* 2. Cols. 1328f.

1323a Nibley, H. "From the Odes of Solomon," *The Message of the Joseph Smith Papyri.* Salt Lake City, Utah: Deseret, 1975. Pp. 263-66.

1323b Nibley, H. *Since Cumorah: The Book of Mormon in the Modern World.* Salt Lake City, Utah: Deseret, 1967. See esp. pp. 72-74.

1324 Phanourgakēs, B.D. "Odes of Solomon," *ThEE* 12. Cols. 563-65. [in Greek]

1325 Philonenko, M. "Conjecture sur un verset de la onzième Ode de Salomon," *ZNW* 53 (1962) 264.

1326 Quasten, J. "The Odes of Solomon," *Patrology.* Utrecht-Antwerp: Spectrum, 1962. Vol. 1, pp. 160-68.

1327 Ragot, A. "De l'essénisme au christianisme," *Cahiers du Cercle Ernest-Renan* 19 (1973) 5-24.

1328 Rudolph, K. "Gnosis und Gnostizismus, ein Forschungsbericht," *ThRu* 34 (1969) 121-75, 181-231. See esp. pp. 214-24.

1329 Rudolph, K. "War der Verfasser der Oden Salomos ein 'Qumran-Christ'? Ein Beitrag zur Diskussion um die Anfänge der Gnosis," *RQ* 4 (1964) 523-55.

1330 Sanders, J.T. "The Odes of Solomon," *The New Testament Christological Hymns: Their Historical Religious Background* (SNTS MS 15) Cambridge: CUP, 1971. Pp. 101-20.

1331 Schmid, J. "Oden Salomons," *LTK²* 7. Pp. 1094f.

1332 Schnackenburg, R. "Early Gnosticism," *Jesus in His Time,* ed. H.J. Schultz; trans. B. Watchorn. Philadelphia: Fortress, 1971. Pp. 132-41.

1333 Schnackenburg, R. *Das Johannesevangelium* (HTKNT 4) Freiburg: Herder, 1965. Vol. 1, see esp. pp. 124-31. [ET by K. Smyth. New York: Herder; London: Burns and Oates, 1968.]

1334 Schulz, S. "Salomo-Oden," *RGG³* 5. Cols. 1339-42.

1335 Smith, D.M. "Johannine Christianity: Some Reflections on its Character and Delineation," *NTS* 21 (1975) 222-48. See esp. pp. 240-44.

1336 Terzoli, R. "Le Odi di Salomone," *Il tema della beatitudine nei padri siri* (Ricerche di Scienze Teologiche 11) Rome: Morcelliana, 1972. Pp. 17-28.

1337 Vööbus, A. "Neues Licht zur Frage der Originalsprache der Oden Salomos," *Muséon* 75 (1962) 275-90.

1337a [Wirt, S.E.] "The Odes of Solomon: Masterpieces of Christian Devotion from the First Century," *Decision* 55440 (Oct. 1975) 8f., 14.

1338 Yamauchi, E.M. "The Odes of Solomon," *Pre-Christian Gnosticism.* Grand Rapids, Mich.: Eerdmans, 1973. Pp. 91-94.

Psalms of Solomon

This pseudepigraphon is preserved in two main traditions:
Syriac and Greek. The former was re-edited recently by W.
Baars (no. 1340) and the latter is found in A. Rahlfs' convenient collection (no. 1355; also see Baars, "A New Fragment of
the Greek Version of the Psalms of Solomon," *VT* 11 [1961] 441-
44). English translations have been published, from the Syriac
by J.R. Harris and A. Mingana (*The Odes and Psalms of Solomon*.
2 vols. Manchester: University of Manchester; London, New York:
Longmans, Green & Co., 1916-1920. Vol. 1, text and facsimile;
vol. 2, transl.) and from the Greek essentially by G.B. Gray
(*APOT* 2. Pp. 631-52). The often-cited book by G.H. Box was
never published although authoritative publications for over
sixty years have noted it with an appended "*N.V.*" or "non con-
sulté." (It was supposed to have been *The Odes and Psalms of
Solomon* [TED 1.6].)

The date of these psalms is around the middle of the first
century B.C. since Psalms of Solomon 2:30-35 refers to the
death of Pompey in 48 B.C. The original language is now generally recognized to be Hebrew (S. Holm-Nielsen, no. 1353, p.
551; H. Braun, no. 1341; U. Rappaport, no. 1356; P. Winter,
no. 1358).

These psalms should be considered related neither with
the Dead Sea Scrolls (cf. the distinctions Holm-Nielsen perceives, no. 1351), nor with the Pharisees (cf. R.B. Wright,
no. 1360; contrast M. Delcor, no. 1343; M. Black in *IDB* 3, p.
777 [!]; and A.-M. Denis, no. 24, p. 64). There is no convincing evidence to link them with a defined sectarian group
(cf. Winter, no. 1358; Rappaport, no. 1356). We are becoming
aware not only that the Pharisees represented a wide range of
ideas, including apocalyptic, but also that there were other
groups within Judaism not represented by the usual sectarian
categories. The psalms are Palestinian, and may have been composed in Jerusalem (cf. Braun, no. 1341; Denis, no. 24, pp.
60-69; Wright, no. 1360, p. 150, n. 8).

The eighteen psalms, like the Odes of Solomon, are composed in the style of the Davidic Psalter. They are clearly
Jewish, although J. Ephron (no. 1346) thinks they are Christian. The psalms are characterized by affirmations of the need

to praise God (3:1-3; 8:40; 15:3), the righteousness of God
(2:19; 8:32; 10:6), the continuous help from God (5:7; 6:3-5;
7:6; 15:1; 16:3f.; 17:3), the destruction of sinners (3:13-15;
13:10; 14:4-6; 15:7, 9-15; 16:5), and the resurrection to eternal life for those who fear God (3:16; 13:9; 14:2f., 6). Running throughout is the conviction that Israel is united with
God by a covenant (cf. esp. 9:16-19; 10:5; 17:7).

The most influential passage, at least in modern scholar-
ship, is the eschatological and messianic passage in 17:23-51.
The Messiah (MŠYḤ' MRY' --christos kuriou, vs. 36), however, is
not accurately defined as militant, despite the frequent inter-
pretations in recent publications. He does "purge Jerusalem"
from foreign domination, but he will not lead an army or an-
nihilate with the sword or bow (vs. 37). He shall destroy the
oppressing nations "by the word of his mouth" (BMLT PWMN--
en logō stomatos autou, vs. 27; cf. vss. 39, 41).

R. Wright at Temple University has been directing a team
that is preparing a new collation of the Greek based upon
eleven manuscripts, two of which he found recently in the Vatican Library shelved incorrectly. Wright is working toward a
critical edition, with text, introduction, notes, and commentary.

Preserved in the Pseudepigrapha Library at Duke University
are copies of the following Syriac manuscripts: Mingana 331,
B.M. Add. 14538, John Rylands Library Cod. Syr. 9.

See the works listed above under Prayer. See also nos.
87, 108, 115, 162, 234, 330, 369, 375, 403, 465, 471, 478.

1339 Baars, W. "An Additional Fragment of the Syriac Version
      of the Psalms of Solomon," VT 11 (1961) 222f.

1340 Baars, W., ed. "Psalms of Solomon," Peshiṭta. Part 4,
      fasc. 6 (1972) i-vi, 1-27.

1341 Braun, H. "Salomo-Psalmen," RGG³ 5. Cols. 1342f.

1342 Brock, S.P. "Psalms of Solomon," Clarendon edition.

1343 Delcor, M. "Salomón, Salmos de," Enciclopedia de la
      Biblia 6. Col. 401.

1344 Denis, A.-M. "Les Psaumes de Salomon," Introduction. Pp.
      60-69.

1345 Enslin, M.S. "Psalmen Salomos," BHH 3. Cols. 1520f.

1346 Ephron, J. "The Psalms of Solomon, the Hasmonean Decline and Christianity," *Zion* 30 (1965) 1-46. [in Hebrew]

1347 Giannopoulos, B.N. "Solomon (Psalms of)," *ThĒE* 11. Cols. 266f. [in Greek]

1348 Glatzer, N.N. "Thou Art Our King," *Judaic Tradition*. Pp. 68-72.

1349 Goodenough, E.R. "Astronomical Symbols," *Jewish Symbols* 8 (1958) 167-218. See esp. p. 204.

1350 Goodenough, E.R. "The Tree," *Jewish Symbols* 7 (1958) 87-134. See esp. p. 127.

1351 Holm-Nielsen, S. "Erwägungen zu dem Verhältnis zwischen den Hodajot und den Psalmen Salomos," *Bibel und Qumran*. H. Bardtke Festschrift, ed. S. Wagner. Berlin: Evangelische Haupt-Bibelgesellschaft, 1968. Pp. 112-31.

1352 Holm-Nielsen, S. "Psalmen Salomos," *JSHRZ* 4, in press.

1353 Holm-Nielsen, S. "Salomos Salmer," *GamPseud* 5 (1970) 548-95.

1354 Oswalt, J. "Psalms of Solomon," *ZPEB* 4. Pp. 947-49.

1355 Rahlfs, A., ed. "Psalmi Salomonis," *Septuaginta* 2. Pp. 471-89.

1356 Rappaport, U. "Solomon, Psalms of," *EncyJud* 15. Cols. 115f.

1357 Salomonsen, B. "Salomos Salmer," *GDBL* 2. Cols. 678f.

1358 Winter, P. "Psalms of Solomon," *IDB* 3. Pp. 958-60.

1359 Wright, R.B. "Psalms of Solomon," Doubleday edition.

1360 Wright, R.B. "The Psalms of Solomon, the Pharisees and the Essenes," *SCS* 2. Pp. 136-54.

Testament of Solomon [and Solomon Cycle]

The Testament of Solomon is extant in unedited Semitic manuscripts (viz. Bib. Nat. Fonds Syriaque 194, ff. 153a-156b; Vat. ar. 448, ff. 39r-54r; cf. G. Graf, *Geschichte*, p. 210) and in Greek. The latter was edited by C.C. McCown (*The Testament of Solomon* [Untersuch. z. N.T. 9] Leipzig: Hinrichs, 1922. Pp. 3*-120*), and translated into English from an earlier edition by F.C. Conybeare ("The Testament of Solomon," *JQR* 11 [1898] 1-45).

This pseudepigraphon is neither so late nor so early as some older scholars claimed. McCown (esp. pp. 105-08) argued

persuasively for an early third-century A.D. date for the
original compilation (so also J.B. Frey in *DBSup* 1, col. 456;
K. Preisendanz in Pauly-Wissowa n.B. Sup. 8 [1956] cols. 684-
90, esp. col. 689; A.-M. Denis, no. 24, p. 67), which incor-
porates a first-century A.D. Jewish composition (McCown's
siglum *d*). Scholars correctly do not follow Conybeare's contention (p. 12) that the original Jewish work is to be identified with the Solomonic incantations cited by Josephus near
the end of the first century A.D. (*Ant.* 8.2, 5). Josephus does
not appear to be referring to a particular text but to the numerous liquid traditions about Solomon's control over demons
(see the discussion on the Solomonic cycle below and L. Ginzberg's "Solomon Master of the Demons," *Legends*, vol. 4, pp.
149-54 and related notes). McCown (pp. 38-43) argued that the
original language is Greek (so also Preisendanz, col. 689; J.
Petroff, no. 1367), except for a possible Semitic original in
recension A in the list of *decani* (18:24-40 [H]). He suggested
that the provenance, in ascending order of probability, is
Galilean, Egyptian, or Asian; the section containing the list
of *decani*, however, is Egyptian (p. 42). Frey (col. 456) proposed an Egyptian provenance for the entire work.

The pseudepigraphon is either a Jewish composition which
was eventually reworked by a Christian (so Conybeare, pp. 11f.;
Frey, col. 455; Ginzberg, *Legends*, vol. 6, p. 292; B.M.
Metzger, no. 1365) or a Christian writing which incorporated
some Jewish material (McCown, pp. 108f.). Clearly Christian
passages are found in sections 54, 65, and 122 (cf. 71 and
104). These passages emphasize the cross and virgin birth.

The Testament of Solomon contains 130 sections, according
to Conybeare's translation (26 chapters according to McCown's
edition of the longest recension). The work is called a testament because Solomon writes the *diathēkēn* (130=26:8) in order
that those who read it may pray and heed the last things (*tois
eschatois*). This exhortation mirrors Solomon's egregious
error, his lust for a Shunammite girl and subsequent idolatry.
Earlier (66=15:13) Solomon states that he wrote his testament
before his death so that the children of Israel would know the
powers and shapes of the demons, and the names of the angels
who have power over them.

The pseudepigraphon recounts how Solomon is able to build the Temple by defeating demons and employing their skills by means of a ring and its seal given to him by the Archangel Michael. Solomon's greatness is acknowledged by a visit from the Queen of the South, who is a witch, and by a letter from the king of the Arabs. Solomon succeeds in building the Temple only to fall into idolatry through lust for a Shunammite girl.

If the Testament of Solomon is not late, as early scholars claimed, then it belongs in the Pseudepigrapha. In light of the emphasis upon demons and angels and the central concern for the Temple it will be interesting to see if there is a relation between this pseudepigraphon and the Qumranic Temple Scroll (cf. Y. Yadin, "The Temple Scroll," *New Directions in Biblical Archaeology*, eds. D.N. Freedman and J.C. Greenfield. Garden City, N.Y.: Doubleday, 1971; pp. 156-66).

It might be helpful briefly to draw attention to the vast amount of apocryphal literature attributed to Solomon. Besides the Odes, Psalms, and Testament of Solomon, which are featured herein, twelve Solomonic apocrypha may be listed: 1) Questions of the Queen to Solomon, which is extant in Armenian and translated by J. Issaverdens (*UWOT*. Pp. 137-43; cf. also the two recensions of "Concerning the Books of Solomon," pp. 144-47); 2) Solomon and Kitovras, which is preserved in Slavonic (cf. Ja.S. Lur'e, no. 1364a); 3) Solomon and Saturn, which is extant in Anglo-Saxon and which M.R. James identified with the lost *Interdictio* or *Contradictio Salomonis* listed in the *Decretum Gelasianum* (8.5, 332--*LAOT*. Pp. 51-53); 4) a quantity of Solomonic magical works, mostly too late for our interest, especially the *Clavicula* (cf. McCown, p. 100; Preisendanz, cols. 696f.; Denis, no. 24, pp. 67-69; W.M. Watt, "The Queen of Sheba in Islamic Tradition," in J.B. Pritchard [ed.], no. 1367a, pp. 104-14; B. Bagatti, nos. 1361, 1362; O. Löfgren, no. 1364); 5) Solomon and the Power of Women (cf. M. McNamara, *The Apocrypha in the Irish Church*. Dublin: Dublin Institute for Advanced Studies, 1975; p. 28); 6) Instructions of David to Solomon (cf. L. Leroy, "Instruction de David à Salomon: Fragment traduit de l'arabe," *Revue de l'orient chrétien* 20 (1915-1917) 329-31; Graf, *Geschichte*, p. 209); 7) Solomon's Warning to Rehoboam (cf. Graf, *Geschichte*, p. 209); 8) Concerning the

Death of Solomon (cf. Graf, *Geschichte*, p. 209); 9) History
of Solomon's Palace (cf. Graf, *Geschichte*, p. 210; Watt in
Pritchard [ed.], no. 1367a, pp. 104-14, esp. p. 87); 10) Judgment of King Solomon (cf. Graf, *Geschichte*, p. 210); 11) Story
of Aphiḳia, who is the wife of Jesus the son of Sirach, vizier
of King Solomon (cf. M.D. Gibson, *Apocrypha Arabica* [Studia
Sinaitica 8] London: Clay, 1901; pp. xi-xiii [intr.], 58-67
[in Arabic numbering, Karshuni and Arabic texts], 59-63
[transl.]; Graf, *Geschichte*, pp. 211f.); 12) *Kebra Nagast*
(Glory of the Kings), which is a medieval romance in Ethiopic
of which chapters 21-63, 84-94, and 113-17 contain traditions
about the Sheba-Solomon cycle (cf. Watt in Pritchard [ed.],
no. 1367a, pp. 104-14, esp. p. 109).

These pseudepigraphical compositions should not be branded
a priori as medieval forgeries and discarded from considera-
tion. It is clear both that in their present form they are
very late and that some preserve ancient traditions. Prior to
the eleventh century, medieval compositions, especially Geor-
gios Hamartolos' *Brief Chronicle*, were built upon earlier traditions, and shortly thereafter the Crusades opened numerous
and varied channels that enriched western culture with eastern
legends, especially ancient haggadic and pseudepigraphical oral
and literary traditions. Some Solomonic traditions are undeni-
ably concretized in the cathedrals at Canterbury, Chartres,
Amiens, and Rheims, perhaps immortalized in Handel's "Solomon,"
and certainly buried in the plays of Pedro Calderón de la
Barca, who studied diverse Solomonic pseudepigrapha according
to P.F. Watson ("The Queen of Sheba in Christian Tradition,"
in Pritchard [ed.], no. 1367a, pp. 115-45, esp. pp. 135f.).
Some art forms certainly betray apocryphal traditions and need
examining by specialists (cf. B. Bayer, no. 1362a). For example, a South German woodcut in G. Boccaccio's *De Claris
Mulieribus* portrays a pile of books burning behind the Queen
of Sheba, who stands before a seated Solomon. The pile of
burning books may mirror the sixteenth-century dispute between
Catholics and Protestants, as Watson suggests (in no. 1367a,
p. 130); it may also witness to the tradition that Solomon
ordered his books to be burned (cf. the two recensions of
"Concerning the Books of Solomon," in Issaverdens, pp. 144-47).

For discussions pertaining to the cycle of Solomon see M. W. Montgomery's "Solomon, in Arabic Literature" (*Jewish Encyclopedia* 11 [1905] 444f.), H.Z. Hirschberg's "Solomon, in Islam" (no. 1363a), M. Seligsohn's "Solomon, Apocryphal Works" (*Jewish Encyclopedia* 11 [1905] 446-48), G. Salzberger's *Die Salomonsage in der semitischen Literatur* (Berlin: M. Schmersow, 1907 [*N.V.*]), McCown's *The Testament of Solomon* (pp. 90-104), Preisendanz' contribution in Pauly-Wissowa (n.B. Sup. 8 [1956] cols. 660-704), and Denis' *Introduction* (pp. 66-69). Special concern for Solomonic pseudepigrapha in other Jewish writings, such as Targum Sheni and the Zohar, is to be found in Seligsohn's "Solomon, in Rabbinical Literature and Legend" (*Jewish Encyclopedia* 11 [1905] 438-44), Ginzberg's *Legends* (vol. 4, pp. 125-76; vol. 6, pp. 277-303, esp. pp. 292f.), L.H. Silberman's "The Queen of Sheba in Judaic Tradition" (in Pritchard [ed.], no. 1367a, pp. 65-84), and A. Rothkoff's "Solomon, in the Aggadah" (no. 1367b).

While working in the Bibliothèque Nationale I came across some unexamined pseudepigrapha that are connected with Solomon. Syriac 194, folios 153a-156b, is a recension of portions of the Testament of Solomon extant in Karshuni. This paper manuscript dates from the sixteenth century and contains 204 folios.

Grec 2419 on folios 218r-226r (219v-223v are blank) contains magical traditions attributed to Solomon. The text is corrupt. The same manuscript on folios 266v to 270v contains a copy of the Testament of Solomon, which was examined and discussed by McCown (his siglum W; see esp. pp. 25-27).

Grec 2511 on folios 244r-251r (251v is blank, 251r is one half of a sheet) preserves a text entitled "The Repeated Accomplishments of Solomon Which Were Compiled by the Friends of Hezekiah, the King of Judaea." The manuscript is in a neat fifteenth-century script.

Grec 854 on folio 201v contains a "Prayer of Solomon" in a polished, but difficult to read, thirteenth-century script.

Grec 1021 on folios 184v-185v preserves a text which begins: "The error of Solomon is that he took wives from the Gentiles." The fifteenth-century script is clear and easy to read. My initial impression is that most of these can be

linked with the homilies of the Fathers, especially those by
John Chrysostom and Ephraem Syrus.

See also nos. 67, 365.

1361   Bagatti, B. "Altre medaglie di Salomone cavaliere e loro
        origine," *Rivista di Archeologia Christiana* 47 (1971)
        331-42.

1362   Bagatti, B. "I Giudeo-Cristiani et l'Anello di Salomone,"
        RSR 60 (1972) 151-60.

1362a   Bayer, B. "Solomon, in the Arts," *EncyJud* 15. Cols.
        108-11.

1363   Giannopoulos, B.N. "Solomon (Testament of)," *ThĒE* 11.
        Col. 267. [in Greek]

1363a   Hirschberg, H.Z. "Solomon, in Islam," *EncyJud* 15. Col.
        108.

1364   Löfgren, O. "Der Spiegel des Salomo," Widengren Fest-
        schrift. Vol. 1, pp. 208-23.

1364a   Lur'e, Ja.S. "Une légende inconnue de Salomon et Kito-
        vras dans un ms. du XVe s.," *RESl* 43 (1964) 7-11.

1365   Metzger, B.M. "Salomos Testament," *BHH* 3. Col. 1653.

1366   Naldini, M. "Un frammento esorcistico e il *Testamento di
        Salomone*," *Studia Florentina: Alexandro Roncini Sexa-
        genario Oblata*. Rome: Edizioni dell'Ateneo, 1970. Pp.
        281-87.

1367   Petroff, J. "Solomon, Testament of," *EncyJud* 15. Cols.
        118f.

1367a   Pritchard, J.B., ed. *Solomon & Sheba*. London: Phaidon,
        1974.

1367b   Rothkoff, A. "Solomon, in the Aggadah," *EncyJud* 15. Cols.
        106-08.

1368   Salomonsen, B. "Salomos Testamente," *GDBL* 2. Col. 679.

1369   Whittaker, M. "Testament of Solomon," Clarendon edition.

Five Apocryphal Syriac Psalms
(Five Psalms of David, Psalms 151-155,
11QPs^a 151 [=Syriac 1], 11QPs^a 154
[=Syriac 2], 11QPs^a 155 [=Syriac 3])

Some Syriac manuscripts preserve five apocryphal psalms,
frequently entitled Psalms of David. An edition of the Syriac
was published by M. Noth ("Die fünf syrisch überlieferten
apokryphen Psalmen," *ZAW* 48 [1930] 1-23; repr. in M. Delcor,

no. 1374), and a critical edition of the Syriac was published
recently by W. Baars (no. 1370). The Five Syriac Psalms were
translated by W. Wright ("Some Apocryphal Psalms in Syriac,"
Proceedings of the Society of Biblical Archaeology 9 [1887]
257-66) and by A. Mingana, who also appended a facsimile of
Mingana Syr. 31 ("Some Uncanonical Psalms," *Woodbrooke Studies.*
Cambridge: Heffer, 1927. Vol. 1, pp. 288-92 [transl.], pp.
293f. [facsimile]). The Hebrew text of Syriac Psalms 1, 2, and
3 has been found in Qumran Cave Eleven; these have been edited
with an English translation by J.A. Sanders (no. 1380). The
first psalm is also extant in Greek, since the Psalter in the
Septuagint contains 151 psalms (Sanders, no. 1380, pp. 54f.,
60, conveniently juxtaposes the Greek and Hebrew; for the Latin
version see R. Weber, no. 1395).

The prerequisite, unfortunately sometimes ignored, for an
understanding of these five psalms is the recognition that they
must be examined separately. The first three Syriac Psalms are
at least as old as the Qumran Psalms Scroll, which was copied
in the first half of the first century A.D. (Sanders, no. 1380,
p. 9; J. Strugnell, no. 1391d, p. 207). Syriac Psalm 1 is the
oldest, and is pre-Christian, and perhaps pre-Qumranian (Sanders, nos. 1380, 1384, 1387; J. Carmignac, no. 1372; W.H.
Brownlee, no. 1371). Most scholars (viz. Sanders, nos. 1380,
1383, 1387; A. Hurvitz, nos. 1377j, 1378; S. Talmon, no. 1393;
J.A. Goldstein, no. 1377b; R. Polzin, no. 1378k; and S.B.
Gurewicz, no. 1377d) conclude that both Psalm 1 and the others
date from the hellenistic period; thus they reject both the
contention, which was never developed, that Psalm 1 is earlier
than the sixth century B.C. (cf. W.F. Albright, no. 1369a),
and the interpretation that it is late and Karaitic (cf. S.B.
Hoenig, no. 1377g, p. 332).

Several scholars have concluded that one or more of these
psalms were composed by the Essenes (viz. M. Philonenko,
"L'origine essénienne des cinq psaumes syriaques de David,"
Sem 9 (1959) 35-48; *idem*, nos. 1378i, 1378j; Delcor, "Cinq
nouveaux psaumes esséniens?" *RQ* 1 (1958) 85-102; *idem*, nos.
1374, 1375; A. Dupont-Sommer, no. 1376; cf. F. Christ, no.
1373b). Most contend correctly that while some passages can
be interpreted in line with Essene theology, there are not

sufficient data to conclude that they are Essene (viz. Sanders, no. 1387, p. 73; Carmignac, no. 1372; Brownlee, no. 1371; A.S. van der Woude, no. 1397, p. 35). There is a consensus that the original language of at least the first three Syriac Psalms is Hebrew.

Psalm 1 apparently consists of two originally separate psalms, Psalm 151A and Psalm 151B, which recount respectively how David was elevated from a common shepherd to the anointed ruler (7 vss.) and how he defeated the Philistine Goliath (11QPs^a is fragmentary; cf. Syr. MS Mingana 31). Psalm 2 contains 20 verses which exhort the worshipper to glorify God. Psalm 3, of 19 (in Hebrew) or 21 (in Syriac) verses, is a personal thanksgiving (*individuelles Danklied*) because the Lord answered the sinner's cry. Psalm 4 is a plea to be delivered from the lion and the wolf who prey upon the "flock of my father"; hence it is a David pseudepigraphon (cf. 1Sam 17:34-37). Psalm 5 is a personal thanksgiving for deliverance, and is conceivably also a David pseudepigraphon since the psalmist was about to be devoured "by two (wild) beasts."

The early date and pseudepigraphical character indicate that these Psalms should be contained in the Pseudepigrapha. It is improbable that 11QPs^a is either the earliest Jewish prayer-book, as M.H. Goshen-Gottstein (no. 1377c) and Talmon (nos. 1393, 1393a; according to Sanders, no. 1385, p. 96, Talmon has now abandoned this hypothesis) suggested, or a "library edition" of the already canonized Psalter, as P. Skehan (nos. 1391, 1391a, 1391b) claims. The presence of so-called apocryphal psalms within the "Psalter" indicates that the distinction between canonical and apocryphal psalms was not clarified before the advent of Christianity (cf. Sanders, nos. 1380, 1381, 1382, 1382a, 1383, and esp. 1385; and Hurvitz, no. 1378).

An unexamined version of Psalm 151 is contained in Syriac MS 7 in the John Rylands University Library of Manchester. This sixteenth-century manuscript contains the psalm after the subscription appended to the Psalter and before the Magnificat.

Psalm 151 is being translated for the new edition of the RSV Apocrypha, under the chairmanship of B.M. Metzger. For a full bibliographical report on the Qumran Psalms Scroll that

includes reviews see J.A. Sanders, no. 1385. The following
list is limited to specific discussions on the Syriac Psalms.

See the sections on the Pseudepigrapha and the Dead Sea
Scrolls and Prayer.

1369a Albright, W.F. *History, Archaeology and Christian Humanism*. New York: McGraw-Hill, 1964. See p. 35. [Archaisms in Ps 151 suggest a date "in the seventh-sixth centuries B.C."]

1370 Baars, W., ed. "Apocryphal Psalms," *Peshiṭta*. Part 4, fasc. 6 (1972) i-x, 1-12.

1370a Barasch, M. "The David Mosaic at Gaza," *Eretz-Israel* 10 (1971) 94-99, pls. 51, 52. [in Hebrew; English summary p. xi.]

1371 Brownlee, W.H. "The 11Q Counterpart to Psalm 151, 1-5," *RQ* 4 (1963) 379-87.

1372 Carmignac, J. "La forme poétique du psaume 151 de la grotte 11," *RQ* 4 (1963) 371-78.

1372a Carmignac, J. "Nouvelles précisions sur le psaume 151," *RQ* 8 (1975) 593-97.

1373 Carmignac, J. "Précisions sur la forme poétique du psaume 151," *RQ* 5 (1965) 249-52.

1373a Charlesworth, J.H. and J.A. Sanders. "Five Apocryphal Syriac Psalms of David," Doubleday edition.

1373b Christ, F. "11QPs[a] XVIII," *Jesus Sophia: Die Sophia-Christologie bei den Synoptikern* (ATANT 57) Zurich: Zwingli, 1970. Pp. 39-42. [Contains a translation with notes on Syr Ps 2.]

1373c Colella, P. "Il testo ebraico del Salmo 151," *RivB* 14 (1966) 365-68.

1373d Dahood, M. Review of J.A. Sanders, no. 1380. *Bib* 47 (1966) 141-44. [The length of the review and the reputation of the reviewer allow us to break the rule not to include reviews.]

1374 Delcor, M. "Cinq psaumes syriaques esséniens," *Les hymnes de Qumran (Hodayot)*. Paris: Letouzey et Ané, 1962. Pp. 299-319. [In an appendix are reprinted the Syriac texts published by M. Noth in *ZAW* 48 (1930) 1-23.]

1375 Delcor, M. "Zum Psalter von Qumran," *BZ* n.F. 10 (1966) 15-29. [Discusses Syr Pss 1, 2, and 3.]

1375a Dupont-Sommer, A. "David et Orphée," *Séance publique annuelle des Cinq Académies* (26 October 1964). [12 pp.]

1375b Dupont-Sommer, A. "Explication de textes hébreux décou-
       verts à Qumrân (suite)," *Annuaire du Collège de France*
       66 (1966) 359-61. [*N.V.*]

1376 Dupont-Sommer, A. "Le psaume CLI dans 11QPs^a et le pro-
       blème de son origine essénienne," *Sem* 14 (1964) 25-62.

1376a Dupont-Sommer, A. "Le psaume hébreu extra-canonique
       (11QPs^a, col. XXVIII)," *Annuaire du Collège de France*
       64 (1964) 317-20. [*N.V.*]

1376b Ebied, R.Y. "A Triglot Volume of the Epistle to the
       Laodiceans, Psalm 151 and Other Biblical Materials,"
       Bib 47 (1966) 243-54. [The article contains the Hebrew
       of Ps 151 from a seventeenth-century manuscript.]

1377 Fitzmyer, J.A. "Detailed Analysis of the Contents of
       11QPs^a," *The Dead Sea Scrolls: Major Publications and
       Tools for Study* (Sources for Biblical Study 8)
       Missoula, Mont.: Scholars Press, 1975. Pp. 37f.

1377a Flusser, D. "Qumrân and Jewish 'Apotropaic' Prayers,"
       IEJ 16 (1966) 194-205. [Discusses Syr Ps 3.]

1377b Goldstein, J.A. Review of J.A. Sanders, no. 1380. *JNES*
       26 (1967) 302-09. [The length of the review and the
       quality of the scholar permit us to include a book
       review.]

1377c Goshen-Gottstein, M.H. "The Psalms Scroll (11QPs^a): A
       Problem of Canon and Text," *Textus* 5 (1966) 22-33.

1377d Gurewicz, S.B. "Hebrew Apocryphal Psalms from Qumran,"
       AusBR 15 (1967) 13-20. [ET of Syr Ps 1.]

1377e Habermann, A.M. "Three New Non-Canonical Psalms from the
       Scroll Found in the Desert of Judah," *Môlad* 2, 7 (1968)
       94-98. [*N.V.*]

1377f Hoenig, S.B. "The Dead Sea Psalms Scroll," *JQR* 58 (1967)
       162f.

1377g Hoenig, S.B. "The Qumran Liturgic Psalms," *JQR* 57 (1967)
       327-32.

1377h Hurvitz, A. "The Form of the Expression 'Lord of the
       Universe' and Its Appearance in Psalm 151 from Qumran,"
       Tarbiz 34 (1965) 224-27. [in Hebrew]

1377i Hurvitz, A. "The Language and Date of Psalm 151 from
       Qumran," [E.L. Sukenik Festschrift] *Eretz-Israel* 8
       (1967) 82-87. [in Hebrew; English summary pp. 70f.]

1377j Hurvitz, A. "Observations on the Language of the Third
       Apocryphal Psalm from Qumran," *RQ* 18 (1965) 225-32.

1378 Hurvitz, A. "Psalms, Apocryphal," *EncyJud* 13. Cols. 1302f.

1378a Lebram, J.C. "Die Theologie der späten Chokma und häre-
       tisches Judentum," *ZAW* 77 (1965) 202-11.

1378b Lührmann, D. "Ein Weisheitspsalm aus Qumran (11QPs[a] XVIII)," *ZAW* 80 (1968) 87-98.

1378c Magne, J. "Orphisme, pythagorisme, essénisme dans le texte hébreu du psaume 151?" *RQ* 8 (1975) 508-47.

1378ca Magne, J. "Recherches sur les psaumes 151, 154 et 155," *RQ* 8 (1975) 503-07.

1378d Magne, J. "Les textes grec et syriaque du psaume 151," *RQ* 8 (1975) 548-64.

1378da Magne, J. "Le verset des trois pierres dans la tradition du psaume 151," *RQ* 8 (1975) 565-92.

1378e Meyer, R. "Die Septuaginta-Fassung von Psalm 151:1-5 als Ergebnis einer dogmatischen Korrektur," *Das Ferne und Nahe Wort*. L. Rost Festschrift, ed. F. Maass. Berlin: Töpelmann, 1967. Pp. 164-72.

1378f Moraldi, L. "Dal Rotolo del Salmi (11QPs[a])," *I Manoscritti di Qumrān*. Turin: Unione Tipografico-Editrice Torinese, 1971. Pp. 465-94.

1378g Ovadia, A. "The Synagogue at Gaza," *Qadmoniyot* 1 (1968) 124-27. [in Hebrew]

1378h Philonenko, M. "David-Orphée sur une mosaïque de Gaza," *RHPR* 47 (1967) 355-57.

1378i Philonenko, M. "Une expression qumrânienne dans le Coran (fils de la fosse)," *Atti del III Congresso di Studi Arabi e Islamici*. Ravello, 1966; Naples, 1967. Pp. 553-56. [*N.V.*]

1378j Philonenko, M. "Une tradition essénienne dans le Coran," *RHR* 170 (1966) 143-57.

1378k Polzin, R. "Notes on the Dating of the Non-Massoretic Psalms of 11QPs[a]," *HTR* 60 (1967) 468-76.

1379 Rabinowitz, I. "The Alleged Orphism of 11QPss 28, 3-12," *ZAW* 76 (1964) 193-200. [A "Responsum" by J.A. Sanders appears on p. 200.]

1380 Sanders, J.A. "The Apocryphal Compositions," *The Psalms Scroll of Qumrân Cave 11 (11QPs[a])* (*DJD* 4) Oxford: Clarendon, 1965. Pp. 51-99.

1381 Sanders, J.A. "Cave 11 Surprises and the Question of Canon," *McCQ* 21 (1968) 284-98; repr. *New Directions in Biblical Archaeology*, eds. D.N. Freedman and J.C. Greenfield. Garden City, N.Y.: Doubleday, 1971. Pp. 113-30.

1382 Sanders, J.A. *The Dead Sea Psalms Scroll*. Ithaca, N.Y.: Cornell University, 1967. [11QPs[a] plus fragment E. See esp. Part III, "The Apocryphal Compositions," and Appendixes.]

1382a Sanders, J.A. "The Dead Sea Scrolls--A Quarter Century of Study," *BA* 36 (1973) 110-48.

1382b Sanders, J.A. "Palestinian Manuscripts 1947-1972," *JJS* 24 (1973) 74-83.

1383 Sanders, J.A. "Pre-Masoretic Psalter Texts," *CBQ* 27 (1965) 114-23.

1384 Sanders, J.A. "Ps. 151 in 11QPss," *ZAW* 75 (1963) 73-86.

1385 Sanders, J.A. "The Qumran Psalms Scroll [11QPs[a]] Reviewed," *On Language, Culture, and Religion: In Honor of Eugene A. Nida*, eds. M. Black and W.A. Smalley. The Hague: Mouton, 1974. Pp. 79-99. [Contains a complete bibliographic report.]

1386 Sanders, J.A. "The Scroll of Psalms (11QPss) from Cave 11: A Preliminary Report," *BASOR* 165 (1962) 11-15.

1387 Sanders, J.A. "Two Non-Canonical Psalms in 11QPs[a]," *ZAW* 76 (1964) 57-75.

1388 Sanders, J.A. "*Variorum* in the Psalms Scroll (11QPs[a])," *HTR* 59 (1966) 83-94.

1389 Sen, F. "El Salmo 151 merece añadirse al Salterio como obra maestra," *CB* 29 (1972) 168-73.

1389a Sen, F. "Traducción y comentario del Salmo 154, por primera vez en castellano," *CB* 29 (1972) 43-47.

1390 Siegel, J.P. "Final *Mem* in Medial Position and Medial *Mem* in Final Position in 11QPs[a]: Some Observations," *RQ* 7 (1969) 125-30.

1391 Skehan, P.W. "The Apocryphal Psalm 151," *CBQ* 25 (1963) 407-09.

1391a Skehan, P.W. "A Broken Acrostic and Psalm 9," *CBQ* 27 (1965) 1-5. [Discusses Ps 155.]

1391b Skehan, P.W. "*Jubilees* and the Qumran Psalter," *CBQ* 37 (1975) 343-47.

1391c Stern, H. "Un nouvel Orphée-David dans une mosaïque du vi[e] siècle," *Comptes rendus des séances de l'Académie des Inscriptions et Belles-Lettres pendant l'année 1970*. Paris: Klincksieck, 1970. Pp. 63-79. [Discusses Ps 151.]

1391d Strugnell, J. "More Psalms of 'David,'" *CBQ* 27 (1965) 207-16.

1392 Strugnell, J. "Notes on the Text and Transmission of the Apocryphal Psalms 151, 154 (=Syr. II) and 155 (=Syr. III)," *HTR* 59 (1966) 257-81.

1393   Talmon, S. "Hebrew Apocryphal Psalms from Qumran," *Tarbiz*
        35 (1966) 214-34. [in Hebrew; English summary pp. II-
        III.]

1393a   Talmon, S. "Pisqah Be'emsa' Pasuq and 11QPs^a," *Textus* 5
        (1966) 11-21.

1393b   Ufenheimer, B. "Psalms 152 and 153 from Qumran: Two More
        Apocryphal Psalms," *Môlad* 22 (1964) 328-42. [See Y.
        Yadin's critique, no. 1397a.]

1394   Viaud, G. "Le psaume 151 dans la liturgie copte," *BIFAO*
        67 (1969) 1-8. [Prints the Coptic text.]

1395   Weber, R., *et al.* "Psalmus CLI," *Biblia Sacra*. Vol. 2,
        p. 1975.

1395a   Weiss, R. "Addenda Concerning Psalm 151," *Massa'* (29 Jan-
        uary 1965) 2. [in Hebrew; *N.V.*]

1395b   Weiss, R. "Tehillîm, Mizmôr 151," *Massa'* (15 May 1964).
        [in Hebrew; *N.V.*]

1396   Westermann, C. "Psalmen, syrische," *BHH* 3. Cols. 1522f.

1397   Woude, A.S. van der. "Die fünf syrischen Psalmen (ein-
        schliesslich Psalm 151)," *JSHRZ* 4 (1974) 29-47.

1397a   Yadin, Y. "Psalms from a Qumran Cave," *Môlad* 22 (1964)
        643-65. [Critique of B. Ufenheimer, no. 1393b.]

Thallus

Thallus apparently was a Samaritan who lived in Rome in
the first century A.D. (cf. Josephus, *Ant.* 18.6, 4) and wrote
a universal history (Theophilus of Antioch, for example, quotes
from Thallus' work and refers to it as follows: *kata gar tēn
Thallou historian* [*Ad Autol.* 3.29; cf. Theophilus of Antioch.
Ad Autolycum, ed. and trans. R.M. Grant. Oxford: Clarendon,
1970; pp. 144f.]). This work is lost, except for eight scattered fragments which were collected and edited by F. Jacoby
(*Die Fragmente der griechischen Historiker*. Berlin: Weidmann,
1929. Vol. 2B, pp. 1156-58) but were never collectively, to my
knowledge, translated into English.

B.Z. Wacholder (no. 1399; also see no. 574d) argues that
the evidence is inconclusive that Thallus was a Samaritan, concluding that he was probably a heathen. Unfortunately the
available data are ambiguous.

It is interesting but not necessarily significant that
Thallus recorded an eclipse in the year 29, which is either

the year of the Crucifixion or one year before.

See Fragments of Historical Works.

1397b Denis, A.-M. "Thallus," *Introduction*. Pp. 267f.

1398 Wacholder, B.Z. "Thallus," Doubleday edition.

1399 Wacholder, B.Z. "Thallus," *EncyJud* 15. Col. 1045.

Theodotus

Like Philo the Epic Poet and Ezekiel the Tragedian, Theodotus was a Jewish epic poet. His *Concerning the Jews* (*Peri
Ioudaiōn*) is lost except for selections in Greek preserved
through Alexander Polyhistor by Eusebius (*Pr. ev.* 9.22, 1-11).
These have been reprinted recently by A.-M. Denis (no. 23, pp.
204-07). An English translation was published by E.H. Gifford
(Eusebius. *Preparation for the Gospel*. Oxford: Clarendon,1903).

Theodotus' work obviously predates Alexander Polyhistor
and probably dates from the early portions of the second century B.C. The concern for Shechem (*Sikima*) leads some scholars
(viz. Denis, no. 24, p. 272; B.Z. Wacholder, no. 1402) to claim
that Theodotus was a Samaritan. One could argue, however, that
this hypothesis is unattractive for the following reasons:
Alexander Polyhistor entitled Theodotus' epic *Peri Ioudaiōn*;
a concern for Jacob, Dinah, and Shechem would be natural in a
chronicle since these traditions were cherished by Jews of all
sects (including the Samaritans); Eusebius extracts only a
portion from the epic, leaving no clue to the contents of the
remainder; at least two sections do not fit a Samaritan thesis:
the mention that the Shechemites were immoral ("regarded
neither bad nor good") and, compared to the brief note on the
name Shechem, the relatively long section on how Levi and
Simeon murdered Sychem and Emmor. In favor of a Samaritan
hypothesis is the description of Shechem as "the holy town"
(*hieron astu*); but another possible translation is "the
splendid town." The work was composed in Greek.

The 47 extant hexameters from *Concerning the Jews* can be
divided into four interrelated episodes. First, it is explained that Sikima derives its name from Sikimus the son of
Emmor, who founded the city. The physical setting and attributes of Shechem are then praised. Second, Jacob's life is

summarized with emphasis placed upon his settling in Shechem
and the description of his only daughter, Dinah, "whose bright
face/ and faultless form a noble soul expressed." Third,
Sychem (Sikimus) falls in love (*erasthēnai*) with Dinah, seizes
her and takes her home, and deflowers (*phtheirai*) her. Later
with his father he asks Jacob for permission to marry Dinah.
Jacob is willing only if all the Shechemites undergo circum-
cision and follow the Jewish customs. Fourth, Emmor attempts
to persuade his subjects to be circumcised, but he and his son
are murdered by Simeon and Levi, who believe they are doing
God's will.

Consult Fragments of Poetical Works.

1400   Reicke, B. "Theodotus," *BHH* 3. Col. 1967.

1401   Wacholder, B.Z. "Theodotus," Doubleday edition.

1402   Wacholder, B.Z. "Theodotus," *EncyJud* 15. Cols. 1102f.

Testaments of the Twelve Patriarchs

This important work is extant in two main recensions: the
Greek, which was re-edited recently by M. de Jonge (no. 1437;
he has nearly completed the *editio maior*, cf. no. 1434d; see
S. Agourides, no. 1403); and the Armenian, which has been
edited in part recently by M.E. Stone (nos. 1457, 1454a; cf.
nos. 1455, 1456; see the early edition by S. Hovsepean, *Non-
Canonical Books of the Old Testament*. Venice: Armenian Press
of St. Lazarus, 1896 [in Armenian; *N.V.*]). A Hebrew fragment
of the Testament of Naphtali (1:6-12) was found among the Dead
Sea Scrolls (cf. J.T. Milik, *Ten Years of Discovery in the
Wilderness of Judaea*, trans. J. Strugnell. London: SCM, 1959;
pp. 34f.). Aramaic fragments of the Testament of Levi were
found in the Cairo Geniza (cf. P. E. Kahle, *Cairo Geniza*, 2d.
ed. Oxford: Blackwell, 1959; p. 27 [observe the contradiction
between the note and the text]), and in Qùmran Caves 1 (1QTLevi
ar; cf. Milik, "Testament de Lévi," *DJD* 1, pp. 87-91, pl. XVII)
and 4 (4QTLevi ar[a]; cf. Milik, "Le Testament de Lévi en
araméen: Fragment de la grotte 4 de Qumrân (Pl. IV.)," *RB* 62
(1955) 398-406. For a discussion of the Aramaic fragments of
Levi see D. Haupt, no. 1428.). English translations of the
Testaments of the Twelve Patriarchs have been published by R.

Sinker (*ANF* 8. Pp. 3-38) and R.H. Charles (*The Testaments of the Twelve Patriarchs*. London: Black, 1908; *idem*, *APOT* 2. Pp. 282-367; repr. [TED] London: S.P.C.K., 1917); these translations were based upon the Greek. For a translation based upon the Armenian see J. Issaverdens (*UWOT*. Pp. 237-320).

The Testaments probably obtained a form recognizably similar to that which we know around 100 B.C. The testaments are apparently based upon an ancient core, which may have been the Testament of Joseph, as intimated above under that particular entry, as well as the Sin-Exile-Return passages and the Levi-Judah sections (cf. esp. J. Becker, no. 1406, pp. 172-82, and de Jonge, no. 1434c). These twelve testaments were probably redacted by a later Jew, perhaps in the first century B.C., as Becker suggests (no. 1406, esp. p. 376), and were certainly interpolated and infrequently reworked by "Christians" over a period of centuries, beginning around A.D. 100 because of the dependence upon the Gospel According to John (Becker, no. 1406, pp. 375f.; cf. also J. Jervell, no. 1432).

The conclusions stated in the preceding paragraph should not be considered the emerging consensus among critical scholars. While there continue to be considerable differences of opinion, these are not nearly so extreme as they were a decade ago. Most scholars readily perceive evidence of redactional activity, admit that some passages are clearly Christian (viz. TSim 6:7c; TLevi 10:2f., [18:6-14?]; [TJud 24:2f.?]; TAsh 7:3b; TJos 19:8, 11b [cf. J. Jeremias, no. 1431, and B. Murmelstein, no. 1443]; TBenj 9:[2?], 3f.; 10:7b, 8b, 9b), and conclude that as a whole the Testaments are pre-Christian. Few critics are now willing to follow A. Dupont-Sommer ("Le Testament de Lévi (xvii-xviii) et la secte juive de l'Alliance," *Sem* 4 (1952) 33-53; *idem*, *The Essene Writings from Qumran*, trans. G. Vermes. New York: Meridian, 1962; see esp. pp. 299-305) and M. Philonenko, his student (*Les interpolations chrétiennes des Testaments des Douze Patriarches et les manuscrits de Qumran* (Cahiers de la RHPR 35) Paris: Presses universitaires de France, 1960; *idem*, no. 1447), who situate the Testaments within the community that produced the "Dead Sea Scrolls"; yet some relationship is--and should be--seen between them. Likewise, no scholar now affirms that the Testaments were written near

the end of the second century A.D. and were composed by a
Christian, as M. de Jonge once suggested (*The Testaments of
the Twelve Patriarchs: A Study of Their Text, Composition and
Origin*. Assen: Van Gorcum, 1953 [repr. 1976]); and it is unjust
to ignore that, as C.H. Dodd later changed his position regarding realized eschatology, so de Jonge (cf. nos. 1434c, 1436),
open to new discoveries and fresh insights, has altered his
conclusions. He now affirms that the Testaments may have
reached their present form around A.D. 150, and, although not
composed by a Christian author, they were redacted by a Christ-
ian(s) who preserved much Jewish material--more than he earlier
admitted. De Jonge, however, needs to clarify how much Jewish
material and how many testaments he thinks the Christian "redactor" inherited (cf. no. 1434a, p. 199). Hence today the
debate centers around the date when we can speak about the
Testaments in a form generally similar to that which we inherit, and around the issue of which passages can be lifted
out as the ancient core and as the "Christian" layers. A un-
animous agreement on these questions is precluded by the impossibility of always distinguishing between Jewish and Christian ideas--certainly a Christian interpolator can add, for
example, passages that could be read as meaningful from a purely Jewish perspective, and indubitably a Christian redactor
can disguise almost everything--and by the awareness that Judaism and early Christianity mutually influenced each other and
that both represent incredibly complex, even contradictory,
heterogeneous phenomena--as we have seen intermittently
throughout the preceding pages.

The attempt to discover the original language of the
Testaments must be related to the theory of composition. It
is significant that most scholars, including de Jonge (cf. no.
1434a, p. 197), now affirm that some portions were composed in
a Semitic language, either Hebrew or Aramaic, and that the
Christian sections, and perhaps even some of the Jewish additions, were composed in Greek. For excellent surveys of contemporary research on the Testaments see Becker, no. 1406, pp.
129-58, and de Jonge, nos. 1434c and 1434a.

The Testaments of the Twelve Patriarchs preserve the
testaments reputed to have been left by the sons of Jacob.

Reuben, lamenting that he took advantage of Bilhah, his
father's concubine, while she was drunk and naked, warns his
sons in a misogynous fashion to be wary of women. Simeon
also claims that fornication is the mother of all evils (5:3).
Levi, who describes a dream in which he ascends into the heavens, urges his sons to teach their children to read (13:2),
prophesies the future of the Jewish nation until the advent of
a new priest, and exhorts his sons to choose the light and the
Law. Judah, who was an extremely fast runner, warns his sons
about the evil influences of being drunk with wine and of
being in love with money, and prophesies the advent of a sin-
less man who shall rise from them to inherit the kingdom.
Issachar, who in contrast to Reuben claims that he was never
attracted by women (3:5) and was not conscious of committing
a sin (7:1), foretells the events of the last times in which
his descendants will forsake the Lord and follow Beliar but
will be delivered by the Lord if they return to him. Zebulun,
claiming to have sinned only in thought (1:4), predicts the
future in which he and the righteous shall be resurrected but
the wicked destroyed, and exhorts his sons to be good to *all*
men (chps. 6, 7, 8). Dan laments his betrayal of Joseph, warns
his sons about the evils of anger and wrath (chps. 2, 3, 4, 5),
and exhorts them to love the Lord and one another. Naphtali,
who has two dreams about future events (chps. 5, 6), exhorts
his sons to be united to Levi and Judah, from whom salvation
shall rise to Israel, and to obey the commandments so that
"the Lord may love you" (8:10). Gad, confessing his sin, the
desire to kill Joseph because of hatred, warns his sons about
"the spirit of hatred" which works with Satan, and exhorts
them to cleave to the love of God and love each other. Asher
warns about the two ways and the two inclinations, exhorts his
sons to follow the truth, and foretells the future: his descendants shall sin, be captured and scattered by enemies, and
eventually be gathered together by God. Joseph, who recounts
inter alia how he successfully endured the repeated attempts
by the Egyptian woman to seduce him (chps. 3, 4, 5, 6, 7, 8, 9)
because the Lord was with him, exhorts his sons to love one
another--even concealing another's faults (17:1f.), and doing
good to him who wishes you evil (18:1f.)--and sees a vision of
future events, notably a virgin who bears a lamb who eventually

215

destroys all the beasts (19:8) and saves Israel (19:11). Benjamin, who exhorts his children to follow Joseph's example by
loving the Lord and keeping his commandments, foretells that
their evil deeds will cause the removal of the kingdom of the
Lord; this calamity, however, is followed by the restoration
of the Temple, the return of the twelve tribes, the resurrection of all men (some to glory and others to shame), and the
advent of the "beloved of the Lord."

J.T. Milik is working on the Aramaic and Hebrew fragments,
and will publish them in SVTP. M. Philonenko is finishing a
monograph on the Testaments of the Twelve Patriarchs.

Consult the publications listed under the Pseudepigrapha
and the Dead Sea Scrolls. See also nos. 4, 67, 84, 87, 108,
175, 234, 299, 303, 317, 320, 322, 330, 368f., 375, 465, 471,
477f., 935, 996, 998, 1480, 1494.

1403 Agourides, S. *Testaments of the Twelve Patriarchs*.
     Athens: Theologikēs Scholēs, 1973. [in Greek]

1404 Andersen, H.G. "Testaments of the Twelve Patriarchs,"
     ZPEB 5. Pp. 679-82.

1405 Becker, J. "Testamente der zwölf Patriarchen," *JSHRZ* 3
     (1974) 15-163.

1406 Becker, J. *Untersuchungen zur Entstehungsgeschichte der
     Testamente der zwölf Patriarchen* (AGAJU 8) Leiden:
     Brill, 1970.

1407 Bertrand, D.A. "Les interpolations des *Testaments des
     Douze Patriarches*," *Le baptême de Jésus: Histoire de
     l'exégèse aux deux premiers siècles*. Tübingen: Mohr,
     1973. Pp. 36-38.

1407a Böcher, O. *Der johanneische Dualismus im Zusammenhang des
      nachbiblischen Judentums*. Gütersloh: Mohn, 1965.

1408 Braun, F.-M. "Les Testaments des XII Patriarches et leurs
     rapports avec le bas-judaïsme," *Jean le théologien*
     (Etudes bibliques) Paris: Lecoffre, 1964. Vol. 2, pp.
     233-51.

1409 Burchard, C. "Neues zur Überlieferung der Testamente
     der zwölf Patriarchen: Eine unbeachtete griechische
     Handschrift (Athos, Laura I 48) und eine unbekannte
     neugriechische Fassung (Bukarest, Bibl. Acad. 580
     [341])," *NTS* 12 (1966) 245-58.

1410 Burchard, C. "Zur armenischen Überlieferung der Testa-
     mente der zwölf Patriarchen," *Studien*. Pp. 1-29.

1411   Caquot, A. "La double investiture de Lévi (Brèves remar-
       ques sur *Testament de Lévi*, VIII)," Widengren Fest-
       schrift. Vol. 1, pp. 156-61.

1412   Chrēstou, P.K. "Testament of the Twelve Patriarchs,"
       ThĒE 4. Cols. 1135f. [in Greek]

1413   Delcor, M. "Patriarcas, Testamentos de los doce,"
       Enciclopedia de la Biblia 5. Cols. 932f.

1414   Denis, A.-M. "Les Testaments des Douze Patriarches,"
       Introduction. Pp. 49-59.

1415   Eltester, W., ed. *Studien zu den Testamenten der zwölf
       Patriarchen* (BZNW 36) Berlin: Töpelmann, 1969.

1416   Flusser, D. "Patriarchs, Testaments of the Twelve,"
       EncyJud 13. Cols. 184-86. [for Hebrew version see
       Encyclopedia Mikra'ith 6 (1971) 689-92.]

1416a Gaylord, H.E. Jr. and Th. Korteweg. "The Slavic Version,"
       Studies on T12P. Pp. 140-43.

1416b Geller, B. "Joseph in the Tannaitic Midrashim," SCS 5.
       Pp. 139-46.

1417   Glatzer, N.N. "A New Priesthood," *Judaic Tradition*. Pp.
       66f.

1418   Gnilka, J. "2 Cor. 6:14-7:1 in the Light of the Qumran
       Texts and the Testaments of the Twelve Patriarchs,"
       Paul and Qumran, ed. J. Murphy-O'Connor. London:
       Chapman, 1968. Pp. 48-68.

1419   Goodenough, E.R. "Astronomical Symbols," *Jewish Symbols*
       8 (1958) 167-218. See esp. p. 204.

1420   Goodenough, E.R. "The Bull," *Jewish Symbols* 7 (1958)
       3-28. See esp. pp. 25-27.

1421   Goodenough, E.R. "Jewish Royalty," *Jewish Symbols* 9
       (1964) 117-96. See esp. pp. 195f.

1422   Goodenough, E.R. "Miscellaneous Fertility Symbols," *Jew-
       ish Symbols* 8 (1958) 71-118. See esp. p. 94.

1423   Goodenough, E.R. "Symbolism of Dress," *Jewish Symbols* 9
       (1964) 124-74. See esp. p. 169.

1424   Goodenough, E.R. "The Tree," *Jewish Symbols* 7 (1958)
       87-134. See esp. p. 126.

1425   Goodenough, E.R. "Victory and Her Crown," *Jewish Symbols*
       7 (1958) 135-71. See esp. p. 169.

1426   Goodenough, E.R. "Wine in Jewish Cult and Observance,"
       Jewish Symbols 6 (1956) 126-217. See esp. pp. 134, 183.

1427 Grelot, P. "Quatre cent trente ans (Ex. XII, 34): du
      Pentateuque au Testament araméen de Lévi," *Hommages à
      André Dupont-Sommer*, eds. A. Caquot and M. Philonenko.
      Paris: Adrien-Maisonneuve, 1971. Pp. 383-94.

1427a Harrelson, W. "Patient Love in the Testament of Joseph,"
      SCS 5. Pp. 29-35.

1427b Harrington, D.J. "Joseph in the Testament of Joseph,
      Pseudo-Philo, and Philo," SCS 5. 127-31.

1428 Haupt, D. *Das Testament Levi: Untersuchungen zu seiner
      Entstehung und Überlieferungsgeschichte*. Halle Disser-
      tation, 1969.

1428a Hollander, H.W. "The Ethical Character of the Patriarch
      Joseph: A Study in the Ethics of *The Testaments of the
      XII Patriarchs*," SCS 5. Pp. 47-104.

1428b Hollander, H.W. "The Relationship between MS. Athos Laura
      I 48 (*l*) and MS. Athos Laura K 116," *Studies on T12P*.
      Pp. 116-19.

1429 Hultgård, A. *Croyances messianiques des Test. XII Patr.:
      Critique textuelle et commentaire des passages messi-
      aniques*. Uppsala Dissertation, 1971.

1430 Hultgård, A. "L'universalisme des Test. XII. Patr.,"
      Widengren Festschrift. Vol. 1, pp. 192-207.

1431 Jeremias, J. "Das Lamm, das aus der Jungfrau hervorging,"
      ZNW 57 (1966) 216-19.

1432 Jervell, J. "Ein interpolator interpretiert: Zu der
      christlichen Bearbeitung der Testamente der zwölf
      Patriarchen," *Studien*. Pp. 30-61.

1432a Jonge, H.J. de. "Additional Notes on the History of MSS.
      Venice Bibl. Marc. Gr. 494 (*k*) and Cambridge Univ.
      Libr. Ff 1.24 (*b*)," *Studies on T12P*. Pp. 107-15.

1432b Jonge, H.J. de. "La bibliothèque de Michel Choniatès et
      la tradition occidentale des Testaments des XII Patri-
      arches," *Studies on T12P*. Pp. 97-106.

1432c Jonge, H.J. de. "The Earliest Traceable Stage of the
      Textual Tradition of the Testaments of the Twelve
      Patriarchs," *Studies on T12P*. Pp. 63-86.

1433 Jonge, H.J. de. "Les fragments marginaux dans le ms. *d*
      des Testaments de XII Patriarches," *JSJ* 2 (1971) 19-
      28; repr. *Studies on T12P*. Pp. 87-96.

1433a Jonge, H.J. de. "Die Patriarchentestamente von Roger
      Bacon bis Richard Simon," *Studies on T12P*. Pp. 3-44.

1434 Jonge, H.J. de. "Die Textüberlieferung der Testamente der
      zwölf Patriarchen," *ZNW* 63 (1972) 27-44; repr. *Studies
      on T12P*. Pp. 45-62.

1434a Jonge, M. de. "Christian Influence in the Testaments of
       the Twelve Patriarchs," *Studies on T12P*. Pp. 193-246.

1434b Jonge, M. de. "The Greek Testaments of the Twelve Patri-
       archs and the Armenian Version," *Studies on T12P*. Pp.
       120-39.

1434c Jonge, M. de. "The Interpretation of the Testaments of
       the Twelve Patriarchs in Recent Years," *Studies on
       T12P*. Pp. 183-92.

1434d Jonge, M. de. "The New editio maior," *Studies on T12P*.
       Pp. 174-82.

1435   Jonge, M. de. "Notes on Testament of Levi II-VII,"
       Travels in the World of the Old Testament. M.A. Beek
       Festschrift, eds. M.S.H.G. Heerma van Voss, *et al*.
       Assen: Van Gorcum, 1974. Pp. 132-45.

1436   Jonge, M. de. "Recent Studies on the Testaments of the
       Twelve Patriarchs," *SEA* 36 (1971) 77-96.

1436a Jonge, M. de. *Studies on the Testaments of the Twelve
       Patriarchs: Text and Interpretation* (SVTP 3) Leiden:
       Brill, 1975.

1436b Jonge, M. de. "Testament Issachar als "typisches Testa-
       ment": Einige Bemerkungen zu zwei neuen Übersetzungen
       der Testamente der zwölf Patriarchen," *Studies on
       T12P*. Pp. 291-316.

1437   Jonge, M. de, ed. *Testamenta XII Patriarcharum Edited
       According to Cambridge University Library MS Ff. 1.24*,
       2d ed. (PVTG 1) Leiden: Brill, 1970.

1438   Jonge, M. de. "Testaments of the Twelve Patriarchs,"
       Clarendon edition.

1438a Jonge, M. de. "Textual Criticism and the Analysis of the
       Composition of the Testament of Zebulun," *Studies on
       T12P*. Pp. 144-60.

1438b Jonge, M. de and T. Korteweg. "The New Edition of the
       Testament of Joseph," SCS 5. Pp. 125f.

1439   Kee, H.C. "Testaments of the Twelve Patriarchs," Double-
       day edition.

1439a Kolenkow, A.B. "The Narratives of the TJ and the Organi-
       zation of the Testaments of the XII Patriarchs," SCS 5.
       Pp. 37-45.

1439b Korteweg, T. "Further Observations on the Transmission of
       the Text," *Studies on T12P*. Pp. 161-73.

1439c Korteweg, T. "The Meaning of Naphtali's Visions," *Stud-
       ies on T12P*. Pp. 261-90.

1440 Macky, P.W. *The Importance of the Teaching on God, Evil and Eschatology for the Dating of the Testaments of the Twelve Patriarchs.* Princeton Theological Seminary Ph.D., 1969.

1440a Martin, R.A. "Syntactical Evidence of a Semitic *Vorlage* of the Testament of Joseph," SCS 5. Pp. 105-21.

1441 Milik, J.T. "Testament de Lévi (Pl. XVII)," *DJD* 1. Pp. 87-91. [lQTLevi ar = TLevi 8:11 (?)]

1442 Milik, J.T. "Le Testament de Lévi en araméen: Fragment de la grotte 4 de Qumrân," *RB* 62 (1955) 398-406.

1443 Murmelstein, B. "Das Lamm in Test. Jos. 19:8," *ZNW* 58 (1967) 273-79.

1443a Nickelsburg, G.W.E. Jr., ed. *Studies on the Testament of Joseph* (SCS 5) Missoula, Mont.: SBL, 1975.

1444 Otzen, B. "'Belial' i det Gamle Testamente og i Senjøde-dommen," *DTT* 36 (1973) 1-24.

1445 Otzen, B. [in] *GamPseud* 7 (1974) 677-789. [*N.V.*]

1445a Pervo, R.I. "The Testament of Joseph and Greek Romance," SCS 5. Pp. 15-28.

1446 Philonenko, M. "Juda et Héraklès," *RHPR* 50 (1970) 61f.

1447 Philonenko, M. "Testamente der zwölf Patriarchen," *BHH* 3. Col. 1955.

1447a Purvis, J.D. "Joseph in the Samaritan Traditions," SCS 5. Pp. 147-53.

1448 Rengstorf, K.H. "Herkunft und Sinn der Patriarchen-Reden in den Testamenten der Zwölf Patriarchen," *La littérature juive entre Tenach et Mishna*, ed. W.C. van Unnik (RechBib 9) Leiden: Brill, 1974. [*N.V.*]

1449 Rost, L. "Testamente der XII Patriarchen," *RGG*[3] 6. Cols. 701f.

1450 Salomonsen, B. "Testamenter, De Tolv Patriarkers," *GDBL* 2. Cols. 958-60.

1451 Segalla, G. "Il problema della volontà libera nell'apo-calittica ebraica e nei 'Testamenti dei 12 Patriarchi,'" *Divus Thomas* 88 (1967) 108-16.

1452 Shemer, B.-A. *The Messianic Idea of the Testaments of the Twelve Patriarchs.* [Tel Aviv]: University of Tel Aviv, 1970. [in Hebrew]

1453 Slingerland, H.D. *The Testaments of the Twelve Patriarchs: A History of Research with Attendant Conclusions.* Union (New York) Ph.D., 1973.

1453a Smith, E.W. Jr. "Joseph Material in Joseph and Asenath
       and Josephus Relating to the Testament of Joseph," SCS
       5. Pp. 133-37.

1454 Smith, M. "Testaments of the Twelve Patriarchs, The,"
       IDB 4. Pp. 575-79.

1454a Stone, M.E. *The Armenian Version of the Testament of
       Joseph: Introduction, Critical Edition, and Transla-
       tion* (T&T 6, Pseudepigrapha Series 5) Missoula, Mont.:
       SBL, 1975.

1455 Stone, M.E. "The Armenian Version of the Testaments of the
       Twelve Patriarchs--Selection of Manuscripts," *Zion* 49
       (1975) forthcoming.

1456 Stone, M.E. "The Jerusalem Manuscripts of the Testaments
       of the Twelve Patriarchs--Samples of Text," *Zion* 44
       (1970) 29-35.

1457 Stone, M.E. *The Testament of Levi: A First Study of the
       Armenian Manuscripts of the Testaments of the XII
       Patriarchs in the Convent of St. James, Jerusalem, with
       Text, Critical Apparatus, Notes and Translation.* Jeru-
       salem: St. James, 1969.

1458 Thomas, J. "Aktuelles im Zeugnis der zwölf Väter,"
       Studien. Pp. 62-150.

1459 Thornton, T.C.G. "Jewish Bachelors in New Testament
       Times," *JTS* 23 (1972) 444f.

1460 Tsakonas, V. "The Teaching Concerning the Messiah in the
       Testaments of the Twelve Patriarchs," *Timetikos tomos
       V.M. Vellas*. Athens, 1969. Pp. 687-93. [in Greek; *N.V.*]

1461 Turdeanu, E. "Les Testaments des Douze Patriarches en
       slave," *JSJ* 1 (1970) 148-84.

1462 Villalón, J.R. "Sources vétéro-testamentaires de la doc-
       trine qumranienne des deux messies," *RQ* 8 (1972) 53-63.

1463 Widengren, G. "Royal Ideology and the Testaments of the
       Twelve Patriarchs," *Promise and Fulfilment*. S.H. Hooke
       Festschrift, ed. F.F. Bruce. Edinburgh: T. & T. Clark,
       1963. Pp. 202-12.

Apocalypse of Zephaniah
(*Apocalypse of Sophonias, Anonymous Apocalypse*)

This pseudepigraphon is lost, except for a brief quotation
by Clement of Alexandria (*Strom.* 5.11, 77, 2; repr. by A.-M.
Denis, no. 23, p. 129) and for probable remnants in two sets
of fragments: one in Sahidic Coptic of fourteen pages on early
fifth-century papyri and the other in Akhmimic Coptic of
eighteen pages on late fourth-century papyri, both of which

were edited by G. Steindorff (*Die Apokalypse des Elias, Eine Unbekannte Apokalypse und Bruchstücke der Sophonias-Apokalypse: Koptische Texte, Übersetzung, Glossar* [TU n.F. 2.3a] Leipzig: Hinrichs, 1899. Pp. 110-44 [Sahidic text; cf. pp. 169f. for transl. of first page], 34-65 [Akhmimic text; cf. pp. 149-55 for transl.]). An English translation, which is literally linked to the Coptic, was published by H.P. Houghton ("The Coptic Apocalypse," *Aegyptus* 39 [1959] 40-91, 170-210; see esp. pp. 42-67 [transl. of Sah. frag.], pp. 76-83, 87-91 [transl. of Akh. text]).

The *terminus ad quem* of the early Jewish pseudepigraphon is clearly the end of the second century A.D. since Clement of Alexandria quoted from it by name (*hupo Sophonia*); but it is impossible to know the date of composition. The extent of the work, according to Nicephorus, was 600 lines. The Apocalypse of Sophonias is also mentioned in the List of Sixty Books, Pseudo-Athanasius' List, and the Slavic List.

Some extremely important questions need to be researched. Do the Sahidic leaves represent the same text? Is that text the Apocalypse of Sophonias as Houghton suggests (contrast Steindorff and Riessler)? If so why does Sophonias' name appear only on the first leaf? How are the two sets of Coptic fragments related? Are the Akhmimic fragments, which are frequently called the Anonymous Apocalypse, another recension of the Apocalypse of Zephaniah, as suggested by M.R. James (*LAOT*, p. 73) and P. Riessler (no. 62, p. 1274)? The parallels between these sets of Coptic fragments and the Apocalypse of Paul are sometimes striking (compare Akh. text 7:5ff. with ApPaul 10:31; cf. R. Meyer, no. 1469). What is the relationship between the traditions? Was A. Harnack correct in assuming that the Apocalypse of Paul is dependent upon the pre-fifth-century Christian redaction of the Apocalypse of Zephaniah (cf. Harnack's *Geschichte der altchristlichen Literatur bis Eusebius*, 2d. ed. Leipzig: Hinrichs, 1958. Part 2, vol. 1, pp. 571-73)? While the Coptic fragments reveal considerable influence from Christians (cf. H. Weinel in Gunkel Festschrift, p. 163), there is a Jewish original (cf. J.B. Frey in *DBSup* 1 [1928] col. 457). How faithfully do these fragments now preserve the original Jewish text? Hopefully some day we may be closer to answering these questions.

It might be helpful to summarize the characteristics of
the three sources that may derive ultimately from the Apocalypse of Zephaniah: the quotation in Clement, the Sahidic fragments, and the Akhmimic text. Clement appeals to a text attributed to Sophonias (the Greek name for Zephaniah) in which the
prophet is lifted into the fifth heaven where he sees angels,
called lords (*kurious*), who dwell in temples of salvation sing-
ing hymns to God. This tradition is reminiscent of some passages in the Testament of Levi, 2 Enoch, 3 Baruch, and especially the Ascension of Isaiah.

The first Sahidic page describes what Sophonias (*anok
Sophōnias*) sees: a soul being flayed by 5,000 angels for its
sins. The Angel of the Lord·then takes him to a large region
in which he sees countless angels with frightening appearances.
The second page unfortunately is illegible.

The remaining twelve Sahidic pages contain predictions
about the King in the West, who shall kill the King of Wanton-
ness. Despite appearances to the contrary he is the Son of
Lawlessness. The Virgin struggles against this impostor and
is joined by sixty just ones who show that the Son of Lawlessness is not the Anointed One. The Anointed One eventually
sends angels from heaven. The text ends with an apocalyptic
vision of the judgment and the end of the earth.

The longer Akhmimic text does not mention Sophonias (or
Zephaniah) but describes how the Seer, led by the Angel of the
Lord, sees the entire earth and learns that the departed
righteous dwell in a place of perpetual light. Almost all of
the apocalypse describes the tortures of the wicked, some of
whom are identified (viz. the three sons of Joatham the priest).

1464 Altendorf, [?]. "Apokalypse Zephanjas," *JSHRZ* 5, in press.

1465 Denis, A.-M. "Les fragments grecs de l'Apocalypse de
        Sophonie," *Introduction*. Pp. 192f.

1466 Geoltrain, P. "Zephanja-Apokalypse," *BHH* 3. Col. 2233.

1467 Helmbold, A.K. "Zephaniah, Apocalypse of," *ZPEB* 5. P.
        1051.

1468 Lacau, P. "Remarques sur le manuscrit akhmimique des
        apocalypses de Sophonie et d'Elie," *JA* 254 (1966)
        169-95.

1469   Meyer, R. "Zephanja-Apokalypse," RGG^3 6. Cols. 1900f.

1470   Rist, M. "Zephaniah, Apocalypse of," *IDB* 4. P. 951.

1471   Schneemelcher, W. "Apocalypse of Sophonias (Zephaniah),"
       trans. E. Best. HSW. Vol. 2, pp. 751f.

1472   Wintermute, O.S. "Apocalypse of Zephaniah," Doubleday
       edition.

Apocalypse of Zosimus
(Narrative of Zosimus, Testament of Zosimus,
The Abode of the Blessed, History of the Rechabites,
History of the Sons of Jonadab, Son of Recab)

The Apocalypse of Zosimus is extant in numerous ancient
languages; it was obviously popular in many areas (cf. R.H.
Ramsey, no. 1477). The most important are the Ethiopic, which
was edited by E.A.W. Budge ("The History of the Blessed Men
Who Lived in the Days of Jeremiah the Prophet," *The Life and
Exploits of Alexander the Great*. London: Clay, 1896. Vol. 1,
pp. 355-76); the Syriac, which was edited by F. Nau ("La
légende inédite des fils de Jonadab, fils de Réchab, et les
îles fortunées--texte syriaque," *RevSem* 7 [1898] 54-75); and
the Greek, which was edited most recently by M.R. James
("Narratio Zosimi," *Apocrypha Anecdota* [T&S 2.3] Cambridge:
CUP, 1893. Pp. 96-108). English translations have been published from the Ethiopic by Budge (*Life and Exploits*, vol. 2,
pp. 555-84; see also Budge, *The Book of the Saints of the
Ethiopian Church*. Cambridge: CUP, 1928. Vol. 3, pp. 784-87)
and from the Greek by W.A. Craigie (*ANF* 10. Pp. 220-24).

    This work has received little critical research, except
for the publication of texts. It is surprising that scholars
who work on the Pseudepigrapha have ignored it. Those who
know about it brand it as medieval because its present form
is late, perhaps as late as the sixth century as James contended (*Apocrypha Anecdota*, p. 95; cf. also Nau, *RevSem* 6
[1898] 264). A mere cursory examination of James' discussion,
however, reveals that he places the present evolved form of
the work in the sixth century, at the latest, and intimates
intermittently that the Jewish original must be much earlier
(cf. the discussion of the antiquity of the traditions by A.
Zanolli, "La leggenda di Zosimo secondo la redazione armena,"
Giornale della Società Asiatica Italiana n.s. 1 [1924] 146-62;

see esp. pp. 146-51). Like many of the compilations discussed herein, the Apocalypse of Zosimus contains an ancient core over which are superimposed more than one later layer of tradition.

The nature of the present monograph precludes a discussion of the literary history of this work. For the present a brief outline of an hypothesis must suffice. The work consists of twenty-two chapters (cf. James, pp. 96-108; and Craigie, pp. 220-24) of which possibly the first and certainly the last were appended later because only they are written in the third person, while chapters two to twenty-one are in the first person. It is not surprising to perceive accretions appearing at the end and beginning of a text; in fact the Armenian recension (cf. Zanolli, p. 153) even adds to chapter one the idea that Yovsimios lived on a mountain on Schizia, an island in the Ionian Sea. Also belonging to this latest level is the last sentence of chapter twenty-one, which defines the work as Zosimus' testament (*hē diathēkē autē*). Chapters nineteen to twenty-one were appended earlier to the work, because Zosimus' name does not appear in them and the narrative is out of character for this powerless monk. These chapters appear to be a remnant of an early account of Jesus' conquest of the Devil (*ho Diabolos*) during the forty days of temptation, because forty days are mentioned more than once, because only the traditions attributed to Jesus aptly fit the Devil's lamentation ("Woe is me that by one man I have lost the world [These chapters are under the influence of Rom 5.], for he has conquered me by his prayer."), and because the judgment of the Devil suggests Jesus' authority ("Then I dismissed him, dispatching [him] and the demons with him into the eternal fire."). Attributing chapters nineteen to twenty-one to another literary stratum explains why Zosimus' tablets (*tas plakas*) are called "the book" (*tēn biblon*) in chapter nineteen, and why Satan (chaps. 6, 18) is called the Devil only in chapters nineteen, twenty, and twenty-one. Chapters two and fifteen-b through eighteen are earlier prefixed and suffixed additions to the core because the name Zosimus appears in them nine times. These appear to be by the same scribe since the river is called Eumeles only in chapters two and fifteen-b. Either the scribe of this stratum was a Christian, or his work was redacted by a Christian. The remainder of the document, chapters three

through fifteen-a, is the core in which the name of Zosimus
does not occur and which appears to be Jewish with frequent
indications that the original was composed in a Semitic
language (viz. "lamented with great lamentation," chps. 6 and
7; "rejoiced with great joy," chp. 7). In the core, which is
an apocalypse, the seer is called "a man of God" (chp. 4),
"the man of vanity" (chp. 5), or simply "man" (chp. 6). The
allocation of chapters one and six to two different literary
strata explains the contradiction between Zosimus' unworthiness
(*ouk ei axios*) and the man's worthiness (*kai katexiōsen me*).
The parallels in the core with The Lost Tribes indicate that it
may have been composed around A.D. 100. Behind these chapters,
however, there seems to be a very ancient core, chapters seven
through nine, which concerns the history and present abode of
the descendants of Rechab, the son of Jonadab, who were not
scattered over the earth but are in a place encircled by an
abyss and a cloud (chp. 9). Chapters six and ten, with their
impressive similarities, appear to reveal that the evolution
moved centrifugally from chapters seven through nine. Since
the ancient core, the Rechabite text, claims that God turned
away his anger from Jerusalem (chps. 7 and 8) and that God's
mercy came to Jerusalem (chp. 7), it would be unwise to ignore
the possibility that this oldest section is a Jewish work that
predates the fall of Jerusalem in A.D. 70.

If the above analysis is generally correct, then it is
possible that the ancient core and the core, because of their
Semitic flavor and concern for Jerusalem, were written somewhere in Judaea. This suggestion is corroborated, but of
course not proved, by the superscription in a British Library
Syriac Manuscript of the work (B.M. Add. MS 12174, f. 209v):
"But it was translated from Hebrew into Greek, and then from
Greek into Syriac by the Holy Mar Jacob of Edessa." It is difficult, therefore, to agree with K. Kunze (no. 1475), who
claims that this work was composed in Greek in the sixth century. We can be relatively certain that the original is Jewish
and has been redacted by Christians (so also G. Graf,
Geschichte, p. 214; J.-C. Picard, no. 1476; Nau, *RevSem* 6
[1898] 265; L. Ginzberg, *Legends*, vol. 6, p. 409).

The above hypothesis may be outlined as follows:

V.	Testament of Zosimus	(chps. 1 and 22)
IV.	Jesus' Conquest of the Devil	(chps. 19-21)
III.	Christian Additions	(chps. 2,15b-18)
II.	Apocalypse	(chps. 3-6,10-15a)
I.	Rechabite Text	(chps. 7-9)

An unexpected confirmation of some of this hypothesis comes
from the Syriac tradition. This version ends with chapter 16
and is entitled "The History of the Blessed Sons of the
Rechabites" (B.M. Add. MS 12174, f. 209v).

Although Picard (no. 1476) rightly sees some interesting
parallels to the Dead Sea Scrolls, there is no compelling reason to conclude that any part of this work was composed by an
Essene, or refers to the exit of the Essenes from Jerusalem.
Possible parallels between the later strata and the Therapeutae
need to be researched carefully. V. Nikiprowetzky (no. 162,
pp. 22-38) has correctly drawn attention to numerous Greek
ideas that may have influenced the composition of some portions
of the work. These and the rabbinic and other Jewish parallels
mentioned by Ginzberg (*Legends*, vol. 6, p. 409) need to be researched.

In his Canon Nicephorus mentions a text entitled the
Apocalypse of Zosimus (*tēn Apokalupsin Esdra kai Zōsima*). James
(*Apocrypha Anecdota*, p. 94) reported "no reason to doubt" that
Nicephorus was referring to the document discussed herein.
A.-M. Denis (no. 24, p. 95) prefers to conclude that he was
thinking about the Visions of Zosimus (see the end of this
entry below), because astrological works are listed in this
section of the Canon. An examination of Nicephorus' Canon (for
the Greek text see James, *Apocrypha Anecdota*, p. 94) reveals
that in 3.1-3 are noted the so-called brontologia, selēnodromia,
and kalandologia; and these, as we saw above while examining
the Treatise of Shem, probably are not about alchemy, as are
the Visions of Zosimus (see below). In 4.1-3 are listed the
Apocalypses of Esdra and Zosimus, and the Two Testimonies of
Gregory. It seems better to follow James' advice.

In its present evolved Greek form the Apocalypse of Zosimus is a testament (chp. 21), preserved and popularized by a
certain Cryseas (chp. 22), concerning the visit of Zosimus (or
an anonymous man) to the abode of the blessed ones. Worthy of
special note are the means by which Zosimus reaches the land

of the blessed and the description of their daily life (*hē
dioikēsis*). He is led by God out of his cave, but forty days
later he nearly faints from exhaustion. After three days of
praying he is carried by a camel until he reaches a river and
a wall of cloud over or through which no one can pass. After
praying Zosimus is lifted by one tree and passed to another on
the opposite side of the river where there is a paradisiacal
land in which the blessed ones live waiting joyously for the
time, which each knows, when an angel comes for the soul. The
blessed appear naked, for they wear only the garment of immortality and are free from the vanity of the world. Food is
abundant and water, sweeter than honey, flows from the roots
of trees. The blessed, who write on stone tablets with their
fingernails, have an occupation, which is to pray day and
night (cf. OdeSol 16:1f.). Even in marriage the blessed are
chaste, having intercourse only to produce two children, one
for a similar marriage and the other for virginity. They are
free from sin, torment, disease, and pain, possessing peace,
patience, and love. Besides the Christian strata, there are
occasional Christian interpolations which are usually inserted
at the end of a chapter (see chps. 12, 15).

If this work is an expanded Jewish apocryphal composition
and not a late monastic legend, then it should be included
within the Pseudepigrapha.

The essential hero in the story should be distinguished
from the Roman bishop and the Greek historian called Zosimus.
The Apocalypse of Zosimus should not be confused with the
Visions of Zosimus, which were written by Zosimus of Panapolis
in the third century A.D., and which are about alchemy, excit-
ing the interest of the renowned psychoanalyst C.G. Jung
("Einige Bemerkungen zu den Visionen des Zosimos," *Eranos-
Jahrbuch* 5 [1937] 15-54).

Photographs or microfilms of almost all manuscripts of
this work are preserved in the Pseudepigrapha Library at Duke
University.

E.G. Martin, under the guidance of Professor J.H. Charlesworth, is writing a dissertation on the original language,
date, and literary history of the Apocalypse of Zosimus.

See works listed under The Lost Tribes. See also nós.
162, 440, 1188.

1473   Charlesworth, J.H. "History of the Sons of Jonadab, Son
        of Rechab," Doubleday edition.

1474   Gnoli, G. "Zosimo e Zoroastro: a proposito di 'maga,'"
        *Annali (dell') Instituto Universitario Orientale di
        Napoli* 16 (1966) 273ff. [*N.V.*]

1475   Kunze, K. "Zosimo, monaco della Scizia, beato(?),"
        Bibliotheca Sanctorum. Rome: Instituto Giovanni XXIII
        della Pontificia Università Lateranense, 1969. Vol. 12,
        col. 1502.

1476   Picard, J.-C. "L'Histoire des Bienheureux du Temps de
        Jérémie et la Narration de Zosime: arrière-plan his-
        torique et mythique," *Pseudépigraphes*, ed. M. Philo-
        nenko. Pp. 27-43.

1477   Ramsey, R.H. *No Longer on the Map*. New York: Ballantine,
        1972. See esp. pp. 62-74.

1478   Tubiana, J. "A propos du 'Livre des Mystères du Ciel et
        de la Terre,'" *Atti del Convegno Internazionale di
        Studi Etiopici*. Rome: Accademia Nazionale dei Lincei,
        1960. Pp. 403-08.

SUPPLEMENT

ACKNOWLEDGMENTS

The preparation and completion of this Supplement is
possible because of the international cooperation of specialists who periodically send me offprints and full bibliographical information on their own publications, because of the help
of my assistants in the Center, and the cooperation of the
librarians in the Duke Divinity School Library. H. M. Orlinsky
and G. MacRae have served as my mentors from the early stages
of this work; G. W. E. Nickelsburg has guided this reprint
with Supplement through Scholars Press. My greatest debt and
fullest appreciation are to M. J. H. Charlesworth, a former
librarian in Florida, who moved to Durham, when her husband
(and my father) passed away; she labored long and with pleas-
ure on this tool, so essential for work on the Pseudepigrapha.
She is the one who compiled the index.

J. H. Charlesworth, Director
International Center on
  Christian Origins
Box 4735
Duke University
Durham, NC 27706

May 1979

231

TABLE OF CONTENTS FOR SUPPLEMENT

234

236

INTRODUCTION TO THE SUPPLEMENT

The preceding work was completed in the spring of 1976. Since then I have noted 750 additional entries on the Pseudepigrapha. The increase is significant; moreover, the Supplement contains 264 additional names of scholars. It is clear that more scholars are recognizing that research on late Old Testament writings, Christian origins, early rabbinics, and Patristics must include in a significant way the study of the Pseudepigrapha. These developments and the fact that *The Pseudepigrapha and Modern Research* has been out-of-print for at least a year demand a reprinting of this monograph with a "Supplement."

Included in the following bibliographical update are works cited incompletely in the former work, the "Publications that Arrived Too Late for Inclusion" (former numbers 1479-1494), and the additional articles and books. Publications listed in G. Delling's superb *Bibliographie* (TU 106.2; see no. 21a), as stated above (pp. 15, 30), were deleted from my earlier lists. These are now reinserted; hence, included herein, are all the publications (known to me) on the Pseudepigrapha from 1960 until the spring of 1979.

Guidelines

The rules that have guided the compilation of the Supplement are similar to those articulated above (pp. 15-32), except for the decision to include entries even if they are in Delling. The rules may be summarized as follows:

1. Publications are included only if they treat one or more of the pseudepigrapha in a substantial fashion.
2. Reprints are included only either if they contain recent additions, or if they are reproductions of extremely important publications.

237

3. Works on the Dead Sea Scrolls are cited only if
    they include significant comments on the Pseud-
    epigrapha or on the fragments of pseudepigrapha
    found in the Qumran caves.

4. Publications on the Old or New Testament,
    Apocalypticism, and Gnosticism are included only
    if they significantly discuss one or more of the
    documents in the Pseudepigrapha.

Additional Pseudepigrapha

Research completed over the last three years has convinced me that we must add under the Pseudepigrapha the
following four documents: the Apocalypse of Daniel, the
Hellenistic Synagogal Prayers, the History of Joseph, and
the Prayer of Jacob. Brief introductions, according to the
guidelines given above (p. 30), precede the bibliographical
entries for each of these pseudepigrapha. Three pseudepigrapha are treated differently than before. The Testament of
Adam is now discussed as a separate entry and not subsumed
under the "Cave of Treasures" (see pp. 91f.); a new introduction to it explains the reasons behind this decision. The
"Apocalypse of Zosimus" (or "Narrative of Zosimus") is now
listed under another title, under which it circulated, which
more adequately demonstrates its inclusion among the pseudepigrapha; it is now called, following the (beginning of the)
title in Syriac MS D (B.M. Add. 12174): "The History of the
Blessed Ones, the Sons of Rechab." The Testament of Abraham,
the Testament of Isaac, and the Testament of Jacob are called
the "Testaments of the Three Patriarchs," because they are
organically related--the Testament of Jacob was inspired by
the first two, and the Testament of Isaac by the Testament of
Abraham--and because in the *Apostolic Constitutions* (16.16, 3)
they are probably referred to as the books "of the three patriarchs."

Order and Numbers for Additional
Bibliographical Entries

The 750 new bibliographical entries are arranged according to the subject or document that is central to them. As in

the preceding pages, pseudepigrapha are arranged alphabetically (see the preceding Table of Contents). Under each listed pseudepigraphon entries are arranged alphabetically. Numbers are assigned so that they relate to the numbers above. For example, publications that follow directly after entry no. 27 are given the numbers 27a, 27b, 27c, etc. Items that go between number 1378c and 1378ca are numbered 1378ca. This procedure of giving the new entries numbers related to those above should facilitate the rapid examination of related publications.

New Translation Projects

Since the publication of the monograph three major translation projects have developed. In Tokyo the Pseudepigrapha is being translated into Japanese, under the editorship of M. Sekine and S. Arai, and is titled *Kyūyaku Giten* (see no. 49a). In Madrid the Pseudepigrapha is being translated into Spanish, under the editorship of A. Díez Macho, and is titled *Los Apocrifos del Antiguo Testamento* (see no. 19a). In Paris the Pseudepigrapha is being translated into French, under the editorship of M. Philonenko and A. Dupont-Sommer, and is titled *Écrits intertestamentaires* (see no. 14c).

Additional Abbreviations

Abbreviations are explained above (pp. 1-14). Additional abbreviations are as follows:

1. *Periodicals, Series, Encyclopedias, and Societies*

AION	*Annali (dell') Instituto [Universitario] Orientale di Napoli*
BInstEstHel	Boletín del Instituto de Estudios Helénicos
BWANT	Beiträge zur Wissenschaft vom Alten und Neuen Testament
CiuDios	*Ciudad de Dios*
DBSup	*Supplément au dictionnaire de la Bible*
EncRel	Gozzini, M., ed. *Enciclopedia delle Religioni*. 6 vols. Florence: Vallecchi, 1970-76.

ExpT	*Expository Times*
Explor	*Explor: A Journal of Theology*
FGH	Jacoby, F. *Die Fragmente der griechischen Historiker.* Berlin: Weidmann, 1940-1943 [repr. 1954].
IDBS	*Interpreter's Dictionary of the Bible, Supplementary Volume*
NHS	Nag Hammadi Studies
OCA	*Orientalia Christiana Analecta*
RuBi	*Ruch Biblijny i Liturgiezny*
SJLA	Studies in Judaism in Late Antiquity
Theol	*Theologia* (Gk)
TRE	Krause, G. and G. Müller, eds. *Theologische Realenzyklopädie.* Berlin: Gruyter, 1977-.
TS	*Theological Studies*
*VT*Sup 28	Boer, P. A. H. de, ed. *Congress Volume: Edinburgh 1974* (Supplements to *VT* 28) Leiden: Brill, 1975.
WMANT	*Wissenschaftliche Monographien zum Alten und Neuen Testament*

2. Books

BETL 46	Delcor, M., ed. *Qumrân: Sa piété, sa théologie et son milieu (Bibliotheca Ephemeridum Theologicarum Lovaniensium 46)* Paris-Gembloux: Leuven University Press, 1978.
EHR 2	Philonenko, M., ed. *Mystères et syncrétismes* (Etudes d'histoire des religions 2) Paris: Geuthner, 1975.
EHR 3	Philonenko, M., ed. *L'Apocalyptique* (Études d'histoire des religions 3) Paris: Geuthner, 1977.
NOAB: Expand. Ed.	*New Oxford Annotated Bible with the Apocrypha: Expanded Edition.* Ed. H. G. May and B. M. Metzger. N.Y.: OUP, 1977.
SBL 1973 Seminar Papers	MacRae, G., ed. *Society of Biblical Literature 1973 Seminar Papers: One Hundred Ninth Annual Meeting, 8-11 November 1973, Palmer House, Chicago, Illinois* 2 vols. Cambridge, Mass.: SBL, 1973.
SBL 1976 Seminar Papers	MacRae, G., ed. *Society of Biblical Literature 1976 Seminar Papers: One Hundred Twelfth Annual Meeting, 28-31 October 1976, Stouffer's Riverfront Towers, St. Louis, Mo.* Missoula, Mont.: SBL, 1976.

SBL 1977 Seminar Papers	Achtemeier, P. J., ed. *The Society of Biblical Literature One Hundred Thirteenth Annual Meeting Seminar Papers: 28-31 December 1977, San Francisco Hilton and Tower--San Francisco, Ca.* [Missoula, Mont.]: SBL, 1977.
SBL 1978 Seminar Papers	Achtemeier, P. J., ed. *Society of Biblical Literature 1978 Seminar Papers. Vol. I: One Hundred Fourteenth Annual Meeting, 18-21 November 1978, Marriott and Monteleone Hotels, New Orleans, La.* Missoula, Mont.: SBL, 1978.
SCS 6	Nickelsburg, G. W. E. Jr., ed. *Studies on the Testament of Abraham* (Septuagint and Cognate Studies 6) Missoula, Mont.: Scholars Press, 1976.
Studia Patristica 12	Livingstone, E. A., ed. *Studia Patristica: Vol. XII* (TU 115) Berlin: Akademie-Verlag, 1975.
Wright Festschrift	Campbell, E. F. and R. G. Boling, eds. *Essays in Honor of George Ernest Wright.* Missoula, Mont.: Scholars Press, 1976.

5. *Pseudepigrapha*

ApDan	Daniel, Apocalypse of
HelSynPr	Hellenistic Synagogal Prayers
HistJos	History of Joseph
PrJac	Prayer of Jacob
AbRech	Rechabites, Abode of
HistRech	History of the Blessed Ones, the Sons of Rechab
T3P	Testaments of the Three Patriarchs

BIBLIOGRAPHY: ADDITIONAL INTRODUCTIONS
AND PUBLICATIONS

General

See also no. 90la̲b̲.

la   Agourides, S. *The Apocrypha of the Old Testament.*
        Athens, 1973. Vol. 1. [modern Greek translation
        of Jub, Tl2P, lEn, LetAris]

2a   Aland, K. "Apokryphen," *Repertorium der Griechischen
        Christlichen Papyri: I, Biblische Papyri* (Patris-
        tische Texte und Studien 18) Berlin, New York:
        Walter de Gruyter, 1976. Pp. 363-92. [A report
        on papyri that contain AsIs, ApEz, lEn, 2Bar, ApEl,
        OdesSol, and TSol.]

4a   Baier, W. "Liturgie und Kult in der frühjüdischen
        Welt und Umwelt," *Archiv für Liturgiewissenschaft*
        19 (1978) 175-92.

7a   Benoit, A. "Les mystères païens et le christian-
        isme," EHR 2 (1975) 73-92.

7b   Bloch, J. "Outside Books," *The Canon and the Masorah
        of the Hebrew Bible: An Introductory Reader,* ed.
        by S. Leiman. New York: KTAV, 1974.

lla   Brox, N. *Falsche Verfasserangaben: Zur Erklärung
        der frühchristlichen Pseudepigraphie* (Stuttgarter
        Bibelstudien 79) Stuttgart: KBW, 1975.

llb   Brox, N., ed. *Pseudepigraphie in der heidnischen
        und jüdisch-christlichen Antike* (Wege der Forschung
        484) Darmstadt: Wissenschaftliche Buchgesellschaft,
        1977.

llc   Brox, N. "Zum Problemstand in der Erforschung der
        altchristlichen Pseudepigraphie," *Festschrift für
        Endre Ivánka,* ed. K. Schubert and N. Brox. Salz-
        burg: Müller, 1974.

lld   Byrns, C. G. *The Phenomenon of Christian Interpola-
        tions into Jewish Apocalyptic Texts: A Biblio-
        graphical Survey and Methodological Analysis.*
        Vanderbilt Ph.D., 1977. [B. discusses ApAb, TAb,
        VAE (ApMos), 3Bar, lEn, 2En, 4Ezra, AscenIs, SibOr,
        Tl2P.]

243

14a   Charlesworth, J. H. "Focus on the Pseudepigrapha," *The Circuit Rider* 2.10 (1978) 6-8.

14b   Charlesworth, J. H. "A History of Pseudepigrapha Research: The Re-emerging Importance of the Pseudepigrapha," *Aufstieg und Niedergang der Römischen Welt*, Vol. II 19,1; pp. 54-88.

14c   Charlesworth, J. H. "New Developments in the Study of the *Écrits Intertestamentaires*," *BIOSCS* 11 (1978) 14-18.

19a   Charlesworth, J. H. "Translating the Apocrypha and Pseudepigrapha: A Report of International Projects," *BIOSCS* 10 (1977) 11-21.

19b   Chilton, B. "A Cornucopia of Targum and Pseudepigrapha Studies from Scholars Press," *Journal for the Study of the Old Testament* 8 (1978) 61-70.

21a   Delling, G. ed. *Bibliographie zur jüdisch-hellenistischen und intertestamentarischen Literatur 1900-1970* (TU 106²) Berlin: Akademie, 1975. (See p. 32, note 35 above.)

26a   Dentan, R. C. "Apocrypha, Old Testament," *Encyclopaedia Britannica*. Chicago: Encyclopaedia Britannica, 1970. Vol. 1, pp. 117-19. [D. includes 4Ezra, PrMan, and "Other Apocryphal Works: Pseudepigrapha."]

26b   Díez Macho, A. "El medio ambiente judío en el que nace el cristianismo," *La iglesia primitiva: medio ambiente, organización y culto* (Biblioteca de estudios bíblicos 7) Salamanca: Sígueme, 1974. Pp. 83-150.

27a   Dinzelbacher, P. "Die Visionen des Mittelalters: Ein geschichtlicher Umriss," *ZRGG* 30 (1978) 116-28.

27b   Dumville, D. N. "Biblical Apocrypha and the Early Irish: A Preliminary Investigation," *Proceedings of the Royal Irish Academy* (Vol. 73, Sect. C, No. 8) Dublin: Royal Irish Academy, 1973. Pp. 299-338.

27c   Dunand, F. "Les mystères égyptiens aux époques hellénistique et romaine," EHR 2 (1975) 11-62.

27d   Eissfeldt, O. *Einleitung in das Alte Testament unter Einschluss der Apokryphen und Pseudepigraphen sowie der apokryphen- und pseudepigraphenartigen Qumran-Schriften;* 4th ed. Tübingen: Mohr, 1976.

27e   Feldman, L. H. "Egyptian Jewish Literature," *The New Encyclopaedia Britannica: Macropaedia*. Chicago: Encyclopaedia Britannica, Inc., 1974. Vol. 10, pp. 313f.

27f   Feldman, L. H. "Hengel's *Judaism and Hellenism* in
       Retrospect," *JBL* 96 (1977) 371-82.

27g   Feldman, L. H. "Palestinian Literature," *The New
       Encyclopaedia Britannica: Macropaedia*. Chicago:
       Encyclopaedia Britannica, Inc., 1974. Vol. 10,
       p. 314.

27h   Fischer, K. M. "Anmerkungen zur Pseudepigraphie im
       Neuen Testament," *NTS* 23 (1976) 76-81.

28a   Flusser, D. "Intertestamental Literature," *The New
       Encyclopaedia Britannica: Macropaedia*. Chicago:
       Encyclopaedia Britannica, Inc., 1974. Vol. 10,
       pp. 931-38.

28b   Flusser, D. "Palaea Historica: An Unknown Source
       of Biblical Legends," *Scripta Hierosolymitana* 22
       (1971) 48-79.

33b   [Geoltrain, P.] "Typologie et fonction de la pseud-
       égraphie comme phénomène littéraire," *École
       Pratique des Hautes-Etudes*. RelAn 82 (1973) 187-
       90.

35a   Gowan, D. E. *Bridge Between the Testaments: A
       Reappraisal of Judaism from the Exile to the Birth
       of Christianity* (Pittsburgh Theol. Mon. Ser. 14)
       Pittsburgh: Pickwick, 1976. [One of the few
       books that does not limit discussion of the Pseud-
       epigrapha to Charles' canon. Addressed to the
       beginning student.]

37a   Grelot, P. "Sacred Literature in the Hellenistic
       Era," *Introduction to the Bible*, trans. G. P.
       Campbell. New York: Herder and Herder, 1967.
       Pp. 245-72, also see pp. 212-29, 273-90.

39a   Grudem, W. "Alphabetical Reference List for Old
       Testament Apocrypha and Pseudepigrapha," *Journal
       of the Evangelical Theological Society* 19 (1976)
       297-313.

41a   Hammershaimb, E. "Om lignelser og billedtaler i de
       gammeltestamentlige Pseudepigrafer," *SEA* 50 (1975)
       36-65. [concerns Parables and Metaphors in the
       Old Testament Pseudepigrapha]

41b   Hatt, J. J. "Interprétation et syncrétisme dans la
       religion gauloise," *EHR* 2 (1975) 117-26.

44a   Karabidopoulou, I. "The Problem of the Pseudepigra-
       pha," *Deltion Biblikon Meleton* 5 (1977/1978) 178-
       80. [In mod. Gk; it concentrates on the problem
       of pseudonymity and the canonical pseudepigrapha.]

44b   Knibb, M. A. "The Exile in the Literature of the
        Intertestamental Period," *HeyJ* 17 (1976) 253-72.

44c   Kolenkow, A. B. "The Genre Testament and Forecasts
        of the Future in the Hellenistic Jewish Milieu,"
        JSJ 6 (1975) 57-71.

49a   _____. *Kyūyaku Giten I-II*, ed. Japan Biblical
        Institute, 2 vols. Tokyo: Kyobunkwan, 1975.
        [translation of the Pseudepigrapha into Japanese]

50a   Lange, N. R. M. de. *Apocrypha: Jewish Literature
        of the Hellenistic Age* (Jewish Heritage Classics
        Series) New York: Viking, 1978. [includes Jub,
        LAB, JosAsen, 4Ezra, LetAris, PssSol]

52a   Marrow, S. B. "Apocrypha and Pseudepigrapha," *Basic
        Tools of Biblical Exegesis (Subsidia Biblica* 2)
        Rome: Biblical Institute, 1976. Pp. 69-73. [M.
        lists only the basic works for beginning students.]

53a   May, H. G. and B. M. Metzger, eds. *The New Oxford
        Annotated Bible with the Apocrypha: Expanded
        Edition*. New York: OUP, 1977. [contains 4Ezra,
        PrMan, Psl51, 3Mac, 4Mac]

53b   Ménard, J. E. "La gnose à l'epoque du syncrétisme
        gréco-romain," EHR 2 (1975) 95-113.

53c   Ménard, J. E. "Pseudonymie," *DBSup* 48 (1973) 246-52.

56a   Moeller, H. R., ed. *The Legacy of Zion. Intertes-
        tamental Texts Related to the New Testament*.
        Grand Rapids, Mich.: Baker, 1977. [Included
        among the selections are excerpts from 7 pseud-
        epigrapha: PssSol, 1En, T12P, TJob, Jub,
        EzekTrag, LivPro.]

58a   Neusner, J. "The History of Earlier Rabbinic Juda-
        ism: Some New Approaches," *History of Religions*
        16 (1977) 216-36. [N. correctly laments that most
        Jewish scholars tend to jump from biblical to
        tannaitic literature. The immense literature in
        between must not be ignored.]

58b   Nibley, H. W. "The Expanding Gospel," *Brigham Young
        University Studies* 7 (1965) 3-27.

60a   Paul, A. "Intertestament," *Cahiers Évangile* 14
        (1975) 72.

60b   Paul, A. "Bulletin de littérature intertestamen-
        taire," *RSR* 64 (1976) 541-56. [reviews recent
        publications on the Pseudepigrapha]

60c   Paul, A. "Bulletin de littérature intertestamen-
        taire: Du Judaïsme ancien au Judéo-Christianisme,"
        RSR 66 (1978) 343-87.

60d   Pauwen, E. *La Bible éclaircie et ses apocryphes.*
       Brussels: Musin, 1972.

60e   Pedersen, S. "Die Kanonfrage als historisches und
       theologisches Problem," *Studia Theologica* 31
       (1977) 83-136.

61a   Philonenko, M., ed. *Mystères et syncrétismes*
       (EHR 2) Paris: Geuthner, 1975.

63a   Robinson, O. P. and C. H. Robinson. *Christ's
       Eternal Gospel: Do the Dead Sea Scrolls, the
       Pseudepigrapha, and Other Ancient Records Chal-
       lenge or Support the Bible?* Salt Lake City,
       Utah: Deseret, 1976. [The subtitle shows that
       the book is apologetic; the answer is that the
       documents "support" the Bible. It is sad that
       the book was not written by one of the brilliant
       and informed scholars in the Mormon community.]

66a   Rubinkiewicz, R. "Research on the Slavonic Old
       Testament Apocrypha During the Last Decade,"
       *RuBi*28 (1975) 235-38. [in Polish]

67a   Sandmel, S. "The Best Known Pseudepigrapha," *Juda-
       ism and Christian Beginnings.* New York: OUP,
       1978. P. 487.

82a   Stone, M. E. "Armenian Canon Lists III--The Lists
       of Mechitar of Ayrivankᶜ (c. 1285 C. E.)," *HTR*
       69 (1976) 289-300.

83a   Stone, M. E. "Pseudepigrapha," *IDBS* (1976) 710-12.

87a   Surburg, R. F. *Introduction to the Intertestamental
       Period.* St. Louis, Mo.: Concordia, 1975.

92a   Walter, N. "Jüdisch-hellenistische Literatur im
       Rahmen der 'Griechischen Christlichen Schriftstel-
       ler' und der 'Texte und Untersuchungen,'" *TU* 120
       (1977) 173-77.

92b   Widmann, H. "Die literarische Fälschung im Alter-
       tum. Bemerkungen zu Wolfgang Speyers Monographie,"
       Antiquariat 23 (1973) 169-74.

History

See also nos. 574a, 901a, 913a, 1112a.

92c   Alon, G. *Jews, Judaism and the Classical World:
       Studies in Jewish History in the Times of the
       Second Temple and Talmud,* trans. I. Abrahams.
       Jerusalem: Magnes, 1977.

248

96a   Blenkinsopp, J. *Prophecy and Canon: A Con-*
        tribution to the Study of Jewish Origins
        (Univ. of Notre Dame Center for the Study of
        Judaism and Christianity in Antiquity 3)
        Notre Dame: University of Notre Dame Press,
        1977.

96b   Bowman, J. *The Samaritan Problem: Studies in the*
        Relationships of Samaritanism, Judaism, and
        Early Christianity (Pittsburgh Theol. Mono.
        Ser. 4) Pittsburgh, Pa.: Pickwick, 1975.

99a   Conzelmann, H. and A. Lindemann. "Neutestament-
        liche Zeitgeschichte--die Umwelt des Urchristen-
        tums," *Arbeitsbuch zum Neuen Testament*. Tübingen:
        Mohr, 1975. Pp. 119-78.

99b   Davies, P. R. "Hasidim in the Maccabean Period,"
        JJS 28 (1977) 127-40.

100a   Doikos, D. "The Samaritan Schism," *Gregorios*
        Palamas 57 (1974) 3-21. [in Greek]

100b   Dunn, J. D. E. *Unity and Diversity in the New*
        Testament: An Inquiry into the Character of
        Earliest Christianity. Philadelphia: West-
        minster, 1977.

100c   Ellison, H. L. *From Babylon to Bethlehem: The*
        Jewish People from the Exile to the Messiah.
        London: Blackwell, 1976.

100d   Feldman, L. H. "Hengel's *Judaism and Hellenism* in
        Retrospect," *JBL* 96 (1977) 371-82.

101a   Finkelstein, L. "An Ancient Tradition About the
        Beginnings of the Sadducees and the Boethusians,"
        Studies and Essays in Honor of Abraham A. Neuman,
        ed. M. Ben-Horin, B. D. Weinreb, and S. Zeitlin.
        Leiden: Brill, 1962. Pp. 622-38.

101b   Foerster, W. *From the Exile to Christ: A Historical*
        Introduction to Palestinian Judaism, trans. G. E.
        Harris. Philadelphia: Fortress, 1964, repr. 1976.

103a   Grelot, P. "From the Conquests of Alexander to the
        Christian Era," *Introduction to the Bible*, trans.
        G. P. Campbell. New York: Herder and Herder,
        1967. Pp. 230-44.

103b   Hayes, J. H. and J. M. Miller, eds. *Israelite and*
        Judaean History. (The Old Testament Library)
        Philadelphia: Westminster, 1977.

103c   Hengel, M. *Juden, Griechen und Barbaren: Aspekte*
        der Hellenisierung des Judentums in vorchristlicher
        Zeit (*SBS* 76) Stuttgart: Katholisches Bibelwerk,
        1976. [an expanded version of Hengel's chapters
        in the Cambridge History of Judaism, N.Y.P.]

104a   Hengel, M. *Die Zeloten: Untersuchungen zur
        jüdischen Freiheitsbewegung in der Zeit von
        Herodes I. bis 70 n. Chr.* (AGAJU 1) Leiden:
        Brill, 1976.

104b   Hengel, M. "Zeloten und Sikarier: Zur Frage nach
        der Einheit und Vielfält der jüdischen Befreiungs-
        bewegung 6-74 nach Christus," *Josephus-Studien*
        [O. Michel Festschrift], ed. O. Betz, K. Haacker,
        M. Hengel. Göttingen: Vandenhoeck, 1974. Pp.
        175-96.

104c   Hessert, Paul, ed. "Galilee and Regionalism,"
        Explor 3 (1977) 1-96. [A valuable summary of
        archeological excavations in Galilee and assess-
        ment of this region during the turn of the era.]

104d   Hoenig, S. B. "The New Schürer," *JQR* 67 (1976-1977)
        47-54.

105a   Isser, S. J. *The Dositheans: A Samaritan Sect in
        Late Antiquity* (SJLA 17) Leiden: Brill, 1976.
        [A provocative and persuasive argument that
        Dositheus was "an early first century A.D. eschato-
        logical figure among the Samaritans," who was
        aligned to an old Samaritan sect that was "hereti-
        cal" and became eponymously named after him.]

108a   Levine, L. I. *Caesarea Under Roman Rule* (SJLA 7)
        Leiden: Brill, 1975.

108b   Loftus, F. "The Anti-Roman Revolts of the Jews and
        the Galileans," *JQR* 68 (1977) 78-98.

108c   Lohse, E. *The New Testament Environment*, trans.
        J. E. Steely. Nashville: Abingdon, 1976. [one
        of the best introductions available]

109a   Luke, K. "Society Divided by Religion: The Jewish
        World of Jesus' Time," *Biblebhashyam* 1 (1975) 195-
        209.

109b   McCullough, W. S. *The History and Literature of the
        Palestinian Jews from Cyrus to Herod: 550 B.C. to
        4 B.C.* Toronto: Univ. Press, 1975. [a survey
        addressed to "the ordinary reader"]

109c   MacMullen, R. *Enemies of the Roman Order: Treason,
        Unrest, and Alienation in the Empire.* Cambridge,
        Mass.: Harvard, 1966.

109d   Maier, J. *Geschichte der jüdischen Religion: Von
        der Zeit Alexander des Grossen bis zur Aufklärung
        mit einem Ausblick auf das 19./20. Jahrhundert.*
        Berlin, New York: Gruyter, 1972. See esp. pp.
        7-396.

109e   Manrique, A. "El bautismo en el judaísmo contemporáneo de Jesús," *CiuDios* 189 (1976) 207-20.

109f   Meyer, R. "Bemerkungen zum Literargeschichtlichen Hintergrund der Kanontheorie des Josephus," *Untersuchungen zu Josephus, dem antiken Judentum und dem Neuen Testament,* ed. O. Betz, *et al.* Göttingen: Vandenhoeck und Ruprecht, 1974. Pp. 285-99.

109g   Meyers, E. M. "Galilean Regionalism as a Factor in Historical Reconstruction," *BASOR* 221 (1976) 93-101. [reprinted in Wright Festschrift, pp. 93-101]

110a   Millar, F. "The Background to the Maccabean Revolution: Reflections on Martin Hengel's Judaism and Hellenism," *JJS* 29 (1978) 1-21.

110b   Mor, M. "More Bibliography on the Samaritans (With Emphasis on Samaritanism and Christianity)," *Henoch* 1 (1979) 99-122. [This publication lists numerous bibliographical reports.]

112a   Noja, S. "Contribution à la bibliographie des Samaritains," *AION* 33 (1973) 98-113.

112b   Oppenheimer, A. *The ᶜAm Ha-Aretz: A Study in the Social History of the Jewish People in the Hellenistic-Roman Period* (ALGHJ 8) Leiden: Brill, 1977.

113a   Pummer, R. "Aspects of Modern Samaritan Research," *Église et Théologie* 7 (1976) 171-88.

113b   Pummer, R. "The Present State of Samaritan Studies: I," *JSS* 21 (1976) 39-60.

113c   Pummer, R. "The Present State of Samaritan Studies: II," *JSS* 22 (1977) 27-47.

114a   Roshwald, M. "Marginal Jewish Sects in Israel," *International Journal of Middle East Studies* 4 (1973) 328-43.

116a   Safrai, S., *et al.,* eds. *The Jewish People in the First Century: Historical Geography, Political History, Social, Cultural and Religious Life and Institutions,* vol. 2 (*Compendia Rerum Iudaicarum ad Novum Testamentum* 1.2) Amsterdam: Van Gorcum, 1976.

116b   Safrai, S. *Das jüdische Volk im Zeitalter des Zweiten Tempels* (Information Judentum 1) Neukirchen-Vluyn: Neukirchener Verlag, 1978.

251

116c   Sandmel, S. *Judaism and Christian Beginnings.*
       New York: OUP, 1978.

119a   Schnider, F. "Propheten in der Umwelt des NT,"
       Jesus der Prophet (Orbis Biblicus et Orientalis 2)
       Göttingen: Vandenhoeck, 1973. Pp. 26-37.

119b   Schubert, K. *Jesus im Lichte der Religionsge-
       schichte des Judentums.* Vienna: Herold, 1973.

123a   Smallwood, E. M. *The Jews Under Roman Rule: From
       Pompey to Diocletian* (SJLA 20) Leiden: Brill,
       1976.

123b   Smith, M. "Rome and Maccabean Conversions: Notes
       on 1Macc. 8," *Donum Gentilicium*, ed. C. K. Barrett.
       [Daube Festschrift] Oxford: OUP, 1978. Pp. 1-7.

125b   Vermes, G. "Ancient Rome in Post-Biblical Jewish
       Literature," *Post-Biblical Jewish Studies* (SJLA 8)
       Leiden: Brill, 1975. Pp. 215-24.

125c   Walter, N. "Frühe Begegnungen zwischen jüdischem
       Glauben und hellenistischer Bildung in Alexan-
       drien," *Neue Beiträge zur Geschichte der Alten
       Welt.* Berlin: Akademie, 1964. Vol. 1, pp. 367-78.

125d   Weiss, R. "Supplements to the Samaritan Bibliog-
       raphy," *AION* 35 (1975) 265-73.

126a   Whitelocke, L. T. *The Development of Jewish Religi-
       ous Thought in the Inter-Testamental Period.* New
       York: Vantage, 1976.

       The Pseudepigrapha and Art

128a   Philonenko, M. "David humilis et simplex. L'inter-
       prétation essénienne d'un personnage biblique et
       son iconographie," *Académie des inscriptions &
       belles-lettres.* Paris: Klincksieck, 1977. Pp.
       536-48. [P. argues persuasively for the influ-
       ence of Ps 151 upon the portraits of David in
       the tenth-century "Psautier de Paris."]

128b   Schubert, K. "Das Problem der Entstehung einer
       jüdischen Kunst im Licht der literarischen Quellen
       des Judentums," *Kairos* 16 (1974) 1-13.

128c   Vikan, G. *Illustrated Manuscripts of Pseudo-
       Ephraem's Life of Joseph and the Romance of Joseph
       and Aseneth.* Princeton Ph.D., 1976.

The Pseudepigrapha and the Dead Sea Scrolls

See also nos. 27d, 63a, 210e-f, 280a, 307e-f, 307h, 313a, 317a, 347a, 370a, 480a, 717a, 725c, 728a, 749b, 752d, 752e, 769a̲b̲c̲, 1046a, 1052a̲b̲, 1055b, 1186a, 1236a, 1269c, 1353c, 1369b-c-d, 1417a, 1417c, 1439d.

136a   Caquot, A. "Pseudépigraphes de l'AT et documents Qumran," *École Pratique des Hautes-Études*, Section: ReligAnnuaire 80 (1971) 210-14.

142a   Dupont-Sommer, A. *Trente Années de Recherches sur les manuscrits de la mer morte (1947-77)* (Académie des Inscriptions et Belles-Lettres) Paris: Institut de France, 1977.

144a   Fitzmyer, J. A. and D. J. Harrington. *A Manual of Palestinian Aramaic Texts (Second Century B.C.- Second Century A.D.)* (*Biblica et Orientalia* 34) Rome: Biblical Institute, 1978. [contains the 10 Enoch fragments, 1QTLevi ar, 4QTLevi ar^a]

The Pseudepigrapha and Gnosticism

See also nos. 53b, 240b, 253b, 266a, 449b-e, 524a, 526a, 530a, 532a, 536a, 539a-b-c, 538a, 542a, 543a, 746a, 762a, 827a, 824b, 827b, 1318a.

181a   Robinson, J. M. "Jewish Gnostic Nag Hammadi Texts," *Protocol of the Third Colloquy: 22 May 1972*, ed. W. Wuellner (Protocol Series of the Colloquies of the Center for Hermeneutical Studies in Hellenistic and Modern Culture 3) Berkeley, CA: Center for Hermeneutical Studies, 1975. Pp. 1-3. [Also see the major part of this volume: contributions by A. Henrichs, W. Shumaker, D. Winston, and M. Schwartz.]

184a   Scopello, M. "Un rituel idéal d'intronisation dans trois textes gnostiques de Nag Hammadi," *Nag Hammadi and Gnosis: Papers Read at the First International Congress of Coptology (Cairo, December 1976)*, ed. R. McL. Wilson. Leiden: Brill, 1978. Pp. 91-95. [S. draws attention to parallels between TLevi, 2En and some Nag Hammadi texts.]

The Pseudepigrapha and the New Testament

See also nos. 197a, 201a, 202a, 250a, 267a, 281a, 282a,
299b, 299d, 315b, 319b, 323a, 327a, 334e, 336a-b, 342c, 348a,
377a, 415a, 444b, 453a, 454a, 523a, 585ab, 622a, 697b, 719d,
722a, 723d, 724c, 758h, 760b, 870a, 948a-b, 1006f, 1022a,
1046a, 1150c, 1215a, 1278a, 1282a, 1297a, 1305a, 1317b, 1336a-b,
1410a, 1412b, 1417a, 1417c, 1449a.

No additional publications.

Apocalyptic

See also nos. 126a, 539c, 688a, 697b, 719d, 751b, 758c-d,
769a, 855a, 1166a.

189a   Alonso Díaz, J.   "Apocaliptica hoy. literatura de
       la resistencia," *SalTerrae* 62 (1974) 894-901.

191a   Anderson, H. "A Future for Apocalyptic?" *Biblical
       Studies: Essays in Honor of William Barclay*, ed.
       J. R. McKay and J. F. Miller. Philadelphia:
       Westminster, 1976. Pp. 56-71.

192a   Barker, M. "Slippery Words III. Apocalyptic,"
       ExpT 89 (1978) 324-29.

192b   Barr, J. "Jewish Apocalyptic in Recent Scholarly
       Study," *BJRULM* 58 (1975) 9-35.

192c   Bauckham, R. J. "The Rise of Apocalyptic," *Themelios*
       3 (1978) 10-23.

192d   Baumgarten, J. "Zum Verhältnis von spätisraelitischer
       und urchristlicher Apokalyptik," *Paulus und die
       Apokalyptik* (*WMANT* 44) Neukirchen-Vluyn: Neu-
       kirchener Verlag, 1975. Pp. 9-53.

193a   Beardslee, W. A. "Openness to the New in Apocalyptic
       and in Process Thought," *Process Studies* 3 (1973)
       169-78.

193b   Beek, M. A. "Zeit, Zeiten und halbe Zeit," *Studia
       Biblica et Semitica* [T. C. Vriezen Festschrift],
       ed. W. C. van Unnik and A. S. van der Woude.
       Wageningen: H. Veenman en Zonen, 1966. Pp. 19-24.

194a   Beyerlin, W., ed. and tr. *Near Eastern Religious
       Texts Relating to the Old Testament*, trans. J.
       Bowden. Philadelphia: Westminster, 1978. See
       esp. pp. 118-28.

194b   Böcher, O.   "Die Heilige Stadt im Völkerkrieg:
        Wandlungen eines apokalyptischen Schemas," *Josephus-
        Studien* [O. Michel Festschrift], ed. O. Betz,
        K. Haacker, M. Hengel. Göttingen: Vandenhoeck,
        1974. Pp. 55-76.

194c   Bogaert, P. M.   "La ruine de Jérusalem et les
        apocalypses juives après 70," LD 95 (1977) 123-41.

197a   Carlson, D. C. *Aspects of Suffering Within Certain
        Apocalyptic Texts.* University of Aberdeen Ph.D.,
        1977.

197b   Collins, A. Yarbro.   "The History-of-Religions
        Approach to Apocalypticism and the 'Angel of the
        Waters' (Rev 16:4-7)," *CBQ* 39 (1977) 367-81.

197c   Collins, J. J.   "Apocalypse: Towards the Morphology
        of a Genre," *SBL 1977 Seminar Papers.* Pp. 359-70.

198a   Collins, J. J. *The Apocalyptic Vision of the Book
        of Daniel* (Harvard Semitic Monographs 16) Missoula,
        Mont.: Scholars Press, 1977.

199a   Collins, J. J.   "Cosmos and Salvation: Jewish Wisdom
        and Apocalyptic in the Hellenistic Age," *History of
        Religions* 17 (1977) 121-42.

200a   Collins, J. J.   "Jewish Apocalyptic Against its
        Hellenistic Near Eastern Environment," *BASOR* 220
        (1975) 27-36. [Reprinted in Wright Festschrift,
        pp. 27-36.]

201a   Collins, J. J.   "Pseudonymity, Historical Reviews and
        the Genre of the Revelation of John," *CBQ* 39 (1977)
        329-43.

202a   Coppens, J. "L'Apocalyptique. Son dossier. Ses
        critères. Ses éléments constitutifs. Sa portée
        néotestamentaire," *ETL* 53 (1977) 1-23.

209a   Davies, G. I.   "Apocalyptic and Historiography,"
        Journal for the Study of the Old Testament
        [Sheffield, UK] 5 (1978) 15-28.

209b   Davies, W. D.   "From Schweitzer to Scholem: Reflec-
        tions on Sabbatai Svi," *JBL* 95 (1976) 529-58.

209c   Delcor, M.   "Bilan des études sur l'apocalyptique,"
        LD 95 (1977) 27-42.

210a   Delcor, M.   "Mythologie et apocalyptique," LD 95
        (1977) 143-77.

210b   Dexinger, F. *Henochs Zehnwochenapokalypse und offene Probleme der Apokalyptikforschung* (SPB 29) Leiden: Brill, 1977.

210c   Dunand, F. "L'Oracle du Potier et la formation de l'apocalyptique Égypte," EHR 3. Pp. 39-67.

210d   Dunn, J. D. G. "Apocalyptic Christianity," *Unity and Diversity in the New Testament: An Inquiry into the Character of Earliest Christianity.* London: SCM, 1977. Pp. 309-40.

210e   Dupont-Sommer, A. "Essénisme et apocalypses juives à la lumière des manuscrits de la Mer Morte," *Annuaire du Collège de France* 70 (1970-71) 399-406.

210f   Dupont-Sommer, A. "Essénisme et apocalypses juives à la lumière des manuscrits de la Mer Morte, *Annuaire du Collège de France* 71 (1970-71) 375-91.

210g   Edwards, G. "The Historical Background of Early Apocalyptic Thought," *Scripture in History & Theology: Essays in Honor of J. Coert Rylaarsdam,* ed. A. L. Merrill and T. W. Overholt. Pittsburgh: Pickwick, 1977. Pp. 193-203.

215a   Eyt, P. "Apocalyptique, utopie et espérance," LD 95 (1977) 441-58.

215b   Fahd, T. "La visite de Mahomet aux enfers," EHR 3. Pp. 181-210.

215c   Fischel, H. A. "The 'Four in Paradise'" (*Hagigah, et al.*): Anti-Epicurean Stereotype, Biography, and Parody in the Portrayals of Tannaim," *Rabbinic Literature and Greco-Roman Philosophy: A Study of Epicurea and Rhetorica in Early Midrashic Writings.* (SPB 21) Leiden: Brill, 1973. Pp. 1-34.

217a   Freer, K. O. *A Study of Vision Reports in Biblical Literature.* Yale University Ph.D., 1975. [Although focusing primarily on Dan 7-12, Freer discusses the history of motifs in apocalyptic.]

218a   Fruchon, P. "Sur l'interprétation des apocalypses," LD 95 (1977) 385-400.

221a   Gowan, D. E. "The Exile in Jewish Apocalyptic," *Scripture in History & Theology: Essays in Honor of J. Coert Rylaarsdam,* ed. A. L. Merrill and T. W. Overholt. Pittsburgh: Pickwick, 1977. Pp. 205-23.

227a   Hanson, P. D. "Apocalypse, Genre," *IDBS* (1976) 27f.

256

227b   Hanson, P. D. "Apocalypticism," *IDBS* (1976) 28-34.

228a   Hanson, P. D. *Dynamic Transcendence: The Correla-
        tive of Confessional Heritage and Contemporary
        Experience in a Biblical Model of Divine Activity.*
        Philadelphia: Fortress, 1978.

230a   Hanson, P. D. "Prolegomena to the Study of Jewish
        Apocalyptic," *Magnalia Dei: The Mighty Acts of
        God: Essays on the Bible and Archaeology in Memory
        of G. Ernest Wright,* ed. F. M. Cross, *et al.* New
        York: Doubleday, 1976. Pp. 389-413.

234a   Hartman, S. S. "Fragan om eventuellt iranskt
        inflytande på kristendomens och judendomens
        apokalyptik och djävulsföreställning. Die Frage
        eines eventuellen iranischen Einflusses auf
        Apokalyptik des Judentums und die Teufelsvor-
        stellung," *Svensk Teologisk Kvartalskrift* 52
        (1976) 1-8.

235a   Heintz, J. G. "Note sur l'origine de l'apocalypse
        judaïque à la lumière des 'prophétics akkadiennes,'"
        EHR 3. Pp. 68-87.

238a   Isenberg, S. R. "Millenarism in Greco-Roman Pales-
        tine," *Religion: Journal of Religion and Religions*
        4 (1974) 26-46.

238b   Jacob, E. "Aux sources bibliques de l'apocalyp-
        tique," LD 95 (1977) 43-61.

240a   Kasting, M. D. "Apocalyptic: Resource for Christian
        Hope," *Currents in Theology and Mission* 1 (1974)
        62-67.

240b   Keller, C. A. "Das Problem des Bösen in Apokalyptik
        und Gnostik," *Gnosis and Gnosticism,* ed. M. Krause
        (NHS 8) Leiden: Brill, 1977.

241a   Kippenberg, H. G. "Die Geschichte der Mittelper-
        sischen Apokalyptischen Traditionen," *Studia Iranica*
        7 (1978) 49-80.

242a   Koch, K. "Die mysteriösen Zahlen der judäischen,
        Könige und die apokalyptischen Jahrwochen," *VT* 28
        (1978) 362-64.

247a   Ladd, G. E. "The Revival of Apocalyptic in the
        Churches," *RevExp* 72 (1975) 263-70.

248a   Lambert, W. G. *The Background of Jewish Apocalyptic.*
        London: Athlohe, 1978. [L. draws attention to
        three Babylonian texts and claims the origin of
        apocalyptic is to be seen in light of OT prophecy.]

249a   Lebram, J. C. H. "Apokalyptiek als keerpunt in het
       joodse denken," *Nederlands Theologisch Tijdschrift*
       30 (1976) 271-81.

249b   Lebram, J. C. H. "Apokalyptik und Hellenismus im
       Buche Daniel, Bemerkungen und Gedanken zu Martin
       Hengels Buch über 'Judentum und Hellenismus,'" *VT*
       20 (1971) 519f.

250a   Lincoln, A. T. "Paul the Visionary: The Setting
       and Significance of the Rapture to Paradise in
       II Corinthians XII.1-10," *NTS* 25 (1979) 204-20.

251a   Luck, U. "Das Weltverständnis in der jüdischen
       Apokalyptik, dargestellt am äthiopischen Henoch
       und am 4. Esra," *ZTK* 73 (1976) 283-305.

251b   Luke, K. "Time in the Perspectives of Jewish
       Apocalyptic," *Jeevadhara* [India: Alleppey,
       Kerala] 7 (1977) 132-54.

253a   Martin-Achard, R. "Essai d'évaluation théologique
       de l'apocalyptique juive," *Beiträge zur Alttes-
       tamentlichen Theologie*, ed. H. Donner, R. Hanhart,
       and R. Smend. [Festschrift Walther Zimmerli]
       Göttingen: Vandenhoeck & Ruprecht, in press.

253b   Ménard, J. E. "Apocalyptique et gnose: leur
       eschatologie respective," EHR 3. Pp. 159-77.

253c   Millar, W. R. *Isaiah 24-27 and the Origin of
       Apocalyptic*. Missoula, Mont.: Scholars Press,
       1976.

253d   Monloubou, L., ed. *Apocalypses et Théologie de
       L'Espérance: Congrès de Toulouse (1975)* (LD 95)
       Paris: Cerf, 1977.

259a   Müller, U. B. "Vision und Botschaft," *ZTK* 74 (1977)
       416-48.

263a   Nola, A. M. di. "Apocalittica e apocalissi," *EncRel*
       1. Cols. 516-19.

266a   Perkins, P. "The Rebellion Myth in Gnostic Apoc-
       alypses," *SBL 1978 Seminar Papers*. Vol. 1, pp.
       15-30.

266b   Philonenko, M., ed. *L'Apocalyptique* (EHR 3) Paris:
       Geuthner, 1977.

266c   Philonenko, M. "La sixième vision de *IV Esdras* et
       les 'Oracles d'Hystaspé,'" EHR 3. Pp. 127-35.

267a   Prigent, P. "Le millenium dans l'apocalypse
       johannique," EHR 3. Pp. 137-56.

268a   Raphael, F.   "Esquisse d'une typologie de l'apoc-
        alypse," EHR 3.   Pp. 9-38.

268b   Rapp, F.   "Apocalypse et mouvements populaires au
        Moyen Age," EHR 3.   Pp. 213-32.

276a   Russell, D. S.   "Apocalyptic Literature," *Encyclo-
        paedia Britannica.*   Chicago: Encyclopaedia
        Britannica, 1970.   Vol. 1, pp. 112-15.

277b   Saldarini, A. J.   "The Uses of Apocalyptic in the
        Mishna and Tosepta," *CBQ* 39 (1977) 396-409.

277c   Salvoni, F.   "L'apocalittica-Caratteristiche e
        valore," *Ricerche Bibliche e Religiose* 13 (1978)
        7-42.

280a   Schmidt, J. M.   *Die jüdische Apokalyptik. Die
        Geschichte ihrer Erforschung von den Anfängen bis
        zu den Textfunden von Qumran,* 2nd ed. Neukirchen-
        Vluyn: Neukirchener, 1976.

281a   Schmithals, W.   "Jesus und die Apokalyptik," *Jesus
        Christus in Historie und Theologie* [Conzelmann
        Festschrift], ed. G. Strecker. Tübingen: Mohr,
        1975.   Pp. 59-85.

282a   Schoonheim, P. L.   "Probleme und Impulse der neu-
        testamentlichen Apokalyptik," *Miscellanea Neo-
        testamentica* (NovTSup 47) Leiden: Brill, 1978.
        Pp. 129-45.

284a   Schubert, K.   "Das Zeitalter der Apokalyptik,"
        Bibel und Zeitgemässer Glaube, 2 vols., ed.
        K. Schubert (vol. 1) and J. Sint (vol. 2).
        Munich: Klosterneuburger, 1965-1967.   Vol. 1,
        pp. 263-85.

284b   Schwartz, J.   "Le voyage au ciel dans la littérature
        apocalyptique," EHR 3.   Pp. 89-126.

284c   Silberman, L. H.   "Apocalyptic Revisited: Reflec-
        tions on the Thought of Albert Schweitzer," *JAAR*
        44 (1976) 489-501.

285a   Smith, J. Z.   "A Pearl of Great Price and a Cargo of
        Yams: A Study in Situational Incongruity," *History
        of Religions* 16 (1976) 1-19.   [a significant study
        of the social milieu of apocalyptic literature]

285b   Smith, J. Z.   "Wisdom and Apocalyptic," *Religious
        Syncretism in Antiquity: Essays in Conversation
        with Geo Widengren,* ed. B. A. Pearson. Missoula,
        Mont.: Scholars Press, 1975.   Pp. 131-56.
        Reprinted in *Map is not Territory.* Leiden: Brill,
        1978, pp. 67-87.

285c   Sneed, D. *Visions of Hope: Apocalyptic Themes from Biblical Times.* Minneapolis, Minn.: Augsburg, 1978.

286a   Stemberger, G. "Heilsvorstellungen im nachbiblischen Judentum," *BiKi* 33 (1978) 115-21.

286b   Stiassny, J. "L'occultation de l'apocalyptique dans le rabbinisme," LD 95 (1977) 179-203.

286c   Stone, M. E. "Apocalyptic--Vision or Hallucination," *Milla wa-Milla* 14 (1974) 47-56.

286d   Stone, M. E. "Lists of Revealed Things in the Apocalyptic Literature," *Magnalia Dei: The Mighty Acts of God: Essays on the Bible and Archaeology in Memory of G. Ernest Wright,* ed. F. M. Cross, *et al.* New York: Doubleday, 1976. Pp. 414-52.

293a   Walter, N. "Zur theologischen Relevanz apokalyptischer Aussagen," *Theologische Versuche* 6 (1975) 47-72.

295a   Willi-Plein, I. "Das Geheimnis der Apokalyptik," *VT* 27 (1977) 62-81.

296a   Zeitlin, S. "Dreams and Their Interpretation from the Biblical Period to the Tannaitic Time: An Historical Survey," *JQR* 66 (1975) 1-18.

Special Themes

Theology

See also nos. 100d, 126a, 576a.

296b   Adinolfi, M. "Gli omologhi del sacrificio di espiazione nel giudaismo antico," *Bibbia e Oriente* 20 (1978) 113-22.

297a   Amir, Y. "Die Begegnung des biblischen und des philosophischen Monotheismus als Grundthema des jüdischen Hellenismus," *EvT* 38 (1978) 2-18.

298a   Aune, D. E. "Orthodoxy in First Century Judaism? A Response to N.J. McEleney," *JSJ* 7 (1976) 1-10.

299a   Barth, C. "Diesseits und Jenseits im Glauben des späten Israel," *SBS* 72 (1974) 7-120.

299ab Baumbach, G. "Das Freiheitsverständnis in der zelotischen Bewegung," *Das Ferne und Nahe Wort* (BZAW 105) [Festschrift L. Rost] ed. F. Maass. Berlin: Töpelmann, 1967. Pp. 11-18.

299b   Berger, K. *Die Auffersteherung des Propheten und die Erhöhung des Menschensohnes: Traditionsgeschichtliche Untersuchungen zur Deutung des Geschickes Jesu in frühchristlichen Texten* (Studien zur Umwelt des Neuen Testaments 13) Göttingen: Vandenhoeck & Ruprecht, 1976. [B. includes a discussion of numerous obscure pseudepigrapha.]

299c   Berger, K. "Zur Frage des Traditionsgeschichtlichen Wertes Apokrypher Gleichnisse," *NovT* 17 (1975) 58-76. [B. comments on ApEl, TAsher, Tl2P, 2Bar, 4Ez, TAb, TIs, TJac, LadJac, and *LAB*.]

299d   Bilde, Per. "Gud og Messias som eskatologisk dommer i nytestamentlige og senjødiske tekster," *DTT* 40 (1977) 159-80.

300a   Brauch, M. *Eschatology in Intertestamental Period with Special Reference to the Wisdom of Solomon.* McMaster University Ph.D., 1972.

301a   Cohn-Sherbok, D. "The Jewish Doctrine of Hell," *Religion* 8 (1978) 196-209.

301b   Coppens, J. *De oud- en intertestamentische Verwachting van een eschatologische Heilsmiddelaar* (Mededelingen van Het Koninklijke Academie voor Wettenschappen, Letteren en Schone Kunsten van België, Kl. der Letteren 37, Nr. 3) Brussels: Paleis der Acadamiën, 1975. ["The Eschatological Messenger in the Old Testament and Intertestamental Writings"; in Flemish.]

301c   Cortès, E. *Los discursos de adiós de Gn 49 a Jn 13-17: Pistas para la historia de un género literario en la antigua literatura judía* (Colectánea San Paciano 23) Barcelona: Herder, 1976.

302a   Daniélou, J. "Tertullian's Reaction Against Judaeo-Christianity," *The Origins of Latin Christianity*, trans. D. Smith and J. A. Baker (A History of Early Christian Doctrine Before the Council of Nicea) London: Darton, Longman & Todd; Philadelphia: Westminster, 1977. Vol. 3, pp. 140-76. [The main discussion is on lEn, Book of Adam[!], SybOr.]

303a   Davies, P. R. and B. D. Chilton. "The Aqedah: A Revised Tradition History," *CBQ* 40 (1978) 514-46.

307a   Delcor, M. "Le mythe de la chute des anges et de l'origine des géants comme explication du mal dans le monde, dans l'apocalyptique juive: Histoire des traditions," *RHR* 190 (1976) 3-53.

307b   Delling, G. "Die Bezeichnung 'Söhne Gottes' in der
        jüdischen Literatur der hellenistisch-römischen
        Zeit," *God's Christ and His People* [Studies in
        Honour of Nils Alstrup Dahl] Oslo: 1977. Pp.
        18-29.

307c   Díez Merino, L. "La crocifissione nelle letterature
        ebree antiche (Periodo intertestamentale)," *La
        Sapienza della Croce oggi* 1 (1976) 61-88.

307d   Díez Merino, L. "Jewish Piety Outside the Gospels
        in Galilee After A.D. 70," *Bible Today* 50 (1970)
        81-85.

307e   Díez Merino, L. "El suplicio de la cruz en la
        literatura judía intertestamental," *Liber Annuus*
        26 (1976) 31-120.

307f   Dimant, D. *'The Fallen Angels' in the Dead Sea
        Scrolls and in the Apocryphal and Pseudepigraphic
        Books Related to Them.* Hebrew University Disser-
        tation, 1974. [in Hebrew]

307g   Dumke, J. A. *The Suffering of the Righteous in
        Jewish Apocryphal Literature.* Duke University
        Ph.D., 1980.

307h   Eiss, W. "Der Kalender des nachexilischen Judentums:
        Mit Aussnahme des essenischen Kalenders," *Die Welt
        des Orients* 3 (1964-66) 44-47.

312a   Fischer, U. *Eschatologie und Jenseitserwartung im
        hellenistischen Diasporajudentum* (BZNW 44) Berlin,
        New York: de Gruyter, 1978. [F., a student of
        C. Burchard and H. W. Kuhn, includes in his dis-
        cussion 2En, 3Bar, 4Mac, JosAsen.]

313a   Fujita, S. "The Metaphor of Plant in Jewish Litera-
        ture of the Intertestamental Period," *JSJ* 7 (1976)
        30-45. [F. discusses PsSol 14:3-5; 1En 83f.;
        91:12-17; 93:1-10; Jub 16:26; 36:6; 1QS8:5; CD1:7;
        1QH8.]

315a   Grabbe, L. L. "Orthodoxy in First Century Judaism:
        What are the Issues?" *JSJ* 8 (1977) 149-53.

315b   Gundry, R. H. "Anthropological Duality in the
        Judaism of NT Times," *Sōma in Biblical Theology
        with Emphasis on Pauline Anthropology* (SNTS MS 29)
        Cambridge: CUP, 1976. Pp. 87-109.

315c   Haag, H. "Die Dämonenlehre der Pseudepigraphen,"
        Teufelsglaube. Tübingen: Katzmann, 1974. Pp.
        218-46.

317a   Hengel, M. "Qumran und der Hellenismus," *BETL* 46 (1978) 333-72.

317b   Hengel, M. *Der Sohn Gottes: Die Entstehung der Christologie und die jüdisch-hellenistische Religionsgeschichte.* Tübingen: Mohr, 1975. See pp. 67-73.

319a   Hummel, H. D. "Law and Grace in Judaism and Lutheranism," *Lutheran Quarterly* 21 (1969) 416-29.

319b   Isaacs, M. E. *The Concept of Spirit: A Study of Pneuma in Hellenistic Judaism and its Bearing on the New Testament* (Heythrop Monographs 1) London: Heythrop, 1976.

319c   James, E. O. "The Apocalyptic Paradise," *The Tree of Life: An Archaeological Study* (Sup *Numen* 11) Leiden: Brill, 1966. Pp. 76f.

323a   Jordahl, V. T. *The Doctrine of Immortality Among the Pre-Pauline Christians.* Hull University Ph.D., 1967/68. [*N.V.*]

325a   Kronholm, T. *Motifs from Genesis 1-11 in the Genuine Hymns of Ephrem the Syrian: With Particular Reference to the Influence of Jewish Exegetical Tradition (Coniectanea Biblica* Old Testament 11) Uppsala: Almquist & Wiksell, 1978. [K. includes references to many pseudepigrapha.]

325b   Lange, N. R. M. de, "Origen and the Aqqadah," *Origen and the Jews: Studies in Jewish-Christian Relations in Third-Century Palestine.* London, New York: CUP, 1976. Pp. 123-32, 201-08.

327a   Légasse, S. "Baptême juif des prosélytes et baptême chrétien," *BLE* 77 (1976) 3-40.

332a   McEleney, N. J. "Orthodoxy in Judaism of the First Christian Century: Replies to David E. Aune and Lester L. Grabbe," *JSJ* 9 (1978) 83-88.

334a   Malina, B. J. "Jewish Christianity or Christian Judaism: Toward a Hypothetical Definition," *JSJ* 7 (1976) 46-57.

334b   Marcos, N. F. "Interpretaciones helenísticas del pasado de Israel," *Cuadernos de Filología Clásica* 8 (1975) 157-86.

334c   May, H. S. "The Daimonic in Jewish History (or, the Garden of Eden Revisited)," *ZRGG* 23 (1971) 205-19.

334d   Meloni, P. "Realtà e simbolismo del profumo nel
        mondo antico," *Il Profumo dell'immortalità* (Verba
        Seniorum N.S. 7) Rome: Edizioni Studium, 1975.
        Pp. 3-28. [See esp. "La tradizione biblica
        apocrifa: profumo del paradiso e profumo del
        sacrificio," pp. 14-22.]

334e   Merode, M. de, "'Une aide qui lui corresponde.'
        L'exégèse de Gen. 2, 18-24 dans les écrits de
        l'Ancien Testament, du judaïsme et du Nouveau
        Testament," *Revue théologique de Louvain* 8.3
        (1977) 329-52. [M. discusses Jub, 2En, 4Mac, and
        LAE.]

336a   Nibley, H. "Evangelium Quadraginta Dierum," *VC* 20
        (1966) 1-24.

336ab   Nibley, H. "Treasures in the Heavens: Some Early
        Christian Insights into the Organizing of Worlds,"
        Dialogue 8 (1974) 76-98. [N. discusses 1En, 2En,
        2Bar, 3Bar, T12P, and other apocryphal documents.]

338a   Otzen, B. "Old Testament Wisdom Literature and
        Dualistic Thinking in Late Judaism," VTSup 28
        (1975) 146-57.

339a   Pikaza, J. "Diablo y demonios en el judáismo pre-
        cristiano," *Biblia y Fe* (Madrid) 2 (1976) 36-46.

341a   Rohland, J. P. *Der Erzengel Michael Arzt und Feld-
        herr: Zwei Aspekte des vor- und frühbyzan-
        tinischen Michaelskultes* (ZRGG 19) Leiden: Brill,
        1977. [Special attention is given to 1En, 2En,
        2Bar, LAE, and ApMos.]

342a   Rubinkiewicz, R. "The Kingdom of God and Israel in
        OT Pseudepigrapha," *Królestwo Boże w Piśmie
        Swiętym*, ed. S. Lach and M. Filipiak. Lublin:
        1976. Pp. 123-33. [in Polish]

342b   Sanders, E. P. "The Covenant as a Soteriological
        Category and the Nature of Salvation in Palestin-
        ian and Hellenistic Judaism," *Jews, Greeks and
        Christians: Religious Cultures in Late Antiquity*.
        [W. D. Davies Festschrift], ed. R. Hamerton-Kelly
        and R. Scroggs. Leiden: Brill, 1976. Pp. 11-44.

342c   Sanders, E. P. *Paul and Palestinian Judaism*. Phila-
        delphia: Fortress, 1977; see esp. "Palestinian
        Judaism," pp. 33-428.

342d   Schäfer, P. *Rivalität zwischen Engeln und Menschen:
        Untersuchungen zur rabbinischen Engelvorstellung
        (Studia Judaica 8) Berlin: Walter de Gruyter,
        1975.*

344a   Schubert, K. "Versuchung oder Versucher? Der
        Teufel als Begriff oder Person in den biblischen
        und ausserbiblischen Texten," *Bibel und Liturgie*
        50 (1977) 104-13. [includes a discussion of 1En,
        Jub]

344b   Schultz, D. R. "The Origin of Sin in Irenaeus and
        Jewish Pseudepigraphical Literature," *VC* 32 (1978)
        161-90.

344c   Simon, M. "Jupiter-Yahvé: Sur un essai de théologie
        pagano-juive," *Numen* 23 (1976) 40-66.

345a   Stachowiak, L. "Pouczenia ctyczne w literaturze
        międzytestamentalnej," *Collectanea Theologica* 48
        (1978) 43-62. ["Ethical Admonitions in Inter-
        testamental Literature"; T12P, Jub, 1En.]

345b   Steck, O. H. *Israel und das Gewaltsame Geschick der
        Propheten: Untersuchungen zur Überlieferung des
        Deuteronomistischen Geschichtsbildes im Alten Tes-
        tament, Spätjudentum und Urchristentum (WMANT* 23)
        Neukirchen-Vluyn: Neukirchener Verlag, 1967.
        [See esp. pp. 110-264 in which S. discusses the
        tradition of the violent fate of the prophets and
        martyrs in many of the Pseudepigrapha.]

347a   Talbert, C. H. "The Myth of a Descending-Ascending
        Redeemer in Mediterranean Antiquity," *NTS* 22 (1976)
        418-40.

347b   Talmon, S. "The Emergence of Institutionalized
        Prayer in Israel in the Light of the Qumran
        Literature," *BETL* 46 (1978) 265-84.

347c   Testa, P. E. "I Novissimi e la loro localizzazione
        nella teologia ebraica e giudeo-cristiana," *Liber
        Annuus* 26 (1976) 121-69.

348a   Tsakonas, B. "A Comparative Study of the Term 'Son
        of God,' in St. Paul, the Old Testament, the Hel-
        lenistic World and in Philo," *Theologia* (1966) 1-52.

348b   Tsakonas, B. "'Spirit,' 'Spirits,' and 'Holy Spirit'
        in Jewish and Apocalyptic Writings," *Hē Peri
        Paraklētou: Pneumatos Didaskalia Tou Evangelistou
        Ioannou*. Athens, 1978. Pp. 47-53. [in modern
        Greek]

348c   Turdeanu, É. "Dieu créa l'homme de huit éléments et
        tira son nom des quatre coins du monde," *Revue des
        Études Roumaines* 13-14 (1974) 163-94.

349a   VanderKam, J. "A Typological Analysis of Intertes-
        tamental Pronouncement Stories," *SBL 1977 Seminar
        Papers*. Pp. 279-84.

265

349b   Vermes, G. "The Present State of the 'Son of Man'
       Debate," *JJS* 29 (1978) 123-34.

351a   Whitelocke, L. T. *The Development of Jewish Religi-
       ous Thought in the Inter-Testamental Period.* New
       York: Vantage, 1976.

351b   Williams, S. K. *Jesus' Death as Saving Event: The
       Background and Origin of a Concept* (Harvard Dis-
       sertations in Religion 2) Missoula, Mont.: Scholars
       Press, 1975. [special discussions of AsMos, T12P,
       4Mac]

351c   Wolff, C. *Jeremia im Frühjudentum und Urchristentum*
       (TU 118) Berlin: Akademie-Verlag, 1976. [includes
       LAB, Eupolemus, 2Bar, LivPro, 4Bar, CavTr, Jub]

Dualism

See also nos. 315b, 336ab, 338a, 841a, 1192b.

No additional publications.

Martyrdom

See also nos. 197a, 296a, 299b, 307c, 307e, 307g, 345b,
351b, 441a, 1112b, 1166aa, 1317b.

Messianism

See also nos. 299d, 701a, 841a, 1417a.

359a   Adinolfi, M. "Sul messianismo sacerdotale," *Bibbia
       e Oriente* 19 (1977) 101-11.

368a   Bowker, J. "The Son of Man," *JTS* N.S. 28 (1977) 19-
       48.

370a   Caquot, A. "Le messianisme qumrânien," *BETL* 46
       (1978) 231-47.

370b   Charlesworth, J. H. "The Concept of the Messiah in
       the Pseudepigrapha," *Aufstieg und Niedergang der
       Römischen Welt*, Vol. II 19.1, pp. 188-218.

370c   Charlesworth, J. H. "Messianism in the Pseudepigrapha
       and the Book of Mormon," *Reflections on Mormonism:
       Judaeo-Christian Parallels*, ed. T. Madsen (RSMS 4)
       Provo, Utah: Religious Studies Center, 1978. Pp.
       99-137.

376a   Ferch, A. J. "The Two Aeons and the Messiah in
       Pseudo-Philo, 4 Ezra, and 2 Baruch," *Andrews Uni-
       versity Seminary Studies* 15 (1977) 135-51.

377a   Frankemölle, H. "Jüdische Messiaserwartung und
        christlicher Messiasglaube," *Kairos* N.F. 20 (1978)
        97-109.

392a   Leivestad, R. "Expectation of the Kingdom of God
        and Conceptions of the Messiah in the Time of
        Jesus," *Kirke og Kultur* [*Oslo*] 81 (1976) 593-607.
        [in Norwegian]

393a   Levey, S. H. *The Messiah: An Aramaic Interpretation.
        The Messianic Exegesis of the Targum.* Cincinnati:
        Hebrew Union College, 1974. [L. does not discuss
        the Pseudepigrapha; but this is an important
        related study of cognate literature.]

403a   Penna, R. *Lo Spirito de Cristo: Cristologia e
        pneumatologia secondo un'originale formulazione
        paolina* (Supplementi alla *RivB* 7) Brescia: Pai-
        deia, 1976. [P. includes a discussion of the con-
        cept of the spirit and the Messiah in the Pseud-
        epigrapha.]

406a   Rivkin, E. "Messiah, Jewish," *IDBS* (1976) 588-91.

411a   Schweizer, E. "Menschensohn und eschatologischer
        Mensch im Frühjudentum," *Jesus und der Menschen-
        sohn* [Vögtle Festschrift], ed. R. Pesch, R. Schnack-
        enburg, O. Kaiser. Freiburg, Basel: Herder, 1975.
        Pp. 100-16.

413a   Sint, J. "Messianologie und Eschatologie: Christol-
        ogie als Eschatologie," *Bibel und Zeitgemässer
        Glaube*, 2 vols. ed. K. Schubert (vol. 1) and J.
        Sint (vol. 2). Munich: Klosterneuburger, 1965-
        1967. Vol. 2, pp. 199-228.

413b   Smith, M. "Messiahs: Robbers, Jurists, Prophets
        and Magicians," *American Academy for Jewish Research*
        44 (1977) 185-95.

415a   Vawter, B. "Levitical Messianism and the NT," *The
        Bible in Current Catholic Thought: Gruenthaner
        Memorial Volume*, ed. J. L. McKenzie (St. Mary's
        Theological Studies 1) New York: Herder and Herder,
        1962. Pp. 83-99.

417a   Villiers, P. G. R. de. "The Messiah and Messiahs in
        Jewish Apocalyptic," *Neotestamentica* (1979) 1-29.

Prayer

See also nos. 307d, 319a, 325a, 347b, 498a, 543a, 899c-d,
945a, 1008a, 1012a, 1121a, 1430a.

422a   Charlesworth, J. H. "Jewish Liturgies, Hymns and
        Prayers (c. 167 B.C.E.-135 C.E.)," *Early Post-
        Biblical Judaism and its Modern Interpreters*, ed.
        R. A. Kraft and G. W. E. Nickelsburg. Missoula,
        Mont.: Scholars Press, in press.

Old Testament Names Used Pseudonymously

Abraham

See also nos. 513a, 520b-c, 1019a.

425a   Berger, K. "Abraham II. Im Frühjudentum und Neuen
        Testament," *TRE* 1. Pp. 372-82.

430a   Schein, B. E. "Abraham in the Non-Christian Writings
        of the Greco-Roman Period," *Our Father Abraham*.
        Yale University Ph.D., 1972. Pp. 19-92. [S. dis-
        cusses Jub, TAb, 1En, T12P, *LAB*, ApAb, 4Mac, 2Bar,
        4Ezra.]

Adam

See also no. 554a.

438a   Schäffer, P. "Adam II. Im Judentum," *TRE* 1. Pp.
        424-27.

Elijah

See also nos. 711a, 1187b, 1204b, 1412a.

441a   Bauckham, R. "The Martyrdom of Enoch and Elijah:
        Jewish or Christian?" *JBL* 95 (1976) 447-58.

Enoch

See also no. 1055a.

441b   Grelot, P. "Hénoch et ses écritures," *RB* 82 (1975)
        481-500.

Ezekiel

See also no. 829a̲.

Jeremiah

See also nos. 677b, 681a.

441c   Turdeanu, É.   "La légende du prophète Jérémie en
        roumaine," *Revue des Études Roumaines* 15 (1975)
        145-79.

Moses

See also nos. 515c-d, 829a, 830b, 1221a.

444b   Meeks, W. A.   "Moses in Non-Rabbinic Jewish Sources,"
        *The Prophet-King: Moses Traditions and the
        Johannine Christology* (NovTSup 14) Leiden: Brill,
        1967.   Pp. 100-75.

446a   Wadsworth, M.   "The Death of Moses and the Riddle of
        the End of Time in Pseudo-Philo," *JJS* 28 (1977) 12-
        19.

Noah

See also nos. 744d, 748a.

Seth

See also no. 554a.

449a   Adler, W. "Materials Relating to Seth in an Anonymous
        Chronographer ("Pseudo-Malalas") and in the Chron-
        ography of George Syncellus," *SBL 1977 Seminar
        Papers.*   Pp. 13-15.

449b   Gibbons, J. A.   "The Second Logos of the Great Seth:
        Considerations and Questions," *SBL 1973 Papers.*
        Vol. 2, pp. 242-57.

449c   Klijn, A. F. J.   *Seth in Jewish, Christian and Gnostic
        Literature* (NovTSup 8) Leiden: Brill, 1977.

449d   MacRae, G. W.   "Seth in Gnostic Texts and Traditions,"
        SBL 1977 Seminar Papers.   Pp. 17-24.

449e   Pearson, B. A.   "Egyptian Seth and Gnostic Seth,"
        SBL 1977 Seminar Papers.   Pp. 25-43.

449f   Quinn, E. C.   *The Quest of Seth for the Oil of Life.*
        Chicago: University of Chicago Press, 1962.

449g   Quinn, E. C.   "The Quest of Seth, Solomon's Ship and
        the Grail," *Traditio* 21 (1965) 185-222.

Resurrection and Eschatology

See also nos. 299b, 299d, 300a, 301a-b, 312a, 319c, 323a,
334d, 411a, 413a, 446a, 518a, 697c, 764a, 1165a.

269

453a   Cavallin, H. C. C. *Life After Death: Paul's Argu-
         ment for the Resurrection of the Dead in I Cor 15;
         Part I: An Enquiry into the Jewish Background*
         (*Coniectanea biblica* New Testament 7.1) Lund:
         Gleerup, 1974. [This is an excellent study that
         considers many of the Pseudepigrapha.]

454a   Díez Macho, A. *La Resurrección de Jesucristo y la
         del hombre en la Biblia* (Colección Santiago
         Apóstol) Madrid: Fe Católica, 1977.

454b   Drane, J. W. "Some Ideas of Resurrection in the NT
         Period," *Tyndale Bulletin* 24 (1973) 99-110.

461a   Keller, E. B. "Hebrew Thoughts on Immortality and
         Resurrection," *International Journal for Philosophy
         of Religion* 5 (1974) 16-44.

470a   Nickelsburg, G. W. E. Jr. "Future Life in Inter-
         testamental Literature," *IDBS* (1976) 348-51.

471a   Nötscher, F. *Altorientalischer und alttestament-
         licher Auferstehungsglauben,* new edition with a
         Nachtrag by J. Scharbert. Darmstadt: Wissen-
         schaftliche Buchgesellschaft, 1970.

473a   Pokorný, P. *Die Hoffnung auf das Ewige Leben im
         Spätjudentum und Urchristentum* (Aufsätze und
         Vorträge zur Theologie und Religionswissenschaft
         70) Berlin: Evangelische Verlagsanstalt, 1978.
         Pp. 5-49.

480a   Ulrichsen, J. H. "Troen på et liv etter døden i
         Qumrantekstene," *Norsk Teologisk Tidsskrift* 78
         (1977) 151-63. ["Belief in Life After Death in
         the Qumran Texts."]

Sin

     See also nos. 315c, 334c, 339a, 341a, 342b-c, 344a-b,
880a.

     No additional publications.

Apocalypse of Abraham

498a   Philonenko, M. "Le Poimandrès et la liturgie juive,"
         *Les syncrétismes dans les religions de l'antiquité:
         Colloque de Besançon (22-23 octobre 1973),* ed.
         F. Dunand and P. Lévêque. Leiden: Brill, 1975.
         Pp. 204-11.

498b   Rubinkiewicz, R. "Apokalipsa Abrahama," *RuBi* 27
         (1974) 230-37.

498c   Rubinkiewicz, R.   "Apocalypse of Abraham," Doubleday
        edition.

Testament of Abraham

See The Testaments of the Three Patriarchs.

See also nos. 425a, 430a.

502a   Agourides, S.   "The Testament of Abraham: An Unpub-
        lished Modern Greek Manuscript," *Deltion Biblikōn
        Meletōn* 1 (1972) 238-48. [in modern Greek with
        text]

505a   Cooper, D. S. and H. B. Weber. "The Church Slavonic
        Testament of Abraham," SCS 6.   Pp. 301-26.
        [English translation with introduction]

506a   Delcor, M. "De l'origine de quelques traditions
        contenues dans le Testament d'Abraham," *Religion
        d'Israël et Proche Orient Ancien: Des Phéniciens
        aux Esséniens.* Leiden: Brill, 1976.   Pp. 241-50.
        [Although this is a reprint, it contains signifi-
        cant corrections; cf. p. 250.]

513a   Harrington, D. J. "Abraham Traditions in the Testa-
        ment of Abraham and in the 'Rewritten Bible' of
        the Intertestamental Period," SCS 6.   Pp. 165-72.

515a   Kolenkow, A. B.   "The Angelology of the Testament of
        Abraham," SCS 6.   Pp. 153-62.

515ab   Kolenkow, A. B.   "The Genre Testament and the Testa-
        ment of Abraham," SCS 6.   Pp. 139-52.

515b   Kraft, R. A.   "Reassessing the 'Recensional Problem'
        in Testament of Abraham," SCS 6. Pp. 121-37.

515c   Loewenstamm, S. E.   "The Death of Moses," SCS 6.
        Pp. 185-217. [Revised version and translation of
        article in *Tarbiz* 27 (1958) 142-57]

515d   Loewenstamm, S. E.   "The Testament of Abraham and
        the Texts Concerning the Death of Moses," SCS 6.
        Pp. 219-25.

515e   MacRae, G.   "The Coptic Testament of Abraham," SCS 6.
        Pp. 327-40. [An English translation]

515f   MacRae, G.   "The Judgment Scene in the Coptic
        Apocalypse of Paul," SCS 6.   Pp. 285-88.   [An
        English translation with discussion]

515g   Martin R. A.   "Syntax Criticism of the Testament of
        Abraham," SCS 6.   Pp. 95-120.

518a   Nickelsburg, G. W. E. Jr.   "Eschatology in the
        Testament of Abraham: A Study of the Judgment
        Scene in the Two Recensions," SCS 6. Pp. 23-64.

518b   Nickelsburg, G. W. E. Jr.   "Structure and Message
        in the Testament of Abraham," SCS 6. Pp. 85-93.

518c   Nickelsburg, G. W. E. Jr., ed. *Studies on the
        Testament of Abraham* (SCS 6) Missoula, Mont.:
        SBL, 1976.

520a   Schmidt, F.   "Le monde à l'image du bouclier d'
        Achille: Sur la naissance et l'incorruptibilité
        du monde dans le 'Testament d'Abraham,'" *RHR* 185
        (1974) 122-26.

520b   Schmidt, F.   "Traditions relatives à Abraham dans
        la littérature hellénistique juive [. . . recen-
        sions grecques du Testament d'Abraham . . .],"
        École Pratique des Hautes-Études, Section: Relig-
        Annuaire 80 (1971) 321-23.

520c   Schmidt, F.   "Traditions relatives à Abraham dans
        la littérature hellénistique juive [. . . recen-
        sions grecques du Testament d'Abraham . . .],"
        École Pratique des Hautes-Études, Section: Relig-
        Annuaire 82 (1973) 191-94.

520d   Schmidt, F.   "The Two Recensions of the Testament
        of Abraham: In Which Way did the Transformation
        Take Place?" SCS 6. Pp. 65-83.

522a   Turdeanu, É.   "Le *Testament d'Abraham* en slave et
        en roumain," *Oxford Slavonic Papers* N.S. 10 (1977)
        1-38.

523a   Ward, R. B.   "Abraham Traditions in Early Christian-
        ity," SCS 6. Pp. 173-84.

Apocalypse of Adam

    See also no. 181a.

524a   Belitz, W.   "Bemerkungen zur Adamapokalypse aus Nag-
        Hammadi-Codex V," *Studia Coptica* (BBA 45) (1974)
        159-63.

526a   Betz, O.   "Adam I," *TRE* 1. Pp. 414-23. See pp. 422f.

530a   Erbetta, M.   "Apocalisse di Adamo," *Apocrifi del
        N.T.* Vol. 1, pp. 206-11.

532a   Hedrick, C. W.   *The Apocalypse of Adam: A Literary
        and Source Analysis.* Claremont Graduate School
        Ph.D. 1977.

536a   MacRae, G.   "Adam, Apocalypse of," *IDBS* (1976) 9f.

538a   MacRae, G. W. and D. M. Parrott.   "The Apocalypse
        of Adam (V,5)," *The Nag Hammadi Library: In
        English*, ed. J. M. Robinson and M. W. Meyer.   San
        Francisco: Harper & Row; Leiden: Brill, 1977.
        Pp. 256-64.

539a   Morard, F.   "L'*Apocalypse d'Adam* de Nag Hammadi: Un
        essai d'interpretation," *Gnosis and Gnosticism*,
        ed. M. Krause (NHS 8) Leiden: Brill, 1977.

539b   Morard, F.   "*L'Apocalypse d'Adam* du Codex V de Nag
        Hammadi et sa polémique anti-baptismale," *Revue
        des Sciences Religieuses* 51 (1977) 214-33.

539c   Perkins, P.   "Apocalypse of Adam: The Genre and
        Function of a Gnostic Apocalypse," *CBQ* 39 (1977)
        382-95.

542a   Robinson, S. E.   "The Apocalypse of Adam," *Brigham
        Young University Studies* 17 (1977) 131-53.

543a   Sanders, J. T.   "The Apocalypse of Adam," *The New
        Testament Christological Hymns: Their Historical
        Religious Background* (SNTS MS 15) Cambridge: CUP,
        1971.   Pp. 130-32.

Testament of Adam
[and Adam Cycle]

In the first printing of this monograph I was forced to
rely upon the Syriac text of M. Kmosko (who used 2 Syriac MSS)
and the Arabic text of M. D. Gibson (see p. 91 above).   With
my guidance S. E. Robinson searched for and found eight Syriac
manuscripts of the Testament of Adam; these date from the ninth
to the eighteenth century (see Robinson, no. 546b, pp. 78-88).
Most significantly, in "every Syriac manuscript the Testament
of Adam appears as an independent, self-contained work, and is
clearly entitled 'The Testament of Adam.'" (Robinson, no. 546b,
pp. 79f.)   Robinson has published the first English translation
of the Syriac (see esp. no. 546c; Budge worked from the Ethiopic, Gibson from the Arabic; see p. 91 above).   The Testament
of Adam now appears to have been written in Syriac, perhaps
sometime in the third century.

The Testament of Adam has three sections: The Horarium,
or a description of the praises offered to God and by whom,
according to the hours of the day and night.   The Prophecy, or

Adam's testament, especially to Seth, which foretells the future. The Hierarchy, or an account of the different orders of angels and other heavenly beings.

See also no. 438a.

546a   Reinink, G. J. "Das Problem des Ursprungs des Testamentes Adams," *Orientalia Christiana Analecta* 197 (1972) 387-99.

546b   Robinson, S. E. *The Testament of Adam: An Explanation of the Syriac and Greek Traditions*. Duke University Ph.D., 1978. [to be published in the SBL Dissertation Series]

546c   Robinson, S. E. "Testament of Adam," Doubleday edition.

Life of Adam and Eve

See also no. 341a.

554a   Kolenkow, A. B. "Trips to the Other World in Antiquity and the Story of Seth in the Life of Adam and Eve," *SBL 1977 Seminar Papers*. Pp. 1-11.

556a   Lieberman, S. "Neglected Sources," *Tarbiz* 62 (1972) 42-54. [L. discusses the Slavonic version of LAE.]

Ahiqar

See also no. 248a.

565a   Brock, S. P. "Notes on Some Texts in the Mingana Collection," *JSS* 14 (1969) 205-25. See esp. pp. 205f.

572b   Niditch, S. and R. Doran. "The Success Story of the Wise Courtier: A Formal Approach," *JBL* 96 (1977) 179-93.

An Anonymous Samaritan Text (Pseudo-Eupolemus)

574a   Denis, A.-M. "L'*Historien Anonyme* d'Eusèbe (Praep. Ev. 9, 17-18) et la crise des Macchabées," *JSJ* 8 (1977) 42-49.

Letter of Aristeas

See also no. 344c.

576a   Cothenet, E. "Pureté et impureté . . . Le judaïsme
        hellénistique," *DBSup* 49 (1973) 527f.

583a   Herrmann, L. "La Lettre d'Aristée à Philocrate et
        l'empereur Titus," *Latomus* 25 (1966) 58-77.

585a   Jellicoe, S. "The Occasion and Purpose of the Letter
        of Aristeas: A Re-examination," *NTS* 12 (1965/66)
        144-50.

585ab   Jellicoe, S. "St. Luke and the Letter of Aristeas,"
        JBL 80 (1961) 149-55.

586b   Klijn, A. F. J. "The Letter of Aristeas and the
        Greek Translation of the Pentateuch in Egypt,"
        NTS 11 (1964/65) 154-58.

591a   Müller, K. "Aristeasbrief," *TRE*, 719-25.

592a   Murray, O. "Aristeas and his Sources," *Studia
        Patristica 12*, 123-28.

593a   Orlinsky, H. M. "The Septuagint as Holy Writ and
        the Philosophy of the Translators," *HUCA* 46 (1975)
        89-114.

595a   Pelletier, A. *Lettre d'Aristée à Philocrate* (SC 89)
        Paris: Cerf, 1962.

597a   Shutt, R. J. H. "Notes on the Letter of Aristeas,"
        BIOSCS 10 (1977) 22-30.

602a   Van't Dack, E. "La date de la Lettre d'Aristée,"
        Studia Hellenistica 16 (1968) 263-78.

Aristeas the Exegete

604b   Doran, R. "Aristeas the Exegete," Doubleday edition.

Aristobulus

608a   Collins, A. Yarbro. "Aristobulus," Doubleday edition

611a   Sandelin, K.-G. "Zwei kurze Studien zum alexandrin-
        ischen Judentum," *Studia Theologica* 31 (1977) 147-
        52.

611b   Walter, N. "Anfänge alexandrinisch-jüdischer Bibel-
        auslegung bei Aristobulos," Helikon 3 (1963) 353-
        72.

Artapanus

612<u>a</u>   Collins, J. J.   "Artapanus," Doubleday edition.

614a   Merentitēs, K. I.   *Ho Ioudaios logios Artapanos kai to ergon autou.*   Athens, 1961

2 (Syriac) Baruch

See also nos. 44b, 194b-c, 341a, 376a, 446a, 1192b.

622a   Dautzenberg, G.   "Das Bild der Prophetie im 4 Esra und im SyrBar," *Urchristliche Prophetie: Ihre Erforschung, ihre Voraussetzungen im Judentum und ihre Struktur im ersten Korintherbrief* (BWANT Folge 6, Heft 4) Stuttgart: Kohlhammer, 1975. Pp. 90-98.

634a   Halperin, I.   "Exchanges between Bruscius and Delmedigo," *Studies and Essays in Honor of Abraham A. Neuman, President, Dropsie College for Hebrew and Cognate Learning, Philadelphia,* ed. M. Ben-Horin, *et al.*   Leiden: Brill, 1962. Pp. 637-49.

641a   Klijn, A. F. J.   "Die syrische Baruch-Apokalypse," *JSHRZ* 5 (1976) 103-91.

645a   Rosenthal, J.   "From 'Sefer Alfonso,'" *Studies and Essays in Honor of Abraham A. Neuman, Dropsie College for Hebrew and Cognate Learning, Philadelphia,* ed. M. Ben-Horin, *et al.*   Leiden: Brill, 1962. Pp. 588-621.

649a   Zimmerman, F.   "Translation and Mistranslation in the Apocalypse of Baruch," *Studies and Essays in Honor of Abraham A. Neuman, President, Dropsie College for Hebrew and Cognate Learning, Philadelphia,* ed. M. Ben-Horin, *et al.*   Leiden: Brill, 1962. Pp. 580-87.

3 (Greek) Baruch

656a   Hage, W.   "Die griechische Baruch-Apokalypse," *JSHRZ* 5 (1974) 1-44.

657a   Jacobson, H., "A Note on the Greek Apocalypse of Baruch," *JSJ* 7 (1976) 201-3.

4 Baruch [and Jeremiah (Baruch) Cycle]

671a   Licht, J.   "Paralipomena Jeremiae," *Pinkhos Churgin Memorial Volume,* ed. H. Z. (J. W.) Hirschberg and P. Artzi (Annual of Bar-Ilan University 1) Jerusalem: Kiryath Sepher, 1963. Pp. 66-80.

676a   Robinson, S. E. "4 Baruch," Doubleday edition.

677a   Schmid, H. "Baruch und die ihm zugeschriebene
         apokryphe und pseudepigraphische Literatur,"
         Judaica 30 (1974) 54-70.

677b   Schützinger, H. "Die arabische Jeremia-Erzählung
         und ihre Beziehungen zur jüdischen religiösen
         Überlieferung," *ZRGG* 25 (1973) 1-19.

681a   Turdeanu, É. "La légende du prophète Jérémie
         d'après le chronographe de Sigmaringen (1679-
         1684)," *Revue des Études Roumaines* 15 (1975)
         180-86.

681b   Turdeanu, É. "La légende du prophète Jérémie en
         roumain," *Revue des Études Roumaines* 15 (1975)
         145-79.

Cave of Treasures

No additional publications. See Testament of Adam.

Cleodemus Malchus

685b   Doran, R. "Cleodemus," Doubleday edition.

Apocalypse of Daniel

A comparatively late Byzantine apocalypse, the Apocalypse
of Daniel is extant in Greek. An eclectic text has been
edited and translated into German by K. Berger (no. 688a).
The first English translation, based upon an examination of
the photographs of Manuscript B (Codex Canonicianus Nr. 19,
ff. 145-52, in the Bodleian Library at Oxford), by G. T.
Zervos will be published in the Doubleday edition of the
Pseudepigrapha.

The present form of the Apocalypse of Daniel apparently
dates from the ninth century A.D., since 7:14 appears to refer
to the coronation of Charlemagne as emperor in A.D. 800. It
may preserve much earlier Jewish traditions; it contains elements parallel to such early documents as the Sibylline Oracles (esp. Books 3-5), 2 Baruch, and 4 Ezra. It also seems to
parallel traditions in the Revelation of John, and in a cryptic Christian inscription of the late second century on the
tomb of Aberkios of Hierapolis. These early parallels

indicate this document should (provisionally) be included in
the Pseudepigrapha.

The original language of the Apocalypse of Daniel is
probably Greek. The Septuagint has supplied Old Testament
quotations and the spelling for proper names (see Zervos,
no. 688b).

The document contains two disparate sections: The first
(chps. 1-7) reflects the historical events of the Byzantino-
Arab wars of the eighth century. The second (chps. 8-14) is
an apocalypse, which describes the end of the world, which is
dominated by the Antichrist.

688a   Berger, K. *Die griechische Daniel-Diegese: Eine
        altkirchliche Apokalypse; Text, Übersetzung und
        Kommentar* (SPB 27) Leiden: Brill, 1976. [Accord-
        ing to B., the historical part of this pseudepig-
        raphon dates from the early part of the ninth
        century; the eschatological section may be as
        early as the fourth or fifth century.]

688b   Zervos, G. "Apocalypse of Daniel," Doubleday edi-
        tion.

                        Demetrius

689b   Hanson, J. S. "Demetrius the Chronographer,"
        Doubleday edition.

                    Eldad and Modad

695a   Leiman, S. Z. "The Inverted *Nuns* at Numbers 10:35-
        36 and the Book of Eldad and Medad," *JBL* 93 (1974)
        348-55.

695b   Martin, E. G. "Eldad and Modad," Doubleday edition.

            Apocalypse of Elijah [and Elijah Cycle]

    See also nos. 441a, 719d.

697a   Berger, K. "Zur frage des traditionsgeschichtlichen
        Wertes apokrypher Gleichnisse," *NovT* 17 (1975) 58-
        76.

697b   Black, M. "The 'Two Witnesses' of Rev. 11:3f. in
        Jewish and Christian Apocalyptic Tradition,"
        Donum Gentilicium 1978. Pp. 227-37.

278

697c   Clark, D. G. *Elijah as Eschatological High Priest:*
        An Examination of the Elijah Tradition in Mal.
        3:23-24. University of Notre Dame Ph.D., 1975.
        Pp. 189-234.

701a   McNeil, B. "Coptic Evidence of Jewish Messianic
        Beliefs (Apocalypse of Elijah 2:5-6)," *Revista*
        degli Studi Orientali 51 (1977) 39-45.

702a   Nola, A. M. di. "Elia e Sofonia, Apocalisse di,"
        EncRel 2 (1970) 1142-44.

710a   Stone, M. E. and J. Strugnell, *The Books of Elijah:*
        Parts 1-2 (T&T 18, Pseudepigrapha Series 8)
        Missoula, Mont.: Scholars Press, 1979.

711a   Wieder, A. *The Prophet Elijah in the Development*
        of Judaism (The Littman Library of Jewish Civili-
        zation) London: Routledge & Kegan Paul, 1978.

        1 (Ethiopic) Enoch [and Enoch Cycle]

    See also nos. 44b, 251a, 307b, 341a, 347a, 441b,
1055a.

713a   Adler, W. "Enoch in Early Christian Literature,"
        SBL 1978 Seminar Papers. Vol. 1, pp. 271-75.

715a   Alexander, P. S. "The Targumim and Early Exegesis
        of 'Sons of God' in Genesis 6," *JJS* 23 (1972) 60.

716a   Barr, J. "Aramaic-Greek Notes on the Book of
        Enoch (I)," *JJS* 23 (1978) 184-98.

717a   Black, M. "The Apocalypse of Weeks in the Light of
        4QEn^g," *VT* 28 (1978) 464-69.

719a   Black, M. "The 'Parables' of Enoch (1 En 37-71) and
        the 'Son of Man,'" *ExpT* 88 (1976) 5-8.

719b   Black, M. "The New Creation in 1 Enoch," *Creation,*
        Christ and Culture, ed. R. W. A. McKinney. Edin-
        burgh: Clark, 1976. Pp. 13-21.

719c   Black, M. "The Throne-Theophany Prophetic Commis-
        sion and the 'Son of Man': A Study in Tradition-
        History." *Jews, Greeks and Christians: Religious*
        Cultures in Late Antiquity [W. D. Davies Fest-
        schrift], ed. R. Hamerton-Kelly and R. Scroggs.
        Leiden: Brill, 1976. Pp. 57-73.

719d   Black, M. "The 'Two Witnesses' of Rev. 11:3f. in
        Jewish and Christian Apocalyptic Traditions,"
        Donum Gentilicium: New Testament Studies in
        Honour of David Daube, ed. E. Bammel, C. K. Bar-
        rett, and W. D. Davies. Oxford: Clarendon, 1978.
        Pp. 227-37.

722a   Cantinat, J. *Les Épitres de Saint Jacques et de Saint Jude.* Paris: Lecoffre, 1973. See esp. pp. 270-76.

722b   Caquot, A. "Léviathan et Behémoth dans la troisième 'Parable' d'Hénoch," *Sem* 25 (1975) 111-22.

722c   Caquot, A. "Remarques sur les chap. 70 et 71 du livre éthiopien d'Henoch," *LD* 95 (1977) 111-22.

723a   Casey, M. "The Use of Term 'Son of Man' in the Similitudes of Enoch," *JSJ* 7 (1976) 11-29.

723b   Charlesworth, J. H. "The SNTS Pseudepigrapha Seminars at Tübingen and Paris on the Books of Enoch," *NTS* 25 (1979) 315-23.

723c   Collins, J. J. "Methodological Issues in the Study of 1 Enoch: Reflections on the Articles of P. D. Hanson and G. W. Nickelsburg," *SBL 1978 Seminar Papers.* Vol. 1, pp. 315-22.

723d   Coppens, J. "Miscellanea biblica 33: Le Fils d'homme daniélique, vizir céleste," *ETL* 40 (1964) 72-80.

723e   Coppens, J. "La vision du très-haut en Dan., VII et Hén. Éthiop. XIV," *ETL* 53 (1977) 187-89.

723f   Cortès, E. *Los discursos de adiós de Gn 49 a Jn 13-17: Pistas para la historia de un género literario en la antigua literatura judía* (Colectánea San Paciano 23) Barcelona: Herder, 1976.

724a   Coughenour, R. A. "The Woe-Oracles in Ethiopic Enoch," *JSJ* 9 (1978) 192-97.

724b   Dalton, W. J. "Light From the Book of Enoch," *Christ's Proclamation to the Spirits* (AnBib 23) Rome: Pontifical Biblical Institute, 1965. Pp. 163-76.

724c   Dautzenberg, G. "Das Offenbarungsverständnis im aethiopischen Henoch," *Urchristliche Prophetie: Ihre Erforschung, ihre Voraussetzungen im Judentum und ihre Struktur im ersten Korintherbrief* (BWANT Folge 6, Heft 4) Stuttgart: Kohlhammer, 1975. Pp. 76-89.

725a   Dexinger, F. *Henochs Zehnwochenapokalypse und offene Probleme der Apokalyptikforschung* (SPB 29) Leiden: Brill, 1977.

725b   Dimant, D. "1 Enoch 6-11: A Methodological Perspective," *SBL 1978 Seminar Papers.* Vol. 1, pp. 323-39.

725c   Doeve, J. W.   "Lamech's achterdocht in 1Q Genesis
        Apocryphon," *Nederlands Theologisch Tijdschrift*
        15 (1961) 401-15.

725d   Doeve, J. W.   "De tien-weken-Apokalyps (I Henoch
        93:1-10; 91:12-17):   een Qumrandocument,"
        Vruchten van de Uithof [H. A. Brongers Fest-
        schrift] Utrecht: Theologisch Instituut, 1974.
        Pp. 7-27.

728a   Fitzmyer, J. A.   "Implications of the New Enoch
        Literature from Qumran," *TS* 38 (1977) 332-45.

730a   Glasson, T. F.   "The Son of Man Imagery: Enoch 14
        and Daniel 7," *NTS* 23 (1976) 82-90.

742a   Greenfield, J. C. and M. E. Stone, "The Enochic
        Pentateuch and the Date of the Similitudes,"
        HTR 70 (1977) 51-65.

742b   Grelot, P.   "Hénoch et ses écritures," *RB* 82 (1975)
        481-500.

744a   Hammershaimb, E.   "On Parables and Figurative Say-
        ings in the Old Testament Pseudepigrapha," *SEA*
        40 (1975) 36-65.   [in Danish]

744b   Hanson, P. D.   "Rebellion in Heaven, Azazel, and
        Euhemeristic Heroes in 1 Enoch 6-11," *JBL* 96
        (1977) 195-233.

744c   Hanson, P. D.   "A Response to John Collins'
        'Methodological Issues in the Study of 1 Enoch,"
        SBL 1978 Seminar Papers.   Vol. 1, pp. 307-9.

744d   Hartman, L.   "'Comfort of the Scriptures'--An Early
        Jewish Interpretation of Noah's Salvation, 1 En.
        10:16-11:2," *SEA* 41f. (1976-77) 87-96.

744e   Himmelfarb, M.   "A Report on Enoch in Rabbinic
        Literature," *SBL 1978 Seminar Papers*.   Vol. 1,
        pp. 259-69.

746a   Jas, M.   *Henoch et le fils de l'homme: Datation du
        livre des paraboles, pour une situation de
        l'origine du gnosticisme*.   These Présenteé à la
        Faculté Libre de Théologie Réformée d'Aix-en-
        Provence, 1979.   [J. argues that 1En 37-71 is an
        anti-Christian Jewish polemic.]

748a   Klijn, A. F. J.   "From Creation to Noah in the
        Second Dream-Vision of the Ethiopic Henoch,"
        Miscellanea Neotestamentica (NovTSup 47) Leiden:
        Brill, 1978.   Pp. 147-59.

749a   Knibb, M. A.   "The Date of the Parables of Enoch:
        A Critical Review," *NTS* 25 (1979) 345-59.

749b   Knibb, M. A. (with E. Ullendorff). *The Ethiopic
        Book of Enoch: A New Edition in the Light of
        the Aramaic Dead Sea Fragments*, 2 vols. Oxford:
        Clarendon, 1978.

749c   Kraft, R. A. "Philo (Josephus, Sirach and Wisdom
        of Solomon) on Enoch," *SBL 1978 Seminar Papers*.
        Vol. 1, pp. 253-57.

751a   Lindars, B. "A Bull, a Lamb and a Word: 1 Enoch
        XC. 38," *NTS* 22 (1976) 483-86.

751b   Luck, U. "Das Weltverständnis in der jüdischen
        Apokalyptik dargestellt am äthiopischen Henoch
        und am 4 Esdra," *ZTK* 73 (1976) 283-305.

752a   Marcheselli, C. C. "Come risorgeranno i morti?
        Osservazioni su alcuni letterari di 1 Henoch,"
        Asprenas 23 (1976) 182-208.

752b   Mearns, C. L. "Dating the Similitudes of Enoch,"
        NTS 25 (1979) 360-69.

752c   Mearns, C. L. "The Parables of Enoch," *ExpT* 89
        (1978) 118f.

752d   Milik, J. T. and M. Black, eds. *The Books of Enoch:
        Aramaic Fragments of Qumrân Cave 4.* Oxford:
        Clarendon, 1976.

752e   Milik, J. T. "Écrits préesséniens de Qumrân:
        D'Hénoch à Amram," *BETL* 46 (1978) 91-106.

752f   Milik, J. T. "Fragments grecs du livre d'Hénoch
        (P. Oxy VII 2069)," *Chronique d'Egypte* 46 (1971)
        321-43.

758a   Neugebauer, O. "Notes on Ethiopic Astronomy,"
        Or N.S. 33 (1964) 49-71.

758b   Nibley, H. "A Strange Thing in the Land: The
        Return of the Book of Enoch," *Ensign* (December
        1975) 72-76; (February 1976) 64-68; (March 1976)
        62-66; (April 1976) 60-64; (July 1976) 64-68;
        (October 1976) 76-81; (December 1976) 73-78.

758c   Nickelsburg, G. W. E. Jr. "Apocalyptic and Myth in
        1 Enoch 6-11," *JBL* 96 (1977) 383-405.

758d   Nickelsburg, G. W. E. Jr. "The Apocalyptic Message
        of 1 Enoch 92-105," *CBQ* 39 (1977) 309-28.

758e   Nickelsburg, G. W. E. Jr. "Enoch, Book of," *IDBS*
        (1976) 265-68.

758f   Nickelsburg, G. W. E. Jr. "Enoch 97-104: A Study of the Greek and Ethiopic Texts," *Armenian and Biblical Studies*, ed. M. E. Stone (*Sion*, Suppl. 1) Jerusalem: St. James, 1976. Pp. 90-156.

758g   Nickelsburg, G. W. E. Jr. "Reflections upon Reflections: A Response to John Collins' 'Methodological Issues in the Study of 1 Enoch,'" *SBL 1978 Seminar Papers*. Vol. 1, pp. 311-14.

758h   Nickelsburg, G. W. E. Jr. "Riches, the Rich, and God's Judgment in I Enoch 92-105 and the Gospel According to Luke," *NTS* 25 (1979) 324-44.

760a   Nola, A. M. di. "Enoch, Libri apocrifi di," *EncRel* 9 (1970) 1156-60.

760b   Osburn, C. D. "The Christological Use of 1 Enoch i.9 in Jude 14, 15," *NTS* 23 (1977) 334-41.

760c   Pearson, B. A. "The Pierpoint Morgan Fragments of a Coptic Enoch Apocryphon," SCS 6. Pp. 227-83.

762a   Philonenko, M. "La plainte des âmes dans la *Korê Kosmou*," *Proceedings of the International Colloquium on Gnosticism* (Kungl. Vitterhets Historie och Antikvitets Akademiens Handlingar, Filol.-filos. ser. 17) Stockholm: Vitterhets, 1977. Pp. 153-56.

764a   Rau, E. *Kosmologie, Eschatologie und die Lehrautorität Henoch's: Traditions- und formgeschichtliche Untersuchungen zum äth. Henochbuch und zu verwandten Schriften.* Hamburg Univ. Ph.D., 1974.

769a   Sneen, D. "The First Book of Enoch," *Visions of Hope: Apocalyptic Themes from Biblical Times.* Minneapolis, Minn.: Augsburg, 1978. Pp. 55-70.

769ab   Stone, M. E. "The Book of Enoch and Judaism in the Third Century B.C.E.," *CBQ* 40 (1978) 479-92.

769abc   Suter, D. W. "Apocalyptic Patterns in the Similitudes of Enoch," *SBL 1978 Seminar Papers*. Vol. 1, pp. 1-13.

769abcd   Suter, D. W. "Fallen Angel, Fallen Priest: The Problem of Family Purity in 1 Enoch 6-16," *HUCA* 50 (1979) in press.

769abcde   Suter, D. W. *Tradition and Composition in the Parables of Enoch* (SBLDS 47) Missoula, Mont.: Scholars Press, 1979.

775a   Widengren, G.   "Iran and Israel in Parthian Times
       with Special Regard to the Ethiopic *Book of
       Enoch*," *Religious Syncretism in Antiquity: Essays
       in Conversation with Geo Widengren*, ed. B. A.
       Pearson. Missoula, Mont.: Scholars Press, 1975.
       Pp. 85-129. [= no. 775 republished]

2 (Slavonic) Enoch

See also no. 341a.

800a   Rubinstein, A.   "Observations on the Slavonic Book
       of Enoch," *JJS* 13 (1962) 1-21.

801a   Turdeanu, É.   "Dieu créa l'homme de huit éléments
       ⊙ et tira son nom des quatre coins du monde,"
       Revue des Études Roumaines 13-14 (1974) 163-94.

801b   Turdeanu, É.   "Une Curiosité de l'Hénoch slave:
       Les phénix du sixième ciel," *RESl* 67 (1968) 53f.

801c   Vaillant, A., ed.   *Le Livre des secrets d'Hénoch.
       Texte slave et traduction française* (Textes
       publiés par l'institut d'études slaves 4) Paris:
       Institut d'études slaves, 1976. [a reprint]

3 (Hebrew) Enoch

802a   Alexander, P. S.   "The Historical Setting of the
       Hebrew Book of Enoch," *JJS* 28 (1977) 156-80.

806a   Hengel, M.   "Die jüdische Mystik: Metatron,"
       Der Sohn Gottes. Tübingen: Mohr, 1975. Pp.
       73-75.

Eupolemus

See also no. 248a.

816a   Fallon, F. T.   "Eupolemus," Doubleday edition.

Pseudo-Eupolemus

820a   Doran, R.   "'Pseudo-Eupolemus,'" Doubleday edition.

Apocryphon of Ezekiel

824a   Eckart, K. G.   "Das Apokryphon Ezechiel," *JSHRZ*
       5 (1974) 45-55.

824b   Guillaumont, A. "Une citation de l'apocryphe
         d'Ezéchiel dans l'exégèse au sujet de l'âme
         (Nag Hammadi II, 6)," *Essays on the Nag Hammadi
         Texts in Honour of Pahor Labib*, ed. M. Krause
         (NHS 6) Leiden: Brill, 1975. Pp. 25-39.

826a   Mueller, J. R. and S. E. Robinson. "Apocryphon of
         Ezekiel," Doubleday edition.

827a   Scopello, M. "Les Citations d'Homère dans le
         traité de *l'exégèse de l'âme*," *Gnosis and Gnos-
         ticism*, ed. M. Krause (NHS 8) Leiden: Brill,
         1977. Pp. 3-12.

827b   Scopello, M. "Les *Testimonia* dans le traité de
         L'exégèse de l'âme," *Nag Hammadi* II, 6)," *RHR*
         191 (1977) 159-71.

828a   Stroker, W. D. "The Source of an Agraphon in the
         Manichaean Psalm-Book," *JTS* 28 (1977) 114-18.
         [Jesus' saying, "I am near to you, like the
         clothing of your body," seems to come from an
         apocryphal book of Ezekiel.]

Ezekiel the Tragedian

See also no. 444b.

829a   Holladay, C. R. "The Portrait of Moses in Ezekiel
         the Tragedian," *SBL 1976 Seminar Papers*. Pp.
         447-52.

829b   Kraus, C. "Ezechiele Poeta tragico," *Rivista di
         Filologia* 96 (1968) 164-75.

830a   Robertson, J. "Ezekiel the Tragedian," Doubleday
         edition.

830b   Snell, B. "Die Jamben in Ezechiels Moses-Drama,"
         Glotta 44 (1966) 25-32.

833a   Zwierlein, O. *Die Rezitationsdramen Senecas* (Beiträge
         zur klassischen Philologie 20) Meisenheim am
         Glon: Hain, 1966. [See esp. pp. 138-46:
         "Ezechiels Exagoge."]

4 Ezra [and Ezra Cycle]

See also nos. 44b, 194b-c, 250a, 251a, 266c, 347b, 376a,
446a, 751b, 1052b, 1192b.

834a   Alonso Díaz, J. "En lucha con el misterio: El
         alma judía ante los premios y castigos y la vida
         ultraterrena," *Palabra Inspirada* 2 (1967) 107-14.

836a   Daniélou, J. "V Esdras," *The Origins of Latin
       Christianity*, trans. D. Smith and J. A. Baker
       (A History of Early Christian Doctrine Before
       the Council of Nicea) London: Darton, Longman &
       Todd; Philadelphia: Westminster, 1977. Vol. 3,
       pp. 17-31.

837a   Dautzenberg, G. "Das Bild der Prophetie im 4 Esra
       und im SyrBar," *Urchristliche Prophetie: Ihre
       Erforschung, ihre Voraussetzungen im Judentum
       und ihre Struktur im ersten Korintherbrief* (BWANT
       Folge 6, Heft 4) Stuttgart: Kohlhammer, 1975.
       Pp. 90-98.

838a   Dinzelbacher, P. "Die Vision Alberichs und die
       Esdras-Apokryphe," *Studien und Mitteilungen zur
       Geschichte des Benediktiner-Ordens und seiner
       Zweige* Ottobeuren: Winfried-Werk, 1976. Pp.
       435-42.

841a   Ferch, A. J. "The Two Aeons and the Messiah in
       Pseudo-Philo, 4 Ezra, and 2 Baruch," *Andrews
       University Seminary Studies* 15 (1977) 135-51.

841b   Frankowski, J. "The Third Book of Esdras," *RuBi*
       26 (1973) 4-7. [in Polish]

841c   Gero, S. "'My Son the Messiah': A Note on 4Esra
       7:28-29," *ZNW* 66 (1975) 264-67.

852a   Hammershaimb, E. "On Parables and Figurative
       Sayings in the Old Testament Pseudepigrapha,"
       SEA 40 (1975) 36-65. [in Danish]

853a   Koch, K. "Esras erste Vision: Weltzeiten und Weg
       des Höchsten," *BZ* N.F. 22 (1978) 46-75.

855a   K'urc'ikidze, C'., ed. *Georgian Version of Old
       Testament Apocrypha*, 2 vols. Tiblisi:
       Metsnierebay, 1970-1973. [in Russian]

855b   Luck, U. "Das Weltverständnis in der jüdischen
       Apokalyptik dargestellt am äthiopischen Henoch
       und am 4.Esra," *ZTK* 73 (1976) 283-305.

856a   May, H. G. and B. M. Metzger, eds. "The Second
       Book of Esdras," *NOAB: Expand. Ed.* Pp. 23-
       62.

857a   Metzger, B. M. "The Fourth Book of Ezra (The Ezra
       Apocalypse with Christian Supplements)," Double-
       day edition.

860a   Müller, U. B. "Die griechische Esra-Apokalypse,"
       JSHRZ 5 (1976) 85-102.

860b   Muñoz León, D.   "El 4º de Esdras y el Targum
        Palestinense (Las dos primeras visiones:
        3, 1-6, 34)," *Estudios Bíblicos* 33 (1974)
        323-55.

860c   Muñoz León, D.   "El 4º de Esdras y el Targum
        Palestinense (La tercera visión: 6, 38-9, 25),"
        Estudios Bíblicos 34 (1975) 49-82.

863a   Nola, A. M. di.   "Esdra, Apocrifi di," *EncRel*
        2 (1970) 1198-1202.

866a   Rubinkiewicz, R.   "Un Fragment Grec de IVe Livre
        d'Esdras (Chapitres XI et XII)," *Le Muséon* 89
        (1976) 75-87.

866b   Schneemelcher, W.   "Esra," *RAC* 6 (1966) 595-612.

868a   Schwartz, J.   "Sur la date de *IV Esdras*," *Mélanges
        André Neher*, [ed.?] Paris: Adrien-Maisonneuve,
        1975. Pp. 191-96.

870a   Stanton, G. N.   "5 Ezra and Matthean Christianity
        in the Second Century," *JTS* 28 (1977) 67-83.

870b   Steck, O. H.   "Die Aufnahme von Genesis 1 in
        Jubiläen 2 und 4 Esra 6," *JSJ* 8 (1977) 154-82.

871a   Stone, M. E.   *The Armenian Version of IV Ezra*
        (University of Pennsylvania Armenian Texts and
        Studies 1) Missoula, Mont.: Scholars Press,
        1979.

876a   Stone, M. E.   "A New Manuscript of the Syro-Arabic
        Version of the Fourth Book of Ezra," *JSJ* 8 (1977)
        183f.

879a   Stone, M. E.   "Two Discoveries Relating to the
        Apocryphal Books of Ezra," *Sion* (in press and in
        modern Armenian).

880a   Thompson, A. L.   *Responsibility for Evil in the
        Theodicy of IV Ezra: A Study Illustrating the
        Significance of Form and Structure for the Mean-
        ing of the Book* (SBLDS 29) Missoula, Mont.:
        Scholars Press, 1977.

880b   Turdeanu, É.   "Dieu créa l'homme de huit éléments
        et tira son nom des quatre coins du monde,"
        Revue des Études Roumaines 13.4 (1974) 163-94.

881a   Zimmermann, F.   "Underlying Documents of IV Ezra,"
        JQR 51 (1960/61) 107-34.

Apocalypse of Ezra

888a   Wahl, O. *Apocalypsis Esdrae, Apocalypsis Sedrach, Visio Beati Esdrae* (PVTG 4) Leiden: Brill, 1977.

Questions of Ezra

889a   Stone, M. E. "The Questions of Ezra," *The Armenian Version of IV Ezra* (University of Pennsylvania Armenian Texts and Studies 1) Missoula, Mont.: Scholars Press, 1979. P. 40.

Revelation of Ezra

890a   Fiensy, D. A. "Revelation of Ezra," Doubleday edition.

Vision of Ezra

See also no. 838a.

890b   Berger, K. "Zur Frage des Traditionsgeschicht-lichen Wertes Apokrypher Gleichnisse," *NovT* 17 (1975) 58-76.

890c   Brock, S. P. "Notes on Some Texts in the Mingana Collection," *JSS* 14 (1969) 205-25. See esp. pp. 210f. [The "Vision of Ezra" is actually the Syriac Apocalypse of Ezra.]

891a   Mueller, J. R. "Vision of Ezra," Doubleday edition.

892a   Wahl, O. *Apocalypsis Esdrae, Apocalypsis Sedrach, Visio Beati Esdrae* (PVTG 4) Leiden: Brill, 1977.

892b   Wahl, O. "Vier neue Textzeugen der 'Visio beati Esdrae,'" *Salesianum* 40 (1978) 583-89.

Hecataeus of Abdera

894a   Stern, M. and O. Murray, "Hecataeus of Abdera and Theophrastus on Jews and Egyptians," *Journal of Egyptian Archaeology* 59 (1973) 159-68.

Pseudo-Hecataeus

897aa   Doran, R. "'Pseudo-Hecataeus,'" Doubleday edition.

Hellenistic Synagogal Prayers

Books seven and eight of the *Apostolic Constitutions* apparently contain remnants of Jewish synagogal prayers. The Greek text was edited by F. X. Funk (*Didascalia et Constitutiones Apostolorum* Paderborn: Libraria Ferdinandi Schoeningh, 1905 [repr. 1960]). English translations are available by W. Whiston (with revisions) in *The Ante-Nicene Fathers* (ed. J. Donaldson. [orig. Edinburgh, 1868] repr. Grand Rapids, Michigan, 1970; vol. 7, pp. 385-508), and by E. R. Goodenough in his *By Light, Light* (New Haven, Conn.; London: Yale University Press, 1935; pp. 306-508).

In 1893 K. Kohler discovered these Jewish prayers in the *Apostolic Constitutions* ("Ueber die Ursprünge und Grundformen der synagogalen Liturgie: Eine Studie," *Monatsschrift für Geschichte und Wissenschaft des Judenthums* N.F. 1 [1893] 441-51, 489-97; also see his "*Didascalia*," *Jewish Encyclopedia*, vol. 4, pp. 588-95; and his "The Essene Version of the Seven Benedictions as Preserved in the VII Book of the Apostolic Constitutions," *HUCA* 1 [1924] 410-25). In 1915-1916 W. Bousset who did not know of Kohler's work, argued that there are Jewish prayers preserved in the *Apostolic Constitutions* ("Eine jüdische Gebetssammlung im siebenten Buch der apostolischen Konstitutionen," *Nachrichten von der Königlichen Gesellschaft der Wissenschaften zu Göttingen*; Philologische-historische Klasse 1915 [Berlin: Weidmann, 1916; pp. 438-85). Bousset influenced E. R. Goodenough (*By Light, Light*, pp. 306-508).

The date of these Jewish prayers must be between 150 B.C. --because both Mattathias and Judas are mentioned (6:12, 7:13)--and A.D. 150, so that they could be incorporated into Christian liturgy. It seems impossible to discern their provenance. Greek seems to be the original language; the Greek flows smoothly and does not indicate a Semitic substratum; and the Old Testament quotations are from the Septuagint.

At least 16 prayers are extant. They praise God's acts in creation and history, and often extol his attributes in the terms of hellenistic philosophy.

899b   Charlesworth, J. H. "Christian and Jewish Self-Definition in Light of the Christian Additions to the Apocryphal Writings," *Judaism from the Maccabees to the Mid-Third Century*, ed. E. P. Sanders and A. I. Baumgarten. Philadelphia: Fortress, in press.

899c   Charlesworth, J. H. "Jewish Liturgies, Hymns and Prayers (c. 167 B.C.E.-135 C.E.)," *Early Post-Biblical Judaism and its Modern Interpreters*, ed. R. A. Kraft and G. W. E. Nickelsburg. Missoula, Mont.: Scholars Press, in press.

899d   Fiensy, D. A. and D. R. Darnell, "Hellenistic Synagogal Prayers," Doubleday edition.

Testament of Hezekiah

See Ascension of Isaiah.

Fragments of Historical Works

See also nos. 27e, 334b, 604b, 612a, 685b, 689b, 816a, 820a, 897aa.

901a   Stern, M. "The Jews in Greek and Latin Literature," *The Jewish People in the First Century: Historical Geography, Political History, Social, Cultural and Religious Life and Institutions*, ed. S. Safrai, *et al.* (Compendia Rerum Iudaicarum ad Novum Testamentum 1.2) Amsterdam: Van Gorcum, 1976. Vol. 2, pp. 1101-59.

901ab   Stern, M., ed. *Greek and Latin Authors on Jews and Judaism*. Vol. I: *From Herodotus to Plutarch*. Jerusalem: Israel Academy of Sciences and Humanities, 1974.

901abc   Strugnell, J. "Fragments of Lost Judeo-Hellenistic Works--General Introduction, with a Note on Alexander Polyhistor," Doubleday edition.

Testament of Isaac

See the Testaments of the Three Patriarchs.

Ascension of Isaiah [and Isaiah Cycle]

913a   Burgmann, H. "Gerichtsherr und Generalankläger: Jonathan und Simon," *RQ* 9 (1977) 3-72.

942a   Turdeanu, É. "La Vision d'Isaïe: Tradition
        orthodoxe et tradition hérétique," [The Com-
        memorative Volume for *the 1100 Anniversary for
        Cyril and Methodius*, ed. ?] Thessalonike, 1968.
        Vol. 2, pp. 291-318. [Book's title is in mod.
        Greek, from an offprint received from T.]

Martyrdom of Isaiah

See preceding entries.

Ladder of Jacob

943a   Lunt, H. "Ladder of Jacob," Doubleday edition.

Prayer of Jacob

Preserved in the Deutsche Staatsbibliothek in Berlin
(DDR) is a papyrus fragment (P. gr. 13895) from the fourth
century A.D.; it contains 26 lines of a "Prayer of Jacob."
The Greek text was published by K. Preisendanz (*Papyri Graecae
Magicae: Die griechischen Zauberpapyri*, 2 vols. Leipzig,
Berlin: Teubner, 1928-1931. Vol. 2, pp. 148f; but cf.
1006a). An English translation will be published by Charles-
worth (no. 945a).

The prayer is obviously Jewish, is similar to the magical papyri, and was intended to be used liturgically. It
must date from at least the fourth century; and since it was
found in Cairo it is possible that the provenance is Egyptian.

The prayer invokes the "Father of the Patriarchs," whose
cosmic powers, and graciousness to Abraham are extolled, and
who is said to sit both upon "the holy mountain Sinai," and
the "sun Iaō." The author does not ask for forgiveness, as
in the Prayer of Manasseh, but for his prayer to be heard,
and for wisdom.

945a   Charlesworth, J. H. "Prayer of Jacob," Doubleday
        edition.

Testament of Jacob

See also the Testaments of the Three Patriarchs.

948a   Nordheim, E. von. "Das Zitat des Paulus in 1 Kor
        2:9 und Seine Beziehung zum koptischen Testa-
        ment Jacobs," *ZNW* 65 (1974) 112-20.

948b   Sparks, H. F. D.   "1 Kor 2:9 a Quotation from the Coptic Testament of Jacob?" *ZNW* 67 (1976) 269-76.   [S. says "no" to E. von Nordheim's argument (no. 948a) that 1 Cor 2:9 quotes the TJac.]

Jannes and Jambres

959a   Maraval, P.   "Fragments grecs du livre de Jannes et Jambré (Pap. Vindob. 29456 et 29828 verso)," *Zeitschrift für Papyrologie und Epigraphik* 25 (1977) 199-207.

962a   Pietersma, A.   and R. T. Lutz, "Jannes and Jambres," Doubleday edition.

Testament of Job

972a   Glatzer, N. N.   "Jüdische TJob-Deutungen in den ersten christlichen Jahrhunderten," *Freiburger Rundbrief* 26 (1974) 31-34.

980a   Preuss, H. D.   "Jahwes Antwort an Hiob und die sogennante Hiob-literatur des alten Vorderen Orients." *Beiträge zur alttestamentlichen Theologie*, ed. H. Donner, R. Hanhart, and R. Smend.   [Festschrift Walther Zimmerli] Göttingen: Vandenhoeck & Ruprecht, in press.

Joseph and Asenath [and Joseph Cycle]

See also no. 128c.

986a   Berger, K.   "Jüdisch-hellenistische Missions-literatur und apokryphe Apostelakten," *Kairos* 17 (1975) 232-48.   [B. follows and discusses Burchard's assessment that JosAsen is an example of "jüdisch-hellenistischer Missions-literatur."]

986b   Brock, S. P.   "Notes on Some Texts in the Mingana Collection," *JSS* 14 (1969) 205-25.   See esp. pp. 206f.

987a   Burchard, C.   "Joseph und Aseneth Neugriechisch," *NTS* 24 (1977) 68-84.

989a   Burchard, C.   *Untersuchungen zu Joseph und Aseneth: Überlieferung-Ortsbestimmung* (WUNT 8) Tübingen: Mohr, 1965.

992a   Delcor, M.   "Un roman d'amour d'origine théra-peute: Le Livre de Joseph et Asénath," *Bulletin de Littérature Ecclésiastique* 63 (1962) 3-27.

292

992b   Delling, G. "Einwirkungen der Sprache der
        Septuaginta in 'Joseph und Aseneth,'" *JSJ*
        9 (1978) 29-56.

994b   Gispert-Sauch, G. "Brhadāraṇyaka Upaniṣad 1.3.28
        in Greek Literature?" *Vidyajyoti* 40 (1976) 177-
        80.

997a   Kee, H. C. "The Socio-Religious Setting and Aims
        of 'Joseph and Asenath,'" *SBL 1976 Seminar
        Papers*. Pp. 183-92.

1001a   Pervo, R. I. "Joseph and Asenath and the Greek
        Novel," *SBL 1976 Seminar Papers*. Pp. 171-81.

1001b   Philonenko, M. "Initiation et mystère dans
        Joseph et Aséneth: Initiation," *Contributions
        to the Theme of the Study-Conference of the
        International Association for the History of
        Religions, Held at Strasburg, September 17th
        to 22nd 1964* (Sup *Numen* 10) Leiden: Brill,
        1965. Pp. 147-53.

1005a   Philonenko, M. "Un mystère juif?" EHR 2 (1975)
        65-70.

1006a̲   Preisendanz, K. *Papyri Graecae Magicae: Die
        griechischen Zauberpapyri*, new ed. by A. Hen-
        richs, 2 vols. Stuttgart: Teubner, 1973,
        1974. [For the "Prayer of Jacob," use the new
        edition; cf. p. 139 above.]

1006b   Smith, E. W. Jr. *Joseph and Asenath and Early
        Christian Literature: A Contribution to the
        Corpus Hellenisticum Novi Testamenti*. Clare-
        mont Graduate School Ph.D., 1974.

1006c   Stehly, R. "Une Citation des Uphanishads dans
        Joseph et Aséneth," *RHPR* 55 (1975) 209-13.

1006d   Suski, A. "Joseph and Asenath. Introduction,
        Translation from the Greek, Commentary," *Studia
        Theologica Varsaviensia* 16 (1978) 199-240.
        [S. bases his translation on Philonenko's
        edition of the Greek text. in Polish]

1006e   Szepcssy, T. "The Joseph and Aseneth Story and
        the Ancient Novel," *Antik Tanulmányok* 20 (1973)
        158-68. [in Polish]

1006f   Tachau, P. *'Einst' und 'Jetzt' im Neuen Testa-
        ment*. Göttingen University Ph.D., 1969.

1006g   Vikan, G. "Illustrated Manuscripts of the Romance
        of Joseph and Asenath," *SBL 1976 Seminar Papers*.
        Pp. 193-208.

History of Joseph

Extant partially in papyri in the Louvre Museum (Gk. papyrus no. 7738a), the Bodleian Library (Gr. th.f. 15 [P] and Gr. th.e. 9 [P]), and the British Museum is a text that seems to be a "History of Joseph." The sixth or seventh century papyrus leaves in the British Museum were published by H. J. M. Milne (*Catalogue of the Literary Papyri in the British Museum*. London: Trustees, 1927; pp. 187-90). Recently more papyrus fragments have been identified (see Zervos, no. 1007a). The first English translation will be published by G. Zervos (no. 1007a). The original language seems to be Greek; the provenance may be Egyptian, because the papyrus was found in the Fayum.

The document is a midrashic expansion of Genesis 41:39-42:38, which relates the account of Joseph in Egypt, the famine, and the visit of his brothers. As in Joseph and Asenath (25:6, 29:11), Joseph is elevated and called king.

1007a   Zervos, G.   "History of Joseph," Doubleday edition.

Prayer of Joseph

1008a   Hengel, M.   "Das Gebet Josephs," *Der Sohn Gottes*. Tübingen: Mohr, 1975. Pp. 76f.

1012a   Smith, J. Z.   "The Prayer of Joseph," *Map is not Territory* (SJLA 23) Leiden: Brill, 1978. Pp. 24-66. [A reprint of Smith's major study (n. 1012) plus a significant "Afterword," p. 66]

Testament of Joseph

See the Testaments of the Twelve Patriarchs.

Jubilees

See also nos. 44b, 742b, 870b.

1014a   Baars, W. and R. Zuurmond.   "The Project for a New Edition of the Ethiopic Book of Jubilees," *JSS* 9 (1964) 67-74.

294

1019a   Brock, S. P.   "Abraham and the Ravens: A Syriac
         Counterpart to Jubilees 11-12 and its Implica-
         tions," *JSJ* 9 (1978) 135-52.

1019b   Caglio, E. T. M.   "Lo jubilus e le origini della
         salmodia responsoriale," *Bibbia e Oriente* 19
         (1977) 205-14.

1022a   Cortès, E.   *Los discursos de adiós de Gn 49 a
         Jn 13-17: Pistas para la historia de un género
         literario en la antigua literatura judía*
         (Colectánea San Paciano 23) Barcelona: Herder,
         1976.

1023a   Cothenet, É.   "Pureté et impureté . . . Le *Livre
         des Jubilés*," *DBSup* 49 (1973) 509-11.

1028a   Derrett, J. D. M.   "A Problem in the Book of
         Jubilees and an Indian Doctrine," *ZRGG* 14 (1962)
         247-62.

1036a   Hilgert, E.   "The Jubilees Calendar and the Origin
         of Sunday Observance," *Andrews Univ. Seminary
         St.* 1 (1963) 44-51.

1041a   Lipscomb, W. L., "A Tradition from the Book of
         Jubilees in Armenian," *JJS* 29 (1978) 149-63.

1046a   Noack, B.   "The Day of Pentecost in Jubilees,
         Qumran, and Acts," *ASTI* 1 (1962) 73-95.

1047a   Pummer, R.   "The Book of Jubilees and the Samari-
         tans," *Église et Théologie* 10 (1979) 147-78.

1052a   Schultz, J. P.   "Two Views of the Patriarchs:
         Noachides and Pre-Sinai Israelites. Verfolgt
         die beiden Bilder der Patriarchen in der frühen
         jüdischen Überlieferung," *Texts and Responses:
         Studies Presented to N. N. Glatzer*, ed. M. A.
         Fishbane.   Leiden: Brill, 1975. Pp. 41-59.

1052ab   Sharvit, B.   "The Sabbath of the Judean Desert
         Sect," *Beth Mikra* 67 (1976) 507-16.   [in Hebrew]

1052b   Steck, O. H.   "Die Aufnahme von Genesis 1 in
         Jubiläen 2 und 4 Esra 6," *JSJ* 8 (1977) 154-82.

1055a   VanderKam, J. C.   "Enoch Traditions in Jubilees
         and Other Second-Century Sources," *SBL 1978
         Seminar Papers*.   Vol. 1, pp. 229-51.

1055b   VanderKam, J. C.   "The Textual Affinities of the
         Biblical Citations in the Genesis Apocryphon,"
         JBL 97 (1978) 45-55.

1055c   VanderKam, J. C. *Textual and Historical Studies
         in the Book of Jubilees* (Harvard Semitic
         Monographs 14) Missoula, Mont.: Scholars Press,
         1977.

1056a   Weinfeld, M. "Pentecost as a Festival of the Giving of the Law," *Immanuel* 8 (1978) 7-18.

Liber Antiquitatum Biblicarum

See Pseudo-Philo.

See also nos. 446a, 1055b.

The Lost Tribes

1062a   Godbey, A. H. *The Lost Tribes: A Myth, Suggestions, Towards Rewriting Hebrew History*. Duke University Press, 1930; repr. with prolegomenon by M. Epstein [and H. M. Orlinsky]. New York: KTAV, 1974.

3 Maccabees

1072a   Freidhof, G. *Zur ersten Übersetzung des 3. Buches der Makkabäer im Ostslavischen: Slavistische Studien zum VII Int. Slavistenkongress in Warschau 1973*. Munich: Trofenik, 1925. Pp. 75-80.

1075a   Hanhart, R. *Zum Text des 2. und 3. Makkabäerbuches* (Mitteilungen des Septuaginta-Unternehmens der Akademie der Wissenschaften in Göttingen 7) Göttingen: Vandenhoeck & Ruprecht, 1961.

1078a   May, H. G. and B. M. Metzger, eds., "The Third Book of the Maccabees," *NOAB: Expand. Ed.* Pp. 294-308.

1082a   Nola, A. M. di. "Maccabei, III e IV Libri dei," *EncRel* 3 (1971) 1776-79.

1084a   Rüger, H.-P. "Apokryphen des Alten Testaments," *TRE*. Vol. 1, pp. 289-316.

4 Maccabees

See also no. 351b.

1089a   Breitenstein, U. *Beobachtungen zu Sprache, Stil und Gedankengut des Vierten Makkabäerbuches*. Basel, Stuttgart: Schwabe, 1978.

1102a   May, H. G. and B. M. Metzger, eds., "The Fourth Book of the Maccabees," *NOAB: Expand. Ed.* Pp. 309-29.

1103a   Nola, A. M. di. "Maccabei, III e IV Libri dei," *EncRel* 3 (1971) 1776-79.

1110a   Verme, M. del, "L'apocrifo giudaico IV Maccabei
        e gli atti dei martiri cristiani del II
        secolo," *Rivista de scienze teologiche* N.S. 23
        (1976) 287-302.

5 Maccabees [and Maccabean Cycle]

1112a   Flusser, D. "Der lateinische Josephus und der
        hebräische Josippon," *Josephus-Studien* [O.
        Michel Festschrift], ed. O. Betz, K. Haacker,
        M. Hengel. Göttingen: Vandenhoeck & Ruprecht,
        1974. Pp. 122-32.

1112b   Rougé, J. "Le *de mortibus persecutorum*, 5e livre
        des Macchabées," *Studia Patristica 12*, 135-43.
        [Using 2 Maccabees Lactantius wrote an account
        of the suffering of Christians which is a
        veritable 5th Bk. of the Maccabees--not what
        has been called 5 Mac.]

Prayer of Manasses

1121a   May, H. G. and B. M. Metzger, eds., "The Prayer
        of Manasseh," *NOAB: Expand. Ed.* Pp. 219f.

1125a   _____ "La prière de Manassé," *Les Livres
        Apocryphes de l'Ancien Testament.* Metz:
        l'Eglise Neo-Apostolique de France, 1972.
        P. 232.

1125b   Rüger, H. P. "Apokryphen des Alten Testaments,"
        TRE. Vol. 1, pp. 289-316.

Pseudo-Menander

1135a   Treu, K. "Aspekte Menanders," *Kairos* N.F. 19
        (1977) 22-34, esp. p. 34.

Apocalypse of Moses

See also no. 341a.

1143a   Quinn, E. C. *The Quest of Seth for the Oil of
        Life.* Chicago: University of Chicago Press,
        1962. [Q. argues that the Seth story was taken
        from the ApMos 9:2-13:6.]

Assumption of Moses

See TMos.

Prayer of Moses

See Pseudo-Philo.

Testament of Moses

See also nos. 446, 351b, 515c.

1150a   Brandenburger, E.   "Himmelfahrt Moses," *JSHRZ* 5
        (1976) 59-84.

1150b   Collins, A. Yarbro, "Composition and Redaction
        of the Testament of Moses 10," *HTR* 69 (1976)
        179-86.

1150c   Collins, A. Yarbro, "The Political Perspective
        of the Revelation to John," *JBL* 96 (1977) 241-
        56.

1165a   Kretschmar, G.   "Auferstehung des Fleisches:
        Zur Frühgeschichte einer theologischen Lehr-
        formel," *Leben Angesichts des Todes: Beiträge
        zum theologischen. Problem des Todes. Helmut
        Thielicke zum 60. Geburtstag,* ed. B. Lohse and
        H. P. Schmidt. Tübingen: Mohr, 1968. Pp.
        101-37.

1166a   Licht, J.   "Taxo, or the Apocalyptic Doctrine of
        Vengeance," *JJS* 12 (1961) 95-103.

1166aa Loftus, F.   "The Martyrdom of the Galilean
        Troglodytes (B.J. i 312-3; A. xiv 429-30). A
        Suggested Traditionsgeschichte," *JQR* 66 (1976)
        212-23.

1171a   Priest, J.   "Some Reflections on the *Assumption
        of Moses,*" *Perspectives in Religious Studies*
        4 (1977) 92-111.

1176a   Santo, C. de.   "The Assumption of Moses and the
        Christian Gospel," *Int* 16 (1962) 305-10.

Book of Noah

See 1 Enoch and Jubilees.

Pseudo-Orpheus

1182a   Lafargue, M.   "A Jewish Pseudo-Orphic Hymn,"
        Doubleday edition.

Paraleipomena Jeremiou

See 4 Baruch.

Philo the Epic Poet

1183aa   Attridge, H. W.   "Philo the Epic Poet," Doubleday Edition.

Pseudo-Philo

See also nos. 446a, 1055b.

1186a   Bogaert, P. M.   "Les Antiquités Bibliques à la
lumière des découvertes de Qumrân: Observations sur l'hymnologie et particulièrement sur
le chapitre 60," *BETL* 46 (1978) 313-31.

1187b   Clark, D. G.   "Liber Antiquitatum Biblicarum,"
*Elijah as Eschatological High Priest: An
Examination of the Elijah Tradition in Mal.
3:23-24.*   University of Notre Dame Ph.D., 1975.
Pp. 168-81.   [C. includes a discussion of
Elijah in T12P and *LAB*.]

1192a   Dietzfelbinger, C.   *Pseudo-Philo: Liber Antiquitatum Biblicarum.*   Göttingen University Ph.D.,
1964.

1192b   Ferch, A. J.   "The Two Aeons and the Messiah in
Pseudo-Philo, 4 Ezra, and 2 Baruch," *Andrews
University Seminary Studies* 15 (1977) 135-51.

1197a   Harrington, D. J.   "Biblical Geography in Pseudo-
Philo's *Liber Antiquitatum Biblicarum*," *BASOR*
220 (1975) 67-71.   [reprinted in Wright Festschrift, pp. 67-71]

1204b   Hayward, R.   "Phinehas--the same is Elijah: The
Origins of a Rabbinic Tradition," *JJS* 29 (1978)
22-34.

1204c   Horst, P. W. van der.   "Seven Months' Children in
Jewish and Christian Tradition," *ETL* 54 (1978)
346-60.

1209a   Scheiber, A.   "Lacrimatoria and the Jewish
Sources," *IEJ* 25 (1975) 152f.

1210a   Wadsworth, M.   "A New Pseudo-Philo," *JJS* 29 (1978)
186-91.   [an extensive review of D. J. Harrington *et al.*'s *Pseudon-Philon*]

1213a   Zéron, A.   *The System of Pseudo-Philo.*   Tel Aviv
University Ph.D., 1969.

Pseudo-Phocylides

1213a   Castanien, D. G.   "Quevedo's Translation of the
Pseudo-Phocylides," *Philological Quarterly* 40
(1961) 44-52.

1214a   Farina, A. *Silloge Pseudofocilidea* (Collana di
         Studi Greci 37) Naples, 1962.

1215a   Horst, P. W. van der. "Pseudo-Phocylides and the
         New Testament," *ZNW* 69 (1978) 187-202.

1215b   Horst, P. W. van der. *The Sentences of Pseudo-
         Phocylides: With Introduction and Commentary*
         (SVTP 4) Leiden: Brill, 1978.

1216a   Keydell, R. "Phokylides," *Der Kleine Pauly* 4
         (1971) 806f.

Fragments of Poetical Works

See Aristobulus, Ezekiel the Tragedian, and Theodotus.

See also nos. 27e, 1182a, 1183aa.

1221a   Attridge, H. W. "Fragments of Pseudonymous Greek
         Poetry," Doubleday edition.

1221b   Strugnell, J. "Fragments of Lost Judeo-
         Hellenistic Works--General Introduction, With
         a Note on Alexander Polyhistor," Doubleday
         edition.

1221c   Walter, N. *Untersuchungen zu den Fragmenten der
         jüdisch-hellenistischen Historiker.* Theologi-
         cal Habilitationsschrift, Halle, 1967.

1221d   Walter, N. "Zur Überlieferung einiger Reste
         früher jüdisch-hellenistischer Literatur bei
         Josephus, Clemens und Euseb," *Studia Patristica*
         7 [TU 92] (1966) 314-20.

1221e   Zeegers-Vander Vorst, N. "Les versions juives et
         chrétiennes du fr. 245-7 d'Orphée," *L'Antiquité
         Classique* 39 (1970) 475-506.

Lives of the Prophets
(Deaths of the Prophets, Triumphs of the Prophets, Pseudo-Epiphanius)

1225a   Jonge, M. de. "Christelijke elementen in de Vitae
         prophetarum," *Nederlands Theologisch Tijdschrift*
         16 (1961/62) 161-78.

The History of the Blessed Ones, the Sons of Rechab

1229a   Brock, S. P. "Notes on Some Texts in the Mingana
         Collection," *JSS* 14 (1969) 205-25. See esp.
         pp. 215f.

300

1229b   Charlesworth, J. H.   "The History of the Blessed
         Ones, the Sons of Rechab," Doubleday edition.

1229c   McNeil, B.   "The Narration of Zosimus," *JSJ* 9
         (1978) 68-82.

1229d   Martin, E. G.   *The Account of the Blessed Ones:
         A Study of the Development of an Apocryphon on
         the Rechabites and Zosimus (The Abode of the
         Rechabites)*, Duke University Ph.D., 1979.

Apocalypse of Sedrach

1231b   Holler, W. M.   "The Ordinary Man's Concept of
         Nature as Reflected in the Thirteenth-Century
         French *Book of Sydrac*," *The French Review* 48
         (1975) 526-38.

1234b   Sharf, A.   "'The Vision of Daniel' as a Byzantine-
         Jewish Historical Source," *Bar-Ilan* 4-5 (1967)
         197-208; English summary on pp. LI-LII.   [in
         Hebrew]

1235b   Wahl, O.   *Apocalypsis Esdrae, Apocalypsis Sedrach,
         Visio Beati Esdrae* (PVTG 4) Leiden: Brill,
         1977.

Treatise of Shem

1236a   Charlesworth, J. H.   "Jewish Astrology in the
         Talmud, Pseudepigrapha, the Dead Sea Scrolls,
         and Early Palestinian Synagogues," *HTR* 70
         (1977) 183-200.

1236b   Charlesworth, J. H.   "Rylands Syriac Ms. 44 and
         a New Addition to the Pseudepigrapha: The
         Treatise of Shem, Discussed and Translated,"
         BJRULM 60 (1978) 376-403.

Sibylline Oracles

See also nos. 109c, 327a, 347a.

1246a   Ebied, R. Y. and M. J. L. Young, "An Unrecorded
         Arabic Version of a Sibylline Prophecy,"
         Orientalia Christiana Periodica 43 (1977) 279-
         307.

1247a   Flusser, D.   "An Early Jewish-Christian Document
         in the Tiburtine Sibyl," *Paganisme, Judaisme,
         Christianisme* [M. Simon Festschrift] Paris:
         Boccard, 1978.

1247b   Flusser, D.   "The Four Empires in the Fourth
         Sibyl and in the Book of Daniel," *Israel Ori-
         ental Studies* 2 (1972) 148-75.

1248a   Frankowski, J. "The Sibylline Oracles," *RuBi*
        26 (1973) 261-70. [in Polish]

1260a   Kocsis, E. "Ost-West Gegensatz in den jüdischen
        Sibyllinen," *NovT* 5 (1962) 105-10.

1263a   Momigliano, A. "La Portata Storica dei Vaticini
        sul Settimo Re nel Terzo Libro degli Oracoli
        Sibillini," *Forma Futuri: Studi in Onore di
        Cardinale Michele Pellegrini.* Turin: Bottega
        d'Erasmo, 1975. Pp. 1077-84.

1267a   Noack, B. "Der hervoragende Mann und der beste
        der Hebräer (Bemerkungen zu Or. Sib. V, 256-
        259)," *ASTI* 3 (1964) 122-46.

1269a   Nola, A. M. di. "Sibille; Sibillini; Libri;
        Sibillini, Oracoli," *EncRel* 5 (1973) 1042-44,
        1244f., 1245-50.

1269b   Nolland, J. "Sib Or III, 265-94: An Early Mac-
        cabean Messianic Oracle," *JTS* 30 (1979) 158-67.

1269c   Peretti, A. "Echi di dottrine esseniche degli
        Oracoli Sibillini giudaici," *La Parola del
        Passato* 85 (1962) 247-95.

1271a   Salanitro, G. "Osservazioni critiche al testo
        degli 'Oracoli sibillini,'" *BInstEstHel* 6
        (1972) 75-78.

                    Odes of Solomon

1276a   Baarda, Tj. "'Het Uitbreiden van mijn Handen is
        zijn Teken': Enkele notities bij de gebedshoud-
        ing in de Oden van Salomo," *Loven en Geloven.*
        [H. N. Ridderbos Festschrift.] Amsterdam:
        Bolland, 1975. Pp. 245-59.

1278a   Barrett, C. K. "The Odes of Solomon," *The Gospel
        According to St. John: An Introduction with
        Commentary and Notes on the Greek Text.* 2d ed.
        Philadelphia: Westminster, 1978. P. 65, cf.
        pp. 112f., 501.

1282a   Braun, H. "Entscheidende Motive in den Berichten
        über die Taufe Jesu von Markus bis Justin,"
        *Gesammelte Studien zum Neuen Testament und
        Seiner Umwelt,* 2d ed. Tübingen: Mohr, 1967.
        Pp. 168-72.

1282b   Bruns, J. E. *The Forbidden Gospel.* New York:
        Harper and Row, 1976. See esp. pp. 22-28,
        33-34, 48-50.

1289a   Charlesworth, J. H. "Haplography and Philology:
        A Study of Odes of Solomon 16:8," *NTS* 25 (1979)
        221-27.

1289b   Charlesworth, J. H. "Odes of Solomon," *IDBS*
(1976) 637f.

1293a   Charlesworth, J. H. *The Odes of Solomon: The
Syriac Texts* (T&T 13, Pseudepigrapha Series 7)
Missoula, Mont.: Scholars Press, 1977. [This
book is a corrected reprint of no. 1292.]

1297a   Dautzenberg, G. "Prophetie, Gemeindeleitung und
Logienüberlieferung," *Urchristliche Prophetie:
Ihre Erforschung, ihre Voraussetzungen im
Judentum und ihre Struktur im ersten Korinther-
brief* (BWANT Folge 6, Heft 4) Stuttgart: Kohl-
hammer, 1975. Pp. 24-28.

1298a   Drijvers, H. J. W. "Die Oden Salomos und die
Polemik mit den Markioniten im Syrischen
Christentum," *Symposium Syriacum 1976* (OCA 205)
Rome: Pontificium Institutum Orientalium
Studiorum, 1978. Pp. 39-55.

1300a   Ehlers, B. "Kann das Thomasevangelium aus Edessa
Stammen?" *NovT* 12 (1970) 284-317, esp. pp. 300f.

1301a   Emerton, J. A. "Notes on Some Passages in the
Odes of Solomon," *JTS* N.S. 28 (1977) 507-19.

1302a   Erbetta, M. "Odi di Salomone," *Apocrifi del N.T.*
Vol. 1, pp. 608-58.

1305a   Gero, S. "The Spirit as a Dove at the Baptism of
Jesus," *NovT* 18 (1976) 17-35.

1313a   Köbert, R. "Ode Salomons 20,6 und Sir 33,31,"
Biblica 58 (1977) 529f.

1316a   Langbrandtner, W. "Die Oden Salomos," *Weltferner
Gott oder Gott der Liebe* (Beiträge zur biblischen
Exegese und Theologie 6) Frankfurt, Las Vegas:
Lang, 1977. Pp. 156-68.

1317a   McNeil, B. "Le Christ en vérité est Un," *Irénikon*
2 (1978) 198-202.

1317b   McNeil, B. "The Odes of Solomon and the Sufferings
of Christ," *Symposium Syriacum 1976* (OCA 205)
Rome: Pontificium Institutum Orientalium Studiorum, 1978. Pp. 31-38.

1317c   McNeil, B. *The Provenance of the Odes of Solomon:
A Study in Jewish and Christian Symbolism.* University of Cambridge Ph.D., 1977. [M. claims
the OdesSol are contemporaneous with Hermas,
Polycarp, Valentinus, and the author of 4Ezra
1f.]

1318a   Ménard, J.-E. "Le repos, salut du gnostique,"
Revue des Sciences Religieuses 51 (1977) 71-88.

1325a   Pokorný, P. "Das Sogenannte Evangelium Veritatis
         und die Anfänge des Christlichen Dogmas," *Listy
         Filologické* 87 (1964) 51-59.

1336a   Tosato, A. "Il battesimo di Gesù e le Odi di
         Salomone," *Bibbia e Oriente* 18 (1976) 261-69.

1336b   Tosato, A. "Gesù e gli Zeloti alla luce delle
         Odi di Salomone," *Bibbia e Oriente* 19 (1977)
         145-53.

1336c   Tsakonas, V. "Die Oden Salomos," *Theol* 44 (1973)
         389-605; 45 (1974) 129-646.

1336d   Tsakonas, V. *The Odes of Solomon: Introduction,
         Translation and Commentary.* Athens, 1974. [in
         modern Greek]

1336e   Vielhauer, P. "Die Oden Salomos," *Geschichte der
         urchristlichen Literatur.* Berlin: Gruyter,
         1975. Pp. 750-56.

1336f   Vogl, A. "Oden Salomos 17, 22, 24, 42: Über-
         setzung und Kommentar (hrgb. B. McNeil)," *Oriens
         Christianus* 62 (1978) 60-76.

1337a   Vööbus, A. "Solomon, Odes of," *Encyclopaedia
         Britannica.* Chicago: Encyclopaedia Britannica,
         Inc., 1971. Vol. 20, p. 878.

                      Psalms of Solomon

1339a   Baars, W. "A New Fragment of the Greek Version of
         the Psalms of Solomon," *VT* 11 (1961) 441-44.

1342a   Delcor, M. *"Psaumes de Salomon,"* DBSup 48 (1973)
         214-45.

1350a   Hann, R. R. *A Prolegomenon to the Textual Criti-
         cism of the Psalms of Solomon.* Temple Univer-
         sity, Ph.D., 1977.

1353a   Jonge, M. de. *De toekomstverwachting in Psalmen
         van Salomo.* Leiden: Brill, 1965.

1353b   Nola, A. M. di. "Salomone, Salmidi," *EncRel* 5
         (1973) 765-67.

1353c   O'Dell, J. "The Religious Background of the
         Psalms of Solomon: Re-evaluated in the Light
         of the Qumran Texts," *RQ* 3 (1961) 241-57.

1354a   Pokorný, P. "Concerning the Eighteenth Psalm of
         Solomon," *Křest'anská Revue* 42 (1975) 151-57.
         [in Czek.]

1357a   Schüpphaus, J. *Die Psalmen Salomos: Ein Zeugnis Jerusalemer Theologie und Frömmigkeit in der Mitte des vorchristlichen Jahrhunderts* (ALGHJ 7) Leiden: Brill, 1977.

1357b   Trafton, J. L. *A Critical Examination of the Syriac Version of the Psalms of Solomon.* Duke University Ph.D., 1981.

Testament of Solomon

1362b   Duling, D. C. "Testament of Solomon," Doubleday edition.

Five Apocryphal Syriac Psalms

See also no. 128a

1369b   Auffret, P. "Structure littéraire et interprétation du Psaume 151 de la Grotte 11 de Qumrân," *RQ* 34 (1977) 163-88.

1369c   Auffret, P. "Structure littéraire et interprétation du Psaume 154 de la Grotte XI de Qumrân," *RQ* 36 (1978) 513-45.

1369d   Auffret, P. "Structure littéraire et interprétation du Psaume 155 de la Grotte XI de Qumrân," *RQ* 35 (1978) 323-56.

1370b   Baumgarten, J. M. "Perek Shirah, an Early Response to Psalm 151," *RQ* 36 (1978) 575-78.

1378ca   Magne, J. "Le psaume 154 et psaume 155," *RQ* 34 (1977) 95-111.

1378caa   Magne, J. "'Seigneur de l'univers' ou David-Orphée? Défense de mon interprétation du Psaume 151," *RQ* 34 (1977) 189-96.

1378daa   May, H. G. and B. M. Metzger, eds., "Psalm 151," *NOAB: Expand. Ed.* Pp. 330f.

1390a   Skehan, P. "Again the Syriac Apocryphal Psalms," *CBQ* 38 (1976) 143-58.

1391ca   Strelcyn, S. "Le psaume 151 dans la tradition éthiopienne," *JSS* 23 (1978) 316-29.

Thallus

No additional publications. See Fragments of Historical Works.

Theodotus

1399a   Bull, R. J. "A note on Theodotus' Description of Shechem," *HTR* 60 (1967) 221-28.

1399b   Fallon, F. T. "Theodotus," Doubleday edition.

Three Patriarchs, Testaments of the
[and Abraham Cycle]
see
Testaments of Abraham, Isaac and Jacob

See also nos. 425a, 430a.

1402a   Sanders, E. P. "Testament of Abraham," Doubleday edition.

1402b   Sanders, E. P. "Testaments of the Three Patriarchs," Doubleday edition.

1402c   Stinespring, W. F. "Testament of Isaac," Doubleday edition.

1402d   Stinespring, W. F. "Testament of Jacob," Doubleday edition.

Testaments of the Twelve Patriarchs

See also nos. 44b, 327a, 351b, 359a, 752e.

1408a   Braun, F. M. "Les Testaments des XII patriarches et le problème de leur origine," *RB* 67 (1960) 516-49.

1410a   Cantinat, J. *Les Épitres de Saint Jacques et de Saint Jude*. Paris: Lecoffre, 1973. See esp. pp. 20-24.

1411a   Charlesworth, J. H. "Reflections on the SNTS Pseudepigrapha Seminar at Duke on the *Testaments of the Twelve Patriarchs*," *NTS* 23 (1977) 296-304.

1412a   Clark, D. G. "The Testaments of the Twelve Patriarchs," *Elijah as Eschatological High Priest: An Examination of the Elijah Tradition in Mal. 3:23-24*. University of Notre Dame Ph.D., 1975. Pp. 92-105.

1412b   Cortès, E. *Los discursos de adiós de Gn 49 a Jn 13-17: Pistas para la historia de un género literario en la antigua literatura judía* (Colectánea San Paciano 23) Barcelona: Herder, 1976.

1412c   Cortès, E. "El 'Testamento de Benjamín' a la luz
         de la literatura targúmica: Comentario al
         libro de J. Becker sobre los 'Testamentos de los
         doce Patriarcas,'" *Estudios Franciscanos* 76
         (1975) 159-76.

1412d   Cothenet, É. "Pureté et impureté . . . Appendice.
         Les Testaments des XII Patriarches," *DBSup* 49
         (1973) 526f.

1417a   Gnilka, J. "Die Erwartung des messianischen
         Hohenpriesters in den Schriften von Qumran und
         im Neuen Testament," *RQ* 2 (1959/60) 395-426.

1417b   Gnilka, J. "Der Hymnus des Zacharias," *BZ* N.F.
         6 (1962) 215-38.

1417c   Gnilka, J. "2 Kor 6, 14-7, 1 im Lichte der
         Qumranschriften und der Zwölf-Patriarchen-
         Testamente," *Neutestamentliche Aufsätze. Fest-
         schrift für Prof. Josef Schmid zum 70. Geburts-
         tag*, ed. J. Blinzler, *et al.*, Regensburg:
         Pustet, 1963. Pp. 86-99.

1426a   Grelot, P. "Quatre cents trente ans (Ex 12, 40):
         Note sur les Testaments de Leví et de 'Amram,"
         *Homenaje a Juan Prado. Miscelanea de estudios
         biblicos y hebraicos.* Madrid: Consejo Superior
         de Investigaciones Científicas, 1975. Pp. 571-
         84.

1427aa   Harrelson, W. "Patient Love in the Testament of
         Joseph," *Perspectives in Religious Studies* 4
         (1977) 4-13. [= no. 1427a republished]

1428aa   Hollander, H. W. "The Influence of the Testaments
         of the Twelve Patriarchs in the Early Church:
         Joseph as Model in Prochorus' Acts of John,"
         Orientalia Lovaniensia Periodica 9 (1978) 75-81.

1430a   Jacobson, H. "The Position of the Fingers During
         the Priestly Blessing," *RQ* 34 (1977) 259f.

1435a   Jonge, M. de. "Once More: Christian Influence in
         the Testaments of the Twelve Patriarchs," *NovT*
         5 (1962) 311-19.

1438c   Jonge, M. de and H. W. Hollander, H. J. de Jonge,
         Th. Korteweg. *The Testaments of the Twelve
         Patriarchs: A Critical Edition of the Greek
         Text* (PVTG 1.2) Leiden: Brill, 1978.

1438d   Kee, H. C. "The Ethical Dimensions of the Testa-
         ments of the XII as a Clue to Provenance," *NTS*
         24 (1978) 259-70.

1439d   Larsson, E. "Qumranlitteraturen och de tolv
         patriarkernas testamenten," *SEA* 25 (1960) 109-
         18.

1443b   Nola, A. M. di. "Testamenti dei Dodiei Patri-
         archi," *EncRel* 5 (1973) 1773-77.

1447a   Prato, G. L. "Excursus 4: confronto con Test.
         Aser I,3-5; V,1ss e 1QS III,13-IV,26," *Il
         problema della teodicea in Ben Sira* (AnBib 65)
         Rome: Biblical Institute, 1975. Pp. 55-58,
         also see pp. 276-78 re. TNaph.

1448a   Robinson, P. A. "To Stretch out the Feet: A
         Formula for Death in the Testaments of the
         Twelve Patriarchs," *JBL* 97 (1978) 369-74.

1448b   Rodriguez-Herranz, J. C. "Los testamentos de los
         XII Patriarcas. El problema de su género
         fontal," *Miscelánea Comillas* 31 (1973) 161-99.

1449a   Rubinkiewicz, R. "Ps LXVIII 19 (= Eph IV 8)
         Another Textual Tradition or Targum?" *NovT* 17
         (1975) 219-24.

1450a   Schwartz, J. "Du Testament de Lévi au Discours
         véritable de Celse," *RHPR* 40 (1960) 126-45.

1452a   Slingerland, H. D. "The Testament of Joseph:
         A Redaction-Critical Study," *JBL* 96 (1977) 507-
         16.

1456a   Stone, M. E. "New Evidence for the Armenian Ver-
         sion of the Testaments of the Twelve Patri-
         archs," *RB* 84 (1977) 94-107.

1457a   Stone, M. E. "Testaments of the Twelve Patri-
         archs, The," *IDBS* (1976) 877.

Apocalypse of Zephaniah

1469a   Nola, A. M. di. "Elia e Sofonia, Apocalisse di,"
         EncRel 2 (1970) 1142-44.

Apocalypse of Zosimus
see
The History of the Blessed Ones, the Sons of Rechab

INDEX OF MODERN SCHOLARS

Numbers in italic refer to pages; those in roman to bibliographical entries. The abbreviation "f." after a number denotes the page or entry immediately following. Some entries (e.g. 1377f) are designated by number and letter.

Bagatti, B. *199*, 1361f.

Baier, W. 4a

Baillet, M. 131f., 1015-17, *161*

Baker, A. 821

Baker, J. A. 303, *141*, 302a, 836a

Baltzer, K. 299

Balz, H. R. 5

Bamberger, B. J. 434, 487, 504

Bammel, E. 719d

Banks, J. S. 363

Barabas, S. 608

Barasch, M. 1370a

Barclay, W. 93

Bardtke, H. 1285

Barker, M. 192a

Barnard, L. W. 1278

Barnes, W. E. *123*, *131*

Barr, J. 897, 192b, 716a

Barrett, C. K. *190*, 123b, 719d, 1278a

Barth, C. 299a̲

Barton, J. M. T. *29*, 912

Bate, H. N. *184*

Batiffol, P. *137*

Bauckham, R. J. 192c, 441a

Bauer, J. B. 6, 92

Bauer, W. 1279

Baumbach, G. 299a̲b̲

Baumgarten, A. I. 899b

Baumgarten, J. M. 1018, 192d, 1370b

Baumgartner, W. 7, *157*, 1114

Baumhauer, O. 364

Baumstark, A. *183*

Bayer, B. *200*, 1362a

Beardslee, W. A. 193, 193a

Becker, J. *30*, *212f.*, 1405f.

Beckwith, R. T. 133f.

Beek, M. A. 193b

Belitz, W. 524a

Beltz, W. 525f.

Ben Horin, M. 101a, 634a, 645a, 649a

Benoit, A. 413, 7a

Bensly, R. L. *183*

Berchem, [?] van 89

Berger, K. *29*, 299a, 365, 1019, 299b-c, 425a, 688a, 697a, 890b, 986a, *276*

Bernard, J. H. *189*

Bertrand, D. A. 1239, 1280 1407

Best, E. 708, 823, 1471

Betz, H. D. 194, *139*

Betz, O. *29*, 135, 366, 443, 497, 104b, 526a, 109f., 1112a

Beurlier, E. *154-56*

Beutler, J. 357

Beyerlin, W. 194a

Bezold, C. *91*

Bianchi, U. 173, 530, 548, 1138, 1207

Bickerman, E. J. 689

Bidawid, R. J. *111*, 834

Bilde, P. 299d

Billerbeck, P. *133*

Bischoff, B. 1240

Black, M. *15*, 96, 120, 136, 150, 185, 300, 367, 564, *95f.*, 717-19, *195*, 1385, 697b, 717a, 719a-d, 752d

Bleeker, C. J. 439, 472, 794

Blenkinsopp, J. 96a

Blinzler, J. 1417c

Bloch, J. 7b

Böcher, O. 1407a, 194b

Böhlig, A. 174, *72*, 527-29

Boer, P. A. H. de *28*, *240*

Ziegler, J.   603, 833
Ziegler, K.   *168*
Zimmermen, F.   649a, 881a
Zink, J. K.   882, 1132
Zuntz, G.   604
Zuurmond, R.   *144*, 1014a
Zwierlein, O.   833a